This Is NOT a Fire Drill

This Is NOT a Fire Drill

Crisis Intervention and Prevention on College Campuses

Rick A. Myer
Richard K. James
Patrice Moulton

WILEY

JOHN WILEY & SONS, INC.

This book is printed on acid-free paper. ∞

Library of Congress Cataloging-in-Publication Data:

Myer, Rick.
  This is not a firedrill : crisis intervention and prevention on college campuses / Rick A. Myer, Richard K. James, Patrice Moulton.
       p. cm.
    Includes bibliographical references and indexes.
    ISBN 978-0-470-45804-4 (pbk. : acid-free paper)
    ISBN 978-0-470-92677-2 (ebk)
    ISBN 978-0-470-92678-9 (ebk)
    ISBN 978-0-470-92679-6 (ebk)
    1. Universities and colleges—United States—Administration.   2. Crisis management—United States.   3. Crisis intervention (Mental health services)—United States.   4. Traumatic shock.   I. James, Richard K., 1942–   II. Moulton, Patrice, 1961–   III. Title.
    LB2866.M94   2011
    378.1'9713–dc22
                                        2010036019

No matter how many plans are developed and steps taken to prevent crises, they will happen. Crises can be small or large, modest or intense, yet all send waves throughout a campus.

This book is dedicated to the survivors of the many crises that have occurred on university and college campuses. Making meaning out of a situation in which you have little to no control, and most of the time no warning, is challenging to say the least. We respectfully acknowledge the struggle you've gone through.

We also dedicate this book to the countless people who have provided support following disasters on university campuses. Being with survivors following a disastrous event and helping them start the healing process requires courage and fortitude. We salute your willingness to give of yourself.

Finally, we dedicate this book to the people charged with the coordination of the recovery of a campus following a tragic event. Administrators and crisis management teams are faced with the unenviable task of making sense out of chaos. Your efforts may go unnoticed and be criticized by some, but not by us. Our hats are off to you.

Contents

Acknowledgments

Special thanks to Kathryn Heidke, Jennifer Duhon, and Sarah Prud'homme, students at Northwestern State University of Louisiana. Your efforts in helping us write this book are appreciated.

Thanks also to Jamie N. Brownfield, Nancy N. Fair, Nickole R. Kopcha, Cristinia Kumpf, Kelley B. McNichols, Helena Ng, and Mary Rudberg, enrolled in the ExCES doctoral program at Duquesne University. The input and assistance you gave were invaluable in the completion of this book.

1

. . . Or a Tornado or Earthquake Drill

Miracle on 34th Street is a Christmas classic, a movie about a little girl who wanted to believe in Santa Claus, but her mom, an upwardly mobile executive at Macy's, was a hardnosed realist who dismissed Santa Claus as a myth. If you have seen the movie, you will perhaps remember the character of Kris Kringle, who was played by Ed Gwenn. One of the great scenes in that movie was when Kris Kringle told a mother that Gimbel's department store, a competitor of Macy's, had the particular toy she was looking for. At first the manager was appalled and wanted to fire Kris, but then when upper management found out that it increased customer respect and loyalty, everybody on the sales staff was told to be helpful and direct customers to other stores if Macy's didn't have the particular product they were looking for. We're going to do the same thing here. If you are really serious about the business of preventing, intervening, and following up in the traumatic wake of violence on your campus, we believe there are three books that need to make the cut on your reading list.

The first book is by Eugene Zdziarski and his associates, *Campus Crisis Management* (2007). It is a comprehensive guide to planning, prevention, response, and recovery of environmental, facility, and human crises in a college setting. It takes an in-depth look at the intricacies of managing all kinds of crisis on a college campus.

The second book is Nicoletti, Spencer-Thomas, and Bollinger's *Violence Goes to College* (2001). It's about 10 years old, but it is still a really great book for understanding, preventing, and planning how to stop violence on college campuses. It covers a variety of violence typologies and also provides information on how to build intervention strategies to combat potentially virulent episodes that can metastasize and spread across a campus.

The third book is Grayson and Meilman's *College Mental Health Practice* (2006), which gives a graphic portrayal of what practitioners in college counseling centers are dealing with in regard to contemporary students. These editors have done an excellent job of providing the reader with a comprehensive view of the legal and ethical, developmental, and diversity issues that undergird a variety of mental disorders and acute and chronic crises that go far beyond homesickness, flunking English, and broken romances.

We think so highly of these authors and what they have to say that we have referenced them a lot in this book. Now that we have told you about these three great books, you may be wondering why in the world you bought this one. So why, indeed, read this book? We do believe there is a reason, and here's why. Those other great books are *about* what goes on in a crisis. This book is what you *do* in a human impact crisis on a college campus. It is further very specific in the kind of crisis with which it deals. Unlike the Zdziarski and associates (2007) book, which covers a wide variety of kinds of crises, this book deals with what to do with human beings who are the causative agents and victims of a crisis. As such, this book is tasked with trying to make predictable what is often unpredictable and chaotic and with giving form and substance to that which is often as concrete and tangible as fog to the emotive, cognitive, and behavioral responses of college students (and maybe some professors and administrators as well) who are attempting to negotiate a crisis caused by either themselves or others. It also attempts to deal with the fog that can surround and engulf the system when it attempts to deal with a crisis. To that end, it indeed is not a book about lockstep fire drill plans.

It would be nice if humans behaved like Skinner's rats and pigeons and lived on nice linear reinforcement schedules. It would certainly make planning for crises a whole lot easier. The problem is that they don't, and it is perhaps an understatement to say that college students *really* don't. It is also concerned with how the systems respond, sometimes in a not-so-linear manner. Therefore, this book is about giving you some very hands-on examples of what to do with students who are potentially violent toward themselves or others and how the system might respond to those problems. It doesn't give you an example of *every* type of violent situation you may encounter. Please don't be put out if the particular crisis you are grappling with is not covered. What we are attempting to do is give you the general tactics and strategies, along with some specific prevention, intervention, and postvention logistics and techniques that will allow you to apply them to almost any human-made crisis you are likely to be confronted with on a college campus.

We have divided this book into two parts. The first part deals with the system. The second part deals specifically with individuals. Following are brief descriptions of what the specific chapters are about.

Chapter 2, *Boilerplate: The Basics of Crisis Intervention*. This chapter covers the definitions, types, and dynamics of crisis. We discuss the basic building blocks of theory and terminology a person needs to know to talk about and understand the field of crisis and crisis intervention. A good deal of ink and paper in this chapter is devoted to multicultural issues and how they may affect crises on college campuses.

Chapter 3, *Herding Cats: Organizing a Crisis Response*. Who does what and when, and how do they do it? Boundary problems, ethical and legal issues, sharing of responsibility, and other critical issues in administration of a comprehensive crisis intervention plan are covered.

Chapter 4, *Duller Than Dirt . . . More Valuable Than Gold: Policies and Procedures*. This chapter examines setting up policies and procedures governing how crises will be handled. Critical issues such as information sharing, retrieval, and storage are covered. Notification, privacy, and other legal and ethical issues that evolve from a crisis are examined.

Chapter 5, *The Best of Times and the Worst of Times: The Tale of Two Laws.* Two tragedies on college campuses have changed the landscape of confidentiality. The death of
Tatiana Tarasoff at the hands of Prosenjit Poddar in 1969 affected the way mental health
professionals manage clients who are homicidal. The Virginia Tech shooting spree by
Seung-Hui Cho on April 16, 2007, may have even a larger impact on the way universities address the issue of students who may become violent. This chapter discusses these
cases and their influence on crisis management and intervention.

Chapter 6, *Reality Check: Entry into the System.* This chapter is a discussion of difficulties in entry into and training issues in changing an entrenched system that has
many constituencies that may pay lip service but resist the complexities inherent in a
comprehensive crisis intervention program. How buy-in is created, who is responsible,
and how they are trained to deal with a campus crisis are detailed.

Chapter 7, *What You See Is What You Get . . . or Maybe Not: Assessment of the System.*
In crisis intervention, assessment of the system is as important as individual assessment
of persons in crisis. Continuous assessment from precrisis to postcrisis functioning in
the system is critical for understanding and ameliorating the crisis. This chapter examines how and why organizational triage assessment for crisis occurs and what can be
learned from it.

Chapter 8, *No Rest for the Weary: System Recovery After a Crisis.* This chapter addresses
components of what the system does in the traumatic wake of human crises, including
memorial, political, and legal issues. We consider the potential emergence of acute stress
disorder in the system, and contextual modeling in understanding the impact of what
happened through use of an eight step intervention model.

Chapter 9, *Not Buying a Pig in a Poke.* This chapter covers basic understanding and
use of the Triage Assessment Scale for Students in Learning Environments (TASSLE)
across affective, behavioral, and cognitive components of a crisis, as well as use of a
threat assessment team to determine potential lethality.

Chapter 10, *Basic Training.* This chapter explains and illustrates the basic listening
and responding skills an average person needs to know and be able to use during a
crisis.

Chapter 11, *One Day at a Time: Survivorship in the Aftermath.* This chapter discusses
individual needs and system support responses to the individual and the role of mourning, stages of grief, Critical Incidents Stress Debriefing, and psychological autopsy of the
individual in helping survivors deal with the traumatic wake.

Chapter 12, *Leadership Checklist: Preparing Your Campus for Crisis.* This chapter details a checklist summary of the things you need to do to get your crisis prevention and
intervention plan for human dilemmas up and running.

If those topics fit into your game plan about what you need to do in crisis containment, then you are in the right place. Before we go any further, though, we want to give
you a brief history of crisis intervention in general and at college campuses in particular.
We do this because we are great believers in the admonishment that those who don't
understand history are condemned to repeat it. In other words, if you don't know where

you have been, then how in the world do you know where you are or where you are going?

A BRIEF HISTORY OF CRISIS INTERVENTION

Depending on your view of the origin of our species, crisis has been around for humans since Eve got interested in a fruit tree or a herd of woolly mammoths stampeded through an Ice Age Cro-Magnon camp. However, for most people, the concept of crisis and crisis intervention comes to the fore only when large-scale natural disasters, such as hurricanes and earthquakes, affect huge parts of the ecosystem and large segments of the population. Historically, crisis intervention is most commonly seen as piling up sandbags on flooding rivers or searching debris for survivors after a tornado or earthquake. Crisis intervention in the form of direct support to humans has been stereotypically seen as disaster relief by such organizations as the Red Cross or Salvation Army providing tents and serving food. Currently, the most discussed and cussed agency identified with disasters and trauma is probably the Federal Emergency Management Agency (FEMA).

As we have moved into the 21st century, the view of crisis intervention as sandbags and soup kitchens has changed as terror acts such as the Oklahoma City bombing, 9/11, and secondary school shootings such as Columbine have been brought to us in living horror in real time by new video technology. Although the Red Cross and the Salvation Army have been involved in disaster relief for more than a hundred years, FEMA has been in existence for only about 30 years. Furthermore, not until the last two decades or so has any organization given much time or thought to the mental health aspect of broadband crisis intervention for large populations afflicted by traumatic events. That unsettling fact has been particularly so in regard to colleges, where wide-scale violence and crisis were not perceived as part of that bucolic, ivory tower atmosphere. To say that environment has now changed would be a bit more than an understatement.

Suicide Intervention

Because of its high incidence in the typical college age group, suicide is certainly part of our focus in this book. Suicide prevention is probably the oldest organized crisis intervention program, starting with the National Save-a-Life League phone line in 1906 (Bloom, 1984). There are now hundreds of crisis suicide hotlines, including the national suicide prevention lifeline at 1-800-273-TALK (8255). Edwin Shneidman (2001) is known as the father of modern suicidology, and his landmark research on suicide has spanned more than six decades of work in trying to figure out why people kill themselves. Suicide is probably one of the most thoroughly researched mental health issues in the world. Clearly, suicide, along with drug addiction, has large implications for college-age populations who are at risk for both, as well as the potential for violence that goes with them (Meilman, Lewis, & Gerstein, 2006; Nicoletti et al., 2001; Silverman, 2006).

Cocoanut Grove Survivors

However, the real benchmark and foundation blocks for the birth of crisis intervention came with the Cocoanut Grove nightclub fire in 1942, when more than 400 people perished. Eric Lindemann (1944), who treated many of the survivors, found that they seemed to have common emotional responses and need for psychological assistance and support. Out of Lindemann's work came the first notions of what may be called "normal" grief reactions to a disaster. Gerald Caplan (1961) was also involved in working with Cocoanut Grove survivors. His experience led to some of the very first theoretical attempts to explain what a crisis is and the first basic rudiments of crisis intervention with traumatized individuals (Caplan, 1964).

Social Movements

To really understand the evolution of crisis intervention, though, is to understand that several social movements have been critical to its development and that these did not start fully formed as crisis intervention groups by any means. Three of the major groups that have helped shape crisis intervention into an emerging specialty have been Alcoholics Anonymous (AA) members, Vietnam veterans, and participants in the women's movement in the 1970s. AA worked long and hard to make alcoholism become recognizable as a disease rather than a character deficit. The veterans pushed the government and the medical establishment to recognize that veterans contracted something more than combat fatigue in Vietnam. The National Organization of Women (NOW) opened the drapes on domestic violence and lobbied state and federal legislatures and authorities to construct laws and prosecute offenders of physical and sexual assault against women and children. Although their commissioned intentions and objectives had little to do with the advancement of crisis intervention as a clinical specialty, these groups had a lot to do with people who were desperate for help and weren't getting any. The groups all started as grassroots movements and, through continuous self-organizing efforts, became political forces that local, state, and federal governments couldn't ignore (James, 2008, pp. 7–9).

As a result, governments and institutions were forced into acting because of intense political pressure from these social interest groups turned political action groups. A classic example of unwillingness to acknowledge an emerging mental health issue was the entrenched and regressive policies of the 1960s and early 1970s Veterans Administration (VA) toward returning Vietnam veterans. It was the intense political pressure that was brought to bear on the VA to deal with the thousands of Vietnam veterans who were returning home with terrifying behaviors, disturbing personality changes, and severe cognitive disturbances that forced them to act years after these behavioral anomalies first came to their attention (MacPherson, 1984); later, such problems came to be known as post-traumatic stress disorder (American Psychiatric Association, 1980). Because of the continuous publicity and lobbying efforts of AA,

NOW, and the Vietnam veterans' organizations, the medical establishment, insurance companies, the government, and finally society in general were forced to recognize these as legitimate and widespread social issues that could give birth to identifiable mental disorders. These bureaucracies grudgingly started to provide resources and treatment for these maladies and the resulting human crises these disorders created. As you shall soon see, university systems have not exactly been paragons of leadership in recognizing and dealing with their own human crises and their traumatic wakes either.

HISTORY OF CRISIS ON COLLEGE CAMPUSES

There was a fairly long history of horrific mass murders on college campuses prior to Virginia Tech and Northern Illinois University. The classic example is Charles Whitman, who in 1966 used the 307-foot Texas Tower as an almost impregnable sniper position at the University of Texas in Austin to kill 14 people and wound dozens of others before he died. There were two rather ominous outcomes of that murderous rampage. The first was news coverage (radio) on-site in real time. This was one of the first times that an ongoing shooting rampage received real-time media coverage. What we now take for granted in regard to real-time news coverage was extraordinary in 1966 and certainly set the stage for some of the traumatic ramifications that media coverage of violence and disaster has for us today. Second, it most likely resulted in the creation of the country's first SWAT teams because an outgunned Austin police department had to rely on citizens bringing their high-powered hunting rifles to the scene of what became a war zone.

Richard Speck's 1966 mass murder of student nurses in Chicago, Ted Bundy's serial killing of co-eds at Florida State in 1978, and Danny Rolling's 1990 murder of co-eds at the University of Florida and Santa Fe Community College all got national headlines, yet these sociopathic killers were not directly linked to those institutions of higher learning, so there was no clear urgency to institute protective measures for the student populations. Along with these highly publicized murders, there were many other types of violence on college campuses. These included date rapes, hazing, hate assaults, alcohol-fueled riots, lethal drinking binges, and suicides that were quietly shoved under the carpet by universities that shunned negative publicity (Nicoletti et al., 2001, pp. 5–13).

The plain and simple fact until the recent past has been that not many universities had certified and trained police departments and instead used a variety of security services that were ill equipped to handle the kinds of problems that would assail colleges and universities in the latter part of the 20th century. Therefore, it is no accident that a number of references in this book and many of the procedures and techniques used here have been developed by law enforcement (Miller, 2006; Slatkin, 2005; Strentz, 2006; Thompson & Jenkins, 2004). Further, until the 1990s, there was no clear, organized mental health approach or, for that matter, tested mental health intervention techniques for dealing with the aftermath of a traumatic event.

Any organized effort to deal with the aftermath of traumatic experiences with survivors of such aforementioned murders and other types of violence and trauma would be years down the road, both in regard to intervention with affected populations that resulted from events like the University of Texas clock tower murders and prevention of similar occurrences. In that era, counseling centers, if they existed at all on college campuses, mainly dealt with financial aid issues, academic failures, or personal adjustment problems such as homesickness or broken relationships. As a rather vivid anecdote of that era, it is noteworthy that one of the authors of this book was assigned to the new director of the brand-new (1966) university personal counseling center as the author's classroom practicum supervisor for his master's degree field experience. This assignment was made because it was felt that the director of that new center didn't have enough to do to keep him busy so he ought to be assigned a faculty course load as part of his duties! How do you suppose a harried director of a college counseling center today might feel about that assignment?

Things have certainly changed in regard to the felt need for counseling centers to deal with severe mental health issues and crisis intervention on the contemporary college campus. Counseling centers are now under severe pressure because of the universal budget cuts facing institutions of higher education, increased student usage, severity of presenting problems, legal and political pressures, and expectations to engage in not only standard psychology intervention but also crisis intervention, prevention, and postvention (Grayson, 2006, pp. 1–11; Kadison & DiGeronimo, 2004, pp. 1–8). While it is easy to cast blame on counseling centers for not spotting and stopping tragedies like the one at Virginia Tech, it should be understood that a perfect storm of the aforementioned problems can easily subvert and sabotage the best-laid plans and intentions of counselors and counseling centers. As Grayson (2006, p. 11) points out, in the eyes of the campus community, nothing is more important than preventing crises that can result in murder and mayhem. The problem is that predicting who will and who will not become violent is terribly difficult and that the consequences of labeling a student as a false-positive lethal risk carries heavy moral, ethical, and legal consequences. The current issues of violence faced by universities do not just fall on the shoulders of overburdened counseling centers. Their historical antecedents also rest on knowing, reporting, and disseminating knowledge of campus violence, which, until the murder of Jeanne Clery, were woefully inadequate.

The Clery Act

Historically, there has been a perceived reticence of colleges and universities to report the true number of crimes or criminal acts on their campuses because of the bad publicity it generates. That attitude changed dramatically with the murder of Jeanne Clery on the campus of Lehigh University in 1986. Clery's parents subsequently found out that Lehigh had been covering up a number of violent crimes on campus. They sued the university and used the money they received in an out-of-court settlement to start a campaign to end campus violence and lobby Congress to require colleges and universities to disclose the crime rates on their campuses (Nicoletti et al., 2001, p. 9).

Subsequent lobbying of Clery's parents to require colleges to publicize criminal acts on campus resulted in the passage of what has become known as the Jeanne Clery Disclosure of Campus Security Policy and Crime Statistics Act. In brief, this act requires colleges and universities to report crime on their campuses in yearly reports to the FBI and also institute informational and educational services to its constituencies about crime and crime prevention (20 U.S.C. § 1092(f), 1990).

Additional amendments have been made to that act. Probably the most significant occurred after the Virginia Tech shootings. Congress passed the Higher Education Opportunity Act (HEOA) (PL 110-315, 2008), which adds a statement of "emergency response and evacuation procedures" to the Clery Act Annual Security Report (ASR) produced by institutions of postsecondary education. This policy disclosure has a "shall include" statement that the institution will "immediately notify the campus community upon the confirmation of a significant emergency or dangerous situation involving an immediate threat to the health or safety of students or staff" on campus (as defined in the act). The act also expands hate crime reporting to include larceny-theft, simple assault, intimidation, and vandalism. Warnings may be withheld only if they would compromise efforts to contain the emergency. While this "shall include" clause sounds definite and concrete about what should happen, it leaves wiggle room for the administration to make a judgment call about the degree of threat. Thus, the same incident might cause one university to make an immediate notification to its constituency while another university might not.

Further, HEOA expands the existing statement of policy on the law enforcement authority of campus security personnel to include a disclosure about whether institutions have agreements, such as a written memorandum of understanding (MOU), with state and local police for the investigation of alleged crimes. Finally, it also includes protection in the form of a whistleblower protection and antiretaliation clause that establishes safeguards for whistleblowers by prohibiting any retaliatory action against any individual "with respect to the implementation of any provision" of the Clery Act. Now why do you suppose that particular piece of legislation got put into the Clery Act? If you are curious about why a whistleblower clause would be put in this amendment, we suggest you read Roy's (2009) *No Right to Remain Silent: The Tragedy at Virginia Tech* to get an idea of why that particular piece of legislation got written so that administrations couldn't cover their tracks by muzzling or threatening employees.

So, do you possibly think there still might be some administrators around who would exact revenge on an employee who sought to bring a potentially violent situation to the light of day?

THE CONTEMPORARY COLLEGE SCENE

Study after study portrays a far different contemporary student population in place on college campuses than previous generations, in regard to both who they are and what kinds of mental health problems they bring to campus. A major question is whether the general student population in the United States is becoming more pathological, or is it because the population itself is changing? That change is due in part to the Rehabilitation Act of 1973 and the Americans with Disabilities Act of 1990, which made college campuses more receptive and accommodating to people with existing mental illnesses. This issue has become so important that the *Journal of College Counseling* devoted its Fall 2005 issue to the topic of severe and persistent mental illness. In recent years, counseling centers have reported an increase in mental health problems, as well as the increased severity of problems associated with college students, when compared with students 5, 10, and 20 years earlier (Arkoff et al., 2006; Benton, Robertson, Tseng, Newton, & Benton, 2003; Bishop, 2006; Erdur-Baker, Aberson, Barrow, & Draper, 2006; Grayson & Meilman, 2006; Kadison & DiGeronimo, 2004; Mowbray et al., 2006; Owen & Rodolfa, 2009; Schwartz, 2006; Yorgason, Linville, & Zitzman, 2008). These are not just typical homesickness, roommate, or romance problems, but serious pathology with the trappings of a community mental health center.

As recently as 2009, Owen and Rodolfa (2009) reported that more than 90% of college students report being stressed, 40% report being so distressed that it interferes with their academic and social functioning, and nearly 10% report seriously contemplating suicide. Similar statistics were found by Kadison (2006) and Field, Elliot, and Korn (2006). According to Mowbray and associates (2006), approximately 15% of college students have a diagnosable mental illness such as major depression, bipolar disorder, schizophrenia and other psychotic disorders, severe anxiety disorders (including obsessive-compulsive disorder), and eating disorders. Gallagher (2004) found in a survey of college counseling directors that 24% of the students turnstiling through their counseling centers were on psychotropic medication.

While these statistics are sobering, they may in fact minimize the problem. These statistics identify students who actually use counseling centers. Many of these students make one or two sessions and then drop out because of time commitments, desire for quick fixes, or a view of counseling centers as just another student service rather than a serious therapeutic endeavor. Many more students don't use counseling centers at all because they can't get an appointment, don't believe they have time due to other demands in their lives, see it as an embarrassing and humiliating stigma, or just don't believe they have a problem (Grayson, 2006; Kadison & DiGeronimo, 2004).

Thus, there is a good deal of debate over the real versus perceived influx of pathology in the mental health status of college students (Mowbray et al., 2006; Yorgason et al., 2008). There are some allegations that only a handful of students who need counseling services seek them (Yorgason et al., 2008), and most epidemiologic studies of college mental health relate to data derived from those students who present themselves to the attention of mental health facilities. It would be a mistake to confuse these usage rates with actual illness rates in the general study body (Reifler, 2006). Whether the incidence of psychopathology is higher or lower in the general student population is a good question. Following are some of the reasons that make us think it is probably not lower.

Psychotropic Medication

The development of psychotropic medication allows students with mental illnesses to now function in an academic environment. The problem is that people go off their medication because of side effects they don't like, don't have money to buy medication, or just plain forget to take their medication, particularly when they are living independently for the first time in their lives, and Mom isn't there to make them take their vitamins or risperidone. The problem of medication compliance is so well known to police departments that these individuals have become known as Pete and Repete for the numerous times they come into contact with police after going off their medication.

Nontraditional Students

A second issue is the influx of nontraditional students into the contemporary university setting. Nontraditional students generally fall into one or more of the following categories: older, geographically and vocationally transient, veterans, married or unmarried with children, physical or mental handicapping conditions, holding down a couple of jobs, first-generation college students, and minority. They don't typically graduate in four years and may show up with a combination of transcripts from numerous colleges and numerous majors from earlier attempts at college that were aborted by a variety of the stressors that go with the foregoing categories. Each of those categories holds its own particular basket of stressors that, when combined with the stress of trying to get a college education, can lead to psychopathology and acting out in self-destructive ways.

Traditional Students

Traditional students certainly have their fair share of stressors as well. In generations past, a high school diploma would have been an admission ticket into a job with higher pay and higher prestige. Today, for many students, getting a bachelor's degree is merely an admission ticket into a graduate or professional degree program. Pressures to perform not just well but exceedingly well as an undergraduate are tremendous. Grade inflation due to student grievances and complaints when they don't receive high grades is endemic and exerts a great deal of pressure on professors to ease their performance criteria (Kadison & DiGeronimo, 2004, p. 50). However, academic pressures are not the only stressors that assail Frederick Freshman or Sarah Sophomore.

Developmental Issues

Beyond experiencing the normal crises that accompany transition from high school into college, students' new environment and the developmental issues of newfound freedom that go with it get large numbers of these traditional students in trouble. They experiment and engage in all manner of risky behaviors that include binge drinking and promiscuous and unprotected sex, sleep deprivation from way too much fun or way too much studying, dietary problems that result from too many supersize pizzas grabbed on the run, eating disorders that range from bulimia to anorexia, self-destructive behaviors such as taking drugs and self-mutilation, and being homesick, socially and emotionally isolated, and clinically depressed in an environment that is not only new and strange but also may be perceived as hostile. The accompanying crises that invariably go with these 18- to 21-year-olds when these stressors pile up and are not dealt with ripple out and affect not only the students themselves but also those surrounding them (American College Health Association, 2003; Grayson, 2006; Kadison & DiGeronimo, 2004).

The potential cause for having one of the greatest developmental crises in life is the simple act of walking onto a university campus as an entering freshman. College is a time of identity crisis for those students who still identify themselves by their high school activities (Kadison & DiGeronimo, 2004, p. 14). For many students, they shift from big man (or woman) on campus in high school to anything but that in college. Listen to one of our doctoral students: "I was the fastest man on my football team in our small rural high school. For that matter, I was the fastest halfback in our conference. When I went to Tech and ran my first wind sprint, I wasn't faster than any of the other running backs and flankers and maybe a little slower. Welcome to Division One football! Talk about creating a crisis of confidence!"

Kadison and DiGeronimo (2004, pp. 5–89) eloquently describe the many developmental issues and challenges that new freshmen on campus walk smack into as they make the transition from the safe, secure, and predictable environment of home into the strange, exotic, and sometimes threatening world of the university setting. Students experience new social and sexual standards of behavior, drug and alcohol use, freedom from parental controls, and getting used to a new roommate who may be the diametrical opposite in everything from clothing to political beliefs. While most students face these developmental issues head-on and move through them, some students will be overcome by the tsunami of new ideas, increased competition, divergent views, and different cultures that engulfs them. The result may be a tidal wave of helplessness and hopelessness that overcomes them. They then become prime candidates for a smorgasbord of intrapersonal and interpersonal issues that can lead to severe crises and most likely will be the faces into which the residence hall workers, administrators, counselors, police, and professors who are reading this book will be peering.

But as we have seen, developmental crises are not the only types of crises that the college crisis worker is likely to encounter, and each of the other crises carries its own multicultural baggage. From that standpoint, a major component of any crisis intervention is being aware of the influence and impact of the cultural background that both the student and the crisis worker bring into the situation.

Diversity and Multiculturalism

Another issue that is now part of the campus scene and factors into the crisis equation on college campuses is the wide range of diversity that embodies most colleges and universities. The word *university* is probably synonymous with the concept of diversity and multiculturalism, given the variety of nationalities, races, creeds, religions, ethnicities, socioeconomic levels, political views, sexual preferences, geographic locales, and about everything else one could think of that somehow differentiates one person from another. This human mélange makes a university setting a petri dish where different people with vastly different backgrounds come together for the first time and attempt to start to grow in this strange new culture. Everyone who enters must adapt or fail to receive a college degree. In the last general census, college enrollment increased 62% for students of color (U.S. Census Bureau, 2001), and "color" is only one part of the diverse group of individuals who are entering colleges and universities in the United States in the 21st century.

Foreign students make up a large population of the diverse students on contemporary college campuses and are assailed with all of the developmental issues that American students face plus language difficulties when struggling with American idioms and euphemisms, different learning styles in American classrooms, problems with student visas, and difficulty in entering, exiting, and reentering the country under the current terrorist alert. They run into different social customs, different foods, and different plumbing that compound the daily dilemmas they face in just surviving (Kadison & DiGeronimo, 2004, pp. 59–64).

Being a minority can mean a not-so-fast Caucasian football halfback on a largely very fast African American backfield, an African American in a largely Caucasian political club, a Hispanic in a largely African American and Caucasian criminal justice program, a female in a largely male civil engineering major, a lesbian in largely heterosexual theology program, an Indonesian Muslim in a Business 201 class with Christian and Jewish Americans, or anybody who has few "us" in a college situation with lot more of "them." These students will most likely experience real or perceived problems adjusting to campus life that the majority won't. Those problems may come in a variety of forms. Is the student's social life pinched off by shunning from the majority or by admonitions from home to stick with your own kind? Do academic problems result from intellectual inaptitude or a lack of support systems and role models? Does a poor grade in a class result from a majority professor's bias, or is it because of misperceptions based on and brought in from the home culture? All of the foregoing may certainly be due to the fact that everyone who enters the college scene for the first time may be considered culturally different and unassimilated, given that most will indeed be strangers in a strange land. We will have a good deal more to say about the concepts of diversity and multiculturalism in Chapter 2, the boilerplate chapter, because we think it is one of the critical variables to be considered in any crisis intervention plan.

SUMMARY

There are several great books about violence and crisis and about violence and crisis intervention on college campuses. This book is not so much about those topics but more about how to do them. It is also not a book about all the kinds of crises that may afflict a college. It is a book on human-made crises and prevention, intervention, and postvention strategies in regard to those crises. This chapter has detailed a brief history of both the general state of the need for crisis intervention as it has evolved in the last century in the United States and its more specific evolution on college campuses.

REFERENCES

American College Health Association. (2003). *National college health assessment: Reference group executive summary spring 2002*. Baltimore, MD: Author.

American Psychiatric Association. (1980). *Diagnostic and statistical manual of mental disorders-technical revision* (3rd ed.). Washington, DC: Author.

Arkoff, A., Meredith, G. M., Bailey, E., Cheang, M., Dubanoski, R. A., Griffin, P. B., & Niyekawa, A. M. (2006). Life review during the college freshman year. *College Student Journal, 40,* 263–269.

Benton, S. A., Robertson, J. M., Tseng, W., Newton, F., & Benton, S. L. (2003). Changes in counseling center client problems across 13 years. *Professional Psychology: Research and Practice, 34,* 66–72.

Bishop, J. B. (2006). College and university counseling centers: Questions in search of answers. *Journal of College Counseling, 9,* 6–19.

Bloom, B. L. (1984). *Community mental health: A general introduction* (2nd ed.). Pacific Grove, CA: Brooks/Cole.

Caplan, G. (1961). *An approach to community mental health*. New York: Grune & Stratton.

Caplan, G. (1964). *Principles of preventive psychiatry*. New York: Basic Books.

Erdur-Baker, O., Aberson, C. L., Barrow, J. C., & Draper, M. R. (2006). Nature and severity of college students' psychological concerns: A comparison of clinical and nonclinical national samples. *Professional Psychology: Research and Practice, 37,* 317–323.

Field, L. D, Elliot, M. S., & Korn, P. R. (2006). A successful community-based intervention for addressing college student depression. *Journal of College Student Development, 47,* 105–109.

Gallagher, R. P. (2004). *National survey of college counseling center directors*. Alexandria, VA: International Association of Counseling Services Inc.

Grayson, P. A. (2006). Overview. In P. A. Grayson & P. W. Meilman (Eds.), *College mental health practice* (pp. 1–20). New York: Routledge.

Grayson, P. A., & Meilman, P. W. (Eds.). (2006). *College mental health practice*. New York: Routledge.

Higher Education Opportunity Act of 2008. PL 110-315 §122 Stat 3078 (2008).

James, R. (2008). *Crisis intervention strategies* (6th ed.). Belmont, CA: Brooks/Cole-Cengage.

Jeanne Clery Disclosure of Campus Security Policy Crime and Statistics Act of 1990§ 20 U.S.C. §1092 (f) (1990).

Kadison, R. (2006). College psychiatry 2006: Challenges and opportunities. *Journal of American College Health, 54,* 338–340.

Kadison, R., & DiGeronimo, T. F (2004). *College of the overwhelmed: The campus mental health crisis and what to do about it.* San Francisco, CA: Jossey-Bass.

Lindemann, E. (1944). Symptomatology and management of acute grief. *American Journal of Psychiatry, 101,* 141–148.

MacPherson, M. (1984). *Long time passing: Vietnam and the haunted generation.* New York: Doubleday.

Meilman, P. W., Lewis, D. K., & Gerstein, L. (2006). Alcohol, drugs, and other addictions. In P. A. Grayson & P. W. Meilman (Eds.), *College mental health practice* (pp. 195–214). New York: Routledge.

Miller, L. (2006). *Practical police psychology.* Springfield, IL: Charles C Thomas.

Mowbray, C. T., Megivern, D., Mandiberg, J. M., Strauss, S., Stein, C. H., Collins, K., & Lett, R. (2006). Campus mental health services: Recommendation for change. *American Journal of Orthopsychiatry, 76,* 226–237.

Nicoletti, J., Spencer-Thomas, S., & Bollinger, C. (2001). *Violence goes to college: The authoritative guide to prevention and intervention.* Springfield, IL: Charles C Thomas.

Owen, J., & Rodolfa. E. (2009). Prevention through connection: Creating a campus climate of care. *Society for College and University Planning, 37,* 26–33.

Reifler, C. B. (2006). Epidemiological aspects of college mental health. *Journal of American College Health, 54,* 372–376.

Roy, L. (2009). *No right to remain silent: The tragedy at Virginia Tech.* New York: Harmony Books/Crown Publishing.

Schwartz, A. J. (2006). Are college students more disturbed today? Stability in the acuity and qualitative character of psychopathology of college counseling center clients 1992–1993 through 2001–2002. *Journal of College Health, 54,* 327–337.

Shneidman, E. (2001*). Comprehending suicide: Landmarks in 20th century suicidology.* Washington, DC: American Psychological Association.

Silverman, M. M. (2006). Suicide and suicidal behaviors. In P. A. Grayson & P. W. Meilman (Eds.), *College mental health practice* (pp. 303–324). New York: Routledge.

Slatkin, A. (2005). *Communication in crisis and hostage negotiations.* Springfield, IL: Charles C Thomas.

Strentz, T. (2006). *Psychological aspects of crisis negotiation.* Boca Raton, FL: Taylor & Francis.

Thompson, G. J., & Jenkins, J. B. (2004). *Verbal judo: The gentle art of persuasion.* New York: HarperCollins.

U.S. Census Bureau. (2001). *U.S. Census 2000.* Washington, DC: U.S. Printing Office.

Yorgason, J. B., Linville, D., & Zitzman, B. (2008). Mental health among college students: Do those who need services know about and use them? *Journal of College Health, 57,* 173–181.

Zdziarski, E. L., Dunkel, W. D., & Rollo, J. M. (Eds.). (2007). *Campus crisis management: A comprehensive guide to planning, prevention, response, and recovery.* San Francisco: Jossey-Bass.

2

Boilerplate: The Basics of Crisis Intervention

This chapter provides a general overview of crisis intervention in an institution of higher learning from both an administrator's and a practitioner's point of view. Indeed, at times, if you are an administrator in a university system when a crisis arises, you may see yourself as a lot more of the latter than the former. Because most of you are neophytes to the business of crisis intervention, this chapter discusses the general boilerplate of what crisis theory and crisis intervention are and what we would expect any beginning practitioner to know and understand about crisis theory and its application. Please be aware that when we speak of a crisis intervention practitioner, we do not necessarily mean the staff at your counseling center or any psychologists or psychiatrists you have under contract with the university. Lots and lots of licensed professional health service providers have little training or expertise in this newly emergent field of psychotherapy. Further, within the field, there are various performance levels of crisis intervention that range from first aid to highly specialized interventions. We deal extensively with what first-line providers need to know and do in Chapters 9 and 10. What these chapters have to offer in the way of techniques and intervention can be taught to virtually any staff member. These basic listening and responding skills are indeed sometimes called "psychological first aid" (Raphael, 1986; Slaikeu, 1990). Once again, though, if one doesn't know how to apply this first aid, advanced degrees in human service work do little good. We don't mean or imply that we are holier than thou or your counseling staff. We just know that in our field there are a lot of people who have never been taught this stuff. It may interest you to know that the national accrediting agency for counseling, the Council for Accreditation of Counseling and Related Educational Programs (CACREP, 2009) has mandated that crisis intervention be a part of an accredited counseling curriculum in the 2009 standards. We are not aware of any other major accrediting body that has, as of this date, mandated crisis intervention training as part of a required curriculum, other than the National Association of School Psychologists, and those fine folks are not likely to be performing a service function in your university. Therefore, you need to check out your human services staff in regard to just how much they do know about the stuff we are talking about in this book.

There are many definitions of *crisis* as they apply to both individuals and systems. The following definitions represent a good overview of what the experts think *crisis* is. These definitions also set the stage for the remainder of the book. For an individual:

1. A crisis arises from a traumatic event that is unpredictable and uncontrollable. There is an inability to influence it by one's actions. The nature of the event changes values and priorities, and indeed changes everything (Sarri, 2005, pp. 19–24).
2. People are in a state of crisis when they face an obstacle to important life goals—an obstacle that is, for a time, insurmountable by the use of customary methods of problem solving. A period of disorganization ensues, a period of upset, during which many abortive attempts at a solution are made (Caplan, 1961, p. 18).
3. Crisis in a clinical context refers to an acute emotional upset arising from situational, developmental, or sociocultural sources, and results in a temporary inability to cope by means of one's usual problem-solving devices (Hoff, Hallisey, & Hoff, 2009, p. 4).
4. Crisis is a crisis because the individual knows no response to deal with a situation (Carkhuff & Berenson, 1977, p. 165).
5. Crisis is a personal difficulty or situation that immobilizes people and prevents them from consciously controlling their lives (Belkin, 1984, p. 424).
6. Crisis is a state of disorganization in which people face frustration of important life goals or profound disruption of their life cycles and methods of coping with stressors. The term *crisis* usually refers to a person's feelings of fear, shock, and distress *about* the disruption, not to the disruption itself (Brammer, 1985, p. 94).
7. Crisis refers to "an upset in the steady state" of the organism. A "steady state" is a total condition of the system in which it is in balance both internally and with its environment, but it is also moving and in dynamic balance. It often has five components which are: A hazardous or traumatic event, a vulnerable state, a precipitating factor, an active crisis state, and the resolution of the crisis (Roberts, 2005, p. 778).
8. A state of active crisis has symptoms of psychological or physiological distress or both. There is an attitude of panic or defeat and a focus on immediate relief from the pain. While a great deal of energy is expended, efficiency in dealing with the crisis and other life issues is generally lowered (Wright, 2003, p. 133).
9. Crisis is a temporary breakdown of coping. Expectations are violated and waves of emotion such as anger, anxiety, guilt, and grief surface. Old problems and earlier losses may surface. The event's intensity, duration, and suddenness may affect the severity of response to the crisis (Poland & McCormick, 1999, p. 6).

To summarize these definitions, for an individual, crisis is a perception or experiencing of an event or situation as an intolerable difficulty that exceeds the person's current resources and coping mechanisms (James, 2008, p. 3). Unless the person obtains relief, the crisis has the potential to cause severe affective, behavioral, and cognitive malfunctioning. While most of the following system crisis definitions are characterized by the concept of *community* as a town, these definitions would also seem to fit the community of a college or university as well.

For the system:

1. Communities in crisis have several characteristics in common with individuals. Within the group there is an atmosphere of tension and fear. Rumors run rampant. Normal functioning is at a standstill and schools and businesses are closed and health and emergency resources may be in short supply. However, crises can also strengthen and mobilize a group (Hoff, Hallisey, & Hoff, 2009, p. 209).
2. Communities in crisis go through chronological stages following a disaster that are known as the impact, heroic/rescue, honeymoon, disillusionment, and reconstruction/recovery phase. Each phase has identifiable characteristics and sequential timelines, and depending on how the various systems in the community react, may move forward positively or not (Roberts, 2005, p. 205).
3. A crisis that threatens the organization is unexpected, demands a rapid response in a short time frame, and threatens its basic values (Hermann, 1963, p. 63).
4. Crises that are community wide carry the potential to help community members care for one another and create opportunities for survivors to understand their obligations to one another and to the earth, and also help the community feel such an obligation (Kalayjian, 1999, p. 99).
5. A crisis is a major unpredicted event that impacts the organization across its employees, products, services, and reputation in unpredictable ways with the potential for negative results (Barton, 1993, p. 2).

As of this writing, there is no clear definition of *crisis* as it relates to systems or, indeed, the disasters that are often its precursors (Shaluf, Ahmadun, & Said, 2003), and this also appears to be true when applied to the university setting. Because of the many variations, models, and missions of universities, it is hard to come up with a fixed definition of what constitutes a crisis. A small college may have a major crisis if one student or one beloved professor is killed in a traumatic accident, whereas it would scarcely create a ripple across the students or faculty of a large university. However, Zdziarski, Dunkel, and Rollo (2007, p. 24) do believe that there are common characteristics in systemic crises that affect organizations such as universities, including a negative event or outcome, the element of surprise, disruption of operations, and a threat to the well-being of the students and staff of the university.

We'd like to think we could do better and come up with a really spiffy definition for crisis in institutions of higher education, but for right now, Zdziarski's (2006, p. 5) definition seems to capture the essence: A crisis is an event, often sudden or unexpected, that disrupts the normal operations of the institution or its educational mission and threatens the well-being of personal property, financial resources, and/or reputation of the institution. To that we would add that depending on how the issue is handled, by whom, and in what time frame, the crisis has the potential to turn into a *transcrisis* that becomes residual and long lasting.

TRANSCRISIS STATES

Individual Transcrisis

Crises have typically been seen as time limited, usually persisting a minimum of a few days (Hoff, Hallisey, & Hoff, 2009, p. 58), to an average of 4 to 6 weeks (Caplan, 1964), and with the maximum being 6 to 8 weeks, at the end of which time the subjective discomfort diminishes (Janosik, 1984, p. 9). We don't entirely agree with that timeline, and here's why. There are three possible outcomes for an individual in crisis. First, and for most people, they can get through the crisis, get it resolved, put it behind them, and return to a precrisis state of psychological equilibrium quickly within those time frames. Second, a number of people can actually come out of the crisis in better shape than they went into it. It may take a while, but they can grow from the crisis and become more resilient to it or to future crises. That's why about half the crisis books you see today have the kangi characters on their front cover to indicate that, within each crisis, there is the opportunity for development and growth. Third, and much more ominous, they can let the crisis overwhelm them, and, if they survive it, the crisis state becomes residual (Hoff, Hallisey, & Hoff, 2009, p. 58); they either contract PTSD or what may be called a *transcrisis state* with *transcrisis points* along the way (James, 2008, pp. 5–6).

Acute Stress Disorder and Post-Traumatic Stress Disorder

If you are familiar with acute stress disorder (ASD) and post-traumatic stress disorder (PTSD), you should understand that they are not necessarily the same as transcrisis states. Both ASD and PTSD are classifiable mental disorders (American Psychiatric Association, 2000) caused by an extremely traumatic event, and very specific criteria must be present for a diagnosis of ASD and PTSD to be made.

The clinical symptoms of ASD look very much like those of PTSD. The major difference is that the disturbance lasts for a minimum of 2 days and occurs within 4 weeks of the traumatic event (American Psychiatric Association, 2000). If individuals are unable to resolve the psychological disturbances that invariably go with traumatic events, they become candidates for PTSD (Harvey & Bryant, 1998).

To have PTSD, a person must have the following conditions and symptoms as specified in the *DSM-IV-TR* (American Psychiatric Association, 2000, pp. 463–468). First, the person must have been exposed to a traumatic event in which he or she was confronted with a circumstance that involved actual or threatened death or serious injury, or a threat to one's own or others' physical well-being. Traumatic events fall into two large categories. First are human-made traumas such as military combat, physical or sexual assault, witnessing a murder or traumatic injury, being held hostage, and severe vehicle accidents. Second are natural disasters such as earthquakes and tornadoes. The person's response to the trauma was intense fear, helplessness, or horror. As a result, he or she has persistent symptoms of anxiety or arousal that were not evident before the traumatic event.

Second, the person persistently reexperiences the traumatic event in at least one of the following ways:

1. Recurrent and intrusive distressing recollections of the event.
2. Recurrent nightmares of the event.
3. Flashback episodes including those that occur on awakening or when intoxicated that may include all types of sensory hallucinations or illusions that cause the individual to dissociate from the present reality and act or feel as if the event were recurring.
4. Intense psychological distress on exposure to internal or external cues that symbolize or resemble an aspect of the traumatic event.
5. Physiologic reactivity on exposure to events that symbolize or resemble some aspect of the trauma, such as a person who was in an earthquake starting to look for cover when a large truck rumbles by and shakes the house.

Third, the person persistently avoids such stimuli in at least three of the following ways:

1. Attempts to avoid thoughts, dialogues, or feelings associated with the trauma.
2. Tries to avoid activities, people, or situations that arouse recollections of the trauma.
3. Has an inability to recall important aspects of the trauma.
4. Has markedly diminished interest in significant activities.
5. Feels detached and removed emotionally and socially from others.
6. Has a restricted range of affect by numbing feelings.
7. Has a sense of a foreshortened future such as no career, marriage, children, or normal life span.

Fourth, the person has persistent symptoms of increased nervous system arousal that were not present before the trauma, as indicated by at least two of the following problems:

1. Difficulty falling or staying asleep.
2. Irritability or outbursts of anger.
3. Difficulty concentrating on tasks.
4. Constantly being on watch for real or imagined threats that have no basis in reality (hypervigilance).
5. Exaggerated startle reactions to minimal or nonthreatening stimuli.

Fifth, the disturbance causes clinically significant distress or impairment in social, occupational, or other critical areas of living. Examples include not being able to keep a job, having a failed marriage, or becoming a substance abuser. The duration of the foregoing symptoms must be more than one month. Both of the foregoing should not be confused with *peritraumatic* symptoms (those that look a lot like ASD and PTSD that commonly occur for almost everyone immediately after the trauma). Peritraumatic symptoms are part and parcel of the traumatic wake of the event and soon dissipate for most people. So given that most people can move through a crisis and get on with their lives, the foregoing symptoms are what you as the intervener will be confronted with if they don't move through the crisis.

ASD and PTSD of Institutions

While there is no official classification that we know of for ASD or PTSD at an institutional level, there are plenty of bad things that can happen if the institution is not planful, resourceful, coordinated, and resilient in getting the system back into homeostasis and equilibrium as soon after the traumatic event as possible. Collective trauma can do the same thing as individual trauma, only it affects the whole system. Collective trauma tears apart the system's social, financial, and physical infrastructure and brings the activities of the college community to a screaming halt. Hurricane Andrew's impact on Florida had the potential to destroy the University of Miami, Florida International University, and Miami–Dade Community College. Hurricane Katrina, which hit New Orleans, came very near to destroying Tulane University, Dillard University, Southern University, the University of New Orleans, Xavier University, and Delgado Community College. That the hurricanes' aftereffects left indelible imprints in the physical structure and collective psyche of the institutions is without question. And very much like what you will see in the individual eight-step crisis intervention model in Chapter 9, social support systems in the form of other universities that came overwhelmingly to the aid of the New Orleans universities and colleges went a long way toward keeping them from perishing (Rollo & Zdziarski, 2007a, pp. 19–21), although at this writing in November 2009, the long-term health of these New Orleans institutions of higher learning is still open to question. So it should be clearly understood that institutions and systems can become traumatized in much the same way as individuals and can have pretty much the same results, depending on what kinds of interventions are employed.

What happens in the passage of time (see the chronosystem in Chapter 7) demarcates whether a salutogenic (healthful) as opposed to a pathogenic (disease) paradigm emerges (Antonovsky, 1980). Antonovsky (1991) proposes that individuals who can see the event as manageable and make some meaningful, coherent sense of it are far more likely to come out of the trauma experiencing salutogenesis as opposed to pathogenesis. Union University in Jackson, Tennessee, and Gustavus Adolphus University in St. Peter, Minnesota, are excellent examples of what we are talking about when we speak of a salutogenic shift. Union University has survived two devastating tornadoes in the span of 10 years, and Gustavus Adolphus's physical structure was also torn to pieces by a tornado. Each time they have survived and prospered because, among other things, they used many of the principles and practices illustrated in this book. Further, their faith-based educational philosophy has helped them emerge from the rubble as stronger and more capable institutions (Bennett, 2004). While secular state universities do not operate from faith-based initiatives or necessarily conceive of spirituality as part of an organized attempt to recover from a disaster, we would propose that much like the spiritual beliefs of individuals we assess during a crisis, those institutions that do not somehow incorporate spirituality and faith into their mission recovery plan are asking for trouble.

Transcrisis States and Points

While ASD and PTSD may be considered transcrisis in nature, the reverse is not true. A great deal of what happens immediately after the onset of a crisis determines whether it will become a psychosis, personality disorder, broken relationship, unresolved grief, lost job, ruined career, academic failure, or a litany of other bad happenings that fly out of a Pandora's box that may all turn into a *transcrisis state*. While the original crisis may appear to have dissipated and been long resolved, it has not. *Transcrisis points* continue to erupt when students come to grips with new developmental stages or other dimensions of the problem. Transcrisis points do not occur in a regular, predictable, linear progression. Much like a chronic respiratory condition, environmental conditions can aggravate it, and the original crisis reappears. If this condition persists and is left untreated, it can lapse into psychological pneumonia and become lethal. This emotional roller coaster may occur frequently and for extended periods of time, ranging from months to years (James, 2008, p. 6). A student gets in a fight with her fiancé, who proceeds to get drunk, drive his sports car into a bridge abutment at 120 miles an hour, and kill himself. Not only is she now grief stricken but also she is guilt ridden because she feels responsible for his death. She may continuously have difficulties with intimate relationships, drink more to resolve her guilt feelings, and wind up in addictions treatment or attempting suicide.

On the surface, the individual may appear to have it all together and be living a perfectly normal life. Yet, this good face is achieved by repressing the material and putting it into what Gestalt therapists (Joyce & Sills, 2001) call "unfinished business." This unfinished business stays locked away in an emotional file drawer and is pulled out over and over again when the individual runs into environmental, situational, or interpersonal stressors that cause the unfinished business to reemerge in maladaptive and pathological ways. The individual may have a dozen breakups, get married and divorced more than once, and even try marriage counseling. The current relationship may even improve temporarily, and a temporary state of equilibrium may ensue, but until the original crisis is dealt with and resolved, little effective resolution will occur (James, 2008, p. 6). Therefore, it is not only the initial crisis with which the intervener must contend but also each transcrisis point, and it should be clearly understood that these are not just developmental minicrises of broken love affairs or athletic defeats, but symptoms of unresolved trauma that can get an individual in deep psychological water in a hurry.

Institutional Transcrisis

We also believe that institutions can suffer from transcrisis states and points. Nicoletti, Spencer-Thomas, and Bollinger (2001, pp. 148–170) give detailed descriptions of how traditional extracurricular activities, festivals, and athletic victory celebrations, all well lubricated with alcohol, can turn into riots. Further, such spontaneous riots can take on a life of their own and become the accepted norm (at least by some of the student population). One of your authors who lived in Urbana, Illinois, as a youngster well remembers the traditional rite of spring when male University of Illinois students besieged women's residence halls demanding panties. These panty raids never turned violent. Although they were given lip service as unacceptable by the university administration, they were, from all appearances, accepted as part of the "sap's starting to flow in the spring" philosophy after a long winter in central Illinois. This campus rite of spring was tacitly tolerated by the university administration with minimal interference by the authorities. The result was that these panty raids generally dissipated on their own.

However, other examples such as the riots at the University of Colorado, Penn State University, and Washington State University were anything but merely a rite of spring. These involved full-scale riots with all the accoutrements of vandalized buildings, overturned and burned cars, street mobs armed with rocks and bottles, calls for police reinforcements, and injuries to both rioters and police. The residual effects of these riots were bad public relations, declining enrollments, the view of these universities as party schools, and a loss of institutional creditability. In essence, the university that attempts to shove a traumatic event under the rug will continue to suffer in a transcrisis state and, much like an individual, is at risk for continued deterioration in both its physical and psychological state. That does not mean that systemically once started, a transcrisis state is forever the only option. If, for example, institutions like Washington State University decide to intervene and change the precipitating events, restructure the environment, change alcohol consumption policies, and engage in comprehensive planning with all of the major constituencies involved—and that absolutely means student inclusion—the transcrisis state will cease to exist (Nicoletti et al., 2001, pp. 153–158).

UNIVERSALITY AND IDIOSYNCRASY

It may seem paradoxical, but for both individuals and systems, crisis is both universal and idiosyncratic. Crisis is universal because no one is immune to breakdown, given the right constellation of circumstances. Neither is any system immune. Crisis is idiosyncratic because what one person may successfully overcome, another may not, even though the circumstances are virtually the same. For the system, even though the type of crisis is the same, and the general response plan is essentially the same, the specific culture and setting of the system makes it highly idiosyncratic, and what is unexpected in one institutional setting may be demanded in another (Rollo & Zdziarski, 2007a, pp. 5–6).

For individuals with depression, generic treatment protocols almost always include some sort of cognitive behavior procedures (Beck, 1995). Yet how those procedures get applied may be very different for each person (Sharff, 2008, p. 351). The same is true of crisis management and containment of violence on college campuses. While crisis management plans, threat assessment teams, and crisis response teams may be part of every system's crisis plan, how they are carried out, by whom, and under what geographical, environmental, cultural, and political constraints makes them very idiosyncratic indeed (Rollo & Zdziarski, 2007b, pp. 73–95; Sherwood & McKelfresh, 2007, pp. 55–71).

Disequilibrium or disorganization accompanies every crisis, whether universal or idiosyncratic (Janosik, 1984, p. 13). It is a fool's errand to believe that one is immune to psychologically traumatic assaults and that one can handle any crisis, no matter how severe or how extended, and be calm, cool, collected, and in control. Thousands of tough veterans of the Vietnam War, the Gulf War, the Iraq War, and the Afghanistan War suffering from PTSD should be living proof that when a crisis boils over, disorganization, disequilibrium, disorientation, and fragmentation of an individual's coping mechanisms can occur no matter how conditioned against psychological trauma the person may be. The same is certainly true of institutions (Nicoletti et al., 2001). Therefore, any crisis intervention plan needs to consider how to adapt what are understood in the world of crisis intervention to be fairly universal responses to the idiosyncratic needs of its population.

THEORIES OF CRISIS AND CRISIS INTERVENTION

A variety of theories have been generated as crisis intervention has evolved. To this point in time, no one theory holds sway. As the field expands, it is likely that more theories that examine environmental, systemic, and contextual elements of crisis will evolve. The following theories are presented to give you a flavor of how crisis theory translates into practice.

Generic or Basic Theory

Less of a theory than an approach, Aguilera (1998, p. 18) proposes that there are certain recognizable patterns of behavior common to all crises that Lindemann (1944, 1956) found in his study of the Cocoanut Grove nightclub fire survivors. Lindemann helped caregivers promote crisis intervention for many sufferers of loss who had no specific pathological diagnosis but who were exhibiting symptoms that appeared pathological and who were going through a well-defined process of grieving. Subsequent research by Caplan (1964) and others has supported the hypothesis that there is a characteristic course to each crisis. Understanding this course is seen as the important component of crisis theory as opposed to the psychodynamics of each individual (Aguilera, 1998, p. 18). Caplan (1964) expanded Lindemann's constructs to the total field of traumatic events.

Caplan believed that crisis resulted from roadblocks to life goals that couldn't be surmounted by usual and customary actions and behaviors. Both Lindemann and Caplan dealt with crisis intervention following psychological trauma by using an equilibrium–disequilibrium approach that can best be called a *stage model of intervention*. The stages in Lindemann's paradigm are (a) disturbed equilibrium, (b) brief therapy or grief work, (c) client's working through the problem or grief, and (d) restoration of equilibrium (Janosik, 1984, pp. 10–12). Caplan linked Lindemann's concepts and stages of grief from traumatic loss to all developmental and situational events and extended crisis intervention to eliminating the affective, behavioral, and cognitive disruptions that caused the psychological trauma in the first place.

Generic or basic crisis theory, following the lead of Lindemann and Caplan, focuses on helping people in crisis recognize and correct temporary affective, behavioral, and cognitive distortions brought on by traumatic events. It is far more concerned with applying these generic principles to all members of a group who have experienced crisis as opposed to the unique differences of one individual (Aguilera, 1998, p. 19).

Psychoanalytic Theory

Psychoanalytic theory (Fine, 1973) is based on the view that the disequilibrium that accompanies a person's crisis can best be understood through gaining access to the individual's unconscious thoughts and past emotional experiences. Psychoanalytic theory presupposes that some early childhood fixation is the primary explanation of why an event becomes a crisis. This theory may be used to help clients develop insight into the dynamics and causes of their behavior as the crisis situation acts on them. Freud's three-part model of id, ego, and superego proposes that these ego states must be kept in equilibrium to avoid unhealthy defense mechanisms and psychopathology (Alexander, 1956). Both basic and psychoanalytic models have been criticized for their strict reliance on the concepts of returning the individual to precrisis homeostasis and equilibrium. Psychoanalytic crisis theory views crisis more in terms of a disease model of pathology rather than as an emotional crisis involving situational, environmental, and contextual factors. As a result, critics believe both basic and psychoanalytic crisis theories discount the ability of the individual to take control and participate in getting through the crisis and instead leave the interventionist in charge of fixing or curing the person (Hoff et al., 2009, p. 8).

We believe that a postmodern view is not entirely tenable. First, there is evidence that what a person brings to the table in a crisis in the form of unfinished business and traumatic incidents are additive and make them more prone to crisis than others (Norris et al., 2002). Second, and more important, we believe that returning people to a precrisis state of equilibrium and homeostasis is tenable and worthwhile. Regaining a sense of self-control in a linear world that has purpose and meaning is critical in getting people through a crisis. While at times people do need very directive intervention, much like a surgeon fixing a broken leg, we believe that people are resilient and can be self-directing, and with the right amount of help—sometimes more and sometimes less—they can once again become masters of their own destiny.

Eclectic or Expanded Crisis Theory

Eclectic or expanded crisis theory was developed because basic theory, which depended on a psychoanalytic approach alone, did not adequately address the social, environmental, and situational factors that make an event a crisis (Hoff et al., 2009, p. 9). As crisis theory and intervention have evolved, it has become pretty clear that an approach that relies on predisposing factors alone as the primary reason that a person is prone to crisis is inadequate. A classic example of the shortfall of this approach is that of Vietnam veterans suffering from PTSD. It was erroneously believed that they were susceptible to psychopathology because of preexisting conditions that had nothing to do with prolonged exposure to combat. Practitioners who first encountered PTSD victims believed that pathology preceding the crisis event was the real cause of the trauma and summarily dismissed the events themselves as the causative factors (Ochberg, 1988, p. 4). As crisis theory and crisis intervention have grown, it has become apparent that given the right combination of developmental, sociological, psychological, environmental, and situational determinants, anyone can fall victim to transient pathological symptoms.

Therefore, eclectic crisis theory draws not only from psychoanalytic theory but also from general systems, ecosystems, adaptation, interpersonal, chaos, and developmental theories. Following are synopses of these major theoretical components of an expanded view. Eclectic theory of crisis intervention is not trying to hit a piñata blindfolded by aimlessly flailing about with random swings of a theoretical bat. It is based on using a combination of theories in an integrated fashion to fit the idiosyncratic problems that each person and institution will have, which, while universal in nature, are individually tailored for treatment.

Systems Theory

Systems theory (Bowen, 1978; Haley, 1973, 1976) is based on the interrelationships and interdependence among people and between people and events. This theory had its start in family therapy and proposes that a family or, for that matter, any member within the family unit cannot be understood without knowing how the family functions as a total unit (Sharff, 2008, p. 482). Systems theory represents a turning away from traditional approaches, which focus only on what is going on within the individual. A standard systems approach to crisis may be thought of as interpersonal rather than intrapersonal. While systems therapy has a good deal of psychoanalytic basis to it and thus may be criticized for many of the same reasons as psychoanalytic and basic crisis theory, it is a first step in starting to see how individuals operate and interact in small and large groups.

In terms of a college environment, it should be readily apparent that a student will have many new families—residence hall floors or pods, fraternities and sororities, clubs and honor organizations for major fields, campus ministries, political organizations, and so on—to adapt to and fit into. When a crisis strikes any member of this microsystem, it has the potential to afflict all members of that system. Reciprocally, how the system reacts impacts the member at the epicenter of the crisis in a positive or negative way, depending on the support or lack thereof that the members of that system provide.

Ecosystems Theory

Ecosystems theory (Bronfenbrenner, 1986, 1995) broadens out the base of systems theory and looks at crisis in relation to the environmental context within which it occurs (Collins & Collins, 2005; Harvey, 1996; James, Cogdal, & Gilliland, 2003; Myer & Moore, 2006). Systemic interactions may occur from the microsystem (residence hall floor, sorority, newspaper staff, etc.) out to the exosystem (college) and then to macrosystems (nation, world) or vice versa. The key to an ecosystem theory is what Bronfenbrenner (1995) called the *mesosystem* (the way communications get transmitted within and between systems). In the contemporary university, technology is king, and the multiple ways both word-of-mouth and technological communication occur and are used are absolutely critical to the outcome of a crisis.

There is great value in looking at crises in their total social and environmental settings—not simply as one individual being affected in a linear progression of cause-and-effect events (Hardy, 1997; Hoff et al., 2009; James, 2008, pp. 569–572). Ecosystems theory comes into play most typically when large-scale disasters affect the university macrosystem, but it also plays a critical part in keeping small crises from metastasizing into larger, uncontrolled ones.

For example, a rumor of bullying, hazing, or assault of a foreign student starts in a residence hall wing. The foreign student tweets across campus about his ugly American roomie to a fellow countryman, who then posts it on Facebook. Other foreign students assemble in front of the administration building and demand an end to the vicious discrimination they are experiencing at the hands of American students. The police in full riot gear are called out, and television camera crews arrive on the scene to upload the demonstration, which is by now becoming unruly. Then CNN picks it up, and an hour later, alarmed parents in a European country get a real-time view of their daughter throwing a brick at a police officer and getting chemically maced for her trouble. In the meantime, frightened and angry community residents beseech every law enforcement agency from the local sheriff to the FBI to do something about the foreign terrorists in their midst. In actuality, the original issue between the foreign student and his American roomie was whose turn it was to go to the snack bar at the university union to get a late-night pizza. What started out as a disagreement between two members of a microsystem has now metastasized into an international incident that includes two exosystems (college and community) and the national and international macrosystem. If you believe this example is a wild exaggeration, then we would urge you to consider how far you might possibly be out of touch with the 21st-century mesosystem on a college campus.

Adaptive Theory

Adaptive theory, as we use the term, proposes that crises are generated through maladaptive behaviors, negative thoughts, and destructive defense mechanisms that are formulated by either the individual or the system. Adaptive theory is not easy to implement because it calls for getting rid of long-held beliefs and suppositions that are ingrained within the individual or the system as the right response. Breaking through destructive defenses that support these erroneous beliefs and suppositions calls for reframing negative self-defeating cognitions to positive growth-promoting ones. By bringing myths to the light of day, exposing them, and introjecting new facts to dispute them, subjective and biased views are changed. Thus, getting rid of faulty defense mechanisms by replacing them with proactive actions and positive self-attributions helps the person overcome the immobility created by the crisis and move to a positive mode of functioning. Adaptive crisis theory is based on the concept that the person's crisis will diminish when these maladaptive coping behaviors are changed to more adaptive, less debilitating behaviors (James, 2008, p. 12).

As maladaptive behaviors are learned, so may adaptive behaviors be learned. Aided by the interventionist, people may learn to replace negative behaviors with new, positive ones. As an example, social norms marketing is a top-down traditional marketing approach that promotes healthy messages for more adaptive behavior and challenges myths about problematic campus issues like high-risk drinking and date rape (Frazier, Valtinson, & Caldwell, 1994; Nicoletti et al., 2001, pp. 58, 138). Its mass-marketing approach is followed up by visits to student groups for candid discussions about these endemic campus problems. While it may seem that such an approach is too simplistic to have any effect on cynical college students, research indicates that it does (Nicoletti et al., 2001, p. 58). Thus, providing information and guidance to individuals who lack the former and could profit from the latter can generate new and more appropriate behaviors that can prevent crises from happening in the first place. Or when they do happen, adaptive theory can help people learn new ways of building coping mechanisms by teaching them new behavioral and cognitive schemas (Beck, 1971) that insulate them from future crises.

It should be readily apparent that adaptive theory also applies to institutions. What the institution does in regard to prevention, intervention, and postvention practices can be either adaptive or maladaptive. It is almost a sure bet, though, that if little prevention is planned, a whole lot is likely to go wrong in the intervention and postvention stages.

Developmental Theory

Probably the greatest developmental stage in students' lives are their undergraduate college years. Because many crises have their bases in developmental stages that humans pass through, developmental theory must play a part in crisis intervention. Developmental stage theorists such as Erikson (1963), Levinson (1986), Levinson and Levinson (1996), Sheehy (1995), and Blocher (2000) believe that movement through various developmental life stages is critical. Erikson's (1963) theory of orderly progression through life stages has particular importance for college-age students because of his belief that each stage is marked by social development as a result of their encounters with their social environment.

The two stages of Erikson's (1963) developmental theory that crosscut the typical college years are Identity versus Role Confusion in adolescence and Intimacy versus Isolation in the young adult years. Erikson particularly viewed the adolescent years as what he called a "normative crisis" stage. That is a stage marked with increased conflicts as teenagers seek to individuate themselves from their families and find their way in an adult world that is filled with a series of role conflicts. These role conflicts have the potential to turn into crises as teenagers attempt to integrate these new, unfamiliar, and sometimes threatening roles into a sense of self. Erikson's second stage that falls squarely into the college years is Intimacy versus Isolation. Once individuals establish a sense of self, they are then faced with the task of developing deep and meaningful relationships, not only with the opposite sex but also with members of their own sex. It doesn't take a rocket scientist to see that many of the troubled individuals who fill up counseling centers and disciplinary board hearings are not moving very well through either of these life stages.

If that weren't enough to guarantee college counseling centers an unending supply of clients, let us now turn to Daniel Levinson (1986; Levinson & Levinson, 1996) and Gail Sheehy (1995). Both authors have spent a good deal of time studying what happens to both men and women when they fail to move through normal maturation and development.

To give an example of what these authors are writing about, one of your authors teaches an undergraduate class in crisis intervention in a five-week summer school night session. It meets four hours a night, two nights a week. To say that it is a fast-moving course is like saying an atomic particle saunters around a nuclear accelerator. The average age of these students is late 30s with some in their 50s and 60s. There are very few traditional college-age students in the class. These nontraditional students may be characterized as first-generation college students who are typically taking care of parents, raising children, holding down one or two blue-collar jobs, and attempting to take six hours of upper division college credit four nights a week for four hours every night Monday through Thursday. Do you suppose they have stressors that lead to crises in their lives? These folks are the prototype of Levinson's and Sheehy's people in that developmental tasks that are not met and accomplished during particular life stages tend to pile up and cause problems. As these adult learners' early needs and wants ran headlong into the demands and expectations of society, these returning students failed to move on to the next life stage. Their postponement of college to meet other demands and expectations means that developmental tasks pile up. These tasks demand attention and cannot be left alone. The typical day-to-day crises that these other familial, occupational, and societal expectations create are now compounded by unreasonable professors' demands and deadlines—particularly in a short-term summer season where voluminous reading assignments, chapter tests, and term papers come endlessly marching day after day after day.

No wonder that stocks in proprietary, online institutions of higher learning soar, with billboards that promise, "You can get our degree in your pajamas!" as these adult learners struggle to meet their outside responsibilities and still fight for a parking space when hoards of students descend at 5 p.m. every night into university evening schools. Failure to navigate these life stages has negative outcomes of decreased job performance, academic failure, divorce, suicide, homicide, stress-related illnesses, substance abuse, and a host of other problems that these adult learners are faced with while attempting to juggle their lives and still finally earn a degree. Given all this, do you really suppose these harried students will decide to make time to go to counseling centers to get psychological tune-ups? When external, environmental, or situational crises that are all too characteristic of people who are struggling with developmental issues emerge and feed into preexisting developmental crises, intrapersonal and interpersonal problems may reach the breaking point (Levinson, 1986).

Interpersonal Theory

Interpersonal theory is based on Carl Rogers's (1977) person-centered approach to counseling, which has as its major building blocks openness, congruence, acceptance, trust, unconditional positive regard, and the self-actualizing tendency that posits that individuals have the ability to raise themselves out of a crisis on their own. The major role of the interventionist is to create an empathic atmosphere that lets individuals increase awareness of their potential to take action by using their own resources. From that standpoint, the theory uses nondirective techniques such as silence, restatement of content, reflection of thoughts and feelings, and open-ended leads to allow persons to feel accepted and start to become masters of their own destinies again. The end goal is that persons will have or regain an internal locus of control (Raskin & Rogers, 1995), which falls directly in line with the goal of crisis intervention to achieve a precrisis state of equilibrium and homeostasis.

If the person continues to believe that fate, the government, the college dean, God, the residence hall director, Mother Nature, Professor James, evil computers, the chief of police, or some other all-powerful and omniscient external force has power over the situation, the crisis will persist. This theory probably has the most utility in the early exploration states of crisis intervention when the interventionist, if at all possible, is trying to determine the context, conditions, thoughts, feelings, behaviors, significant others, and any other information that will give him or her an idea about what is going on. While it is the ideal approach from the standpoint of allowing the individual freedom to choose options, the problem is that many times people in crisis are not anywhere near masters of their own destiny. Indeed, if people are wildly out of control, this value-free and judgment-free approach is going to be about the last approach they need to help them regain stability.

Chaos Theory

Most major crises are chaotic, or at least the person in crisis generally perceives it in that manner. In some ways, chaos theory is an ecosystemic theory because it takes into account the total interaction of the environment as its component parts collide with each other and the individual. Chaos theory is really a sort of theory of evolution when applied to human functioning such as crisis intervention. It is evolutionary in that it is essentially an open-ended, ever-changing, self-organizing system whereby a new system may emerge out of the crisis (Butz, 1995, 1997).

It also recognizes the complexity of the human condition and that interdependence and interaction are key components (Ramsey, 1997) in trying to understand and make sense out of what at first appears to be a mess with no sense or order in it. This theory evolves from what Postrel (1998, p. xv) calls "emergent complex messiness" and forces administrations to deal with a chaotic (crisis) situation—which at first seems to have no sense or solution to it. But, if they are up to the task, they soon move into a self-organizing mode when a critical mass of people come to perceive that they have no way to identify patterns or preplan options to solve the dilemma at hand and are forced to come up with new, creative ways of handling the problem.

The messiness of the crisis lies not in disorder but in an order that is unknown, unpredictable, and spontaneous, an ever-shifting pattern driven by millions of uncoordinated, independent factors that necessitate experimentation yet may finally result in a global clarification of the crisis. In an attempt to attack the chaotic situation, such experimentation may lead to false starts, temporary failure, dead ends, spontaneous innovation, creativity, improvisation, brainstorming, cooperative enterprise, and other evolutionary attempts to make sense of and cope with the crisis. As an example, the chaos of the massacre that Seung-Hui Cho created at Virginia Tech brought to light the broader underlying chaos of a broken mental health system whose various components collided head-on and allowed Seung-Hui Cho's paranoid schizophrenia to continue to blossom until it turned into a massacre. This is an excellent example of chaos theory at work, where unpredictable behavior can spontaneously erupt in what are erroneously believed to be predictable and linear systems (Rogers, 2001).

APPLIED CRISIS DOMAINS

Zdziarski, Rollo, and Dunkel (2007) propose a three-dimensional crisis matrix that involves types, levels, and intentionality of crisis. According to them, types of crises that may occur on a college campus fall into environmental, facility, and human categories. In this book, we are mainly concerned with human crises and only tangentially with facility or environmental crises and only when they apply to the perpetration of human-initiated crises. Crisis in regard to humans encompasses at least four domains: (a) developmental crises, (b) situational crises, (c) existential crises, and (d) ecosystemic crises.

Developmental Crises

Developmental crises are events that occur in the normal flux and flow of human growth and devolvement, as previously indicated in this chapter. College is all about development across every conceivable component of the individual's existence and growth. As such, it should not be any surprise that developmental crises probably lead over any other kind of crises that afflict college-age individuals.

Situational Crises

A situational crisis emerges with the occurrence of uncommon and extraordinary events that an individual has no way of forecasting or controlling (James, 2008, p. 13). Situational crises on college campuses can occur as a result of accidents, riots, serial rapes, assaults and murders, and terrorist or radical attacks on symbols of power. The key to differentiating a situational crisis from other crises is that it is random, sudden, shocking, intense, and often catastrophic. A classic example of such a crisis was the 1999 Texas A&M bonfire construction tragedy that killed 12 students. This tragedy not only killed students but also caused chaos in frantic attempts to obtain information on who was not involved. Communications systems were overwhelmed, and community resources had to be reallocated to deal with the communications breakdown (Rollo & Zdziarski, 2007a).

Existential Crises

An existential crisis includes the inner conflicts and anxieties that accompany important human issues of purpose, responsibility, independence, freedom, and commitment (James, 2008, p. 13). An existential crisis might accompany the realization, from an assistant professor, that he or she will never make a significant and distinct impact on his or her profession and will not be granted tenure. Or a doctoral student comes to the realization after 10 years of starts and stops on a dissertation that it will never be finished. Or a team filled with seniors who had a chance to go to the NCAA finals loses on a heartbreaking last-second desperation shot from the opposition. Or a date turns into a rape from what was thought to be a good friend that the victim was able to confide in. What happens when the realization hits that there is ugly finality in these examples of existential dilemmas?

Existential issues relate to the uncontrollable factors a person is thrown into in the world (being in the auditorium where the Northern Illinois University shootings took place, as opposed to deciding to cut the lecture and go drink coffee in the university union). Existential crises test the beliefs one has about the world and the faith and spiritual values that are placed in it when things go terribly wrong. Finally, existential crises test the beliefs about oneself: the Me, Myself, and I and coming to grips with who this self is (Sharff, 2008, pp. 152–153) when placed in the middle of a traumatic event. While these issues may sound exotic, esoteric, and more in the realm of philosophy as opposed to crisis, they are not. Particularly in a university where a lot of thinking about such issues is fairly common, existential crises are very real, and the crises sometimes become lethal.

Ecosystemic Crises

Ecosystemic crises typically occur when some *natural or human-caused* disaster overtakes a person or a (large or small) group of people who find themselves, through no fault or action of their own, inundated in the aftermath of an event that may adversely affect virtually every member of the environment in which they live. Such crises may occur in the form of natural phenomena such as hurricanes, floods, tidal waves, earthquakes, volcanic eruptions, tornadoes, blizzards, mud slides, drought, famine, and forest or grassland brush fires. The universities in Miami and New Orleans after Hurricanes Andrew and Katrina, Union University in Tennessee and Gustavus Adolphus College in Minnesota after tornadoes, and California State University at Northridge after the Northridge earthquake are vivid examples of ecosystemic crises. Other instances of ecosystemic crises may be *biologically derived*, such as the meningitis epidemic at the University of Illinois at the Urbana-Champaign campus. Or the crisis may spread across all universities in the form of the current severe economic recession (Nicoletti et al., 2001, p. 224; Rollo & Zdziarski, 2007a, p. 13). However, they most certainly can be caused by humans, as in the cases of Virginia Tech and Northern Illinois University.

CRISIS INTERVENTION MODELS

There are essentially three basic crisis intervention models (Belkin, 1984): the equilibrium model (Caplan, 1961, 1964), the cognitive model (Dattilio & Freeman, 2007), and the psycho/social/cultural transition model (Hoff et al., 2009). These three models provide the groundwork for many different crisis intervention strategies and methodologies for individuals and can be adapted to systems. Recently, in response to large-scale crises that have affected thousands if not millions of individuals, a number of ecosystemic models have been developed to deal with how individuals are affected by whole systems in crises or, in fact, how the systems themselves are affected. These models are James, Cogdal, and Gilliland's (2003) adaptation of Bronfenbrenner's (1986, 1995) developmental ecosystem model, Collins and Collins's (2005) developmental-ecological model, and the contextual-ecological model that is detailed throughout this book in delivering crisis services to the university (Myer & Moore, 2006). All these models take the total ecology of the crisis environment into consideration in one way or the other.

The Equilibrium Model

The equilibrium model derives from general systems theory and could more aptly be called an *equilibrium–disequilibrium model*. Gerald Caplan, one of the primary originators of the field of crisis intervention, developed this model (Caplan, 1961, 1964). If people experience problems that cannot be redefined, resolved, or avoided, then tensions continue to rise until some precipitating factor causes a breaking point and previous coping mechanisms no longer work. The individuals then suffer disequilibrium and are in a state of crisis (Golan, 1978) because their usual coping mechanisms and problem-solving methods fail to meet their needs.

The goal of the equilibrium model is to help people recover a state of precrisis equilibrium and homeostasis (Caplan, 1961, 1964). The equilibrium model is probably the most often used in crisis intervention. It seems most appropriate for early intervention, when the person is out of control, disoriented, and unable to make appropriate choices. Until the person has regained some coping abilities, the main focus is on stabilizing the individual. Until the person has reacquired some measure of stability and has some psychological homeostasis, the crisis will not be resolved (Viney, 1976). For example, it does little good to probe the underlying psycho/social/cultural factors that cause a suicidal, depressed person to believe that he or she is worthless until the individual can be stabilized to the point of agreeing that life is worth living for at least another week.

The Cognitive Model

Cognition, or the subjective interpretation of the stressful event through the eyes and ears of the beholder, plays a major part in determining the nature and degree of coping behaviors and whether that event will turn into a crisis (Aguilera, 1998, p. 38). The cognitive model of crisis intervention is based on the premise that crises are rooted in faulty thinking about the events or situations that surround the crisis—not in the events themselves or the facts about the events or situations. The resulting negative appraisals and schemas that people build wind up in black-and-white, all-or-none, catastrophic thinking, where there are no outcomes other than the awfulness, helplessness, and hopeless of the crisis (Beck, Freeman, Davis, & Associates, 2004; Dattilio & Freeman, 2007;

Ellis, 1962). The goal of this model is to help people change the negative self-attributions and irrational ideas they make about themselves or the situation to more positive self-attributions and rational cognitions. Changing the kinds of negative self-talk and thoughts about the crisis to more positive coping statements is critical in changing the dynamics and impetus of the crisis (Meichenbaum, 1977, 2001).

The negative messages that people in crisis send themselves are due to the constant pressure and stress of crisis situations, where they can see no end in sight or hope for a positive outcome. Think of a very bad hair day you have recently had and all the frustration and stress that went into that day. Now think of that day turning into weeks, months, or even years, and you start to get an idea of what persons who have lost their homes and farms to a flood and been foreclosed and are homeless, people who are in constant transcrisis due to a series of broken relationships and abusive childhoods, individuals experiencing long-term, chronic depression, persons suffering unresolved, complicated grief from having lost their entire family in a vehicle accident, or veterans who have rampant cases of PTSD are experiencing. Do you see why they might have a little bit of negative self-talk about the situation and see doom, despair, and agony as some of the primary emotions that go with that bad hair?

This constant negative self-talk soon begets behavior that things are hopeless and they are thus helpless to change anything about themselves, the situation, the environment, or significant others in it. At this point in time, crisis intervention becomes a job of changing the individual's thoughts to more positive feedback loops by practicing and rehearsing new positive self-statements about the situation until the old, negative, debilitating ones are expunged (Meichenbaum, 2001). If people can do this, they gain a more realistic perception of the original event and see it in various shades of gray rather than the absolutistic all-or-none, catastrophic cognitive distortions that are characteristic of this model. Viney (1976) calls this cognitive mastery of the situation. Because cognition is such a critical part of crisis intervention, using the cognitive model seems most appropriate early on in stabilizing the client's thinking and regaining his or her precrisis cognitive equilibrium.

The Psycho/Social/Cultural Transition Model

The psycho/social/cultural model assumes that people are a great deal more than what they inherited from their parents. It also assumes that people are resilient and capable of pulling themselves through a crisis if they have adequate support systems at their disposal. Hoff and associates (2009) believe that helping people in crisis is far more than just restoring them to some hypothetical state of precrisis equilibrium. People may need to incorporate adequate internal coping mechanisms, social supports, and environmental resources to gain autonomous (noncrisis) control over their lives.

A psycho/social/cultural model is all that its complex name implies. That is, crises are complex, and no one theory is adequate to explain all of the physical, emotional, social, and spiritual functions that are involved in the generation and resolution of crisis

(Hoff et al., 2009, p. 20; Kalayjian, 1999). The Adlerian notion of social influence and development of social interest is critical to this approach. Such social influence and interest in involvement with others reaches out beyond the individual and his or her immediate family and friends to the entire community (Ansbacher & Ansbacher, 1978; Sharff, 2008, p. 141). This notion is certainly a key component in our own model's emphasis on obtaining support systems in a crisis. Absence of social supports is a major contributor to the exacerbating effects of the initial crisis (Halpern & Tramontin, 2007, p. 103).

Thus, the psycho/social/cultural model extends out and beyond the individual's microsystem and critically examines and seeks to enlist the larger exosystems in aiding crisis intervention (Myers & Wee, 2005, pp. 221–229). From that standpoint, this model sometimes acts as a social change agent in attempting to alleviate systems and environments that contribute to the potential for crises to occur (Hoff et al., 2009, p. 21). The goal of a psycho/social/cultural approach is to establish preventive methodologies throughout the system and a positive, healthy, strength- and resiliency-based approach rather than a problem-centered pathological view (Bennett, 2004; Clark, 2002; Lukens et al., 2004; Miller, 2003; Strumpfer, 2006; Zinner & Williams, 1999).

With certain kinds of crisis problems, few lasting gains will be made unless the social systems that affect the individual are also changed or the individual comes to terms with and understands the dynamics of those systems and how they affect adaptation to the crisis. The psychosocial transition model seems to be most appropriate after the client has been stabilized or is employed to plan for future disasters.

Diversity and Multicultural Issues

Why are the issues of diversity and multiculturalism important in crisis intervention? In counseling circles, the concept of multiculturalism has achieved such notoriety and fame that it has been called "the fourth force" (Arredondo, 1999; Sue, 1999a, 1999b). If you aren't a counselor, you don't need to worry about the other three "forces," at least in this book. Okay! You aren't a counselor, so why be concerned about the fourth force when the other three don't matter? In the world of counseling, multiculturalism is seen as one of the major driving forces in how counseling gets conducted (Arredondo, 1999; Ivey, 1987; Ober, Peeters, Archer, & Kelly, 2000; Ridley, 1995; Sue, 1992, 1999a, 1999b). How, then, do going to college, understanding multiculturalism, and practicing crisis intervention go together?

A vast majority of the world's population lives by a non-Western perspective, and that is particularly important in relation to 21st-century American universities, which have seen the largest influx of foreign students in their history (U.S. Department of Census, 2001). As one small piece of evidence of this phenomenon, witness one of your authors' amazement at seeing a Sunday afternoon game of cricket being played on an empty parking lot by a group of Indian, Australian, English, and Jamaican students.

Despite the emergence of a more global perspective, much of our approach to the field of counseling and crisis intervention is specific to North American and European cultures (Pedersen, 1998; Ponterotto & Pedersen, 1993). The major problem with that assumption is that at present very little is known about how culture and crises actually do interact, although one thing is becoming clearer as we come to understand the etiology of crises, which is that crisis outcomes do not act on all people, in the same way, all the time (James, 2008). Indeed, it may interest you to know that a number of experts in the field of crisis don't necessarily believe that PTSD is a cause-and-effect outcome of trauma or that it even exists as an identifiable psychological malady. Rather, they suggest, instead of treating the symptoms of PTSD, we would do far better to look at trauma in terms of grief, injustice, faith, and a number of other broader social issues (Silove, 2000).

UNIVERSAL VERSUS A FOCUSED VIEW OF DIVERSITY/ MULTICULTURALISM

There are both universal and focused views on diversity and multiculturalism. A universal view considers not only racial and ethnic minorities but also other minority or special populations. Taken to the extreme, this view has a *beta bias* (Berg-Cross & Pak, 2006). That is, by seeing the universal commonalities in all cultures, interventionists may take the view that universal values far overshadow any specific cultural traits or attributes and thus minimize cultural factors that play into the crisis.

A focused view of diversity/multiculturalism sees it in terms of "visible and racial ethnic minorities" (Sue, Arredondo, & McDavis, 1992). This view, when taken to the extreme, has an *alpha bias* (Berg-Cross & Pak, 2006), which bases one's perceptions on a cookie-cutter notion that fits all individuals of an identifiable race, religion, or nationality into one pigeonhole of sameness. To view diversity/multiculturalism from such a narrow perspective with either an alpha or beta bias is, we believe, asking for a lot of trouble in crisis intervention. Therefore, when we respond to individuals in crisis, we need to see them in the broadest possible terms and understand that both the student's cultural background and individuality within that culture are critical factors.

Ivey (1987) and Arredondo (1999) believe that before any kind of counseling—and we would propose that applies twofold to crisis intervention starts—interveners need to examine their own assumptions, values, and biases regarding racial, cultural, and group differences. That notion is probably exponentially true for crisis workers in college settings, given the wide variety of people with which they are dealing. Kiselica (1998, p. 6) proposes four attributes that interventionists would do well to consider in dealing with diversity in a crisis situation. We have posed questions in regard to these attributes that we believe interventionists need to ask themselves when approaching individuals in crisis:

1.   What skills do I have to deal with culturally different individuals, and if I don't have them, am I willing to take the trouble to learn them? What do I know

about myself, and where do I stand on the alpha-beta continuum in regard to my own stereotypes and biases about Caucasian farm kids who like to bass fish, Asian city kids who play violas, or anybody else who looks, acts, thinks, or feels different from me?

2. Am I willing to do something different to better match the cultures of individuals in crisis than what my traditional game plan usually is?

3. Am I willing to engage culturally different individuals to learn how to do this?

4. What do I know about the culture of different groups that I may have to deal with, and what trouble am I willing to go to in finding out something about them that at least gives me a common ground on which to operate.

CULTURALLY BIASED ASSUMPTIONS

Although you are undoubtedly aware and tolerant of all kinds and types of students with whom you come in contact on your campus, you might want to mentally check yourself against the following 10 culturally biased assumptions (Pederson, 1987):

1. People all share a common measure of so-called normal behavior (p. 17) (the notion that problems, emotional responses, behaviors, and perceptions of crises are more or less universal across social, cultural, economic, or political backgrounds).

2. Individuals are the basic building blocks of all societies (p. 18) (the idea that crisis intervention considers only the individual and not the groups the individual is affiliated with, such as family, athletic teams, friends, political clubs, religious groups, and fraternal organizations).

3. The definition of problems can be limited by academic or professional discipline boundaries (p. 19) (the concept that the identity of the interventionist and the problem are somehow separate from the identity of the police officer, biology professor, campus minister, residence hall director, custodian, or president of the university and their environments and that the crisis does not ripple out into other environments).

4. Western culture depends on abstract words (pp. 19–20) (the idea that others will understand these abstractions in the same way as interveners intend them, particularly when English may be the second language of the person the intervener encounters; further, that the chaotic conditions that often exist in a crisis make even the best communicators difficult to understand).

5. Independence is valuable, and dependencies are undesirable (p. 20) (the endearing and enduring philosophy of Western individualism that people should not be dependent on others or allow others to be dependent on them when the exact, diametric opposite may be true in regard to the cultural origins of the individual, which are highly interdependent).

6. Formal counseling is more important than the natural support systems of the individual in problem resolution (pp. 20–21) (the erroneous presumption that students prefer the intervention offered by professionals over the support of family, peers, and other support systems, which may be compounded when those support systems are not yet in place in a university setting and are often hundreds or even thousands of miles away).

7. Linear thinking is the only kind of logical approach to resolving a problem (pp. 21– 22) (the notion that the way the world works is through a direct cause–effect relationship and that everything can be measured and described in terms of good or bad, appropriate or inappropriate, and/or other common dichotomies, when the individual's cultural background may see tangential, indirect, or even circular thinking as an appropriate way to deal with a problem).

8. Intervention needs to change individuals to fit the system (p. 22) (the idea that the system does not need to change to fit the individual, which may be even more problematic in a university setting that thrives on complex bureaucratic systems that students have little familiarity with in attempting to navigate through it, particularly when dealing with a crisis).

9. The individual's past has little relevance to contemporary events (pp. 22–23) (the presumption that crises are strictly related to here-and-now, real-time situations and that it is a mistake for the interventionist to get hung up in the history of the individual; consider the potential differences between the responses of an American student who has just been notified that his parents have been killed in an auto accident with a drunk driver and the responses of an Iraqi student who has just been notified his parents' car was blown up by a roadside bomb).

10. Professionals who deal with diversity already know all the foregoing assumptions (p. 23) (the idea that if professionals in student personnel services acted in stereotypical, biased, and culturally encapsulated ways, they would be aware of it, and that would include those professionals who wear their multiculturalism on their sleeves but in fact know precious little about multiculturalism and its relationship to crises).

So what do you think? Do any of these apply to you? The point is that if you don't understand your own cultural biases, all of your good intentions may be misinterpreted by individuals from other cultures, whether those cultures originate out of Arkansas or Vietnam.

THE ENVIRONMENT'S IMPACT ON CULTURAL DEVELOPMENT

Meet two freshmen who are now assigned as roommates in Rawls Hall at Central University. Sam Hull is from Lone Oak, Arkansas. He is a Caucasian of Scots-Irish lineage, and his family has been big rice farmers and cattle raisers for four generations in rural

Arkansas. Sam likes to hunt and fish, played football in high school, and was pretty good as an offensive tackle but not good enough to make a college team. Sam is pretty good at math and science. He got a 27 on his ACT, which was good enough to get him into the civil engineering program. His parents are divorced. His family goes back more than a century in the Arkansas delta, and a number of his distant relatives fought for the Confederates in the Civil War. Sam was raised in the Southern Baptist Church, although he isn't a real zealous churchgoer. Besides playing video games, Sam likes to shoot pool and watch football, play progressive country rock with his bass guitar, and drink beer. When he drinks enough beer, he can tend to get a little rowdy. His academic future is most likely going to depend on whether he can form a balance between time at the Lowlife pool hall, e-mails with his high school girlfriend who goes to another university, trips back home to deer hunt, and courses in differential calculus, chemical qualitative analysis, and mechanical physics. Sam puts up a very self-assured front, but he is scared to death and intimidated by this large university, which has twice as many people as his entire county back in Arkansas, but macho guy that he is, he would never admit it.

George Giap is also a new freshman and is from San Francisco. He is a first-generation Vietnamese American who got a scholarship in civil engineering because of his 34 ACT, his outstanding high school academic background, and his ability to play classical music with the viola well enough to also get a music scholarship to Central. His parents, and in fact his whole extended Vietnamese family, are very proud of George as the family's first college student. They all work in a fresh produce store and are very frugal and hardworking. They believe highly in education, since they had no chance to go beyond elementary grades in their Mekong Delta village. They are devout Roman Catholics who were supported by Catholic Charities when they first emigrated to the United States. George is very loyal to his family and e-mails them at least once a week to let them know how things are going. He does not have a girlfriend nor thinks he will have time for one if he is going to succeed in the rigorous engineering program and perform in the university orchestra. His hobbies are playing chess, working Sudoku puzzles, and practicing tai chi in the early morning.

To say that George is mentally and physically disciplined is akin to saying the Marine Corps is mildly interested in mental and physical stamina. The problem is that George is as tightly wrapped emotionally as a San Francisco Bay bridge support cable. He could not endure the shame of failure that it would cast on him or his family. Nobody knows about this terrifying sense that he is probably inadequate to the rigors of the second-year courses he has been placed in because of all his high school AP credits. He is determined to study 20 hours a day, 7 days a week to succeed but wonders why there are only 24 hours in a day. The problem with all that fine determination is that he is more than a thousand miles from home and terribly homesick, and he can't seem to remember a thing he reads in his textbooks.

How well do you think George and Sam are going to get along? They may be roommates only for one semester, but most likely as their personalities and backgrounds rub up against each other, another person who is about to come into their lives is going to have an interesting time dealing with them.

Meet Latavius Blanton Jefferson, or LBJ (not necessarily Lyndon Baines Johnson, as people laughingly say), as most of the residents in Rawls Hall know him by those initials. He is African American and a junior in marketing. His parents have been sharecroppers in Mississippi and most likely worked for somebody very much like Sam Hull's father. His father is dead, and his mother is now working as a domestic in Jackson, Mississippi. He has five brothers and sisters. He is the middle of the five. Two have graduated from college, and two are in high school. LBJ is a gregarious, outgoing, very popular resident hall assistant (RHA). He enjoys working with fellow students, even the knuckleheads who get drunk or do other stupid things. Besides being a gregarious individual who gets along well with others, he believes strongly in self-reliance. He is ambitious, fiercely independent, and the first African American student to ever be elected president of the Young Republican Club at Central University. That position has caused him some grief from other African American students who have more liberal views than he does, but LBJ doesn't care. He also is fairly rigid as far as right versus wrong, but he somewhat tempers that in his dealings with the men on his floor. He would very much like some extra time to study because he'd like to go on for his MBA. He'd also like to spend a little more time with Sherenda, his girlfriend, particularly on Friday and Saturday nights, when he is on duty and has to deal with students who overindulge their alcohol habit. These problems cause some serious disruption to his study and dating plans, and he doesn't have a lot of patience when that happens. This is his second year of being a residence hall assistant, and he has had some very interesting on-the-job training dealing with everything imaginable that a bunch of college-age males can think up to get themselves in trouble—trouble that invariably comes to his attention as a first responder when things go haywire in the residence hall. We will meet these three Central University students again in Chapter 9.

Now take a look at Figure 2.1. It has three figures that look like wastebaskets. Two of them are sitting on top of a large cylinder that represents their new college environment. They represent the developmental ecosystems of origin for both Sam and George. Note that the tops of their wastebaskets are much larger than the bottoms that interface with the college milieu in which they are now operating. That's because their larger area of cultural knowledge is narrowed a great deal as they meet this new environment. Also notice that their wastebaskets don't overlap very much. At present, their cultural backgrounds have very little in common, besides their love of music, albeit very different, and enrollment in an engineering program.

Now consider LBJ's representational wastebasket. Notice that it is almost opposite in proportion to Sam's and George's. His developmental ecosystem of origin still exerts considerable influence on him. However, it is rapidly growing smaller and being replaced by the university ecosystem, which is growing and exerting a larger and larger influence over his development.

This is a nice theoretical diagram, but what does that have to do with the business of crisis and crisis intervention? LBJ has been in the business of getting acculturated at Central University for two years now, so he is way ahead of the game in comparison

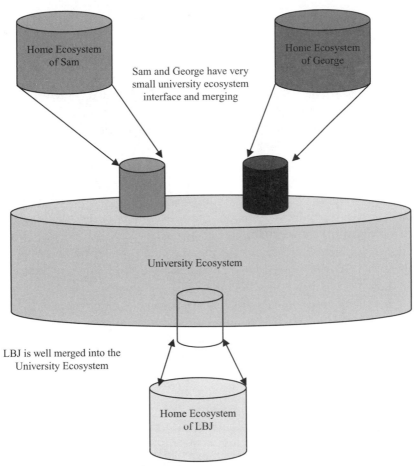

Figure 2.1 Student Interface with Ecosystem

to the two freshmen. However, that may or may not be of help to him if he doesn't understand what the terms *multicultural* and *diversity* really mean, particularly when it comes down to how people adapt when they are under stress, which appears to have at least some basis in what their cultural background is. The interface between the two new freshmen and their RHA represents what Stamm, Stamm, Hudnall, and Higson-Smith (2004) believe can happen in a larger culture context when arriving cultures run headlong into original cultures. While in the Stamm and associates' model the original culture is likely to suffer and have its sustainability put at risk, in this situation it is far more likely that the freshmen are going to find themselves the ones who are radically changed or find themselves somewhere else by their sophomore year. What this means to you is that culture most surely interacts in multiple ways on individuals. Consider the following studies in terms of what effects culture may have on an individual in crisis.

Cultural Impact on Crisis

Norris and Alegria (2006) were interested in understanding what age and culture had to do with how easily a person could catch PTSD. They studied Mexican, Polish, and American males who were disaster survivors. They found that PTSD occurred at higher rates in younger Mexicans, middle-age Americans, and older Poles. Thus, while no common age factor involved in susceptibility to PTSD was found, the cultural context of the specific country of origin and the social roles that age dictated in those countries did impact the development of PTSD.

Oyserman, Coon, and Kemmelmeier (2002) conducted a meta-analysis of collectivist societies to identify if any differences existed. These researchers examined Asian and Latino cultures (nobody does much until the clan, tribe, or group get together and discuss the matter) compared with American and Western Europeans, who were assumed to be in individualistic cultures (take the bull by the horns and get it done!). What they found were that Indonesians were not significantly different from European Americans, Australians, and Germans in regard to individualism and that European Americans were lower in individualism than people from more than half the countries in Latin America. An even more interesting finding is that Americans were significantly higher in collectivism than the Japanese and no different in collectivism than Koreans. So you need to take the point that arbitrarily lumping groups of nationalities into collectivist or individualist societal groups based on a supposition that they ought to be that way because of their perceived cultural values doesn't necessarily work very well.

Now add the crisis intervener into the mix. The crisis interventionist's idea of how to help people is pretty much based on his or her own cultural heritage and what worked for them (Kaniasty & Norris, 1995). The mainstream notion of how one gets through a crisis in the United States is generally a view that centers on individualism. That individualistic view focuses on a high internal locus of control and a belief that through personal effort, psychological homeostasis and equilibrium can start to be regained.

The problem is that a can-do internal locus of control may not always do well with people in crisis whose cultural background is different than the interventionist's. Over and over, when culturally different people are subjected to a traumatic event, they tend to revert to what they know best, their cultural origins (Myers & Wee, 2005; Perilla, Norris, & Lavizzo, 2002; Shelby & Tredinnick, 1995; Weisaeth, 2000). When that cultural worldview is based on an external locus of control that views fate, a higher spiritual power, or the collective wisdom of the clan or tribe as the abiding principles and supports that will get them through the crisis, attempting to impose an individual view of self-reliance is likely to exacerbate rather than help the situation. Understand, then, that no crisis is done in a sterile vacuum, free from the multiple effects of the ecological-cultural background.

So while LBJ may have a greater fund of knowledge about the cultural context within which the two freshmen are operating, he will do well to understand the very different values they bring into the setting. How can somebody who is so different in color, age, experience, background, and knowledge possibly be effective with another person who may be 180 degrees different in each of these dimensions? It's pretty clear that Sam or George, if he gets into trouble, is not going to be able to dial up a crisis interventionist who is his mirror image. What they have is LBJ, and if LBJ is to be helpful to them, he must be acutely sensitive to the emerging needs of the individual. He will need to be able to prize that person in regard to his or her distinctive individuality in the context of the crisis situation. That may not be easy when the individual combines his cultural individuality with obnoxious and dangerous behavior. Finally, he will need to attempt to remain value free in judging the goodness of the person's efforts, because those efforts may not necessarily fit his own worldview of truth and beauty (Raskin & Rogers, 1995). If he can do that, LBJ will be able to establish a relationship built on trust and credibility, and that has been shown over and over in counseling outcome research to be the critical ingredient in a positive outcome for a client (Capuzzi & Gross, 1995, pp. 12–25). We believe that is no different for the people in the front line of crisis intervention that this book is about.

CULTURALLY EFFECTIVE HELPING

The plain and simple truth is that we don't know a lot about how culture, crises, and crisis intervention interact. Very little research has been done in the area. Certain cultures don't even have words for trauma (Silove, 1998)! However, we do know that deeply held cultural beliefs and previously learned ways of dealing with the world rapidly surface when individuals are placed in a crisis. There is a good deal of evidence that minorities in the United States use mental health services much less than Caucasians do. That underutilization becomes very problematic when a disaster strikes, because research indicates that ethnic minorities tend to suffer more than the majority group (Norris & Alegria, 2006).

Certainly, much human-made crisis revolves around lack of cultural understanding and conflicts between cultures. Eidelson and Eidelson (2003) have documented how distorted beliefs may produce excessive death, suffering, and displacement as a result of conflicts among and between groups regarding ethnicity, nationality, religion, or other social identities and issues. Even though Seung-Hui Cho was diagnosable as a paranoid schizophrenic, his deep alienation from the culture of the university and his view of the privileged students "who spit in his face" added tremendous amounts of energy that fueled the fire of his paranoid rage. Eidelson and Eidelson (2003) found five core beliefs that cause individuals and groups to make dangerous assumptions about people who are different from themselves. These beliefs revolve around the individual's or group's perception of the values of superiority-inferiority, justice-injustice, invulnerability-vulnerability, trust-distrust, and helpfulness-helplessness. Cho's beliefs that he was inferior and had suffered injustice and his distrust that the system would work for him led to the feelings of vulnerability and helplessness that ultimately tilted his paranoia into a murderous rampage.

One of the major problems in crisis intervention with culturally different people is in both sending and receiving communications that are understandable, clearly communicate what we are attempting to do, and do not exacerbate an already potentially volatile situation. While it is impossible to know the nuances of every culture and the subtleties of the client's native language, one of our abiding rules in crisis intervention in which cultural differences are an issue is that they are undoubtedly there in a crisis, and you need to be sensitive to them and proceed with caution.

Making owning statements early on about our cultural ignorance, coupled with a positive, empathic approach, goes a long way in compensating for errors of omission. That approach is particularly true when language may be a barrier. Those owning statements are true whether we are dealing with the rice fields of Sam's parents in Arkansas or the rice fields of George's parents back in Vietnam.

SUMMARY

This chapter summarizes the basic principles of what one needs to know about crisis and crisis intervention. We examine a number of definitions of both individual and systemic crisis. Our general definition for an individual in crisis is that crisis is experiencing an event as an intolerable difficulty that exceeds the person's current resources and coping mechanisms. We have used Zdziarski's (2006) definition of a *crisis* on a college campus as an event that is often sudden or unexpected, disrupts the normal operations of the institution or its educational mission, and threatens the well-being of personal property, financial resources, and/or the reputation of the institution. Two major negative outcomes that may occur after a traumatic event for both individuals and institutions are post-traumatic stress disorder and transcrisis states. Both may have long-term deleterious effects if the resulting crisis is not dealt with in a proactive manner. There are a variety of theories of crisis that include generic or basic, psychoanalytic, eclectic/expanded, systems, ecosystems, adaptive, developmental, interpersonal, and chaos theory. Three crisis intervention models that attempt to make these various theories operational are the equilibrium, cognitive, and psycho/social/cultural transition models. These theories and models deal with the four basic domains of crisis: developmental, situational, existential, and ecosystemic. Finally, the role of multiculturalism/diversity and its impact on crisis and crisis intervention are examined.

REFERENCES

Aguilera, D. (1998). *Crisis intervention: Theory and methodology* (8th ed.). St. Louis, MO: Mosby.

Alexander, F. (1956). *Psychoanalysis and psychotherapy*. New York: W. W. Norton.

American Psychiatric Association. (2000). *Diagnostic and statistical manual of mental disorders* (4th ed.). Washington, DC: Author.

Ansbacher, H. L., & Ansbacher, E. (Eds.). (1978). *Superiority and social interest by Alfred Adler*. Evanston, IL: Northwestern University Press.

Antonovsky, A. (1980). *Health, stress, and coping.* San Francisco: Jossey-Bass.

Antonovsky, A. (1991). The structural sources of salutogenic strengths. In C. Cooper & R. Payne (Eds.), *Personality and stress: Individual differences in the stress process* (pp. 67–104). London: John Wiley & Sons.

Arkoff, A., Meredith, G. M., Bailey, E., Cheang, M., Dubanoski, R. A., Griffin, P. B., & Niyekawa. A. M. (2006). Life review during the college freshman year. *College Student Journal, 40,* 263–269.

Arredondo, P. (1999). Multicultural counseling competencies as tools to address oppression and racism. *Journal of Counseling and Development, 77,* 102–108.

Barton, L. (1993). *Crisis in organizations: Managing and communicating in the heat of chaos.* Cincinnati, OH: Southwestern.

Beck, A. T. (1971). *Cognitive therapy of depression.* Philadelphia: University of Pennsylvania Press.

Beck, A. T. (1995). *Cognitive therapy: Basic and beyond.* New York: Guilford Press.

Beck A. T., Freeman, A., Davis, D., & Associates (2004). *Cognitive therapy of personality disorders.* New York: Guilford Press.

Belkin, G. S. (1984). *Introduction to counseling* (2nd ed.). Dubuque, IA: William C. Brown.

Bennett, S. R. (2004). Case study of the tornado at Gustavus Adolphus College. In R. Lee & D. Casey (Eds.), *Crisis & trauma in colleges and universities* (pp. 1–12). Ellicott City, MD: Chevron.

Berg-Cross, L., & Pak, V. (2006). Diversity issues. In P. A. Grayson & P. W. Meilman (Eds.), *College mental health practice* (pp. 153–172). New York: Routledge.

Blocher, D. H. (2000). *Counseling: A developmental approach* (4th ed.). New York: John Wiley & Sons.

Brammer, L. M. (1985). *The helping relationship: Process and skills* (3rd ed.). Upper Saddle River, NJ: Prentice Hall.

Bronfenbrenner, U. (1986). Ecology of the family as a context for human development: Research perspectives. *Developmental Psychology, 22,* 723–742.

Bronfenbrenner, U. (1995). Developmental ecology through space and time: A future perspective. In P. Moen, G. H. Elder Jr., & K. Luscher (Eds.), *Examining lives in context: Perspectives on the ecology of human development* (pp. 619–647). Washington, DC: American Psychological Association.

Bowen, M. (1978). *Family therapy in clinical practice.* New York: Aronson.

Butz, M. R. (1995). Chaos theory, philosophically old, scientifically new. *Counseling and Values, 39,* 84–98.

Butz, M. R. (1997). *Chaos and complexity: Implications for psychological theory and practice.* Washington, DC: Taylor & Francis.

Caplan, G. (1961). *An approach to community mental health.* New York: Grune & Stratton.

Caplan, G. (1964). *Principles of preventive psychiatry.* New York: Basic Books.

Capuzzi, D., & Gross, D. R. (Eds.). (1995). *Counseling and psychotherapy: Theories and interventions.* Upper Saddle River, NJ: Prentice Hall.

Carkhuff, R. R., & Berenson, B. G. (1977). *Beyond counseling and therapy* (2nd ed.). New York: Holt, Rinehart & Winston.

Clark, R. (2002). Enhancing resiliency in adults, youths, and children: An anticipatory prevention program to help citizens manage life adversities and crises. *Annals of the American Psychotherapy Association 5(5),* 14–15.

Collins, B. G., & Collins, T. M. (2005). *Crisis and trauma: Developmental-ecological intervention.* Lahaska, PA: Lahaska Press.

Council for Accreditation of Counseling and Related Educational Programs. (2009). *Accreditation standards of 2009.* Alexandria, VA: Author.

Dattilio, F. M., & Freeman, A. (Eds.). (2007). *Cognitive-behavioral strategies in crisis intervention* (3rd ed.). New York: Guilford Press.

Eidelson, R. J., & Eidelson, J. I. (2003). Dangerous ideas: Five beliefs that propel groups toward conflict. *American Psychologist, 58,* 182–192.

Ellis, A. E. (1962). *Reason and emotion in psychotherapy.* New York: Lyle Stuart.

Erikson, E. (1963). *Childhood and society* (2nd ed.). New York: Norton.

Fine, R. (1973). Psychoanalysis. In R. J. Corsini (Ed.), *Current psychotherapies* (pp. 1–33). Itasca, IL: F. E. Peacock.

Frazier, P. A., Valtinson, G., & Caldwell, S. (1994). Evaluation of a coeducational interactive rape prevention program. *Journal of Counseling and Development, 73*, 153–158.

Golan, N. (1978). *Treatment in crisis situations.* New York: Free Press.

Haley, J. (1973). *Uncommon therapy.* New York: Norton.

Haley, J. (1976). *Problem-solving therapy.* New York: McGraw-Hill.

Halpern, J., & Tramontin, M. (2007). *Disaster mental health: Theory and practice.* Belmont, CA: Brooks/Cole–Cengage.

Hardy, K. V. (Therapist). (1997). *Family systems therapy.* (Videotape No. 0-205-32931-4, T. Labriola, Producer). In J. Carlson & D. Kjos, *Family systems with Hardy: Psychotherapy with the experts.* Boston: Allyn & Bacon.

Harvey, A., & Bryant, R. (1998). The relationship between acute stress disorder and posttraumatic stress disorder: A prospective evaluation of motor vehicle accident survivors. *Journal of Consulting and Clinical Psychology, 66*, 507–512.

Harvey, M. R. (1996). An ecological view of psychological trauma and trauma recovery. *Journal of Traumatic Stress, 9*, 3–23.

Hermann, C. F. (1963). Some consequences of crisis which limit the viability of organizations. *Administrative Science Quarterly, 8*, 61–81.

Hoff, L. A., Hallisey, B. J., & Hoff, M. (2009). *People in crisis: Clinical and diversity perspectives.* New York: Routledge, Taylor, & Francis Group.

Ivey, A. E. (1987). Cultural intentionality: The core of effective helping. *Counselor Education and Supervision, 26*, 168–172.

James, R. (2008). Crisis intervention strategies. Belmont, CA: Brooks/Cole–Cengage.

James, R. K., Cogdal, P., & Gilliland, B. E. (2003, April). *An ecological theory of crisis intervention.* Paper presented at the American Counseling Association convention, Kansas City, MO.

Janosik, E. H. (1984). *Crisis counseling: A contemporary approach.* Monterey, CA: Wadsworth Health Sciences.

Joyce, P., & Sills, D. (2001). *Skills in Gestalt counseling and psychotherapy.* London: Sage.

Kalayjian, A. S. (1999). Coping through meaning: The community response to the earthquake in Armenia. In E. S. Zinner and M. B. Williams (Eds.), *When a community weeps: Case studies in group survivorship* (pp. 87–99). Philadelphia: Brunner-Mazel.

Kaniasty, K., & Norris, F. (1995). In search of altruistic community: Patterns of social support mobilization following Hurricane Hugo. *American Journal of Community Psychology, 20*, 211–241.

Kiselica, M. S. (1998). Preparing Anglos for the challenges and joys of multiculturalism. *Counseling Psychologist, 26*, 5–21.

Levinson, D. J. (1986). A concept of adult development. *American Psychologist, 4*, 3–133.

Levinson, D. J., & Levinson, J. D. (1996). *The seasons of a woman's life.* New York: Knopf.

Lindemann, E. (1944). Symptomatology and management of acute grief. *American Journal of Psychiatry, 101*, 141–148.

Lindemann, E. (1956). The meaning of crisis in individual and family. *Teachers College Record, 57*, 310.

Lukens, E. P., O'Neill, P., Torning, H., Gubiseh-Avala, D., Batista, M., Chen, T., . . . & Waterman-Cecutti, J. (2004). Building resiliency and cultural collaboration post September 11th: A group model of brief integrative psychoeducation by diverse communities. *Traumatology, 10*, 107–129.

Meichenbaum, D. H. (1977). *Cognitive-behavior modification: An integrative approach.* New York: Plenum.

Meichenbaum, D. H. (2001). Treatment of individuals with anger control problems and aggressive behaviors: A clinical handbook. Clearwater, FL: Institute Press.

Miller, E. D. (2003). Reconceptualizing the role of resiliency in coping and therapy. *Journal of Loss & Trauma, 8*, 239–246.

Myer, R. A., & Moore, H. (2006). Crisis in context theory: An ecological model. *Journal of Counseling & Development, 84,* 139–147.

Myers, D., & Wee, D. F. (2005). *Disaster mental health services.* New York: Brunner-Routledge.

Nicoletti, J., Spencer-Thomas, S., & Bollinger, C. (2001). *Violence goes to college: The authoritative guide to prevention and intervention.* Springfield, IL: Charles C Thomas.

Norris, F. H., & Alegria, M. (2006). Promoting disaster recovery in ethnic-minority individuals and communities. In E. C. Ritchie, P. J. Watson, & M. J. Friedman (Eds.), *Interventions following mass violence and disasters* (pp. 319–342). New York: Guilford Press.

Norris, F., Friedman, M., Watson, P., Byrne, C., Diaz, E., & Kaniasty, K. (2002). 60,000 disaster victims speak: Part I. An empirical review of the literature, 1981–2001. *Psychiatry: Interpersonal & Biological Process, 65,* 207–243.

Ober, C., Peeters, L., Archer, R., & Kelly, K. (2000). Debriefing in different cultural frameworks: Responding to acute trauma in Australian Aboriginal contexts. In B. Raphael and J. P. Wilson (Eds.), *Psychological debriefing: Theory, practice, and evidence* (pp. 241–253). New York: Cambridge University Press.

Ochberg, F. M. (Ed.). (1988). *Post-traumatic therapy and victims of violence.* New York: Routledge Press.

Oyserman, D., Coon, H. M., & Kemmelmeier, M. (2002). Rethinking individualism and collectivism: Evaluation of theoretical assumptions and metaanalyses. *Psychological Bulletin, 128,* 3–72.

Pedersen, P. (1987). Ten frequent assumptions of cultural bias in counseling. *Journal of Multicultural Counseling and Development, 15,* 16–24.

Pedersen, P. (1998). *Multiculturalism as a fourth force.* New York: Brunner/Mazel.

Perilla, J., Norris, F., & Lavizzo, E. (2002). Ethnicity, culture, and disaster response: Identifying and explaining ethnic differences in PTSD six months after Hurricane Andrew. *Journal of Social and Clinical Psychology, 21,* 28–45.

Poland, S., & McCormick, J. S. (1999). *Coping with crisis: Lessons learned.* Longmont, CO: Sopris West.

Ponterotto, J. G., & Pedersen, P. (1993). *Preventing prejudice: A guide for counselors and educators.* Newbury Park, CA: Sage.

Postrel, V. (1998). *The future and its enemies: The growing conflict over creativity, enterprise, and progress.* New York: Free Press.

Ramsey, R. (1997). Chaos theory and crisis intervention: Toward a new meaning of equilibrium in understanding and helping people in crisis. *Child and Family, 1*(3), 223–235.

Raphael, M. (1986). *When disaster strikes: How individuals and communities cope with catastrophe.* New York: Basic Books.

Raskin, N. J., & Rogers, C. R. (1995). Person-centered therapy. In R. J. Corsini & D. Wedding (Eds.), *Current psychotherapies* (5th ed.). Itasca, IL: F. E. Peacock.

Ridley, C. R. (1995). *Overcoming unintentional racism in counseling and therapy: A practitioner's guide to intentional intervention.* Newbury Park, CA: Sage.

Roberts, A. (2005). *Crisis intervention handbook* (3rd ed.). New York: Oxford University Press.

Rogers, C. R. (1977). *Carl Rogers on personal power: Inner strength and its revolutionary impact.* New York: Delacorte.

Rogers, J. R. (2001). Suicide risk assessment. In E. R. Welfel & R. E. Ingersoll (Eds.), *The mental health desk reference* (pp. 259–263). New York: John Wiley & Sons.

Rollo, J. M., & Zdziarski, E. L. (2007a). The impact of crisis. In E. L. Zdziarski, W. D. Dunkel, & J. M. Rollo (Eds.), *Campus crisis management: A comprehensive guide to planning prevention, response, and recovery* (pp. 3–34). San Francisco: John Wiley & Sons.

Rollo, J. M., & Zdziarski, E. L. (2007b). Developing a crisis management plan. In E. L. Zdziarski, W. D. Dunkel, & J. M. Rollo (Eds.), *Campus crisis management: A comprehensive guide to planning prevention, response, and recovery* (pp. 73–96). San Francisco: John Wiley & Sons.

Sarri, S. (2005). *A bolt from the blue: Coping with disaster and acute traumas.* London: Jessica Kingsley.

Shaluf, I. M., Ahmadun, F., & Said, A. M. (2003). A review of disaster and crisis. *Disaster Prevention & Management, 12*, 24–32.

Sharff, R. S. (2008). *Theories of psychotherapy and counseling: Concepts and cases.* Belmont, CA: Brooks/Cole Thomson.

Sheehy, G. (1995). *New Passages.* New York: Random House.

Shelby, J. S., & Tredinnick, M. G. (1995). Crisis intervention with survivors of natural disaster: Lessons from Hurricane Andrew. *Journal of Counseling and Development, 73*, 491–497.

Sherwood, G. P., & McKelfresh, D. (2007). Crisis management teams. In E. L. Zdziarski, W. D. Dunkel, & J. M. Rollo (Eds.), *Campus crisis management: A comprehensive guide to planning prevention, response, and recovery* (pp. 55–72). San Francisco: John Wiley & Sons.

Silove, D. (1998). Is PTSD an overlearnt survival response? An evolutionary learning hypothesis. *Psychiatry, 61*, 181–190.

Silove, D. (2000). A conceptual framework for mass trauma: Implications for adaption, intervention and debriefing. In B. Raphael & J. P. Wilson (Eds.), *Psychological debriefing: Theory, practice, and evidence* (pp. 337–350). New York: Cambridge University Press.

Slaikeu, K. A., (1990). *Crisis intervention: A handbook for practice and research* (2nd ed.). Boston: Allyn & Bacon.

Stamm, B. H., Stamm, H. E., Hudnall, A. C., & Higson-Smith, C. (2004). Considering a theory of cultural loss and loss. *Journal of Loss & Trauma, 9*, 89–111.

Strumpfer, D. J. (2006). The strength perspective: Fortigenesis in adult life. *Social Indicators Research, 77*, 11–36.

Sue, D. W. (1992). The challenge of multiculturalism: The road less traveled. *American Counselor, 1*, 5–14.

Sue, D. W. (1999a, August). *Multicultural competencies in the profession of psychology.* Symposium address delivered at the 107th Annual Convention of the American Psychological Association, Boston.

Sue, D. W. (1999b, August). *Surviving monoculturalism and racism: A personal journey.* Division 45 Presidential address delivered at the 107th Annual Convention of the American Psychological Association, Boston.

Sue, D. W., Arredondo, P., & McDavis, R. J. (1992). Multicultural counseling competencies and standards: A call to the profession. *Journal of Counseling and Development, 70*, 477–486.

U.S. Department of Census. (2001). *U. S Census 2000.* Washington, DC: U.S. Printing Office.

Viney, L. L. (1976). The concept of crisis: A tool for clinical psychologists. *Bulletin of the British Psychological Society, 29*, 387–395.

Weisaeth, L. (2000). Briefing and debriefing: Group psychological interventions in acute stressor situations. In B. Raphael & J. P. Wilson (Eds.), *Psychological debriefing: Theory, practice, and evidence* (pp. 43–57). New York: Cambridge University Press.

Wright, N. H. (2003). *The new guide to crisis and trauma counseling.* Ventura, CA: Regal Books.

Zdziarski, E. L. (2006). Crisis in the context of higher education. In K. S. Harper, B. G. Paterson, & E. L. Zdziarski (Eds.), *Crisis management: Responding from the heart* (pp. 3–24). Washington, DC: NASPA.

Zdziarski, E. L., Dunkel, W. D., & Rollo, J. M. (Eds.). (2007). *Campus crisis management: A comprehensive guide to planning, prevention, response, and recovery.* San Francisco: Jossey-Bass.

Zdziarski, E. L, Rollo, J. M., & Dunkel, W. D. (2007) The crisis matrix. In E. L. Zdziarski, W. D. Dunkel, & J. M. Rollo (Eds.), *Campus crisis management: A comprehensive guide to planning prevention, response, and recovery* (pp. 35–51). San Francisco: John Wiley & Sons.

Zinner, E. S., & Williams, M. B. (1999). *When a community weeps: Case studies in group survivorship.* Philadelphia: Brunner-Mazel.

3

Herding Cats: Organizing a Crisis Response

In the last decade, institutions of higher learning have found themselves at the center of crisis with rather high frequency (Mitroff, Diamond, & Alpasian, 2006). These crises have caused loss of life, loss of a sense of security in higher education, loss of enrollment, injury, and impinged finances (Nicoletti, Spencer-Thomas, & Bollinger, 2001). We expect that the reaction among university officials upon hearing of a crisis on another campus is a mixture of fear—"there but by the grace of God go I"—and denial—"poor bastards, so glad it won't happen here." The key to substantial reduction in these types of losses and to increased security of the learning environment lies in planning through comprehensive crisis and mitigation actions (Mitroff et al., 2006).

This chapter focuses on the practical issues related to crisis management planning as it applies to human impact issues. Although all crisis management plans have common components, we are not going to offer a template for a plan. Your crisis management plan should reflect the uniqueness of your campus. Our discussion is limited to issues related to the human impact of a crisis. Our discussion starts with an overview of terms used in crisis management planning. This section defines these terms and serves as a primer as to how we use them throughout the remainder of the book. The next section outlines the current state of crisis management planning in universities. This discussion focuses on the traps and obstacles crisis management planning faces in university settings. These issues must be overcome to develop a functional crisis management plan. The next section addresses basic building blocks for a crisis management plan, including development of a crisis management team and basic logistical concerns regarding crisis management plans. The chapter closes by talking about the three Cs for building a crisis management plan as it relates to the human impact of a crisis. The three Cs should be integrated throughout your crisis management plan. In this section, we also discuss the development of a pragmatic decision-making model that should be part of any crisis management plan.

CRISIS PLANNING PRIMER: COMMON TERMS

What many universities identify as a crisis management plan is really an emergency response plan (Mitroff et al., 2006). This confusion is understandable, given the various terms used in the literature. Terms such as *crisis management, emergency response, disaster recovery,* and *business continuity* seem to be used interchangeably. Since the Virginia Tech tragedy, terms such as *threat assessment team* and *behavioral intervention team* are also being used, causing even more confusion. This state is not surprising, since crisis management for universities is still in its infancy (Mitroff et al., 2006). This section clarifies the most often used terms by defining the various types of plans and teams that may be found at a university. The configuration of plans and teams at your university may differ from our discussion.

Types of Plans

Five major plans seem to appear consistently in literature addressing crisis management. The first four plans are (a) emergency response plans, (b) business continuity plans, (c) disaster recovery plans, and (d) risk management plans. The fifth, crisis management plan, is sometimes used to mean a comprehensive plan including the first four. However, at other times, a crisis management plan is considered to be a stand-alone plan not related to anything else. The primary differences among these plans lie in the focus and goals of the plans. Figure 3.1 depicts the relationship of these plans with one another. We see the crisis management plan as the overall design for responding to a crisis. The other plans are ancillary components of this plan. Decisions about activating these components depend on two factors: (a) timing and (b) scope of the crisis. Timing simply means where you are in the recovery process. The obvious example is that you would not need to use the emergency response plan several months into the recovery process. Scope involves the overall impact of the crisis on a campus. Crises that have a larger impact on a campus may require that either the business continuity plan or the disaster recovery plan be activated.

Emergency Response Plan

Emergency response plans focus on the first few hours to weeks following a crisis. The aim of these plans is to provide whatever assistance is needed at that time and a method to allow communication with appropriate groups and to conduct damage assessment (Myers, 1999). Major components of these plans include notification systems to minimize physical harm, formulas for responding to a crisis situation, and provision

Figure 3.1 Comprehensive Crisis Management Planning

for emergency health (i.e., physical and psychological) services (Griffin, 2007). For universities, notification systems would include warning about possible violent intruders on campus, as well as warnings about potentially dangerous environmental (e.g., tornado, hurricane, flash flooding) conditions on campus. Emergency response plans also generally include the time-honored and much-practiced fire drills and similar procedures to use when physical safety is threatened. The final major component included in these plans most of the time is procedures for meeting the physical and psychological needs of people directly affected by a crisis. In addition, these plans generally include procedures for working with first responders (e.g., law enforcement and fire departments). These plans might also include agreements with local and possibly even state-level emergency management agencies (Haddow & Bullock, 2003).

Risk Management Plan

Risk management plans (RMPs) involve ongoing evaluation of risks in order to mitigate the potential for a crisis (Myers, 1999). These plans are used to identify weak links that pose a threat to cause a crisis or may prevent an efficient and effective recovery process. Ideally, RMPs examine environmental hazards, technological vulnerabilities, human resource concerns, and any other potential risks that expose an organization to a crisis. Mitroff (2004) discusses the idea that all crises give off signals. Risk management plans can help identify these signals. Myers (1999) recommends that these plans involve regularly scheduled evaluations to maintain awareness of risks. Included in RMPs is a business impact analysis that outlines the expected effect of a crisis if the risks are not addressed.

Business Continuity Plan

Business continuity plans concentrate on one thing: maintaining the daily operation of the university (Pollard & Hotho, 2006). These plans are designed to reduce the impact of a crisis and reduce the time to restore conditions to a state of business as usual (Cerullo & Cerullo, 2004). Business continuity plans are developed to avoid the chaos and confusion that occurs following a crisis. Typically, these plans provide for backup systems so that routine business can be restored as quickly as possible (Savage, 2002). A major focus of these plans tends to be technology (Myers, 1999). Steps involved in these plans include conducting assessments of risks to and impact a crisis may have on routine activities and training in business recovery procedures (Cerullo & Cerullo, 2004; Savage 2002). Attention to issues related to the human impact of a crisis seems to be in relation to the restoration of day-to-day functioning.

Disaster Recovery Plan

The term *disaster recovery plan* is sometimes used interchangeably with *business continuity plan*. The focus for both is restoring the daily operations of the campus; however, the difference lies in the scope of the problem (Cervone, 2006; Zdziarski, Rollo, & Dunkel,

2007). Disasters are natural or man-made events that overwhelm the response capacity of a university (Shaluf, Ahmadun, & Said, 2003). Massive damage, economic loss, disruption of daily activities, injury, and loss of life may occur in a disaster. Disaster recovery planning is intended to address these larger-scale events that cripple a campus. These plans are aimed at minimizing the impact a disaster will have on critical business processes (Toigo, 2000). Business functions in these plans may be rank-ordered from most to least critical function, and a resumption schedule developed (Muecke, 1994). In general, these plans appear to recognize issues related to the human impact of a crisis, but the primary focus is on the restoration of daily business activities as quickly as possible.

Crisis Management Plan

According to Mitroff and Anagnos (2001), a crisis management plan should be a comprehensive plan that addresses any crisis an organization may encounter. These include (a) economic, (b) technological, (c) safety, (d) human resource, (e) reputational, (f) criminal acts, and (g) disasters. A more detailed list is shown in Table 3.1. Crisis management plans generally address all aspects of the recovery process. Examples include technology, restoration of day-to-day functioning, media relations, renovation of facilities if needed, and assistance to the physically injured and psychologically traumatized. Crisis management plans should be developed to deal with anything and everything needed to recover from a crisis. The plans previously discussed can be considered components of a complete crisis management plan.

Many other terms may be used to describe plans developed to address crises on your campus: *crisis mitigation plan, trauma response plan, crisis response plan,* and *crisis recovery plan.* An almost endless list of names could be generated for these plans. Regardless of what it is called on your campus, a comprehensive plan that outlines policies and procedures to support the recovery process is needed on your campus. As we have said previously, we will focus on the aspects of a crisis management plan related to the human impact of crises. However, the ideas and concepts we discuss may be applicable to other problems associated with a crisis.

Types of Teams

The number of groups dealing with crises varies from campus to campus. There really is no right or wrong answer with respect to the number of responsibilities of the teams. Larger universities may have several teams, and smaller institutions may have fewer teams responsible for crisis management. With respect to the human impact of crisis, we recommend three basic teams: (a) a threat assessment team, (b) a crisis response team, and (c) a crisis management team (see Table 3.2). These titles are used periodically in the remainder of the book. However, understand that the titles refer to the function of the team. On your campus, these teams may have different titles. As you read about these teams later in the book, we encourage you to think of the functioning of these teams rather than become bogged down or confused because you may not use these labels on your campus.

Table 3.1 Types of Crises

Economic	Technological	Safety	Human Resource	Reputational	Criminal Acts	Disasters: Natural
Labor strikes	Loss of confidential information	Loss of equipment or material	Death of student, teacher, administrator, staff	Gossip	Vandalism	Earthquake
				Rumors	Kidnapping	Flood
Funding shortfall	Tampering with records	Loss of key facilities	Loss of key administrator	Slander	Workplace violence	Fire
	Loss of computer information				Hostage taking	Hurricane
			Major accident on grounds			Explosion

Table 3.2   Teams

	Threat Assessment Team	Crisis Response Team	Crisis Management Team
Membership	Static	Fluid	Static
Leadership	Varies based on experience and expertise	Senior administrator	Top administrator on campus or his/ her representative
Number on Team	3–5	Varies	10–15
Recovery Phase	Continuous	Emergency and honeymoon phase	All phases of recovery
Responsibility	Assess threats Make recommendations	Respond to needs of anyone affected by the incident	Direct of phases of recovery
Report Structure	Varies but typically senior administration	Crisis management team	Senior administration and possibly trustees

Threat Assessment Team

The use of threat assessment teams (TATs) to identify students who are disruptive to the learning environment is not new, although the labeling of such teams is a recent phenomenon. The practice has been used informally for quite some time, and only recently have universities begun to formalize the functions of these groups (Flynn & Heitzmann, 2008). Development of TATs gained popularity following the Virginia Tech incident (Flynn & Heiztmann, 2008). However, as early as 1986, literature on addressing the increasing numbers of disruptive students can be found in professional journals (Gerald, 1986). Much interest was generated in developing programs to identify potentially violent students after the shooting at Columbine High School (Cornell et al., 2004). Although not in a university setting, the tragedy of this high school captivated the public's attention, with everyone demanding something be done to prevent future incidents such as this one. Early efforts seemed to have focused on prevention through the use of profiling strategies borrowed from law enforcement agencies (Cornell et al., 2004). According to these authors, even though the profiling strategies were modified for use with adolescents and in school settings, success varied in identifying students who posed a real threat.

The composition of TATs varies from campus to campus, but they typically are composed of a set and limited number of people. Membership might include representation from campus security, health services, student affairs, judicial office, residence life, and the counseling center. Usually, two to five people make up this team. At times, other people may attend meetings based on need and to provide first-person information for specific situations. Team membership, as well as leadership of the team, varies because of experience and expertise in this area. Meetings are held regularly but may be called for if a threat is made. These teams operate on a continuous basis and are not directly tied to the recovery process. Ideally, TATs operate independently from teamscharged with addressing crises on university campuses. The office TATs report to varies based on policies and which office has the responsibility to make decisions regarding actions to be taken when someone makes a threat.

Crisis Response Team

Crisis response teams (CRTs), sometimes referred to as emergency response teams, refer to groups that are in the field and have direct contact with victims of the crisis. This group is on call and responds to the immediacy of the situation. Generally, CRTs have a core membership. Core members respond to a crisis as needed. We emphasize *as needed* because not all crisis response team members are needed for every crisis (Sherwood & McKelfresh, 2007). Core membership is likely to include people from campus security, health services, counseling center personnel, campus ministries if your campus has this department, several people from facilities management, staff members from housing, student affairs staff, food services, athletics, and human services. Each of these core members can play an important role in responding to a crisis on your campus. However, not all members are needed for each crisis. Most crisis response teams have the ability to request expansion of the team as needed on a temporary basis. Two reasons give rise to the need for temporary membership on this committee. First, core members may lack the expertise to respond to a specific crisis at a university. In this situation, membership is expanded to provide the needed services and support. Second, the need is so great for a specific crisis that core membership cannot adequately provide the assistance or help that is needed. In these situations, membership is expanded to meet the needs on the campus. An example is the need for additional support after the shootings at Northern Illinois University, Virginia Tech, and to a lesser degree Duquesne University. Although CRTs need to have the ability to function independently to a certain degree, this group typically reports to and takes directions from the crisis management team (Sherwood & McKelfresh, 2007). The freedom to operate independently is needed because CRTs are on the front line, and at times decisions need to be made and support offered with no time to get permission from the crisis management team. The CRTs should be aware of and understand any limits to their ability to make decisions and work on their own.

Crisis Management Team

Crisis management teams (CMTs) provide oversight to the recovery process as well as help a university prepare for a crisis (Sherwood & McKelfresh, 2007). Ideally, this team works throughout the recovery process, yet many times senior administration begins to assume the responsibilities of CMTs after the first few months of the recovery. The specific responsibilities for CMTs vary from campus to campus but generally involve the management of operations associated with recovery. The human impact of crisis responsibilities might include (a) making provisions for follow-up physical and mental health concerns, (b) dealing with personnel concerns, (c) being involved in conflict management, and (d) providing support (e.g., completing paper work for benefits) for anyone needing assistance following a crisis. They may also be called on to address other unanticipated issues related to the human impact of crisis that arise as part of the recovery process.

Membership on CMTs is generally constant; however, other people may be invited to participate for a given crisis situation (Sherwood & McKelfresh, 2007). These invitations would occur when additional expertise is needed. The leadership of CMTs varies but is typically either the top administrator on campus or that person's representative. The number of people on CMTs is normally between 10 and 15. Membership represents major departments or units on a campus. They report to senior administration and possibly the board of trustees or other governance body.

CURRENT STATE OF CRISIS MANAGEMENT PLANNING IN HIGHER EDUCATION

We believe that most institutions of higher learning could physically produce some semblance of a plan for crisis management if called upon to do so. However, many of these plans are not adequate to the task of responding to and resolving crisis events (Mitroff et al., 2006). The real issue, as with most planning, is the actual usefulness of the plan. Developing a comprehensive plan means the plan can be used throughout the recovery process, as well as to address the contextual systemic issues.

Two factors that influence the effective use of crisis management plans are (a) barriers in implementation and (b) barriers to planning. Although it may seem we are simply talking "about" crisis management planning, a working understanding of these factors is needed to avoid banging your head against a proverbial wall. Keeping them in mind as you revise or develop will help you circumvent inefficient and ineffective crisis management plans.

Barriers in Implementation

When a crisis does occur, everyone trusts that plans have been made to respond as needed (Casey, 2004). Unfortunately, this question is all too common: "Does anyone know where the crisis management plan is?" A follow-up question is "Who is in charge of the plan?" Another question might be "How do we activate the plan?" If you think these questions sound like ones that would be asked at your university, the current state of crisis preparedness is not what it ought to be. In fact, if this is true on your campus, should a crisis occur, expect the worse. A careful audit of crisis preparedness needs to be conducted to correct the situation. Seven major traps hamstring many educational institutions when it comes to using their crisis management plans. Together, these spell disaster and an inefficient, possibly prolonged, recovery period.

Compartmentalization

The first pitfall educational institutions fall into when trying to implement a crisis management plan is compartmentalization (Mitroff & Anagnos, 2001). Compartmentalization in universities is all too common. Compartmentalization occurs on campuses when departments and units function as if independent of the others and is played out in behaviors such as not communicating with others or withholding resources. Many reasons can be identified for structuring campuses in this manner, including history, personalities, and politics, to name a few. This compartmentalization slows the decision-making process. Being too slow to make decisions leads to frustration and misinformation and fuels apathy (Caponigro, 2000). Decision-making processes must be streamlined if administrators and CMTs are to respond to the fluidity of a crisis situation.

Limited Focus

A second problem with university crisis plans is the tendency to focus on just addressing individuals during the emergency phase of the crisis. In general, educational institutions are very good at addressing the needs of the individuals; in most cases, that means students (Knotek, 2006). Staff and faculty members are included, but the primary focus remains on students. The standard procedure is to make mental health specialists available to help anyone experiencing undue trauma because of the crisis event. Rooms are set aside, at times mental health specialists are allowed in the classrooms, and memos are sent out to allow anyone who wants to talk with a counselor to be allowed to do so (Griffin, 2007).

On the other hand, for-profit organizations have taken the lead in attending to the overall impact of a crisis on business. The concern is to attend to the collective well-being of the organization, which includes addressing human impact issues. Elaborate plans are developed to ensure that minimal disruption to business will occur, because of problems related to the reactions of the employees. The goal or plan developed by organizations is to map out procedures that decrease the amount of downtime. Neither approach is fatally flawed; both have merit. Yet a comprehensive crisis management plan requires integration of these two philosophies. An integration of these two approaches creates the best opportunity for a university to experience the least disruption to its mission.

Out-of-Date

A third problem with respect to implementation faced in universities is that crisis management plans become dust collectors and out-of-date (Casey, 2004; Grund, 2008). The belief seems to be that once written, the plan is good to go, even if it is several years old. A reason for not updating a plan can be costs. Personnel costs, the expense required to update technologies, and expenditures involved with supplies all can be a factor for having out-of-date plans.

Many times, crisis management plans sit on a shelf and are often buried under other books. When the time comes to implement the plan, someone has to search through reports on enrollment projections, recruitment plans, funding opportunities, faculty production, physical plant utilization, and so on just to find the crisis management plan. Once located, the person has to make sure the crisis management team has the latest copy, and then, and only then, is the plan read, which, by the way, is too late for all practical purposes.

Impulsive Reaction

The fourth concern is that sometimes the CMT, or another group guiding the intervention process, will simply wing it, doing what they think is best (Mitroff et al., 2006). Administrators intellectualize the chances that a crisis will occur and cling to the belief that resolving the crisis is just a matter of leadership (Mitroff, 2004). They make it (i.e., the plan) up as it goes. Sometimes making it up as you go works out wonderfully, but flying by the seat of your pants in crisis situations can also lead to any number of disastrous consequences. Leadership is an issue, but responding to the crisis and implementing a comprehensive intervention is more than leadership. Expertise and knowledge of organizational crisis reactions as well as individual responses to crises is needed. The biggest blunder for institutions depending on this approach is to misunderstand the crisis. Key issues are neglected or ignored, and critical aspects of the impact of the crisis on the university are neglected, as attempts are made to resolve the crisis situation. What often happens is that the CMT uses valuable time reinventing the wheel. One person—the president of the university, the chair of the board of directors, the university counsel, provost, vice president for student affairs, or anyone else—is not able to solely provide all the leadership needed in a crisis situation.

Lack of Practice

The fifth and maybe the most common hazard universities encounter when a crisis on campus occurs is the lack of practice (Grund, 2008; Mitroff et al., 2006). In fact, it is not so much even the lack of practice, but rather the absence of practice altogether. Often budget issues get in the way of practice. Administrators allocate monies to projects viewed as more relevant and, many times, more tangible. Practice of crisis management plans seems to be an extravagance too costly considering the chances a crisis will occur. Although practice may not make the response perfect, it does help everyone understand what needs to happen (Sherwood & McKelfresh, 2007). Research shows that practice does help when it comes to implementing a crisis management plan (FEMA, 2006). With practice, CMTs learns to work together and think like a team.

Failure to Recognize

The sixth, and all too common, obstacle in the planning process is the failure to see a crisis coming (Augustine, 1995; Caponigro, 2000; Fink, 2002). Mitroff and Anagnos

(2001) talk about this idea as signal detection. Sometimes these signals are internal, and at other times they are external. For example, an internal signal could be an increase in the number of students written up for being intoxicated. An escalation of the number of complaints filed by employees might also be viewed as a signal. Each of these signals might be a precursor to possible violence. External signals include the spread of criminal activity closer to campus or the activation of groups with political agendas close to campus. Signals may also be formal or informal, based in technology, or generated by people. Formal signals refer to those that are sought out, such as those gathered from suggestion boxes. Exit interviews can also be used to detect poor morale or other problems that could erupt into a full-blown crisis if not addressed. Informal signals can be found anywhere at any time. These signals seem to pop up and, if identified, can help prevent a crisis from occurring. Examples include a change in the culture on campus or the types of clothes being worn by students. None of these is generally given much attention but can be a sign that the potential for a crisis exists.

Sacred Cows

For some campuses, the seventh downfall is protected individuals or groups. At times, university sacred cows may be a lightning rod for a potential crisis (Nicoletti et al., 2001). Sacred cows are people or groups who are treated differently because of their status on campus. Every campus has these people and groups. Sacred cows are not inherently bad. Think of the beloved custodian who has been around for a long time and who is given some leeway in getting his job done. Or the office assistant who has held her position for many years and is given slack when her work is not up to par. These people have earned the right to a level of leniency due to their commitment and dedication. However, the special status some sacred cows enjoy may signal the makings of a crisis. Students whose parents make significant contributions to the university or the children of trustees may be among the sacred cows. These students may receive special privileges or are not disciplined as severely for infractions. Athletes who are allowed latitude with respect to behaviors are among the sacred cows. The Colorado State problem with recruitment of athletes shows how leniency given to certain groups can explode into a crisis. A crisis plan should include a mechanism to identify and analyze signals that are the precursor to a crisis.

Barriers to Planning

We have identified six barriers to effective crisis management that involve issues ranging from budgets to bureaucracy. Individually, they do not present insurmountable obstacles. However, combined they represent an intricate maze to navigate bureaucracy when revising or developing a crisis management plan. The following list and discussion highlight some of the normative difficulties in planning effectively for crisis situations. Although we discuss each of these barriers individually, be aware that each of these issues interacts with others to create a very interesting and intriguing challenge for the person in charge. The whole is much greater than the sum of these parts.

Structure of Higher Education

Institutions of higher education are well aware of the issues related to silos in education. *Silo* is the vernacular used to describe a disconnect between units, academic departments, and administrative functions. On some campuses, this division is especially apparent between student affairs and academics (Grund, 2008). The concept has become synonymous with barriers to workplace effectiveness, personal agendas, and political conflict (Jacobs, 2009). On college campuses, silos are evident in crisis management planning particularly with respect to issues related to the human impact of crises. Silos cause barriers that are difficult to get around. Typically, these barriers have been established well before a crisis. Barriers are seen in two forms. The first is communication. Crisis management plans must build in methods to allow appropriate communication across the silos on your campus (Eells, 2008). We want to emphasize *appropriate* communication that does not violate professional ethics or state or federal laws. A second, and sometimes more important, consideration involves cooperation. Cooperation among departments and units is critical for the overall management of a crisis. Without cooperation, efforts will be duplicated and resources misused. Again, these obstacles predate your crisis management plan. The plan must be designed to overcome long-standing problems associated with silos.

Politics

Effective crisis management planning can be thwarted if politics rule the process. One way that politics can unduly influence crisis management planning is in the selection of the crisis management and crisis response teams. Collins, in his best-selling motivational leadership book *Good to Great* (2001), says that the first step in moving forward successfully in any major endeavor is determining "who should be on the bus," rather than the destination. He suggests that if the right people are driving the bus, leadership will be in place to get to whatever destination is necessary. He also clearly indicates that getting the wrong people off the bus accelerates a process by removing barriers. Determining who in the institution has previously demonstrated competency or who has specialized training and/ or experience in crisis management planning helps to overcome this barrier. When you are putting together crisis plans and crisis teams, political appointments make zero sense.

During the recovery process, politics can also interfere with decisions to address the crisis. Decisions based on political expediency can backfire during the recovery process. Taking the high ground when you make decisions during the recovery process is imperative. Do whatever it takes to help victims and survivors, regardless of personal agendas, university politics, or external influences. You must also attend to the departments and units that were directly affected by the crisis. If you truly work toward and focus on the goal of assisting your university in crisis, the politics of the crisis response will be lessened, the liability less, and the outcome stronger by not allowing politics to be a barrier.

Paradox of Higher Education

On the outside, higher education appears progressive, with academic programs and curricula on the cutting edge. In fact, universities are decidedly conservative in nature and decision making, much of the time accepting change only if absolutely required. This paradox of being perceived as progressive while being stuck in the status quo creates some unique challenges to the crisis management initiative.

In the past decade, universities have been in the spotlight as they attempted to respond to numerous and varied crises. The institutions are often placed under the public microscope by the media, and leadership is second-guessed regarding every decision before, during, and after a crisis. Even with this type of pressure, leaders of many institutions have not made comprehensive crisis management a priority on their campuses (Mitroff et al., 2006). You can almost hear someone say, "It is not the way we have always done business." This attitude forms a substantial barrier to crisis management planning and intervention on university campuses. Recognition of this barrier is important as you revise or develop your crisis management plan.

Administrative Versus Frontline Perspective

The administrative versus frontline perspective is truly one of the biggest challenges, possibly *the* biggest, in our experience. This barrier involves the intentionality with which crisis management planning occurs. Crisis management planning is put on a to-do list with numerous other projects. Many times completion of the other projects is more visible, such as creation of a service learning component or increased retention of students as opposed to the development of a crisis management plan that is simply a plan just in case it is needed. Crisis management planning, while acknowledged, becomes a low priority on an administrator's to-do list.

The need for a crisis management plan is identified by the board or other governing body. Once the need is identified, an administrator is given the responsibility and, in turn, passes the actual development of the plan onto others. This assignment may have little to do with expertise and more to do with budgets, workloads, or an assortment of options having little to do with crisis management knowledge or experience. The individuals writing the plan may or may not have knowledge about comprehensive crisis planning, may or may not have authority to call on others from across campus or external constituents, and may or may not be the individuals who are actually expected to carry out the plan if needed. For the administration, this is a task that has been acknowledged, responded to, and other than basic reporting on plans when requested, forgotten (until something happens at another university and is in the media or, God forbid, happens on your campus). The staff assigned the task probably struggles to understand what is needed, feeling the responsibility of the assignment and hoping they are not called upon because they know they are not prepared or fully supported in this task. This is a sitting duck position for some poor soul.

FERPA and HIPAA

The Family Educational Rights and Privacy Act (FERPA) of 1974 and the Health Insurance Portability and Accountability Act (HIPAA) of 1996 are not barriers to be overcome but rather a difficulty to be lived with in crisis management planning (Paterson & Colbs, 2008). Both acts were designed to protect individual privacy rights, and they prevent sharing information that may help in crisis management planning and intervention. Two issues surface with respect to this barrier. The first involves the structure of the university. Often university reporting structures complicate decisions about the *appropriate* sharing of information. The issue involves protecting the rights of the individual versus maintenance of a safe working environment. This problem has been an issue in organizations for many years (Braverman, 1999), and FERPA and HIPAA become an issue in crisis management planning for making decisions about the appropriate sharing of information to prevent and/or respond to a crisis. The second issue concerns the debate regarding the applicability of FERPA and HIPAA in crisis situations (Jones, 2003). This issue is hotly debated, with no definitive answer. Unfortunately, no clear answer can be given to resolve the problems associated with this barrier. Crisis management plans must find a way to balance these sometimes competing directives.

Support

Another obstacle is whether professional staff and physical plant staff believe in and are willing to support the plan. Although a great deal of lip service is paid to building crisis management plans (CMPs), lack of real support is a hallmark of such operations (Toigo, 2000). You might assume that few would oppose a full-scale crisis prevention and intervention program in a university, given the current publicity about school violence (Myer, 2009). Yet we are talking about biologists, vice presidents for finance, IT people, English teachers, cooks, the alumni coordinator, computer programmers, secretaries, librarians, custodians, physicists, and sociologists, not to mention students who are cheerleaders, violin players, student senators, presidents of clubs, rush chairpersons for fraternities and sororities, and members of the university chess team. All of these people have other things they need to do and want to do, and they didn't necessarily sign on to be crisis planners or interventionists. For example, faculty at a major university were required to complete a one-hour online course that involved spotting students who might be headed for violence and what to do about them. After 6 months, only about 40% of the faculty at all the schools had taken and passed the online course.

Governance

Governance can also be a barrier to crisis management planning (Grund, 2008). By governance, we mean the representation of control and authority over an institution. In the case of higher education, this means not only the university's senior administrative staff but also the board of directors or trustees and other entities that govern the university. Given the complex and political environment in which institutions of higher learning operate, crisis management needs to be a key element in strategic governance. Trustees, board members, and others in principal positions of leadership should be familiar with an institution's plan. Many of these individuals representing various levels of governance should participate in the institution's crisis management program. The exact makeup of this group will vary, based on whether the university is private or public and if the university is part of a larger system of institutions reporting to a single governing board.

Examining the culture of a university may be a step in helping to overcome governance as a barrier (Tierney, 1988). This examination helps increase awareness and decreases conflict among various levels of the administration. Including the various levels of governance in the crisis management planning and training process will also help you rise above the problems of governance as a barrier to crisis planning. This involvement will permit the clarification of roles and responsibilities in crisis and give credibility to those responsible. The advantage to having all levels of governance involved in planning is the ability to share resources where appropriate, such as training costs. A comprehensive model should incorporate all levels of intervention and resources to appropriately plan for and respond to the array of diverse crises that may occur within the higher education system.

BUILDING BLOCKS FOR CRISIS MANAGEMENT PLANS

The Federal Emergency Management Agency (2003) has published a manual outlining a generic structure for a CMP for institutions of higher education. Others, such as Zdziarski, Rollo, and Dunkel (2007), also have described a basic structure for a CMP. Rather than repeating this information, we want to discuss some basic building blocks to a CMP. These building blocks form a strong foundation for making a CMP operational. Like building a house, the foundation must be poured before walls are put up. Although you see the walls, it is the foundation that supports the house. These building blocks provide the base on which comprehensive CMPs can be built. Ignoring these issues can lead to a collapse of your plan.

The Players

The following players make up what we believe to be a gold or even platinum model of a CMT. A university can do with less than this A-team, but the more that is removed from it, the more it becomes one made of lead. While fewer of these players and resources in it may well work, it still comes down to the fact that somebody is going to have to do the jobs and roles that follow.

Emergency Preparedness Coordinator

This person goes by different names and titles but is tasked as the lead person and coordinator of prevention, intervention, and postvention responses to a campus crisis. The emergency preparedness coordinator or manager is the linchpin in the crisis response team. If this person is not solely designated to the role and has other duties, the institution is asking for trouble, because this is truly a full-time job. Small colleges may be tempted to just have these responsibilities added on as a supplementary task. Size does not make a difference; the coordinator's responsibilities remain surprisingly similar. Responsibilities are still pretty much the same and maybe even more problematic if the college has a security force rather than a police force, a very small student counseling center, and other shortages of resources. The ideal emergency coordinator is experienced in some form of disaster mitigation or crisis intervention, whether in government, armed services, law enforcement, or business. He or she either has a college degree in emergency preparedness or is National Incident Management Systems compliant through courses taken at the Emergency Management Institute of FEMA. In an ideal world, both would be better, but as of this date, there are few programs and few graduates.

Besides knowing logistics, tactics, and strategies for dealing with a systemic disaster, the coordinator should know the individual crisis intervention techniques and strategies detailed in Chapter 10. He or she should have a clear understanding of the objectives and methods of a variety of crisis intervention plans that crosscut both natural and human-caused disasters and range from a suicide-murder to an earthquake. This person also needs to be a good administrator and delegator who can coordinate a number of activities and people under very stressful and chaotic conditions. The EMP must have the autonomy and the backing of the administration to make on-the-spot decisions and not have to wait to move decisions through the bureaucracy (Brock, 2002; Brock, Sandoval, & Lewis, 1996, pp. 68–69; Langelier, 2010; Nicoletti et al., 2001, pp. 72–75; Petersen, 1999; Poland, 2004; Poland & McCormick, 1999).

Information Technology

There are two primary reasons that someone from information technology is part of the team. First and foremost is keeping communication going, or getting it back up and running. In a business climate, this would be one of the most important people on the team for business continuity purposes. However, IT as part of the CMT is not just getting computers going so business can get back to normal. Above all is the safety of the members of the university community, so that means having knowledge of the red phones on campus, the sirens, the computers, the telephones, and the infrastructure that ties them together.

Information Systems

While this person may be one and the same as the information technology member, this person is not so much about getting electrons moving through wires and cyberspace as about coordinating systems with people. If every student's cell phone is set up to get a call from the CMT or every smart classroom's screen can flash a message in the CMT's electronic bulletin board, how does that get out to the right people and when does it happen over what systems? More ominously, information systems will be responsible for determining what classes are in session in which buildings and who are the students and faculty in those classes. This person will also be responsible for finding the parents and relatives of those students and staff members. Finally, if buildings are damaged or destroyed, information systems will have to be responsible for notifying students of those changes. These may seem like mundane issues, but they are anything but mundane to the parties trying to get this information.

Media Liaison

The media liaison is probably second only to the EPM in the critical role he or she plays. This person is at the center of what Nicoletti and his associates (2001, p. 111) call a *communications vortex*. All information pertaining to the crisis passes through the center, and ultimately the media liaison has to decide what and how much information to release. Particularly when there is a possibility that the event is a criminal act, information needs to be tightly controlled. Maintaining control may sound like an easy thing to do, but it is far too easy to give anguished parents who are beseeching the CMT for answers on the safety and whereabouts of their children information that may compromise the investigation or allow the perpetrators to escape (Langelier, 2010).

The media's voracious appetite for news is absolutely phenomenal in the event of a large-scale disaster. In the not-too-distant past, there would be three waves of people to deal with after a crisis. The first would be first responders such as police, firefighters, and EMTs. The second would be the media, and the third would be parents. Given the advent of the cell phone, with its multiple capabilities to make phone calls, tweet messages, take pictures, and send e-mail *during* a crisis, these three waves may now arrive almost simultaneously at the scene, demanding answers, getting in the way, and in fact impeding recovery efforts. Therefore, the media liaison, information systems, and law enforcement are often a miniteam that is under extreme pressure. These groups often coordinate what gets communicated to whom, under what conditions, and during what timelines.

Further, it is one thing for the media liaison to deal with local television, radio, and newspaper reporters; it is quite another thing to deal with national news media. Imagine yourself as media liaison in a scenario of an exploding science building with loss of life and abounding and abundant rumors of how and why the science building and a lot of people in it are now gone. You have national reporters with uplink dishes to satellites for national and international news organizations. Helicopters land on the soccer field and disgorge news teams. Reporters are quizzing faculty, students, and anybody else they can get microphones in front of, while you are trying to stop rumors, control the flow of information, and provide as much information as you can to your constituents.

This scenario should make it very clear that dealing with the media is a major responsibility and should be the sole responsibility of one person specially designated and trained for the job. One of the worst possible scenarios is to let others who may be perceived to be in a position of authority talk to the media. When this happens, the mixed messages accelerate rumors and can spread panic because people now don't know what to believe, and the university loses credibility (Brock et al., 1996, pp. 69–70). The idea is to get the media to help and not hinder the operation. How the media liaison goes about this is a delicate balancing act. Stonewalling is not acceptable. Communicating the truth of what is known and facts that do not compromise an ongoing investigation is important, and later finding out that the information disseminated was anything but the truth must not happen (Siegal, 1994).

Law Enforcement

If there is only a security force on the campus, the university absolutely must have a memorandum of agreement with local law enforcement to come on campus in the event of a major crisis. It is also important that a local law enforcement agent be privy to the planning of the crisis management team. Even if the university does have a police force, it will probably not have enough officers to handle a major crisis. Thus, we agree with Captain Kevin Langelier, special operations officer of the University of Memphis Police Department, that a memorandum of agreement as to how joint law enforcement operations will be conducted is an absolute necessity when you are confronted with a major crisis. Whoever is the law enforcement member of the CMT should be experienced in conducting tactical operations, running command posts, conducting hostage negotiations, and using verbal de-escalation and defusing techniques for violent and mentally ill individuals.

President's Liaison

While we agree with Nicoletti and his associates (2001, p. 75) that presidents must be both visible and vocal in their support of the CMT and be seen as the leader in a crisis, we do not believe they should be members of the CMT, no matter how small the college. Our reasons are as follows: First and foremost, presidents are subject to political pressure. There is no place for politics in an operational CMT that has to make hard and quick decisions that may mean life or death for its constituents. Second, presidents' egos can get in the way. Their subjective responses have little place in the objective world of the CMT. There is no substitute for the knowledge base the CMT has to manage the situation, and presidents frankly put their careers in jeopardy when they attempt to second-guess a CMT. As an example, we are aware of one president who didn't like the recommendations of the CMT in regard to how to triage students suffering from acute stress disorder. He decided that henceforth his secretary would be responsible for making decisions about those cases and that students should be referred to her. She would then inform him of their problems, and he would decide their disposition. We wonder what his length of tenure is going to be after the next crisis.

Therefore, we believe a person designated as the presidential liaison should be named to the committee. The liaison should be seen as a bona fide member of the CMT and have the trust and confidence of the president. The presidential liaison should be able to condense information and relay it rapidly and accurately to the president. The liaison should also be part of the policy committee, if there is a separate one, and be able to rapidly and accurately apprise the CMT of school policy and the president's views on the situation.

Medical Liaison

The medical liaison should have established close links between the local emergency, fire, medical, and mental health systems and the university. A critical component in her or his role and function is planning for medical triage of victims in a crisis. To that extent, the medical liaison should have a good knowledge of trauma medicine and be able to make quick decisions about the extent of injuries people have sustained and what kind of immediate medical care is needed. As the official medical representative of the university, he or she should also have the responsibility of holding debriefings about the current medical status of sick and injured constituents and communicating to parents and staff the medical conditions of those involved in the crisis (Brock et al., 1996, pp. 71–72; Rubin, 1999). Particularly in the case of a death notification, the medical liaison should have a close working relationship with the media person to coordinate how information about people who died will be disseminated. The words used and how they are conveyed when a death occurs are critically important (Kerr, 2009, p. 69). The medical liaison should also be closely associated with the local emergency management agency, so that she or he knows whom to contact and what kinds of resources are available in a disaster. Here again, a memorandum of understanding as to what community emergency medical personnel, hospitals, and other medical services will be available is critical to the university's plan.

Parent Liaison

The parent liaison's job is dealing with parents, period! Keeping parents calm, providing them with information, and furnishing support are critical in containment of a crisis. This person works closely with the media liaison in determining what information and support services are disseminated to parents and how it gets to them. When a part of the community is not fluent in English, provisions for interpreters are important, as well as for translators for all written information that goes out to parents. Because parents may need the services of other components of the team, this school official must have a good working knowledge of each member's role—particularly the mental health service providers (Rubin, 1999).

Mental Health Facilitator

There will be much work for the mental health component of any disaster response, both immediately after the impact phase and for a long time afterwards through recovery. For large-scale disasters, the traumatic wake that ensues calls for coordination of services that will most likely reach far beyond the abilities of the campus counseling center and perhaps local community health systems as well. Therefore, either through partnerships with other mental health providers or through Red Cross disaster relief services, the provision of large-scale mental health services will call for a good deal of coordination (and this is a big *and*) and an understanding of what is involved with wide-scale mental health crisis intervention. To that end, we believe that at least one person on the campus should be Red Cross certified and have been on national call-ups.

This person, the police representative, or both should also be on the TAT. When human-made violence causes the team to go into action, a member of the threat assessment team with knowledge of the perpetrator may be invaluable in intervention.

Provost Liaison

After the impact phase, school will still have to go on. Obtaining building space, determining revised schedules and academic calendars, deciding about graduation requirements, and a host of other academic concerns are common after a crisis. These may seem of minor concern in the immediate aftermath of a disaster. Down the road, they will not be so minor to the students and faculty affected by how well these decisions are thought out.

Residence Life Coordinator

The residence life coordinator, or his or her representative, should be on the committee. Regardless of whether a large-scale disaster directly impacts the residence halls themselves, this is where the students are and a likely hot spot for trouble. Providing services to this large block of students will require knowledge and skills regarding residence life.

Resource Person

This member will need to know where a variety of available supplies are and how to get them from point A to point B in a hurry. This may be a physical plant and planning person, but it may also be someone in food services, the bursar, the comptroller, or anybody else who knows how to get things in a hurry. Depending on the size and type of the crisis, the resource person may need to know how to obtain everything from printer ink to a front loader. This is not a menial job. If the material supplies are not available, including food and drink when a crisis is going full tilt, then everything grinds to a halt (Rubin, 1999). One of your authors found this out the hard way while on patrol with a crisis intervention team police officer. About 5 p.m., a call came in of a suicidal person who had barricaded himself in a house with 5 gallons of gasoline, a gun, and his sister held hostage. During the ensuing standoff, your author and two police officers were pinned inside a SWAT perimeter negotiating with the suicidal individual. We three negotiators were unable to get food or water because of safety concerns and shared one bottle of water, a peanut butter sandwich, and a banana that one of the officers retrieved from her child's lunchbox. The barricade finally ended on a positive note at 4 a.m. the next morning. Suffice it to say, you do not do your best work when you are not only hot and tired, but thirsty and hungry, too.

In summary, you should be able to see that this group of workers demonstrates the expertise that will need to be brought to bear on a major crisis. Redundancy in these personnel is also important, so that if one member of the group is unable to participate, another person from the same expertise area can step into his or her place without creating a gap in the team.

Physical Requirements

The following minimum nuts-and-bolts requirements are critical to a university crisis plan (e.g., Brown & Bobrow, 2004; Conoley & Goldstein, 2004; Gerler, 2004; Kerr, 2009; Langelier, 2010; Slater, 2010; Williams, 2004, 2006; Zdziarski et al., 2007).

Operations/Communications Center

For a very large crisis, a room that will become the nerve center needs to be designated and equipped. Additional phone lines, supplies, and furniture for the CMT; computers with Internet capability; and emergency equipment such as portable phones, flashlights, citizen band and police band radios, and portable generators should be available here. This nerve center will become the center point to an efficient crisis operation. All communications and decisions will flow through here. It should have a second and even a third backup, so that if the disaster disables one center location, it can quickly be relocated.

Break Room

This is a place that is private and allows workers time to relax, eat, make personal phone calls, and rest. Continuous high adrenaline levels for long periods of time are common in a crisis environment, and CMT members need a quiet place to take a breath and relax for a few minutes. It may also double as a debriefing room for crisis intervention team members who are frontline workers.

Information Center

A room large enough to handle a number of media personnel should be equipped with a sound system and visual media equipment. It may also double as a briefing room for parents and relatives of staff.

First-Aid Room

This room should be stocked with first-aid supplies for minor physical problems, of which there are likely to be many.

Counseling Locations

The counseling center may not have enough room to service the number of people who have mental health problems. As many locations as possible need to be identified for crisis counseling offices. Crisis counseling will involve a wide variety of activities that will require different accommodations. For factual briefings and dissemination of psychoeducational materials, auditorium- or cafeteria-size rooms will be needed to handle large groups of people. Classrooms or offices will need to be designated to do triage and provide psychological first aid. Offices will be needed to perform psychological triage and provide individual counseling. If school is in session, a great deal of rescheduling and shuffling of rooms and assignments is going to be necessary and should be planned for ahead of time, or alternative buildings such as churches and office buildings will need to be used.

Other Necessities

On-Site Communications

Dedicated telephone lines, walkie-talkies, citizen and police band radios, message boards both electronic and standard, and computers linked to internal systems and external emergency management agency systems are standard communications equipment. Because telephone lines may be jammed or otherwise inoperable, a central message board should be available for announcements, bulletins, student lists, and other personal information. If possible, dedicated phone lines with the numbers known only to officials and staff responsible for handling the crisis should be available. Walkie-talkies or other handheld communication devices are vital in case normal on-site communication lines are not available. The portable "to go boxes" that K-12 school systems have provide vital hard-copy data such as updated attendance lists, emergency numbers, and parent or guardian names. These hard copies can be used to check off names of survivors and determine where injured are being transported; they can be moved to an alternate site to check off names of students and staff.

Establishing a Phone Tree Among All Staff

In any size crisis, a redundant phone tree is absolutely imperative. Computer systems are fine, but they may not be reliable as a phone tree, particularly if people are not on their computers or cannot access them in a power outage. All staff members of a university need to be informed of a crisis event as soon as there is knowledge of it. The phone tree is critical so that all staff members who are assigned to the CMT can begin to operate in a crisis mode and assume preplanned positions and duties. Messages about the crisis should be written down by each person on the tree. Relying on memory and verbal transmission will guarantee that facts will get commingled with fiction. The CMT members and other faculty and staff need to be aware of what is happening and not go blundering into an ongoing crisis. We have experienced such a lack of communication firsthand, and it is, to say the least, a nightmare.

Procedural Checklist

Although it may seem to be wasting time to go through a procedural checklist when a crisis is going full blast, not doing so is asking for trouble. It is too easy to overlook a critical component of the intervention plan or assume it has been taken care of by somebody else. Pilots run a preflight checklist on aircraft when taking off and landing. Doing so prevents plane crashes. The same is true here.

Building Plans and Infrastructure Schematics

Building plans and schematics of light, communication, steam, gas, sanitary, and water lines are vital to emergency personnel and police. Blueprints and schematics should be available in hard copy. Having them on a computer when the computer won't work does little good. Further, rescue workers need hard copies of such plans.

Provisions

Because crisis personnel may be involved for extended periods of time, food and drink should be provided or be delivered on-site, and that means a refrigerator and at least a microwave. There also ought to be access to a portable generator to power all the foregoing stuff.

THREE Cs OF CRISIS MANAGEMENT PLANNING

Integrated throughout CMPs should be three components: (a) communication, (b) coordination, and (c) consultation. Systematically weaving these three components into your CMP helps to minimize problems throughout the recovery process. *Minimize* is the key word. No CMP is perfect, and no plan is executed to perfection, but you can reduce problems in using the plan by incorporating these components into all parts of the plan. You can also use these components to evaluate your current CMP to understand the weaknesses and strengths of the plan. The more these components are built into it, the more robust the plan.

Although the structures of CMPs are very similar, plans are both generic and idiosyncratic. They are generic in the sense that the same areas should be addressed, including issues related to the human impact of a crisis throughout the recovery process, restoration of day-to-day functioning, and rebuilding, if needed. You cannot plan for every contingency, but you can have a basic plan that fits your particular set of circumstances. So you need to generate a plan that has utility to it, has ease of implementation, and can be understood, practiced, and used (Nicoletti et al., 2001; Rollo & Zdziarski, 2007). Plans are idiosyncratic because of the uniqueness of the university. The CMP of Flagship Land Grant State University will look different from the CMP of Small Private Liberal Arts College. Each campus has its distinctive way of doing things and its own relationships on campus.

Communication

Literature on crisis management typically focuses on communication issues related to talking with the popular media. In fact, some experts say the field of crisis management owes its existence to handling the media following a crisis event (Caponigro, 2000). Yet communication is not simply a public relations issue. Recently, communication has been used to reduce the impact of crisis through notification systems to warn anyone on campus about the possibility of danger (Greenberg, 2007). Communication must also be viewed as a two-way street in which administrators and CMTs give people the opportunity to express their feelings and perceptions (Fink, 2002; Mitroff, 2004). Although this suggestion may seem to go against typical leadership, a crisis is anything but typical. Taking the time to listen to others is a wise decision in the recovery process (Mitroff et al., 2006).

Public Relations

A great deal has been written on public relations during the recovery process. Simply stated, this literature advocates maintaining a positive rapport with all constituencies following a crisis (Caponigro, 2000). Two fundamental suggestions can be gleaned from this literature. The first suggestion concerns making sure that the message given to the media is honest (Fink, 2002). In this day, secrets are very difficult if not impossible to keep. The time-honored saying "honesty is the best policy" is very applicable for CMP. Doing damage control because of misleading the public through deceitfulness or trickery adds another layer to the recovery process. Avoid off-the-cuff comments, and understand that private messages may be seen by others. Understand that the message must be managed so that appropriate information is made public (Caponigro, 2000). This management involves making sure of facts and disclosing them in a timely fashion.

The second suggestion is that communication should take place with anyone with a stake in the recovery process (Fink, 2002; Mitroff et al., 2006). This includes not just students, staff, and faculty members but also vendors, the community, and others who have an association with the university. This communication should involve providing information in a timely fashion about the state of the recovery process. Regular communication is recommended, even if the information is limited. The CMPs should build in methods to maintain public relations that benefit rather than impede the recovery process.

It is crucial that you identify a few core messages that you want to communicate in the crisis and recovery process (Caponigro, 2000; Lawson, 2007). These messages should be communicated on a repeated basis throughout the recovery process. Messages should be simple and to the point. Ambiguous statements lead to speculation and rumors. Misleading statements raise suspicions when new information comes to light. Statements should acknowledge the problem, identify current efforts to address the issues, and express support for anyone affected by the crisis.

Notification

Notification systems have become an important aspect of CMP safety procedures (Sharma, 2008). Ideally, these systems serve two purposes: (a) to alert a campus to possible dangers and (b) to give information regarding the status of incidents on campus. The primary purpose of notification systems is to sound the alarm when potentially dangerous situations arise. These situations range from weapons being used on campus to dangers resulting from natural causes such as tornadoes. When activated, the system uses numerous ways, including electronics (text messages, recorded phone messages, e-mail) and old-fashioned sirens or public address systems (Sharma, 2008) to notify subscribers. A secondary and less recognized use of notification systems is to provide information regarding anything from school closures to all-clear messages after an incident has been resolved. Used in this manner, notification systems can prevent undue stress across campus. For example, in an incident involving possible criminal activity a sample message might be:

> A possible incident involving criminal activity has occurred on campus. Campus police/security and local law enforcement have been contacted. The situation is under control. More information will be given as it becomes available.

Another example of a message to prevent excessive stress for a situation involving a reported environmental hazard might be:

> A report has been made that an odor has been smelled on campus. At this time there does not appear to be any danger. However, if you experience any changes in your current health, please go to the health center immediately to determine the cause for the change. Thank you for attending to this message.

Messages such as these will help to relieve stress. Remember that the person or persons making the decision to use the notification system have more information than the rest of the campus. They know that no dangers exist, but the rest of the campus does not. Timely communication can help to calm the campus as well as prevent rumors from developing.

However, notification systems are only as good as the people making decisions to activate them. Training is important for anyone involved in making the decision to use the notifications system. Awareness of the plan is not enough (Greenberg, 2007); practice in making decisions is important to avoid common mistakes. These mistakes include overuse and underuse (Myer, 2009). Consistent overutilization will result in people ignoring bona fide warnings about realistic threats. In addition, consideration should be given to using more than one person when deciding to use the notifications system. The saying that two heads are better than one applies to activating a campus notification system. In situations involving threats, three heads may even be better than two. If three people are used, we recommend that a senior administrator and head of campus police or security be involved. The other member might be someone from media relations, the board of trustees, another senior administrator, or another person with experience and expertise in making this type of decision.

Another method to guard against making errors in activating notification systems involves developing a set of questions that can be utilized to make the best decision possible. You may think these questions are obvious, and in fact, for the most part, they are. However, when faced with a threat, having a set of questions to answer or guidelines to follow supports high-quality decisions. Making decisions under the pressure of a possible life-and-death situation is not like making decisions about managing the curriculum or which vendor to use to supply smart boards for your campus. Figure 3.2 is a checklist of issues to consider when activating a notification system. This checklist by no means exhausts the forms of threat but can help guide the decision-making process. This checklist considers four key issues (i.e., type, location, timing, and nature) of a threat and will help you sort through the reality of the situation and avoid overreaction or underreaction.

Form of Threat	____ Use of weapon
	____ Weather-related danger
	____ Hazards present (e.g., chemical spill)
	____ Warning of violence
	____ Infectious medical condition
	____ Criminal activity
	____ Disorderly and uncontrollable gathering
	____ Other situation that poses a potential safety issue
Location of Threat	____ On campus
	____ Off campus
Timing of Threat	____ Already occurred
	____ Currently taking place
	____ Warning of future violence
Nature of Threat	____ Confirmed
	____ Unsubstantiated

Figure 3.2   Checklist for Activation of Notification System

Two-Way Street

Crisis management plans should include methods for communication to move up, not just down. People want and need the opportunity to express their feelings and perceptions about the crisis and the recovery process (Fink, 2002; Mitroff, 2004). The need to regain a sense of control is very important in the recovery process (James, 2008). Giving the people on campus and other stakeholders a voice in the recovery process helps everyone regain a sense of control.

You may be a having a knee-jerk reaction, thinking that letting everyone have a voice will only complicate things and confuse the recovery process. You know that decisions need to be made and that letting students, staff, faculty members, and other stakeholders have a voice will result in endless conversations, and nothing will get done. However, you must remember that leadership in crisis is different than when operations are normal (Mitroff, 2004). Allowing input is important to promote ownership in the recovery process. In the first few hours and possibly weeks after a crisis, input is essential to make available resources where help is needed. Later in the recovery process, input from everyone affected by the crisis helps in three ways. Input from stakeholders will make CMTs aware of problems that may have otherwise been missed or ignored. Ideas to support the recovery process may also come to light by allowing input. Trust in the decisions that are being made and the recovery process will also be created. The result is that the recovery process will receive stronger support.

Coordination

Coordination involves working for a common goal and is critical for crisis management planning. Understand that the tasks of coordination change according to the severity of the crisis (Myer & James, 2005) and the passage of time (Myer & Moore, 2006). The more severe the crisis, the more coordination is needed. Time also influences coordination because the problems associated with the crisis will evolve and change. For example, initially coordination might involve organizing volunteers to support anyone who has experienced psychological distress. After a few months, coordination might take the form of managing issues related to conflicts among departments or units that feel forgotten or ignored because of the crisis. In addition, the complexity of college campuses makes coordination critical in the recovery process. Throughout the recovery process, administrators and CMTs must use a balanced approach, meaning that they cannot neglect issues related to the overall impact of the catastrophe on the campus while dealing with the problems involving the few faculty members in the departments in question. Nor can the problems of the limited number of faculty members be overlooked because of concerns involving the campus as a whole. Intervention must be coordinated in a way that promotes recovery for everyone.

Structure

A clear structure for coordinating the campuswide response to the crisis and recovery process is needed. Leadership and procedures need to be spelled out as clearly as possible if the response to the crisis is to be efficient and effective (Dunkel & Stump, 2007). Not having an explicit line of authority leads to anarchy during the recovery process. Leadership should be able to see the big picture and connect the dots in order to organize campuswide efforts for recovery (Mitroff, 2004). However, inflexibility within the structure will also lead to chaos during the recovery process (Sherwood & McKelfresh, 2007). If flexibility is not built into the leadership structure, you may find that the response to a crisis is stalled simply because it is not available. You do not want to find that decisions cannot be made or resources directed because the person who is supposed to make that decision is not available. Leadership from a crisis will evolve as the recovery progresses. Initially, CMTs may be calling the shots, but as the campus returns to a more normal day-to-day functioning, leadership may shift to senior administration and also in part to the heads of departments and units. A key issue with this shift concerns the failure to connect problems with the crisis. Not recognizing the problems associated with the crisis can lead to blunders that can delay recovery (Ren, 2000).

Procedures should also be outlined in order to give direction to the recovery process. What issues are to be addressed first, second, third, and so on? If physical safety is a concern, procedures should be structured to address this issue first (Mitroff & Anagnos, 2001). For crises not involving physical danger, procedures will reflect the values of the university. If a university values scholarship above all else, the procedures described in the CMP will reflect this value. If the university places a high value on program development, the crisis management plan will involve procedures to get this aspect of the university operating as soon as possible. Procedures should be structured in such a way that promotes recovery. As with leadership, procedures need to be flexible and can evolve as recovery progresses. You do not want to be stuck following a procedure that is not working just because it is the procedure. The structure of CMPs should adjust, based on the specifics of the crisis.

Relationships

Prior to a crisis, working relationships, both internal and external, should be established (Dunkel & Stump, 2007). Waiting until a crisis happens to establish contact with people and groups that can support and assist in the recovery process is not a good idea. Meeting directors of agencies while trying to respond to a crisis is too late. You do not want to be looking for people to help in the midst of a crisis. Making contact is more than being aware that expertise is available internally and externally. We strongly recommend that you meet with these people before a crisis occurs on your campus. You want to know the expertise that individuals and agencies can offer. You want to know the name and phone number of the person or persons to obtain assistance. Having established relationships prior to a crisis will help you avoid inviting individuals or groups on campus who are not sympathetic with the values of your university. For example, a well-meaning group who wants to help may also have hidden agendas to proselytize their beliefs to the people they help. The beliefs of these groups may conflict with the stated mission of the university. A zealous religious group bent on converting everyone they contact to their beliefs could result in many problems on the campus of a state university. Establishing relationships with groups prior to a crisis can prevent these problems from happening.

Consultation

Consultation during each step of the model involves making use of someone who can help administrators and CMTs avoid missing important variables (Knotek, 2006). Involvement of consultants may depend on the severity of the crisis. The more severe the crisis, the more likely a consultant is needed. The consultant should be able to help administrators and CMTs maintain a situational awareness (Paton & Jackson, 2002). Situational awareness concerns helping administrators and CMTs to be attentive to the variables in the situation that are critical to the recovery process. Infusing these elements into each step of the model helps you move through the recovery process with as much ease as possible, given the crisis. Dougherty (2009, p. 55) lists several questions that can be used to guide the consultation process: "Why am I here?" "What is my expertise?" "What is likely to happen?" "What will be the result?" and probably most important, "What can go wrong?" If you don't have answers to these questions, you most likely will need to get somebody who does. You will encounter situations you have never faced before that need expertise and support. More will be said about this set of questions in Chapter 6.

Consulting as it applies to issues related to the human impact of a crisis goes beyond mental health concerns (Knotek, 2006). One purpose for a consultant is to help administrators and CMTs wade through the chaos and myriad issues that surface throughout the recovery process. These issues range from logistical concerns involving the implementation of programs and changes in routines to concerns such as conflict management, resistance of some to the change brought about by a crisis, and other problems associated with the human impact of a crisis (Myer & Moore, 2006). Consultants may also be used to provide direct services to people who have been directly affected by a crisis (Duffy & Schaeffer, 2002). For example, a consultant may be assigned to guide victims and families through the bureaucracy and paperwork that might be needed to receive benefits or, in the case of a student, withdraw from the university. It is unlikely this person would be called a consultant, even though that is what he or she is doing.

SUMMARY

Creating CMPs is a complicated process. You have to consider logistical matters as well as political issues. Both can present formidable obstacles as you build an operational CMP. This chapter outlined some of the problems you might encounter as you work through the process on your campus. While all CMPs have common and unique elements, the three Cs (i.e., communication, coordination, consultation) should be woven into the fabric throughout. These elements provide a strong base upon which to either build a CMP or evaluate existing CMPs.

REFERENCES

Augustine, N. R. (1995). Managing the crisis you tried to prevent. In *Harvard Business Review, on crisis management* (pp. 1–32). Boston: Havard Business School Press.

Braverman, M. (1999). *Violence in the workplace.* Newbury Park, CA: Sage.

Brock, S. E. (2002). Preparing for the school crisis response. In J. Sandoval (Ed.), *Handbook of crisis counseling, intervention and prevention in the schools* (2nd ed., pp. 25–38). Mahwah, NJ: Erlbaum.

Brock, S. E., Sandoval, J., & Lewis, S. (1996). *Preparing for crisis in the schools.* Brandon, VT: Clinical Psychology.

Brown, E. J., & Bobrow, A. L. (2004). School entry after a community-wide trauma: Challenges and lessons learned from September 11, 2001. *Clinical Child and Family Psychology Review, 7,* 211–221.

Caponigro, J. R. (2000). *The crisis counselor: A step-by-step guide to managing a business crisis.* Chicago: Contemporary Books.

Casey, D. (2004). During the crisis. In R. Lee & D. Casey (Eds.), *Crisis and trauma in colleges and universities* (pp. 105–112). Ellicott City, MD: Chevron Publishing.

Cerullo, V., & Cerullo, M. J. (2004, Summer). Business continuity planning: A comprehensive approach. *Information Systems Management, 21,* 71–78.

Cervone, H. F. (2006). Disaster recovery and continuity planning for digital libraries. *OCLC Systems and Service, 22,* 173–178.

Collins, J. (2001). *Good to great.* New York: HarperCollins.

Conoley, J. C., & Goldstein, A. P. (Eds.). (2004). *School violence intervention: A practical handbook* (2nd ed.). New York: Guilford Press.

Cornell, D. G., Sheras, P. L., Kaplan, S., McGonville, D., Douglass, J., Elton, A., . . . Cole, J. (2004). Guidelines for student threat assessment: Field test findings. *School Psychology Review, 33,* 527–546.

Dougherty, A. M. (2009). *Psychological consultation and collaboration in school and community settings* (5th ed.). Belmont, CA: Brooks/Cole–Cengage Learning.

Duffy, J., & Schaeffer, M. S. (2002). *Triumph over tragedy: September 11 and the rebirth of a business.* Hoboken, NJ: John Wiley & Sons.

Dunkel, W. D., & Stump, L. J. (2007). Working with emergency personnel and outside agencies. In E. L. Zdziarski, W. D. Dunkel, & J. M. Rollo (Eds.), *Campus crisis management: A comprehensive guide to planning, prevention, response, and recovery* (pp. 121–144). San Francisco: Jossey-Bass.

Eells, G. T. (2008). Identifying and responding to students with mental health needs. *Leadership Exchange, 5,* 16–21.

Family and Educational Rights and Privacy Act, 20 U.S.C. § 1232g: 34cr Part 99 (1974).

FEMA. (2003). *Building a disaster-resistant university.* Emmitsburg, MD: Emergency Management Institute.

FEMA. (2006). *Emergency planning.* Emmitsburg, MD: Emergency Management Institute.

Fink, S. (2002). *Crisis management: Planning for the inevitable.* Lincoln, NE: iUniverse.

Flynn, C., & Heitzmann, D. (2008). Tragedy at Virginia Tech: Trauma and its aftermath. *Counseling Psychologist, 36,* 479–489.

Gerald, A. (1986). Dealing with disruptive college students: Some theoretical and practical considerations. *Journal of American College Health, 34,* 221–225.

Gerler, E. R., Jr. (Ed.). (2004). *Handbook of school violence.* New York: Haworth Press.

Greenberg, S. F. (2007). Active shooters on college campuses: Conflicting advice, roles of the individual first responder, and the need to maintain perspective [Invited commentary]. *Disaster Health and Public Health Preparedness,* 57–61.

Griffin, W. (2007). Psychological first aid in the aftermath of crisis. In E. L. Zdziarski, W. D. Dunkel, & J. M. Rollo (Eds.). *Campus crisis management: A comprehensive guide to planning, prevention, response, and recovery* (pp. 145–181). San Francisco: Jossey-Bass.

Grund, N. (2008). Presidential expectations: Are you making the grade? *Leadership Exchange, 5*, 22–25.

Haddow, G. D., & Bullock, J. A. (2003). *Introduction to emergency management.* Amsterdam: Butterworth Heinemann.

HIPAA. (1996). Health Insurance Portability and Accountability Act of 1996—Senate Conference Report.

Jacobs, J. A. (2009, November). Interdisciplinary hype. *Chronicle of Higher Education.* Retrieved from http://chronicle.com/article/Interdisciplinary-Hype/49191/.

James, R. K. (2008). *Crisis intervention strategies* (6th ed.). Belmont, CA: Brooks/Cole–Cengage.

Jones, G. E. (2003). Crisis intervention, crisis counseling, confidentiality, and privilege. *International Journal of Emergency Mental Health, 5*, 137–140.

Kerr, M. M. (2009). *School crisis prevention and intervention.* Upper Saddle River, NJ: Pearson.

Knotek, S. (2006). Administrative crisis consultation after 9/11: A university's systems response. *Consulting Psychology Journal: Practice and Research, 58*, 162–173.

Langelier, K. (Speaker). (2010). *Emergency planning on an urban campus* [Cassette recording 2010-1- Crisis Intervention Series]. Memphis, TN: Department of Counseling, Educational Psychology and Research, University of Memphis.

Lawson, C. J. (2007). Crisis communication. In E. L. Zdziarski, W. D. Dunkel, & J. M. Rollo (Eds.). *Campus crisis management: A comprehensive guide to planning, prevention, response, and recovery* (pp. 97–119). San Francisco: Jossey-Bass.

Mitroff, I. I. (2004). *Crisis leadership: Planning for the unthinkable.* Hoboken, NJ: John Wiley & Sons.

Mitroff, I. I, & Anagnos, G. (2001). *Managing crises before they happen.* New York: American Management Association.

Mitroff, I. I., Diamond, M. A., & Alpasian, C. M. (2006). How prepared are America's colleges and universities for major crises? Assessing the state of crisis management. *Society for College and University Planning.* Retrieved from http://www.scup.org/page/knowledge/crisis-planning/diamond.

Muecke, D. W. (1994). Justifying recovery testing. In P. J. Rothstein (Ed.), *Disaster recovery testing* (pp. 1–8). Ossining, NY: Rothstein Associates.

Myer, R. A. (2009, December). *Three C's of violence prevention on college campuses.* Presented at the First Annual National Behavioral Intervention Team Association. San Antonio, TX.

Myer, R. A., & James, R. K. (2005). *CD ROM and workbook for crisis intervention.* Pacific Grove, CA: Brooks/Cole.

Myer, R. A., & Moore, H. (2006). Crisis in context: An ecological model. *Journal of Counseling and Development, 84*, 139–147.

Myers, K. N. (1999). *Management guide to contingency planning for disasters.* New York: John Wiley & Sons.

Nicoletti, J., Spencer-Thomas, S., & Bollinger, C. (2001). *Violence goes to college: The authoritative guide to prevention and intervention.* Springfield, IL: Charles C Thomas.

Paterson, P., & Colbs, S. (2008). *In search of safer communities: Emerging practices for students affairs in addressing campus violence.* Unpublished manuscript.

Paton, D., & Jackson, D. (2002). Developing disaster management capability: An assessment centre approach. *Disaster Prevention and Management, 11*, 115–122.

Petersen, S. (1999, April). *School crisis planning.* Workshop at the American Counseling Association World Conference, San Diego, CA.

Poland, S. (2004). School crisis teams. In J. Conoley & A. P. Goldstein (Eds.), *School violence intervention: A practical handbook* (2nd ed., pp. 131–163). New York: Guilford Press.

Poland, S., & McCormick, J. S. (1999). *Coping with crisis: Lessons learned.* Longmont, CO: Sopris West.

Pollard, D., & Hotho, S. (2006). Crises, scenarios and the strategic management process. *Management Decision, 44*, 721–736.

Ren, C. H. (2000). Understanding and managing the dynamics of linked crisis events. *Disaster Prevention and Management, 9,* 12–17.

Rollo, J. M., & Zdziarski, E. L. (2007). Developing a crisis management plan. In E. L. Zdziarski, W. D. Dunkel, & J. M. Rollo (Eds.). *Campus crisis management: A comprehensive guide to planning, prevention, response, and recovery* (pp. 73–96). San Francisco: Jossey-Bass.

Rubin, R. (1999, June). *Crisis intervention.* Paper presented at the American School Counselor Association Convention, Phoenix, AZ.

Savage, M. (2002). Business continuity planning. *Work Study, 51,* 254–261.

Shaluf, I. M., Ahmadun, F., & Said, A. M. (2003). A review of disaster and crisis. *Disaster Prevention and Management, 12,* 24–32.

Sharma, R. (2008). New platforms broaden communication options. *Leadership Exchange, 5,* 36–39.

Sherwood, G. P., & McKelfresh, D. (2007). Crisis management teams. In E. L. Zdziarski, W. D. Dunkel, & J. M. Rollo (Eds.). *Campus crisis management: A comprehensive guide to planning, prevention, response, and recovery* (pp. 55–71). San Francisco: Jossey-Bass.

Siegal, D. (1994). *Campuses response to violent tragedy.* Phoenix, AZ: Oryx Press.

Slater, S. L. (Speaker). (2010). *Emergency planning on an urban campus* [Cassette Recording 2010-1- Crisis Intervention Series]. Memphis, TN: Department of Counseling, Educational Psychology and Research, University of Memphis.

Tierney, W. G. (1988). Organization culture in higher education. *Journal of Higher Education, 59,* 1–21.

Toigo, J. W. (2000). *Disaster recovery planning: Strategies for protecting critical information assets* (2nd ed.). Upper Saddle River, NJ: Prentice Hall.

Williams, M. B. (2004). How schools respond to traumatic events: Debriefing interventions and beyond. In N. B. Webb (Ed.), *Mass trauma and violence: Helping families and children cope. Social work practice with children and families* (pp. 120–141). New York: Guilford Press.

Williams, M. B. (2006). How schools respond to traumatic events: Debriefing interventions and beyond. *Journal of Aggression, Maltreatment & Trauma 12*(1), 57–81.

Zdziarski, E. L., Rollo, J. M., & Dunkel, W. D. (2007). The crisis matrix. In E. L. Zdziarski, W. D. Dunkel, & J. M. Rollo (Eds.). *Campus crisis management: A comprehensive guide to planning, prevention, response, and recovery* (pp. 35–54). San Francisco: Jossey-Bass.

4

Duller Than Dirt . . . More Valuable Than Gold: Policies and Procedures

You will face no harder times than those when crises arise and every decision is placed on display and under a microscope. Why? Because crisis situations provide ample opportunity for everyone to question ethical, legal, and moral dilemmas and the liability inherent to almost any decision made. That makes conversation about policy a bit tricky, since you can't have policy to back up every move, nor can you anticipate all the actions that will need to be taken during any given crisis. This circumstance is what often creates barriers to taking action efficiently and effectively. Most people in administration have had the experience of consulting with legal counsel regarding a problematic situation and being told in various ways that it is better to be consistently wrong than inconsistently right, according to Bickel and Lake (1999).

Policies are needed to provide guidance during chaotic times and to assist in protecting campuses, given the increase in litigation (Cantu-Weber, 1999). However, remember that policies are not intended to be prescriptive. Specific actions dictated by policy set you up to break the rules. Crises create the need to handle situations sometimes in creative ways that fall outside the usual manner of conducting business. Policy should not dictate the actions needed but can provide guidance for the decisions about what actions are needed. Policies are not a crisis management plan. Your crisis management plan is the procedure; policy is the foundation for the plan.

If policies are not in place, many unanswered questions regarding basic philosophy and guidance will become obstacles to the planning process. For instance, at one of the author's universities, there were no policies regarding crisis management when the first crisis planning team began its work. Questions such as "Who would be the primary reporting office?" "Who would house the official student tracking files?" and "Would those files be considered official student documents?" sidetracked and impeded the process of developing a comprehensive crisis management plan. Without policy, the specifics of the plan were almost impossible to write.

Policies are broad statements that reflect the values of your institution. The types of values that often underlie both policy and ethics are very basic in nature and rather universal. The principles used by professional organizations such as the American Psychological Association (2002) and American Counseling Association (2005) to develop codes of ethics are an example of using values. These values include the ideas (a) beneficence (i.e., doing good), (b) nonmaleficence (i.e., doing no harm), (c) fidelity, (d) integrity, (e) justice, and (f) respect of people's rights (Fisher, 2009). These principles or similar ones can serve as a sound foundation for consideration for drafting policy. Principles used by professional organizations are a strong defense if your plans or actions are ever questioned. Someone with a working knowledge of professional ethics as a team member or as an ad hoc member when drifting, writing, and reviewing policy is invaluable.

Ideally, principles based on accepted professional practice will guide most policy writing to support actions on our campuses. Although these principles seem very reasonable to most, at times they appear aspirational in nature for most leaders. However, whatever principles you base policy on do not stand alone. In reality, the overlap often creates conflict for leaders in making difficult decisions. As you are probably all too well aware, being caught between the good of the individual or the few and the good of the many in leadership decisions on higher education campuses happens regularly. Most people believe a person cannot answer to two masters. Yet people are asked on more days than not to respond to issues that require us to (a) balance the good of the system versus the good of the individual, (b) be responsive to numerous constituents of authority and power, (c) work competently, (d) honor our word, (e) maintain integrity, and (f) conduct business in a fair manner. All these responsibilities must be accomplished while showing respect for numerous campus constituents that may be seeking very different responses. A bit overwhelming at best, is it not? And yet, it is the task you have agreed to take on and often the task that leads us to remind ourselves that this is why we are paid the big bucks—to make the hard decisions and stand responsible for them. Having clear understandings of the leadership philosophy, the basic values, and the priority of expectation will assist you in writing policy that will support you in difficult times.

POLICY DEVELOPMENT

Because policy is as individual as each campus, we know of no specific examples of policy that will automatically apply. If you Google "crisis policy and procedure" or "university crisis policy," you will see a plethora of universities that have posted crisis policy and procedures. Deciphering all the many topics that are presented is a daunting process. However, most campus handbooks and policy manuals have sections in common regarding areas such as threats, weapons, violence, civility, harassment, sexual harassment, and discrimination. In addition, there are some general areas to consider for policy development. The list is illustrative, and you will find additional areas on your campus that need policy. These areas include, but are certainly not limited to, use of outside resources, communication, decision making, use of resources, personnel issues, role of technology, tolerance of aggressive behavior, academic/resumption of classes, provision of support (how long, how much), memorial services, leadership, and extra-curricular activities.

Process for Policy Development

If you have ever sat on a committee to write or update any of these policies, you understand the detail that is required to match the expectations of the campus, the requirements of the law, and the needs of the consumer. With respect to crisis intervention and prevention, policies should relate to primary, secondary, and tertiary prevention (Zero Tolerance Task Force, 2008). According to this task force, primary prevention policies target all students regardless of the potential to engage in violent behaviors. This part of the policy might outline the need for general education programs on campus that might help prepare a campus for a crisis. The goal of secondary prevention is to provide support to students, staff, or faculty members who are at risk. Policy at this level could focus on making available programs such as alcohol and drug prevention programs, date violence prevention, and for employees, employee assistance for anyone having difficulties. Policy related to tertiary prevention focuses on providing support for people who have engaged in disruptive or aggressive behaviors. This comprehensive approach to policy development provides a strong foundation for creating a crisis management plan.

The Appendix is an example of a policy that might be found in a manual. This policy addresses the issue of people on campus engaging in threatening behaviors. You will notice the policy describes the types of behaviors that could be considered threatening but leaves open the opportunity for including other behaviors not listed. The insertion of this phrase allows administration flexibility should situations arise that were not specifically listed in the policy (Zero Tolerance Task Force, 2008). In addition, the sample policy also describes a process by which threats can be reported to appropriate authorities on campus. This part of the policy suggests that students, staff, and faculty members take some responsibility in reporting threatening behaviors not just directed at themselves, but also at others. Including this language communicates that responsibility is shared and that anyone can be held accountable for identifying threats on campus.

Figure 4.1 illustrates the links between the mission, vision, and values (both spoken and unspoken) of your university and the process of planning, developing policy, and determining procedures. These links are important elements as you approach policy writing to support crisis management planning. Obviously, the process depicted is not linear in nature but builds upon itself, with each of the components interacting with the others. For example, if your university has a mission statement that includes components of "quality education in a safe learning environment" and "an environment responsive to student needs" and a vision of a systemic approach to providing a progressive, safe, responsive environment for your students, it would be obvious that three of your stated values are quality education, safety, and responsiveness. Therefore, crisis planning would include discussions and sections identifying how your university will respond to crisis in a way that provides as much continuity as possible in the delivery of educational programs; mitigation and risk assessment, and crisis intervention components related to safety; and possibly assessment, identification, and referral

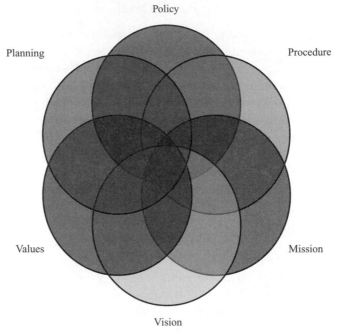

Figure 4.1   Overlap

components for students in need of care (those who may threaten as well as those who may have been threatened or violated). Examples of just a few of the many policies that may be drafted for consideration could include policies for alternative modes of delivering curriculum during recovery from a critical incident; assessment of students at risk; communication and collaboration with external agencies regarding identified students at risk; referral; detention and/or expulsion; and communication regarding students at risk across campus. Once the policies are drafted, you will then begin to spell out the detailed plan of action in procedures. Your procedures will give specifics of the action steps needed and the individuals and/or teams responsible to carry out the goals of the plan.

You might want to consider using your crisis management team for this exercise and to include legal counsel as appropriate to bounce ideas off and also to review final documents. Convene your group and consider a worst-case scenario of crisis on your campus. Brainstorm the actions that would need to be taken to meet the immediate and long-term needs of the individuals affected and the campus as a whole. Consider what the roadblocks might be to making decisions and taking decisive action as needed. Don't limit yourself to the immediacy of the emergency situation (Mitroff, Diamond, & Alpasian, 2006). Consider issues that may surface 1, 2, 4, or 6 months later, up to potentially a year or even longer after the crisis. By identifying these areas, you are considering the ways in which daily operations would have to change in order to move through and recover from the crisis. These are areas for consideration in crisis policy writing. For example, you may want a policy stating who determines an official crisis state on campus; you may need to consider how you would purchase emergency materials outside the typical business procedures. With respect to the human impact of a crisis, issues might include evaluation and retention procedures, along with allowances for time off because of family or personal concerns. Remember, the policy is the broad statement that will provide the overall guidance for the decision-making process. The procedures spell out the details. For instance, your policy regarding purchasing during a crisis may simply state that purchasing procedures may be set aside for official emergency business, once a crisis has been declared. Your procedures would then spell out details, such as who would have the ability to approve purchases, possible limits of purchases, or steps for reimbursement. Consider policies to cover each phase of crisis management: precrisis, crisis, and recovery. These policies should be accessible in your student, staff, and faculty handbooks and in policy and procedure manuals.

Politics in Policy

The caveat to writing policy, as many have learned the hard way, is to consider the politics of policy. The politics of policy means what? Well, for every policy, there are legal, ethical, and moral implications. The following examples illustrate the interaction of policies and politics.

Plagiarism

Although not related to crisis intervention and prevention, plagiarism is a good example of the interface between policies and politics. Standard procedure these days is to have student integrity statements and policies regarding plagiarism. Everyone on campus basically agrees that plagiarism is dishonest and should not be tolerated. This seems very simple and straightforward, right? Wrong. A zero tolerance policy of plagiarism can become very sticky among constituents at any institution. Legally, the policy we are to uphold with zero tolerance is to take action. This action can range from documentation, to investigation, to failure of a paper or course, to removal from a program. However, there may be much conversation about how to handle any given incident of plagiarism, depending on the student involved, the situation, the status of the student within the degree program, the status of the student in the community (we hate to admit this, but it has been known to happen), and the varying opinions of the different factions of campus that may be involved: faculty, administration, judicial affairs, athletics. The campus must think through what zero tolerance means for them and how it is to be enforced. If there can be this much discussion over the right thing to do for such an obvious, simple philosophy of no cheating, then just imagine the politics that can be involved when making decisions and taking actions in the midst of a crisis while often in the public eye.

Clery Act

Another example of the politics in policy might be the policy that is written to carry out various legal mandates, for instance, the policy that dictates the implementation of the Clery Act. This law was enacted to address campus security issues in the hopes of keeping campuses safe. It requires campuses to report crime statistics in annual security reports, provide timely warnings about safety, keep public crime logs, and submit annual crime statistics. This act, in light of the recent scrutiny of college campuses following critical incidents, brings up the controversy of cover-up versus transparency of campus violence. The implications of not reporting range from financial loss to possible loss of life. However, the implications of having a truly transparent campus regarding campus security incidents raises concerns regarding public relations, enrollment, and economics, just to name a few (Goldman, 2007). The law is clear, the policies written to ensure compliance seem simple enough, but the depth of the implementation of the policy is based on the values of the university and the priorities set forth by the leadership regarding transparency of critical issues identified on campus.

DRAFTING POLICY

You will find that there are few rights and wrongs to drafting policy for crisis. Buying something off the rack, so to speak, does not work when developing policy. We know of no one-size-fits-all policy because your school should set policies that fit your institution's primary mission, vision, and values. However, like writing mission statements, some common threads need to be addressed. We would like to suggest discussion questions, not in any given sequential order, to facilitate writing crisis policy. Engaging in discussion using the following prompts will help you sort through concerns related to policy development.

Tips to Facilitate the Process of Policy Writing

- Describe the leadership style of your administration (not public perception, but internal knowledge of how business is conducted regularly). A clear understanding of leadership style will permit you to identify both strengths and possible obstacles to responding to and recovering from a crisis.
- Describe the process you would like to see regarding crisis management on your campus. Brainstorm the various components that would make up your organizational crisis plan. A full and complete plan would include a disaster recovery plan, a crisis response plan (prevention, intervention, recovery), and a risk management plan. Bring your crisis management team (CMT) together to discuss the possible issues that each of these areas would address, what type of resources might be needed, and who and what resources are currently available on your

campus to meet these needs. Use this information to assist in developing your planning teams in each of these areas.

- Identify primary values, both written and unwritten, that drive the actions of your institution. This awareness can serve as a reality check when drafting policy and specifically procedure for managing crisis situations. For example, what is your campus value regarding transparency of critical incidents on campus? This value will affect action steps related to communication with both internal and external constituents. Will the campus be notified of incidents? How will media be handled?

- Identify and list the primary areas, departments, and/or individuals to be involved in the implementation of the crisis plan. For instance, regardless of which location or department is affected directly, any crisis on campus is likely to affect and utilize the offices of student services, finance, university housing, university police, academic affairs, facilities, and campus media.

- Identify which personnel may have decision-making authority during a crisis. List and specify authority in a flowchart if possible. While this list would not work for everyone, it seems that the final authority lies with the president; however, your vice presidents and CMT leader, along with key personnel such as housing director, auxiliary services director, facilities director, and director of the counseling center, come to mind as some of those who need to have authority to take care of business with immediacy. These individuals need to be aware ahead of time about how purchasing can take place during a crisis situation as compared with handling business based on usual daily purchasing policy and procedure.

- Review FERPA and HIPAA rules as well as rules of privacy, privilege, and confidentiality so that everyone is working from the same page regarding sharing of information. A primary issue that needs to be addressed is what type of documentation you may use for tracking incidents on campus, where these documents will be located, who will have access, and whether they will be considered part of an official student record. Your legal counsel will be able to assist you in determining these issues for your campus based on your documentation system already in place.

- Consider guidelines set by the Office of Safety and Health Administration (OSHA) and the implications for responding not only to a crisis but also to the recovery process. The guidelines set by this agency have a particularly significant influence on the recovery process. Human resources and legal counsel should be prepared to help with policy development for crisis management around these guidelines.

- Carefully consider the role of your counseling center. Will they serve as a primary assessment partner or as a primary referral partner? (The counseling center is singled out due to their prior knowledge of many risk factors, combined with rules of confidentiality that do not allow them to share this knowledge before the intensity meets requirements of duty to warn). Virginia Tech has recently changed policy to allow information to be shared about individuals who are deemed a threat to the campus environment. This is a controversial decision that will affect many campuses. Policy and procedure changes are evident in the language of the following excerpts from the responses provided by Virginia Tech Cook Counseling Center to the recommendations in the Investigations Records Report #179-09 (2009) put forth by the Office of the Inspector General for Behavioral Health & Developmental Services following the incidents at Virginia Tech:

○ "The CARE Team meets weekly and maintains records of each of its meetings and the students discussed. The caseload of the CARE Team typically includes 15–20 students weekly including both new cases to be staffed and follow-up with ongoing cases. Students may be referred to CARE Team from a member of the CARE Team or from faculty, staff, or students.

○ "The role of the Cook Counseling Center participants on the CARE Team is primarily consultative given that confidentiality laws preclude sharing of information without the client's permission except in very specific instances including health and safety emergencies. While the Cook Counseling Center may not always share information regarding the students, the majority of cases considered by the CARE Team either result in a referral to the Center or are students currently being treated at the Center." (p. 38)

○ "Procedure on Parental Notification. Following the above procedures, counselors are released from confidentiality to seek support and protection of a student potentially dangerous to self or others. Recent revisions to Virginia code (23-9.2:3.C) now make parental notification mandatory except in limited circumstances. The new code requires notification of the parent(s) of a dependent student (as defined by tax status) when the student is treated by the counseling center or health center and there exists a substantial likelihood that the student may cause harm to self or others by reason of psychological disturbance. The law makes clear provision for an exemption to parental notification if such notification would be likely to cause harm to students—if this exception is exercised, it must be in writing." (p. 36)

○ Regarding students who violate university standards of behavior, whose behavior may indicate a significant psychological disturbance, and who may be considered for "interim suspension" and referred to the Cook Counseling Center for mandatory assessment—"It is incumbent on the counselor for the Cook Counseling Center to notify the student that s/he is acting on behalf of the university, not on behalf of the student, and that the results of the evaluation will be shared with university officials—this clarifies that the counselor is not abrogating the therapist-client relationship and attendant confidentiality restrictions. The decision to issue an interim suspension is not the responsibility of the counselor but of the referring office." (p. 30)

- As stated, these types of changes to policy are very controversial since they definitely reflect a new model regarding client-therapist confidentiality. A recent personal communication (December 30, 2009) with Brett A Sokolow, JD, counselor/advisor for the National Center for Higher Education Risk Management, suggested that this new policy is "ill-considered," due to its potential to undermine the clinical relationship, create incentive for clients to be less than honest, and lessen the likelihood of a long-term relationship with the counselor, which is usually a goal of mandated assessment. The buck is being pushed by past critical incidents to allow more open communication in circumstances of safety. You and your team will have to determine the role and responsibility of your counselors.

- Discuss possible roles and responsibilities of each major constituent of the organization as they relate to crisis management, and identify concerns that might be implicit to each area. Determine who will have primary responsibility, leadership, and authority. This process is completed to determine lines of authority and communication throughout campus, should a crisis occur. This line of authority will be determined by the structure of your campus. There is no way to provide you with a diagram that will fit all campuses. Each division of the campus should bring together leaders of each unit to brainstorm issues to be addressed, should a crisis occur on campus. Use of tabletop scenarios may be helpful in these meetings to get the group thinking about what primary needs might be, given various situations, and what actions would be needed to respond. This exercise will identify questions about who needs approval to take needed action and who has authority to take the needed actions. You will find examples of identified hierarchy of authority in areas such as health services and also housing and university police. You probably have policy and/or procedure in place that can assist the rest of your campus in determining lines of appropriate authority during a crisis. For instance, when health services writes procedures for infectious disease control on campus, it is understood that once the Centers for Disease Control (CDC) become involved, the campus stands down to the line of authority dictated by the CDC regarding infectious disease control procedures. Another example may be your housing staff procedures. It is common for residence assistants to be frontline authority until a crisis occurs, and then they are to report to a director. If campus police are involved, they are to stand down to the authority of campus security procedures; if medical personnel are called to the scene, they all stand down to the authority of the medical personnel as related directly to medical emergency procedures. Being clear about the lines of authority during a crisis is a huge relief and saves time and lives in critical incidents.

- Discuss current communication barriers and possibilities to enhance communication across boundaries. We have identified many barriers to communication on campus that apply to crisis management as well as many other general initiatives on campus. What is important for successful crisis management is to clearly and realistically acknowledge the barriers and to determine the best means of creating collaborative work arrangements between divisions and departments during a time of crisis response and recovery. For instance, if your school has a bit of an issue with communication between student affairs and academic affairs (hard to imagine but possible), the leadership of these two areas need to come together to discuss the specific hurdles that can be foreseen regarding crisis management plans and procedures. Leadership needs to model and maintain an open dialogue throughout the planning process to clearly identify areas of frustration so plans and procedures can be agreed on that specify who, what, when, and how they might work together for the good of the common cause. An example that comes readily to mind is the possibility of the counseling staff providing training and information to faculty and staff regarding signs and symptoms of students in distress following a crisis, or they might train a few key faculty members to serve as trainers for the rest of the faculty. Another example would be to have faculty who have been identified as specialists in crisis intervention on your campus develop and share a training session with counseling staff who may not be trained specifically in crisis management. These two examples seem very obvious and very simple, and yet there are many campuses that do not communicate and allow small barriers to impede their ability to fully respond to critical incidents.

- Brainstorm and list local resources for referral purposes. By thinking through and identifying key partners in your crisis response and recovery, you can consider what types of arrangements will be needed and what types of policy will guide those partnerships. This work must be conducted in advance of critical incidents on campus in order to respond efficiently and effectively when needed. For example, you very well may not have 2 to 3 days following a critical incident to determine how the arrangement will work with a local mental health agency regarding what services they can and are willing to provide. Questions such as reimbursement and the manner of payment for services to individual mental health staff will undoubtedly surface. Ethical issues regarding confidentiality will also arise, and procedures must be ironed out for communication between the campus and the agency.

- Identify and list the steps that need to occur to operationalize your crisis plan. Obviously, the first and foremost priority is the safety and well-being of those directly impacted by the incident. Beyond this initial need, where will you focus? Where might limited resources be allocated? Examples of the areas likely to be in the running are enrollment management, media, auxiliary services, counseling center, health services, and university police. A scenario that comes to mind is the response needed following multiple rapes on a campus. The students directly involved will be the priority. However, the university then has to address the fallout while maintaining the privacy of these individuals. There will be a ripple effect from the incident that includes safety issues, calls from parents, students uncomfortable in their surroundings, and rumors. This fallout requires responses and allocations of resources from housing staff availability, increased security measures, increased hours and availability of counseling staff, enrollment and retention concerns, and public relations issues.

- Identify and list the policy changes that will be needed on your campus to support your crisis plan. You may wish to carefully review your harassment and discrimination policies, purchasing policy, and disciplinary and appeals policy, just to name a few. Once these questions have been discussed, it is time to review your current policies and procedures manuals to determine where the gaps might be. You may have some specific policies regarding faculty, staff, and student behavior under codes of conduct, but you will also want a blanket policy to cover your overall efforts to provide a safe environment for your campus. Your CMT may want to review your current policies and procedures manual for areas that would not serve you well during a crisis. This would be a great exercise for a graduate class in campus leadership, student personnel services, or counseling services. The CMT may wish to partner in this activity to identify questionable policies and/or procedures related to crisis management.
- Consider the role of faith-based institutions and initiatives for your campus. This issue is especially important for crises involving loss of life. Concerns would include supporting memorial services on campus. Policies can address this issue.

Crisis policies are now as important to campus risk management processes as those of harassment, discrimination, and academic integrity because of the increased attention and inherent liability that surrounds campus safety. The crisis policies need to be written with the same thoughtful detail with regard to definition and process. Language should be specific enough to maintain a safe environment and promote full recovery from a crisis. At the same time, policies must provide the flexibility the administration needs to implement and reinforce the crisis management plan. In addition to the blanket policy on threats and violence, your campus will want to determine if there is need for additional standards or updates in the codes of conduct or policies and procedures manuals regarding issues such as, but not limited to, sexual harassment and assault, hazing, hate crimes, discrimination, threats to others, and communication regarding violent threats.

REVIEW OF POLICY DRAFTS

Once drafted, the crisis policies for your campus should be reviewed prior to publishing them and educating your campus community about them. By asking some basic questions regarding your draft, you can clarify and make certain the policy is workable. The following 10-step model is provided to assist you in your review and evaluation of drafts.

10-Step Model to Evaluate New Policies

1. Does the policy reflect the voices of those most closely associated with the subject area? (Include those who assess and those who must implement and enforce.)
2. Does the policy cover the primary issues at hand?
3. Does the policy take into account other legal and ethical mandates (FERPA, HIPAA, OSHA)?
4. Can the policy be reasonably administered?
5. Can the policy be reasonably enforced?
6. Is the policy limited to a single policy topic, or have you tried to cover multiple issues in one policy?
7. Can any of the requirements be interpreted as discriminatory in nature?
8. Is the policy consistent with other campus policies and codes of conduct?
9. Is the policy appropriately cross-referenced to other related policies?
10. Is the policy a good fit for your university mission, vision, values, and goals?

Once the individual or committee has completed the draft, review, and evaluation, and you think you have a final product, allow those constituents who will be directly affected by the policy to provide feedback for consideration. You may wish to have representation of the areas affected by the policy join you for focus groups to gain feedback about the doability of the drafted policy. It is absolutely essential that the equal employment opportunity (EEO) officer for the university and legal counsel provide review and approval prior to formal submission. It may also be necessary to gain board review and approval based upon your university's procedure. This consultation with others will allow for gaps to be addressed and a stronger policy to guide your actions. You would not be the first ever to draft what you consider to be a sound policy, only to hear your legal counsel or board member gasp and say, "You can't do that!" Either you have inadvertently and with the best intentions blatantly contradicted a board policy or procedure, or you have suggested something that would make you more liable than you realized.

When your policies are in place and ready to publish, you may wish to think about distribution beyond the obligatory printing in the appropriate manuals and handbooks. You may want to consider a distribution and education rollout for the material due to the importance of the content in setting the tone for your campus. This process could include distribution and education through in-services, workshops, specifically targeted class lectures, freshman orientation, faculty orientation, community forums, local media, residence hall meetings, parent meetings, newsletters, electronic distribution (e-mails, tweets), or podcasts. Remember that students listen to students, so you may want to consider using campus movers and shakers, also known as peer influencers, to distribute new policies and procedures related to crisis management. You might use your student government association leaders, Greek advisory council, student athletic board, and student organizations council. For faculty and staff, you want to distribute official copies, but you may want to combine personal communication with an update regarding crisis management on campus by visiting departments and sharing this information during regular faculty and staff meetings. Simply providing hard copies will probably waste paper, and the material will end up in the circular file and do your campus little good during a critical incident. Most faculty and staff are ready and willing to discuss safety on campus and want to know expected procedures.

As you consider the policies needed to support actions during critical incidents, you also want to be aware of common legal considerations related to crisis policy and procedures. This awareness will assist you in lessening the liability for your actions during a crisis. The following discusses some of the predictable legal issues that can turn into landmines for your university, if not addressed.

Legal and Ethical Landmines

In earlier times, college campuses seemed to be held separate and rather protected from litigious actions. Today, campuses are being held responsible for providing safe environments for the campus community. The following serves as a brief overview of legal concerns related to crisis management. These represent common emerging themes.

Political Hires

Be aware of the credentials and experience of those being asked to make key decisions during a crisis. For some of these areas, university accreditation requires that you address this concern, but not across the board. This issue goes back to having the right person driving the bus and the right people riding the bus. We all know that credentials alone do not make a professional or guarantee competence, and we each could give great examples of those without credentials but with characteristics to perform jobs exceptionally well. However, when it comes to authority and responsibility for leading in crisis, you want to have both. This is no place for political hires who do not meet minimum standards or for relegating titles and responsibilities to those further down the line so that the university can document that bases are covered. This is an area that can easily come back to bite you, if all goes south in a crisis situation. Individuals are harmed, and those in charge never stood a chance of handling the situation effectively because of inadequate training or lack of expertise.

Personnel Issues

You do not want to find yourself having to justify your hiring and retention practices based on allegations of negligent hiring or negligent retention. These terms are most often used when describing hiring practices that do not screen for prior illegal or violent behaviors and/or retention of employees following reasonable evidence of risk of violence in the workplace. In the psychological world, it has long been believed that the best predictor of future behavior is past behavior (Myers, 1989). This philosophy is a good rule of thumb for hiring and retention practices as well. So, who are you hiring and what are the criteria? What are your policies regarding personnel screening, drug testing, and background checks? What are your policies regarding sanctions following inappropriate or threatening behavior on campus for your faculty, staff, and students?

Off-Campus Sites

The term *campus* takes on a whole extended meaning these days in terms of accountability and liability for student and some employee (only as it relates to official professional roles and responsibilities) behavior. Campus is no longer a single logistical location and seems to include a much broader set of boundaries. A few instances to illustrate this broad definition of campus liability are students at local establishments (bars seem to come to mind), visitors to campus facilities, Greek housing on and off campus, international programs, branch campuses and communities, off-campus parties at private homes, and practicum and internship sites. Many schools have decided to expand the student code of conduct to apply to any site where a student is participating as part of an organized university group or activity. Others have simply expanded the code of conduct to apply to off-campus sites. This then allows the university to address issues through judicial affairs. These are very difficult decisions for a university because of possible litigation from remaining traditional in the campus definition or from expanding the definition.

Criminal Charges

Having students, staff, faculty, or an administrator brought up on criminal charges is always stressful. The university has to take a stance (remember that inaction sends a powerful message to the general public) while awaiting investigation or trial of a serious crime. The dilemma for the university often involves deciding whether to temporarily suspend an individual while waiting for the completed investigation or decision. Regardless of what steps are taken, liability is inherent. Each university has to decide on which side to err. You may be asking yourself what criminal charges have to do with crisis, but just imagine the impact when a faculty member is arrested and brought up on criminal charges for raping a student. This situation is a crisis for the faculty member, the student, and the colleagues and students of the arrested faculty member. The academic vice president has to field calls from parents and also deal with media. Many critical decisions must be made about handling this very fragile and potentially volatile situation. No action, or the faculty member being found guilty, will certainly have repercussions for the campus. If there is early dismissal (often interpreted as guilt) and the faculty member found innocent, you have an entirely different type of crisis on your hands to support faculty and staff.

Violence

Controversy over sharing information regarding a student's history of violence in the student affairs and enrollment management arena is always a challenge. Universities have concerns about unknowingly taking on the baggage of liability from another university by accepting a student who has been expelled for violent acts. Many heated discussions occur about protecting a student's privacy, allowing the opportunity for second (or third, or fourth) chances for an education, reporting laws, and means by which to share information regarding a violent student. Some campuses feel that once they have adequately handled a situation with a violent student on their campus, they have no further responsibilities, and others feel a responsibility to warn but there may be no imminent danger, so there is concern about reporting procedures. The American Association of Collegiate Registrars and Admission Officers (AACRAO, 2002) has debated the issue of transcript notations for disciplinary actions for some time now and recently reported a survey of current practices. Some schools have lobbied for a transcript notation to flag potential issues to possible future institutions. Others are adamant that from a developmental perspective, students deserve the right to screw up within reason, survive the consequences of their behavior, and move on in life without being labeled and having the incident follow. Still others would say that it depends on the intensity of the violent action the student participated in, and to navigate this stance, definitions would become very cumbersome to determine where the line is drawn in terms of both quantity and intensity of student actions. As you can see, this issue is convoluted. Yet campuses continue to struggle, since a certain amount of liability and a lot of media attention follow incidents of campus violence where a past record of violence, often at numerous institutions, is known.

Communication Provision

A provision for communication among departments and units (e.g., psychological, medical, police) is a necessity for protecting your campus. Kitzrow (2003) discussed the special circumstances of working with students who have participated in self-injurious behaviors and those who have returned to campus following an unanticipated early release from a hospital as examples of times when sharing pertinent information can be helpful. Without this information, universities become one more in the lineup of organizations plastered across the news with facts gathered after an incident showing multiple red flags waving wildly and no one catching the danger signal.

The most obvious tool is an informed consent process whereby the student gives permission for you to share information among relevant campus agencies. However, not all students want their identity or the details of their situation shared, which can tie the hands of the professionals who need to communicate to care for students and who also need to look for signs and symptoms of crises on campus. Zdziarski, Dunkel, and Rollo (2007) noted one campus's alternative of having each student, or parents of those who are minors, authorize student health services to provide services and communicate within and between its own agency and the counseling center on campus. When an identified trend of behavior is affecting the learning environment negatively and multiple campus agencies are involved, communication should occur among departments to identify and clarify concerns, identify resources, and coordinate an action plan. In Chapter 9, we introduce the Triage Assessment Scale for Students in Learning Environments (TASSLE) that can be used as a common method to share these concerns. This instrument helps departments use a common language based on a reliable and valid instrument to communicate across campus.

Scope of Practice

Professional standards and the ethics codes of many of those on your campus who are asked to participate require that the helping professional practice "within their professional scope of practice." The interpretation of scope of practice implies they are to provide services only within the boundaries of those areas in which they have specifically been trained and/or supervised. The skill set of crisis intervention is not one that comes with the territory for most counseling, psychology, or social work degrees at this time. This statement means that additional training is required to acquire crisis intervention skills. Providing professional development specific to crisis intervention and management is important for anyone on your campus who has been identified to respond to a crisis situation. This training will ensure that professionals on campus stay abreast of standards of best practice and also current research in the field. This training can be a great resource in updating your crisis plan, training your staff, and supervising the many paraprofessionals and volunteers who want to help during crises.

Duty to Protect and/or Warn

Numerous lawsuits have been filed against universities for failure to provide adequate security or prevent foreseeable harm. The most noteworthy is the previously described *Tarasoff v. Regents of the University of California* of 1976 (Welfel, 2006). Wheeler and Bertram (2008) discuss the controversy regarding liability in the absence of a readily identifiable victim. They report that courts have varied findings of liability based on a range of situations from failing to warn or protect only when there is a resulting personal injury to failing to protect a foreseeable victim within the "zone of danger," meaning probably at risk of harm based on a patient's violent behavior.

Mandatory Reporting

Provisions of law regarding issues such as reporting of child sexual abuse, child neglect, confidentiality, sexual assault, sexual harassment, right of privileged communication, duty to warn, and FERPA regulations should be reviewed regularly through consultation with university attorneys. If critical incident simulation trainings are taking place on campus, it is important to keep these ideas in mind for analysis as part of follow-up discussion. Situational training sessions, followed by solid and honest analyses, will assist you in developing a list of questions for your attorneys so that you can gain the clarification needed to feel confident in the policies and procedures you are relying on in crises.

Suicide

Wheeler and Bertram (2008) state that suicide assessment and appropriate intervention constitutes a "daunting clinical challenge" and a "significant risk of liability" to institutions of higher education. This statement is based on data reported by the American College Health Association (2006) and the Jed Foundation (2006). Examples of the astounding data regarding college-age students who attempt or complete suicide include:

- Completed suicide is the second leading cause of death among college students.
- A projected 1,100 suicides occur on college campuses each year.
- Ninety percent of suicide victims have at least one diagnosable, active psychiatric illness at the time of death, and only 15% of those were in treatment at the time of death.
- Twenty-six to 33% of adolescent suicide victims have made a previous suicide attempt.

These statistics show only the tip of the iceberg regarding the severity and regularity of suicidal ideation, attempts, and completions on our campuses each year. Having highly trained staff and proper policies in place is imperative in protecting your campus as much as possible while dealing with this type of tragic incident.

Language Barriers

Zdziarski and colleagues (2007) discuss the need to address language as a barrier to crisis intervention, which brings with it a responsibility in planning. These authors address the need for and utilization of interpreters as the makeup of college populations becomes more international and diverse. Addressing language needs, particularly in early stages of recovery, when it is not uncommon for individuals to revert to their language of origin to describe experiences, is a critical issue, according to these authors. This issue becomes particularly pressing when dealing with death notifications. Interpreters are often needed to address actions being taken during crises, as well as those of postincident involvement.

Under no circumstances should crisis response teams (CRTs) circumvent legal counsel, campus policies and procedures, or their own professional judgment in their urgency to meet human need during crisis (Lee & Casey, 2004). It is less likely that these legal and ethical landmines will be detonated if your campus takes the time to identify and take liability issues under consideration when formulating policy, procedures, plans, and training activities. Police Crisis Intervention Teams rendezvous and discuss plans of action before entering a hazardous situation. Any competent crisis management team (CMT) should do the same. If the situation is hairy when the first responder reaches the scene, back off and get help.

BASIC RISK MANAGEMENT RECOMMENDATIONS

Risk management takes a coordinated effort (Myer, 2009). Piecemeal efforts lead to confusion and ineffectiveness. The following discussion outlines basic tenets to consider as you move from a discussion on policy to actual procedures.

Risk Management Resource Materials

A notebook containing your most valued crisis management resources, along with your organization's crisis management plan, should stay within reach at all times if you are a top administrator or have been assigned primary crisis responsibilities. In many areas, it is mandatory that CMT and CRT members not only have copies in their offices but also carry it in their vehicles or otherwise have it accessible should they be called to a scene after hours. These resources should contain a minimum of the following: organization chart with contact information (more than office); copies of ethics codes, laws, and statutes that govern actions during critical issues; campus policies; articles or checklists for crisis management; legal and community professional consultation information; and a reminder of your personal philosophy so you have something of value to hang on to when all hell breaks loose. This notebook, along with your formal crisis intervention plan, should be reviewed and updated annually as appropriate to ensure current familiarity.

Training

A great plan is not worth the paper it is written on if the plan does not help those in charge take appropriate action when needed. Consistent training, discussions, role plays, rehearsals, and networking are needed to provide those in authority the opportunity to attain the competence and confidence necessary to address a critical incident. Training may include practice of basic crisis intervention skills as described in Myer and James (2005). Also, there may be good reason to consider a policy regarding basic and ongoing training for those who serve as leaders for your crisis management team and your crisis intervention team.

Peer Consultation

Your crisis management plan will usually identify and provide information about campus responders and also community partners to utilize as needed during a critical incident. You are encouraged to have working alliances with various constituencies throughout your community. These alliances may be spelled out through a combination of memoranda of agreements or through contracts, depending on the levels of services being negotiated. This may require having campus leaders assigned liaison duties to appropriately network and keep track of information that may affect your ability to partner effectively during crisis. You will also want to informally network and consult among your state's colleges and universities. This can be accomplished by asking your vice presidents and directors to share and also to bring information that may be helpful back to your organization from their professional organizations and meetings. Much can be taken from lessons learned by similar institutions that have experienced critical incidents.

Institutional Policies

Have policies for crisis management that provide guidelines for taking action during crisis. Many a phone call has been made to legal counsel requesting guidance, only to be asked: "Do you have a policy about this?" followed by "If you do, follow it" or "If you don't, you need to write one and follow it."

Critical Incident Documentation

The use of documentation during critical incidents is a bit controversial. Some think that by recording information, an institution is raising its liability. If you are flying by the seat of your pants, this can be true, because you are probably documenting steps of incompetence and less than what would be considered reasonable care in a critical incident. However, there are many ways that documentation can assist in justifying and supporting the actions taken during a critical incident and show that reasonable steps were taken to do the right thing in very difficult circumstances. Numerous assessment instruments and checklists have been developed to assist in documenting critical incidents on your campus. In Chapter 9, we introduce you to an instrument called TASSLE that has the ability to assess crises with regard to the level of threat, assist in determining appropriate action based on level of threat, and provide justification for action based on more than a subjective feeling regarding threats on campus. This type of instrument serves multiple purposes in documenting crises and serves as a strong risk management tool. Another instrument, "Triage Assessment Form: Organizations," is described in Chapter 7. This instrument can be used to measure the impact of the crisis on the entire campus, as well as on specific departments or units on campus.

Scope of Competence

Recognize and respect the limitations of professional competence of your administration and staff. Remember that an exceptional administrator may well be a lousy leader during crisis. Those who truly lead well during crisis are a different breed for sure and may not be the first people who come to mind when you think of traditional leadership qualities. James (2008) has identified characteristics of effective crisis workers, including experience, poise, creativity, flexibility, energy, resilience, and mental acuity. Those with primary responsibility need to possess natural crisis leadership characteristics and also secure appropriate education, training, and consultation.

Duty to Warn

Know the law in your state, and identify the specifics regarding the expectation to warn. Does your law require you to communicate a threat against a specifically identified individual who may be victimized, or does your responsibility to communicate encompass a broader construct including foreseeable victims, not specifically identified, but likely targets should the client become violent or carry through on a specific threat? Remember to never share more information than is necessary to protect potential victims if you do need to report a potential danger to others. Always follow your institutional policy when reporting, and document the actions you consider, those you take, and a rationale for each. By law, regardless of specificity, counselors must document and warn in instances of immediate danger to self or others (Wheeler & Bertram, 2008). It would be prudent to work with your legal counsel to determine the definitions of *imminent* and *scope of danger* for your state and campus for use in your policies and procedures.

Suicide

Some very basic risk management practices regarding the handling of suicide on campus include proper training of professionals to conduct adequate evaluation of students (basic screening information to make an appropriate referral to a mental health professional could be provided to all frontline campus employees), having identified appropriate referral sources in place, always considering past treatment and previous behaviors ("the best predictor of future behavior is past behavior"), having clear institutional policies, and always providing follow-up with an at-risk student. Other factors that will serve as protective action include early detection and prevention activity when possible, consultation always in these instances (no professional should have to go this journey alone), and careful documentation.

SUMMARY

It seems that everyone tends to feel better prepared for the crisis that just occurred on another campus and few seem well prepared for the crises in which they find themselves. Luckily, you have the opportunity to learn from the crises that not only you but also others survive. Lessons can be learned about what to do and what not to do. As the field of crisis management continues to grow, more resources become available to work with.

If you are serious about crisis management on your campus, you need to do more than the standard planning document with a cookie-cutter approach. Spend time looking at incidents and lessons learned by others, imagine yourself in their shoes, and look at what resources you might have for responding. You can also look for barriers to success, strengthen weak links that might make you vulnerable to litigation, and set up basic risk management actions.

You have an opportunity prior to a critical incident on your campus to step back and look at how you might align your mission, vision, values, crisis plans, policies, and procedures. Solid policies—those carefully considered, drafted, and reviewed—will provide the general guidance needed during a crisis. They will also help protect you during scrutiny after the fact. The policies need to be specific enough to provide guidance and flexible enough to allow you to be responsive to the specifics of the crisis at hand. Procedures that outline the responsibility, roles, and specific actions needed to accomplish the goals of the crisis plan will carry you through a crisis. Your comprehensive crisis plan, supported by the proper policies and procedures, will allow you to pull together the components to assist you in crafting the needed response to the chaos we call crisis. Resources can be launched in whatever direction is required (which is multiple directions at once in many crises) with the proper plan, policies, and procedures.

REFERENCES

AACRAO. (2002). Academic transcripts and records: Survey of current practices. *Special Report.* Retrieved from http://www.aacrao.org/about/atr.pdf.

American College Health Association. (2006). *NCHA—National college health assessment.* Retrieved from http://www.acha-ncha.org/docs/JACH January 2007 SP 06 Ref Grp.pdf.

American Counseling Association. (2005). *ACA code of ethics.* Alexandria, VA: Author.

American Psychological Association. (2002). *American Psychological Association ethical principles of psychologists and code of conduct.* Retrieved from http://www.apa.org/ethics/code/index.aspx.

Bickel, R. D., & Lake, P. F. (1999). *The rights and responsibilities of the modern university: Who assumes the risk of college life?* Durham, NC: Carolina Academic Press.

Cantu-Weber, J. (1999). Harassment and discrimination: News stories show litigation on the rise. *Change, 31*(3), 38–45.

Fisher, C. B. (2009). *Decoding the ethics code: A practical guide for psychologists* (2nd ed.). Springfield, IL: Charles C Thomas.

Goldman, R. (2007). School accused of covering student's murder. *ABC News.* Retrieved January 29, 2010, from http://abcnews.go.com/US/story?id=3296170&page=1.

James, R. K. (2008). *Crisis intervention strategies* (6th ed.). Belmont, CA: Brooks/Cole–Cengage.

Jed Foundation. (2006). *Important facts about adolescent suicide.* Retrieved October 11, 2006, from http://www.jedfoundation.org/libraryNews_facts.php.

Kitzrow, M. A. (2003). The mental health needs of today's college students: Challenges and recommendations. *NASPA Journal, 41,* 167–181.

Lee, R., & Casey, D. (2004). *Crisis and trauma in colleges & universities.* Ellicott City, MD: Chevron Publishing.

Mitroff, I. I., Diamond, M. A., & Alpasian, C. M. (2006). How prepared are America's colleges and universities for major crises? *Change: The Magazine of Higher Education Learning, 38,* 61–67.

Myer, R. A. (2009, December). *Three C's of violence prevention on college campuses.* Presented at the First Annual National Behavioral Intervention Team Association meeting. San Antonio, TX.

Myer, R. A., & James, R. K. (2005). *Crisis intervention workbook and CD ROM.* Belmont, CA: Thomson Brooks/Cole.

Myers, D. G. (1989). *Psychology* (2nd ed.). New York: Worth.

Nicoletti, J., Spencer-Thomas, S., & Bollinger, C. (2001). *Violence goes to college.* Springfield, IL: Charles C Thomas.

Welfel, E. R. (2006). *Ethics in counseling and psychotherapy: Standards, research, and emerging issues* (3rd ed.). Pacific Grove, CA: Wadsworth.

Wheeler, A. M., & Bertram, B. (2008). *The counselor and the law: A guide to legal and ethical practice.* Alexandria, VA: American Counseling Association.

Zdziarski, E. L., Dunkel, W. D., & Rollo, J. M. (2007). *Campus crisis management: A comprehensive guide to planning, prevention, response, and recovery.* San Francisco: John Wiley & Sons.

Zero Tolerance Task Force. (2008). Are zero tolerance policies effective in the schools? *American Psychologist, 63,* 852–862.

Appendix
Sample Threats Policy

Our policy is to strive to maintain a campus environment free from intimidation or threats. This includes, but is not limited to: intimidating, threatening, or hostile behaviors, harassment, discriminatory acts, physical abuse, vandalism, hazing, sexual assault, hate crimes, arson, sabotage, carrying or use of weapons, or any other act, which, in the administration's opinion, is inappropriate to the campus environment or disrupts the learning environment. In addition, bizarre or offensive comments (direct or indirect) regarding violent events or aggressive behaviors will not be tolerated.

Campus employees or students who feel subjected to any of the behaviors listed above should immediately report the incident to _____ (name of appointed campus representative). All complaints will receive prompt attention and the situation will be investigated. Based on the results of the inquiry, disciplinary action which administration feels is appropriate will be taken.

Campus employees or students who observe or have knowledge of violation of this policy are encouraged to report immediately to _____ (name of appointed campus representative). All reported events will be taken seriously. If an investigation is warranted, we reserve the right to request the cooperation of all incident-related individuals. An employee or student who believes there is a serious and imminent threat to the safety and health of others should report this concern directly to law enforcement authorities.

Reasonable actions will be taken to protect the safety and privacy of those reporting incidents. Malicious reporting will not be tolerated and disciplinary action may be taken should this occur.

Source: Adapted from *Violence Goes to College* (Nicoletti, Spencer-Thomas, & Bollinger, 2001).

5

The Best of Times and the Worst of Times:
The Tale of Two Laws

Charles Dickens's opening line in *A Tale of Two Cities*, "It was the best of times, it was the worst of times," says it well. Crises can be both. The death of Tatiana Tarasoff at the hands of Prosenjit Poddar in 1969 had a momentous impact on practice in the field of mental health. The changes that resulted have become standard practice and built into ethical codes of professional organizations that focus on mental health issues. The tragedy of April 16, 2007, at Virginia Tech has the potential to push the envelope even further. This chapter looks at those two events and the impact each has had on crisis intervention and prevention on college campuses. This discussion concludes by outlining the follow-up system used at the counseling center. We hope this discussion prompts a conversation regarding issues related to communication and violence prevention on your campus.

TARASOFF AND ITS IMPACT ON POLICY

Whenever clients sit down with a licensed mental health worker and start to talk about their problems, a variety of ethical and legal shields to that conversation are erected. These legal shields are particularly strong on a college campus where the Family Educational Rights and Privacy Act (the Buckley amendment, 1974) regulates the transmission of student data, the Americans with Disabilities Act (ADA, 1990) provides protection for people with disabling conditions (mental health being one of those conditions), and the Health Insurance Portability and Accountability Act (HIPAA, 1996) provides for guidelines about the release of medical data. Whenever a client talks to a licensed mental health therapist, state laws provide the therapist and the client the legal shield of *privileged* communication. Further buttressing these shields are national professional organizations' ethical standards of *confidentiality*. These standards developed by professional organizations guide their members in how and to whom what information about a client is disseminated. But the guiding principle for mental health professionals in the delivery of services for severely disturbed and potentially lethal individuals that stands above all these regulations, laws, and standards is the Tarasoff case (*Tarasoff v. Board of Regents of the University of California*, 1976).

The Tarasoff case turned the therapeutic world of therapist confidentiality topsy-turvy and is held as the classic example of a therapist, a supervisory staff, and an institution not adequately dealing with a client threat and subsequently not warning intended victims of that threat. The Tarasoff case came into being when a male client told a University of California college counseling center psychologist of his intentions to murder a young woman. Although the intended victim was not specifically identified, the therapist determined her identity, yet took no steps to warn her of the client's threats. The therapist did write a letter to the campus police about the client's homicidal intentions, and the client was immediately taken into custody for observation. However, after evaluation and the client's promise to stay away from the woman, the man was released.

Because of concerns that ethical confidentiality and the law of privileged communication had been violated, the therapist's supervisor demanded the police return the letter and destroy all copies of the letter and other further written communication about the matter (Thompson, 1983, p. 167). Approximately two months later, the woman was killed. Subsequently, the parents of the victim found out about the exchange of information and sued the university. Lower courts denied the university and the counseling center's culpability, citing both the ethical standard of confidentiality and the law of privileged communication as the basis for the center's decision to withhold information. However, after the rulings of the lower courts were appealed, the State Supreme Court of California found for the plaintiff. In this precedent-setting case, the court found that when a mental health therapist ascertains that a threat is neither remote nor idle in its content, the public good demands that disclosure of the threat to a third party outweighs the benefits of preserving confidentiality (Cohen, 1978). The *Tarasoff* decision has mandated three conditions that are necessary and sufficient for a duty to warn to occur: (a) There must be a special relationship, such as therapist to client; (b) there must be a reasonable prediction of conduct that constitutes a danger; and (c) there must be a foreseeable victim.

This ruling had a domino effect that spread across the United States and changed state laws to mandate that an imminent threat to the health and well-being of a person means that victims, relatives, the authorities, or anyone else in a position to prevent that harm needs to be informed. While this tidal change in duty to warn seems straightforward enough, it is anything but that, as clearly evidenced by the massacre at Virginia Tech, where a perfect storm of these shielding laws, ethical codes, moral principles, fear of reprisal and censure, and communications logjams between and within agencies prevented authorities from reacting to and stopping Seung-Hui Cho from killing 32 people and wounding 14 others.

Therefore, regardless of confidentiality or any other ethical or legal shield, when the client provides information about intent to do harm to himself or herself or another person, rules of confidentiality take on an entirely different perspective due to *Tarasoff*. The mental health professional then must make a decision about whether to inform the authorities, significant others, or a potential victim of such threats and is tasked with taking action to ensure the client does not carry them out. It is almost a sure bet, because of the often emotional and highly volatile world of crisis intervention, that an individual will eventually appear in a college counseling center with such potentially lethal behavior that the mental health professional will have to make a decision about telling someone in order to keep the client or another person safe.

The general rule for determining a clear and present danger is that such a danger is present if a client specifies victim identity ("my roommate"), motive ("revenge"), means ("gun"), and plan ("I'll wait for him after night class when no one's around") (Thompson, 1983, p. 83). Danger is also present if the client is unable to understand what he or she is contemplating, is incapable of exercising self-control, and is incapable of collaborating with the worker. While this strategy sounds good on paper, when practiced it is an entirely different matter, and that became very clear in the Inspector General's report (2009) on the massacre at Virginia Tech.

VIRGINIA TECH INSPECTOR GENERAL REPORT: GOING BEYOND *TARASOFF*

The following summary is an abridged version of the Inspector General for Behavioral Health and Developmental Services of Virginia's report on the review of events of the shooting that occurred on the campus of Virginia Tech. The report includes the responses and implementation efforts of the Cook Counseling Center on that campus to recommendations for policy changes in how mental health services are provided and how and to whom confidential client information that would usually be shielded from the public view is disseminated. The following report could well serve as a tutorial for anyone interested in instituting policy changes in a university's counseling center that could reduce the risk of a lethal client falling through the cracks of the system. We have added comments where relevant to the recommendations of the committee and responses of the center where we believe they have particular relevancy for the readership.

After a thorough review of the history of events that occurred with Seung-Hui Cho and his contacts with both the Virginia Tech counseling center and outside agencies, the following is a synopsis of what went wrong and why a Tarasoff warning was never initiated. First, while Seung Hui made a number of appointments and had some initial preliminary intake interviews with the counseling center, he broke many of them and never formerly became a client with a case file. That caused some gaping holes in communication of his blossoming intent both within and between agencies. When professors, students, and resident hall staff reported his ominous writing and verbal threats, he would recant and say he was joking when confronted with questions of lethality (Inspector General, 2009, pp. 2–20).

Although his writing was very scary, there was no clear target, such as a named person or place. Therefore, when officials in university judicial affairs, professional staff at the counseling center, and professional staff at the local community mental health center did triage assessments, since no specific target was named, no action could be taken. Seung-Hui was hospitalized overnight after voluntarily going to a community mental health center but left the next day since no involuntary psychiatric hold could be placed on him. Once again, he did not meet Tarasoff criteria and maintained he was only joking about his lethal ideation and threats (Inspector General, 2009, pp. 2–20).

The university counseling center, as most counseling centers do, would not take involuntary commitments for counseling by other agencies. In other words, while the English Department Chairperson Dr. Lucinda Roy and other faculty members were frantically trying to get Seung-Hui into counseling, the center would not do anything unless Seung-Hui voluntarily came to the counseling center. Also, the counseling center would not agree to take students who had been put under court order to receive counseling, citing confidentiality, privilege, and privacy act issues that would forbid them from passing information about students to legal entities or university departments or divisions (Inspector General, 2009, pp. 12–14).

VIRGINIA TECH COUNSELING CENTER ACTIONS TAKEN

The Virginia Tech counseling center's response to the Virginia Inspector General's recommendations follow. These recommendations have major ramifications in how and to whom confidential information about the mental health assessment and treatment process is delivered. These changes potentially represent as significant a shift in data handling and information processing of the mentally ill and potentially lethal client as *Tarasoff* and have wide-ranging implications for clients, counseling centers, and universities themselves. In that regard, they have major implications for policy decision making for a university.

First and foremost, following the tragic events of April 16, 2007, the entire process of mandatory outpatient treatment ordered by the courts underwent significant revision and clarification under Virginia law (VA Code 37.2-817). Under these provisions (VA Codes 37.2-817.1 through 37.2-817.3), the community services board in the area in which the patient resides is responsible for developing a treatment plan for mandatory outpatient treatment, implementing the plan, and monitoring compliance with the plan. The counseling center at Virginia Tech was tasked to closely coordinate treatment plans with the local community mental health agency, which would mean trading treatment information on the student (Inspector General, 2009, pp. 26–29).

Thus, a Virginia Tech student who had been evaluated by Access (a formal triage team of the local mental health clinic), who has been subject to a temporary detention order, or who has received a civil commitment would, upon his or her release, continue to receive appropriate treatment, and the case manager of the Virginia Tech counseling center would coordinate follow-up care with any of these agencies.

Compliance with the treatment recommendations of the inpatient facility would be considered a condition of continued enrollment at Virginia Tech (Inspector General, 2009, pp. 26–29).

What this means is that if a student did not agree to a release of personal data or was unwilling to continue treatment, then that student could face sanctions within the university, including an emergency suspension (Inspector General, 2009, p. 28). To that end, the counseling center developed the following letter that would be given to any student mandated to treatment. Titled "Information for Students Referred for Case Management following Temporary Detention Order/Involuntary Hospitalization," this document states:

> If appropriate to your needs, you may receive treatment from the Cook Counseling Center, from an off-campus licensed mental health professional or from the Community Services Board; in either case, care will be coordinated with the Case Manager from the Cook Counseling Center. Should you wish to receive treatment from an off-campus professional, it is imperative that the provider coordinates care with the Case Manger regarding treatment. In the event that treatment recommendations include outpatient commitment, the Cook Counseling Center will coordinate care with the Community Services Board. (Inspector General, 2009, p. 29)

Mandatory Assessment

When a client receives required treatment ordered by another agency, the therapist is then acting on behalf of the agency, and confidentiality of the client's statements cannot always be provided. Under these conditions, it is incumbent on the counselor for the Virginia Tech counseling center to notify the student that she or he is acting on behalf of the university, not on behalf of the student, and that the results of the evaluation will be shared with university officials. This clarifies that the counselor is not abrogating the therapist–client relationship and associated confidentiality restrictions. The following conditions would fall under this provision:

1. Students referred for a mandatory assessment requested by another university office, usually the Office for Student Conduct
2. Students who have been hospitalized for evaluation of danger to self or others who have received a temporary detention order
3. Students whose continued enrollment requires continued counseling and for whom the threat assessment team (TAT) has mandated this
4. Students who have received a mandatory outpatient treatment order from the courts and whose treatment plan from the community service board includes services at the counseling center

A request for a mandatory assessment could come from the following offices:

1. Student Conduct
2. Dean of Students
3. Residential Life
4. TAT (Inspector General, 2009, pp. 29–30)

The staff member of the counseling center would clarify the responsibilities of the student and the counselor when a mandatory assessment is made, as well as to whom any report will be directed. The decision to issue an interim suspension is not the responsibility of the counselor but of the referring office, which should keep the counseling center at arm's length from any disciplinary actions. Whether clients would see it that way is another matter and indeed raises credibility questions about the counseling center (Inspector General, 2009, pp. 29–30).

Temporary Detention Orders

An individual who is suffering from a mental illness, who may cause physical harm to self or others either intentionally or by being unable to care for self, or who is in need of hospitalization and unwilling to be voluntarily hospitalized may receive a temporary detention order and be hospitalized at a psychiatric facility. In all cases, the case manager indicates to the student that, following discharge, the student must continue in treatment with either the counseling center or an off-campus provider until such time that the student is no longer in need of treatment or no longer a Virginia Tech student. The student is asked to sign a release of information allowing the case manager to speak to any treatment provider who works with the student. If the student does not comply with this request and is considered by either the case manager or the treatment provider to still be in need of treatment, the student may face a referral to the Office of Student Conduct for failure to comply (Inspector General, 2009, p. 30).

One wonders when the student is placed under treatment conditions that are deemed coercive, whether the individual would attempt to present a better picture of himself or herself than what is actually true. We have seen this phenomenon occur regularly in court adjudications of domestic violence and addiction problems and see no reason why it would not occur here.

CARE Team

There are two separate entities at Virginia Tech charged with ensuring a safe and supportive campus environment. The CARE Team is focused on support and intervention with students, and the TAT is charged with assessing individuals and situations that may pose a threat to the safety of self and others in the entire community of students, faculty, and staff. These entities are separate in mission and focus, but communication between them is essential. The memberships of the committees intentionally have some overlap so that there is clear communication involved in gathering and transmitting information affecting students. The dean of students, the director of the Cook Counseling Center, the Threat Assessment Program manager, and the deputy chief of police are members of both groups, and the threat assessment investigator is a member of the CARE Team and attends meetings of the TAT (Inspector General, 2009, pp. 37–38).

The Dean of Students Office at Virginia Tech convenes and organizes the CARE Team, which meets every Monday at 11:00 a.m. during the academic year and as needed over the summer months. The mission of the CARE Team is to support and intervene with students whose behavior, physical or emotional health, or academic performance puts them at risk. The goals of the CARE Team include assessing the functioning of students, developing plans of support or intervention, assigning responsibility for follow-up, and monitoring the situation until it is resolved. Given the breadth of the mission for the CARE Team, membership is drawn from a wide range of offices including the following:

1. Student Affairs
2. Dean of Students (Dean, the Associate Dean, and Case Manager)
3. Cook Counseling Center (Director, Case Manager)
4. Judicial Affairs (Director)
5. Residence Life (Director)
6. Services for Students with Disabilities (Director)
7. Health Center (Director)
8. Dean for Undergraduate Registration
9. University Registrar
10. Office of the President
11. University General Counsel
12. Administrative Services
13. University Police Threat Assessment Program Manager and Deputy Chief
14. University Police Threat Assessment Investigator

In addition, the CARE Team may also rely on representatives from other offices as needed, including the Women's Center, the Cranwell International Center, and representatives from academic colleges and departments. The CARE Team meets weekly and maintains records of each of its meetings and the students discussed. The caseload of the CARE Team typically includes 15 to 20 students weekly, including both new cases to be staffed and follow-up with ongoing cases. Students may be referred to the CARE Team from any member of the CARE Team or from faculty, staff, or students (Inspector General, 2009, pp. 37–39).

The role of the Cook Counseling Center participants on the CARE Team is primarily consultative, given that confidentiality laws preclude sharing of information without the client's permission except in very specific instances, including health and safety emergencies. While the Cook Counseling Center may not always share information regarding the students, the majority of cases considered by the CARE Team either result in a referral to the center or are students currently being treated at the counseling center. Counseling center follow-up of CARE Team referrals is immediate. To maintain communication and continuity of care, the notes from the weekly CARE Team are presented the same day at the weekly case conference of the counseling center (Inspector General, 2009, pp. 37–38).

Prior to the case conference, the case manager checks the electronic records of the counseling center to see if each student who was discussed is either being treated at present or has been treated in the past. This information is noted prior to the case conference review, and an alert is placed in the electronic medical record so that the counseling staff is aware of any current or ongoing concerns of the student. Each student is discussed by the staff of the counseling center to ensure that the students' concerns or problems will be addressed, should they seek counseling. Counselors may take material from the case conference and discuss these with the students who are being followed by the CARE Team; with the student's permission, information may be given back to the CARE Team to facilitate communication and/or an intervention with the student. A student experiencing a health and safety emergency may come to the attention of the CARE Team during its weekly meeting, but emergency interventions are not deferred until a meeting of the CARE Team since they may arise at any time and in any area across campus (Inspector General, 2009, pp. 38–39).

The CARE Team at Virginia Tech is an interesting concept. It appears to be a much wider and somewhat looser net to catch students in trouble and provide support for them. It is somewhat unclear as to how actual referrals are made to the team, what kinds of problems might get called to their attention, or how they are assessed as to their validity. Such widespread nets are, in our opinion, double-edged swords. On the one hand, they have much wider coverage and the potential to catch problems early on and get help before disturbed individuals are out of control. On the other hand, students could report other students out of jealousy, anger, or a host of other reasons to get them in trouble. Also, we know of faculty members who become easily alarmed and hysterically believe they are being confronted by dangerous, psychotic students who may be vocal about a low grade but are a long way from the homicidal maniacs these mercurial professors believe them to be. From a protective standpoint and a student help view, there are excellent reasons to have such a program as the CARE Team. However, our belief is that there needs to be campuswide training as to what a team such as CARE does. That training would go a long way toward understanding the difference between legitimate concerns and spurious referrals.

Threat Assessment Team Referral

The university TAT is charged with assessing any situation where a university community member's behavior may represent a potential threat of violence to the safety of the campus community (VA Code 23-31 9.2:10). The university TAT has the responsibility for the assessment and intervention with a community member who may pose a threat (VA Code 23-31 9.2:3C).

The tragedy at Virginia Tech illuminated the importance of assessing individuals who may represent a threat to themselves or others. The results of internal reviews and subsequent legislation in the Commonwealth of Virginia led to the creation of a university TAT. As required by Virginia Code (23.9.2:10), the TAT in a public higher education setting includes representation from academic departments, student affairs, university police, human resources, university counsel, and mental health. The TAT may be called upon to assess threats posed by students, faculty, or staff, but review of threat assessment in higher education reveals that threats are equally or more likely to be posed by individuals who are not members of the academic community.

The director of the Cook Counseling Center serves as the mental health representative to the TAT. The role of the director of the Cook Counseling Center differs on the TAT from that described previously for the CARE Team (Inspector General, 2009, p. 39). Some of these distinctions include the following:

1. The TAT is charged with assessing and intervening with individuals who may pose a threat to the safety of self and others. The director may interview witnesses and individuals whose behavior poses a concern and, in doing so, acts as an agent of the university and not as the therapist of the student. This distinction is critical since confidentiality does not apply when he or she is acting on behalf of the TAT, and the student must be notified of this at the initiation of any interview.

2. In a health and safety emergency, the director may divulge information necessary to ensure a prompt and safe intervention with a student. This may include confidential material gathered by a counselor in the course of treatment with a client. As noted previously, only information critical to ensuring the safety of the student or community is released, and all other information remains confidential. This release of information is considered critical when seeking an emergency custody order from a magistrate or during a hearing for a temporary detention order. Under Virginia Code, the issuance of a temporary detention order is public information since it occurs through a court hearing. If a student is issued a temporary detention order, which is by definition public information, any member of the TAT may share this knowledge with the full team.

3. As part of the risk management strategy, the team may require a student to continue in counseling with a member of the counseling center staff; since enrollment at the university is voluntary, a student may withdraw from the university at any time, but continued enrollment under the evaluation by the university TAT may be contingent on continued counseling. The procedure for working with a student referred by the TAT parallels the procedure for working with mandatory assessments. The student is notified that the counselor is working on

behalf of the university and that this is not a counseling relationship with the attendant confidentiality. The student is notified that the results of the assessment will be shared with the TAT, and the student is asked to sign an informed consent document that acknowledges these facts (Inspector General, 2009, pp. 39–40).

Picture yourself as a student under these conditions. How willing do you think you would be to share your innermost thoughts and feelings? How would you behave and what would you say when the therapist asked you if you had thoughts of killing yourself or others? Do you think you might lie? Do you think you might present a better picture of yourself than what you really felt, out of fear you would go to jail or a mental institution or be expelled from school? One of the most difficult problems therapists face when they deal with individuals who are forced into counseling is that individuals may say things therapists want to hear. Knowing their information will be transmitted to a third party can influence individuals to say things out of expediency. Whether they will do those things or not is another matter entirely.

Speed of Assessment

One of the critical aspects of care for potentially dangerous students is time from contact to time of treatment. With current backlogs at counseling centers across the country, this may be weeks or months. The goal of the triage system at Virginia Tech is to have the student receive an in-person evaluation within 24 hours of the time he or she makes contact. In a situation that is deemed to be an emergency by students, they are encouraged to come in as soon as possible, and they are seen the same day (Inspector General, 2009, pp. 33–34).

When a student arrives for the triage appointment, the student completes two online questionnaires; one asks for demographic information, and the other is a standardized measure of psychological symptoms and distress, Counseling Center Assessment of Psychological Symptoms (CCAPS), which provides normative data measuring student distress. The counselor accesses the completed questionnaires before meeting with the student and signs off on that review. The counselor then spends 30 minutes with the student to assess the current concerns, any psychological symptoms, and the presence or absence of suicidal and homicidal ideation, plans, or intent (Inspector General, 2009, p. 34).

During an interview, the counselor assesses both the content of what the student is saying and how the material is being presented through the mental status portion of the interview. Both aspects are critical. The counselor's job is to assess quickly whether either portion of the presentation requires a more comprehensive assessment to be completed at the present time or through the extended process of the intake appointment. At any point, the counselor may decide that more time is required because of the immediacy of the student's concern and complete a continued assessment. In these circumstances, consultation and engagement of a psychiatric professional may also be necessary. If the student is in crisis, the counselor continues to meet with the student until a plan of action is developed to ensure the student's safety (Inspector General, 2009, p. 34). Very much like standard crisis intervention protocol (James, 2008, p. 38; Ottens, Black, & Klein, 2005), a short-term plan of action is initiated to de-escalate the client and return him or her to a precrisis state of equilibrium.

While this response is absolutely critical, it means having the staff to do it. With universities facing severe budget cuts, it is unlikely that the staff numbers needed to do such assessment on a real-time basis will be forthcoming. Perhaps graduate students doing these triage assessments, as part of their internships, might be an answer. The other problem is that a crisis typically does not happen on a 9-to-5 business day. It is as likely to show up at 1 a.m. Saturday morning as at 1 p.m. Monday afternoon. Who will do the triage on the night shift? Can there be an agreement with a community mobile crisis team or crisis intervention team police officers to do the assessment? Those questions need answers if a comprehensive triage assessment system is to be put into place like Virginia Tech.

Designation of Risk

At the end of each triage interview, the student is assigned to one of three levels: (0) minimal risk, (1) follow-up required, or (2) hospitalization required. If a student is assigned to level 1, the follow-up appointments are noted as "urgent," and the student is seen on a weekly basis. Each student at that level is followed carefully, and there is immediate follow-up with the scheduling of the intake appointment at the next available time. Should a student assigned to a level 1 miss an appointment or call to cancel an appointment, the student must speak with a counselor. Students who are level 2 are the focus of an immediate intervention and seen following the procedures outlined previously for a "health and safety emergency." The counselor completes a triage form for each student in an electronic medical record (Inspector General, 2009, pp. 34–35).

Although the Triage Assessment Scale for Students in Learning Environments (TASSLE) system does not make recommendations as to specific disposition of clients because of the vagaries of differences in settings and state laws, we believe that its scores may be easily wielded to action designations such as the foregoing. If you are starting to get the idea that this sounds like a cardiac emergency care unit at an ER, you are starting to grasp the idea that this is not a business as usual approach to counseling. To that end, as we have stated throughout this book, there had better be center staff who are trained to do this specialized work.

Health and Safety Emergencies

Staff members of the counseling center are always available to assist a student experiencing a health and safety emergency. During office hours, triage times are held throughout the day for evaluation of potential emergencies. Students are often self-referred,

referred by any of the CARE Team members, or by faculty, staff, and family members. In a health and safety emergency, the counselor on call may do whatever is necessary to support and protect students; this includes notifying police, university officials, or community mental health facilities and hospitals to obtain services for the students. Although the counselor attempts to release only the minimum information necessary, the usual restrictions on confidentiality are eased to ensure that students get optimal assistance. Under recent revision to Virginia Code (38.2-804), mental health professionals may share any necessary information with each other and with a magistrate during an emergency custody evaluation, and this revision makes clear that the mental health professional will be immune from civil liability while acting in good faith to protect a client. Under Virginia Code (54.1-2400.1), mental health professionals are also expected to issue a Tarasoff-type warning. The therapist may also notify police to ensure that the client receives a thorough assessment of dangerousness (Inspector General, 2009, pp. 35–36).

It is important to note that Virginia law covers the therapist's actions. If the state in which you reside does not have such protective laws, your best plan is to inform clients that you are not exempt from confidentiality and privileged communication.

Procedure on Parental Notification

Following the preceding procedures, counselors are released from confidentiality to seek support and protection of a student potentially dangerous to self or others. Recent revisions to Virginia Code (23-9.2:3.C) now make parental notification mandatory except in limited circumstances. The new code requires notification of the parent(s) of a dependent student (as defined by tax status) when the student is treated by the counseling center or health center and there exists a substantial likelihood that the student may cause harm to self or others by reason of psychological disturbance. The law makes a clear provision for an exemption to parental notification if such notification would be likely to cause harm to the students; if this exception is exercised, it must be in writing (Inspector General, 2009, pp. 35–36).

Undoubtedly, there is going to be a lawsuit challenging this state law as it butts up against the Family Educational Rights and Privacy Act (FERPA). How notification of parents will ultimately occur or not is a constant and thorny problem for universities. On the one hand, students are mainly adults in the eyes of the law. On the other hand, for most students, whether they are tax dependent on their parents or not, parents are most generally the most critical resource and support in the student's life. As you are well aware of in our use of the Systematic Crisis Intervention Model (James, 2008, p. 38), finding and using a support system is a critical component to stabilizing a crisis.

Record Keeping

Information regarding students at risk may come from sources external and internal to the university who are dealing with out-of-control students, from clients who walk into the counseling center, or from other offices and departments in the university who have had contact with at-risk students. How it gets to a university counseling center and catches somebody's attention in a timely manner, not to mention made sense of, is another matter. Herein are the holes that occurred in Virginia Tech's communication linkages, as there are undoubtedly holes in every other university system in the country.

The counseling center at Virginia Tech did a pretty fair job of tracking students prior to Seung-Hui Cho's rampage. The problem with Seung-Hui was that he didn't trigger the trip wire that would have gotten him completely into the system because he never got past the triage phase. What has happened as a result of that failure at Virginia Tech is that the counseling center now works closely with the local community mental health center to coordinate care for students who may have been hospitalized following temporary detention orders. Similarly, the case manager of the center coordinates care with local psychiatric facilities to ensure continuity of care for students who seek voluntary care (Inspector General, 2009, pp. 41–43).

When a student calls the center, the appointment is made for the next convenient time for the student as a triage appointment. The center uses a standardized form for triage assessments. Notes are kept in electronic form from that appointment and all future appointments. In keeping with the standards of mental health professionals, an electronic file is begun when the student makes contact with the center, and the file is updated for each subsequent visit or contact (Inspector General, 2009, pp. 39–41).

In addition to the direct contacts with students who seek services voluntarily, the Virginia Tech counseling center now consults frequently with faculty, students, parents, and staff who are concerned about students or peers. These consultations are noteworthy as to their high number, with more than 700 consultations per year. The student of concern may be a student never seen in the center or a student who is currently being seen. In either case, the counseling center does not divulge whether a student is a client of the center to the individual calling for a consultation, which may change if there is an exception to confidentiality such as a health or safety emergency (Inspector General, 2009, p. 40).

Since the fall of 2008, the center staff constructs electronic notes from these off-site consultations that are filed as "Non-client" notes under the name of the student of concern so that this environmental issues information is available to the counseling staff if the student seeks an appointment at a later date. When a student calls for the initial appointment, the front office staff does a search for all notes for nonclients and integrates any notes into the current electronic file. For students who are active clients, consultation notes are likewise entered into their current electronic file. Information such as previous treatment records, information from collateral sources, and other contacts is scanned into the current electronic record. Under the client file, all contacts and scanned documents are listed by date (e.g., appointment history), counselor notes, consultations, and scanned documents—as are alerts from the CARE Team or the TAT, if any exist (Inspector General, 2009, pp. 40–41).

Through this process of integrating consultation notes, notes from sources external to the university, and notes from internal committees charged with facilitating a comprehensive review of at-risk students, a more complete assessment of the student is possible for the clinician assigned to work with the student. The counselor or psychiatric professional is responsible for reviewing all of the notes (if any) in the client file prior to a first meeting with the student (Inspector General, 2009, pp. 40–41).

While all the foregoing attention to detail on how information is obtained, integrated, and kept may seem tedious, it is this very kind of information—and its ability to be consolidated into a single document that a therapist could quickly review and gather all pertinent information to base a therapeutic intervention on—that is absolutely critical in giving the counseling center the best possible chance of controlling and containing a potentially violent individual.

Outreach and Follow-Up Activities

Probably the most controversial part, at least from the eyes of professionals in counseling centers, is the Virginia Inspector General's recommendation for individuals of concern who either come to the center's attention through outside agencies or come to the attention of students, faculty, parents, and others and are then reported to the center. That recommendation asks the center to manufacture policies, procedures, and protocols that are designed to enhance their outreach and information sharing with other units and institutions. The case manager within the counseling center has become a linchpin in coordinating activities with these external constituencies. In regard to outside agencies, the case manager is responsible for maintaining and coordinating relationships with community mental health services and with area hospitals with psychiatric facilities. Under a memorandum of understanding with the community mental health center, the case manager is notified when a student has been evaluated by ACCESS, the emergency services unit of the community mental health center, regardless of whether the student was hospitalized or released following an evaluation (Inspector General, 2009, pp. 44–46).

If a student is hospitalized following the issuance of a temporary detention order in one of the area hospitals, the case manager attends the hearings to coordinate the necessary information from the university to the special justice and to provide the necessary linkage for follow-up care after discharge. Students who leave the hospital may return to school or may take a leave of absence to continue intensive treatment elsewhere. In either situation, the case manager seeks a release of information to continue contact with the treatment provider until the student is released from treatment or graduates from the university. The case manager also coordinates care for students who return to Virginia Tech (Inspector General, 2009, pp. 46–47).

In addition, the case manager is the central connection to the university CARE Team. The case manager attends each meeting of the CARE Team, enters relevant notes at the counseling center, and briefs the staff of the center weekly on students who are of concern to the CARE Team. The case manager has access to files maintained by the CARE Team and the files maintained by the Office of Student Conduct for adjudicated cases (Inspector General, 2009, p. 42).

The case manager also coordinates care of students under review by the TAT through interaction with the threat assessment investigator. All requests for mandatory assessments are directed first to the case manager, who, in coordination with the director, decides on the assessment procedure for the student. Within the center, the case manager coordinates care for students entering or leaving the hospital or returning to the university following leave for psychological reasons, as well as care for students who may need more intensive treatment (Inspector General, 2009, p. 42).

Each counselor does a careful assessment of a student's functioning level through triage appointments and later follow-up appointments. On the triage form and for every subsequent appointment, counselors assign students to a "Level." The three levels are 0 for students who are evaluated as a minimal risk of danger to self or others and whose care will generally include counseling until the concern is resolved; 1 for students who may represent significant concern, including functional disturbances related to psychological symptoms, and who are in need of ongoing treatment, including counseling and evaluation for medication; and 2 for students who are in need of immediate intensive treatment, including hospitalization or intensive outpatient treatment. When a student is assigned to level 2, parents are notified in almost all cases. The case manager tracks all students who are at levels 1 and 2 until the concerns are dropped down to a level 0. Every Friday, all professional staff members meet in small groups to discuss students in their care who are at levels 1 or 2. The case manager provides all staff members with a list of their students who are at these levels. Follow-up appointments with students who are at level 1 (or have been 2) are marked *urgent* in the electronic schedule, and counselors must make contact with students at level 1 if they cancel or miss a scheduled appointment (Inspector General, 2009, pp. 41–43).

When a client treated by the center is hospitalized, the case manager notifies the treatment provider of the current status of the student and coordinates discharge planning with the treating professional, the hospital, the community mental health center, and family members. As part of the consultation with other students, faculty, parents, or others, the counselor clarifies (a) whether they have addressed their concerns to the individual of concern and (b) whether the student is willing to seek counseling of his or her own volition. When the answer is affirmative to both of these questions, the counselor provides information to assist in making the referral to the counseling center; this includes ways in which to facilitate an appropriate referral, including ways to gently deal with any resistance. In some cases, the counselor may use the information to initiate contact with the student directly (Inspector General, 2009, pp. 41–43).

In other instances, the individual student, faculty member, parent, or others may not be comfortable in addressing their concerns directly with the student, or the student may have refused to seek counseling on his or her own. The counselor may then seek the permission of the concerned individual to bring the student's name forward to the university CARE Team or TAT to develop an intervention strategy, or the concerned individual may contact other offices (e.g., Dean of Students Office, Residential Life Office) directly to make a plan to engage the student. In either case, the counselor will continue to work with these other offices to engage the student and to coordinate referrals to the center. The counselor will follow up as necessary to ensure that the student has been connected to the appropriate resources on or off campus. In all cases, the referring agent (student, faculty, parents, or staff) is apprised of the outcome of the referral as fully as possible; in some cases, such as ongoing counseling, there may be limitations on what can be shared with the referring agent (Inspector General, 2009, pp. 42–43).

VIRGINIA TECH FOLLOW-UP SYSTEM

After each and every contact, students are assigned a follow-up level. The follow-up level identifies both the need for follow-up with the student and the follow-up course of action. This follow-up level would also apply to students who are referred off campus for services. In addition, the follow-up level should be used for after-hours contacts. Following are the descriptions for each follow-up level and the course of action to be taken in contacting the student:

Follow-Up Level 0

This level represents the majority of the students who are seen at the Cook Counseling Center.

Description: Based on information from the last clinical contact with client and/or from a reliable third party:

1. There is minimal to no risk of danger to self or others.
2. There is low concern about relapse or progression into more acute psychopathology if treatment is discontinued.

Action: No action or follow-up is required. The clinician is free to do whatever is determined as clinically appropriate if a student no-shows or cancels an appointment (e.g., nothing, an e-mail, a phone call). If an off-campus referral is made, the clinician is free to do whatever is determined to be clinically appropriate in terms of follow-up.

Follow-Up Level 1

Students identified with this follow-up level are to be followed very carefully until they are moved to either of the other levels.

Description: Based on information from the last clinical contact with client and/or from a reliable third party:

1. There is indication that potential for danger to self or others may exist.
2. There is potential for progression into more acute psychopathology that would cause risk to self or others.

Action: When a student no-shows or cancels an appointment, the student should be contacted. Students will be phoned unless the student specifies an alternate form of contact (e.g., e-mail). Attempts to contact the student are continued until they are determined to be nonproductive. If the student cannot be reached, administrative consultation occurs, with a new set of decisions made regarding follow-up or lack thereof. If the student is reached, the student's risk level is reassessed. A very clear and concrete description of all efforts made to reach the student is entered in the record.

If the student is reached, the details of the reassessment are included in the record entry.

If the student is reached but is refusing continued treatment, this is to be documented in the record and discussed with an administrator or supervisor. If the student is referred to a medical or mental health provider, follow-up contact with the student is made and continued until transfer of care to another provider is complete. A completed release of information form may assist with this.

The case manager may be utilized for help with follow-up at clinician discretion.

Any follow-up appointments at the counseling center will be scheduled as urgent appointments until the status of the student changes and is documented as such (Inspector General, 2009, pp. 49–50).

Follow-Up Level 2

Students identified with this follow-up level are likely to be placed in an inpatient setting unless there is another acceptable alternative. Upon release, follow-up level will be reassessed.

Description: Based on information from the last clinical contact with the client and/or from a reliable third party: There is a "substantial likelihood" of danger to self and/or others or significant decompensation into disorganized, irrational, and unpredictable behavior. A level 2 follow-up is used for students we would seriously consider hospitalizing, even if they do not miss an appointment.

Action: Every attempt should be made to place the student in a safe and monitored environment to prevent any danger to the student or someone else. If these efforts are unsuccessful, then we will do whatever is necessary to ensure the student's safety (e.g., contact emergency person, contact the dean of students, contact the police, initiate emergency custody order for involuntary hospitalization).

Parents who are financially supporting their student are notified of the student's likelihood of causing serious physical harm to self or others. If there is reason to believe this notification would cause harm to the student or another person, this reason would be documented in the record, and the parent would not be notified. The counseling center case manager will be notified and coordinate follow-up of any student with this follow-up level. The treating counselor may continue treatment with the student if it is assessed to be clinically appropriate at discharge (Inspector General, 2009, p. 42).

SUMMARY

It may seem that we have beaten Virginia Tech's counseling center response to death. Yet, the fact remains that if their remediation efforts had been in place beforehand, Seung-Hui Cho's massacre might well have been prevented. The counseling center at your university will almost always play a large part in determining the eventual outcome of what happens when an individual shows signs of lethal behavior. As simple a thing as streamlining and systematizing records may mean the difference between action occurring and saving people from harm. Had there been a clear path from the Virginia Tech English Department to contact and coordinate with the counseling center and they, in return, conducted outreach to the English Department, the community mental health center, and the courts, Seung-Hui would have not been a client will-o'-the-wisp who was flitting in and out of the counseling system but never really entering into it.

From that standpoint, Seung-Hui is not an exception. Many, many students make some attempt to enter into counseling but then get cold feet and disappear. Thus, given all the other policy issues that are inherent in large-scale human disasters on a college campus, getting policy right, in regard to how students and other individuals who present with potentially violent and lethal behavior, should be a first priority in planning and policy making.

Finally, it is informative to consider the laws passed by the Virginia legislature in direct reaction to the Virginia Tech shooting. These laws push far beyond the boundaries of the original *Tarasoff* legal precedent. Putting these mandates into practice will result in a significant alteration of business as usual, potentially for university counseling centers across the country. Brett A. Sokolow, a lawyer and current president of the National Behavior Intervention Team Association, had this to say about the policies of Virginia Tech: "I believe this policy is ill-considered, mainly because it:

1. Potentially undermines the clinical relationship,
2. Creates incentive for the subject to lie, and
3. It creates less likelihood the subject will enter into a long-term relationship with the counselor, which is one of the potential goals of mandating assessment." (Personal communication, December 30, 2009).

REFERENCES

Americans with Disabilities Act. (1990). PL 110-325.

Cohen, R. N. (1978). *Tarasoff v. Regents of the University of California.* The duty to warn: Common law and statutory problems for California psychotherapists. *California Western Law Review, 14,* 153–182.

Family Educational Rights and Privacy Act. (1974). PL 93-380.

Health Insurance Portability and Accountability Act. (1996). PL 104-1919.

Inspector General. (2009). *Investigation—Records Virginia Tech Cook Counseling Center, Blacksburg, Virginia. Report # 179-09.* Richmond, VA: Office of the Inspector General for Behavioral Health & Developmental Services.

James, R. K. (2008). *Crisis intervention strategies* (6th ed.). Belmont, CA: Brooks/Cole–Cengage.

Mandatory Treatment of Mental Health Patients. (2007). Virginia Codes: 37.2-817.1 through 37.2-817.3.

Ottens, A. J., Black, L. L., & Klein, J. F. (2005). Crisis intervention at college counseling centers. In A. R. Roberts (Ed.), *Crisis intervention handbook: Assessment, treatment, and research* (pp. 416–440). New York: Oxford University Press.

Sharing of Confidential Information. (2008). Virginia Code 38.2-804.

Tarasoff v. Board of Regents of the University of California, 551 P.2d 334 (1976).

Tarasoff Warning. (2008). Virginia Code 54.1-2400.1.

Thompson, A. (1983). *Ethical concerns in psychotherapy and their legal ramifications.* Lanham, MD: University Press of America.

Threat Assessment Team Formation. (2008). Virginia Code 23-31 9.2:3C.

Threat of Violence. (2008). Virginia Code 23-31 9.2:10.

6

Reality Check: Entry into the System

So you have been tasked with putting together a crisis plan by the president of your university, and he or she has given you a strict deadline to get it done. Sounds easy, huh? Well, here comes the hard part—gaining the buy-in of key individuals on campus who believe the issue is critical and important enough to invest their time, energy, and resources into its success. Sure, you are an expert 50 miles away from home, but there are always those individuals on campus who remember every foul-up and dumb decision you have ever made and gleefully hold it against you. As a result, they are not thrilled about the opportunity to work with you and are turned off by the idea of investing their time and effort into a project that presents little possibility for reward and quite possibly a lot of grief.

So what is the solution? You could hire us, or somebody like us, to guide you through the crisis management development process. But we are going to cost you a fair amount of money, which in all honesty could be better spent putting the plan into action. Furthermore, when we get done consulting with you, guess who is still going to be responsible for ensuring things get up and running? That's right—yours truly. So your best bet is to hunker down and direct your own show by employing the principles as outlined in this book.

Of all the topics covered in this book, nothing is more important to your success than gaining entry into the system. If your constituency doesn't buy into what you are about, then the rest of what is in this book can go in the Dumpster. We have already mentioned that administrators are busy administering, professors are busy professoring, students are busy studenting, maintenance people are busy maintenancing, police are busy policing, and everybody is worrying about the economy and trying to keep their jobs. Thus, the last thing on their collective mind is dealing with a campus emergency, since that is clearly somebody else's job. But the fact of the matter is that crisis management and prevention really is everybody's job, as much as a pain in their collective anatomy as it may be. The Justice Department has known for a long time that the best way to abate violence in a community is to get everyone in the community involved in stamping out the nickel-and-dime crimes such as loitering, tagging, graffiti, street garbage, broken windows, abandoned homes, prostitution, gangs, and other petty crimes that beget more violent crimes if left unchecked. If the community allows these low-level crimes to occur because they are too afraid, busy, intimidated, lazy, or unconcerned about their community to get involved, then the potential for bad things to happen to good communities rises exponentially. Now replace the word *community* with *university* or *college,* and you start to understand why we believe there should be a sense of urgency, with every member of the academic community contributing to its safekeeping. Easier said than done, right?

CONSULTING

The way we would propose to gain entry into and buy-in from the system is by using a consulting approach, in which you act as the consultant. To do that, we are going to follow Dougherty's (2009) consultation approach through its entry stage, which has four major components:

- Exploring the organization's needs
- Contracting with the organization
- Physically entering the system
- Psychologically entering the system (p. 53).

However, before any crisis intervention plan can be put into operation, Dougherty (2009) and Brown, Pryzwansky, and Schulte (1991) contend that a number of critical issues need to be addressed. Thus, whether you invite us to start up this program or you do it yourself, the following issues (Caplan, 1970; Cherniss, 1993; Holtz & Zahn 2004; McLean, 2006; Meyers, Parsons, & Martin, 1979; Nicoletti, Spencer-Thomas, & Bollinger, 2001; Stroh & Johnson, 2006) have to be addressed honestly and objectively:

1. *Degree of congruence between the consultant and the consultee system.* In other words, how do your values and beliefs about the issue mesh with the current system? If people do not believe that human-made crisis can be a problem on campus, then you have a sales job ahead of you before you attempt to do anything else.
2. *Skills required to effectively manage the crisis plan development process.* Crisis intervention planning is a complex business. While you are not likely to have the headaches that the Federal Emergency Management Agency (FEMA) director had over Hurricane Katrina, be advised that the responsibility of developing a crisis management plan is not just an add-on to an administrative job. The process demands a combination of the very best of administration, psychology, emergency management, group leadership and facilitation, and policing skills, along with a strong dose of political acumen. Intense training is also required, with Local Emergency Management Agency (LEMA) directors taking countless hours of courses from FEMA every year to stay abreast of issues in the field. There are even undergraduate and graduate majors in emergency management available, so this is also not a job that gets shoved onto a clerk or administrative intern. Thus, one of the very first issues you need to consider is hiring somebody

who can fill the dedicated position of emergency manager. Providing funding for this position in itself demonstrates how much credibility the administration gives to crisis planning.

3. *Amount of resources the university is willing to commit toward change.* In a time of exceedingly sparse and declining funding for both state and private institutions of higher learning, you must determine what resources in the form of personnel, facilities, equipment, time, and administrative priority the system is willing to commit to the crisis management process. A quality crisis management program utilizes all of the aforementioned resources; therefore, any crisis management planner who is asked to skimp in any of these categories is being set up for trouble. We actually believe that no plan is better than an underdeveloped and/or undersourced plan. Such plans can not only hinder the effectiveness of a crisis response but also exacerbate the crisis itself. When dealing with such circumstances, you would most likely be better to turn the whole college program over to the LEMA to administer. Indeed, for many small colleges that lack resources and personnel to carry out a comprehensive intervention program, closely coordinating and creating memoranda of agreement with outside agencies and the local municipalities is probably the best bet of all.

4. *Readiness and motivation of the system to change.* There is a whole field of research in addictions therapy that says until the drug user has contemplated change and becomes motivated to quit, little is likely to happen (Miller & Rollnick, 2002). Likewise, if the constituency in your university isn't ready to change, it is unlikely that it will happen. The job of motivating the constituency to change then falls into someone else's lap—yours. We're not just talking about the custodial staff's motivation; we mean the whole kit and caboodle, from the top administrators on down. Thus, you must consider how much flexibility the administrators have in making preemptive changes and the likelihood of their staffs embracing new directions. It is absolutely critical to ensure that the university president, chancellor, and other top-level administrators demonstrate their support of the crisis plan to all constituents of the university through active participation in the development and implementation process, rather than merely paying lip service to it because of political, public, or media pressure.

5. *Perception of need for the program.* It is almost a given that professors will have very different notions and motivations for either accepting or rejecting any kind of crisis intervention plan that the administration generates. Further, the people actually tasked with providing services on the front lines of any crisis, such as police, maintenance staff, counseling center, and housing personnel, will surely have their own ideas about the logistics, tactics, and strategic planning necessary to make the plan actually work. Thus, soliciting input from and understanding the viewpoints of these various groups is critical to the development of a realistic, effective crisis plan.

6. *Assurance of confidentiality.* Confidentiality is particularly important in crisis planning because of the laws surrounding client/student privacy and individuals with disabilities. Further, in any kind of consultation process, there is a general fear among respondents that talking freely with a change-driven consultant will cost the respondents in terms of job security and administrative disapproval. As a result, any attempt to institute a crisis plan may be met with resistance out of suspicion that what people say will be used against them by the administration or in legal proceedings. Thus, there need to be ironclad guarantees from the administration that what is said by individuals to the planning team stays within the planning team.

7. *Guaranteed protection from legal proceedings.* All involved staff need to be assured that their opinions will be taken seriously and any actions they take in accordance with plan protocols will be nonpunitive. Furthermore, they need to be guaranteed protection from lawsuits and other legal and administrative complaints made against them by disgruntled individuals who maintain they are being persecuted for any numbers of reasons. Although a delicate, sensitive, and mainly unspoken issue, lawsuits by disgruntled employees on the basis of discrimination and harassment are a routine part of doing business for institutional bureaucracies such as universities, state and federal agencies, and the military. As a point in fact, Major Nidal Hasan's extremist religious views and potential for violence were well known before the massacre he perpetrated at Ft. Hood, Texas, on November 5, 2009. Why did his superiors do nothing about it? The answer is simple: fear of being accused of harassment or discrimination. While there certainly are valid complaints of harassment and discrimination, false accusations can end careers, mar reputations, and ruin marriages. Many of the people who are capable of igniting crises are angry, paranoid, hostile, and well versed in accusing others of harassment when their thoughts or actions are called into question. Thus, we cannot emphasize enough the need to broach this subject with key legal and investigative staff early on in the planning process.

8. *Clear understanding of expected outcomes.* It is important to establish the expected outcomes of the crisis planning process in order to help shape the crisis intervention plan and have benchmarks against which to evaluate success. There are several models of plans that will do a good job of primary, secondary, and tertiary intervention, but you must know your end goal in order to select the most appropriate model. Knowing the end goal will also allow you to commit adequate resources to ensure the success of the crisis plan. We recommend that you put together a memorandum of agreement or formal contract detailing the desired outcomes and the contributions all involved parties will make to support the success of the endeavor.

If you take the time to address all of these issues before you proceed, gaining entry into a system shouldn't be a problem.

PRACTICE

A few words about practicing your crisis management plan are needed at this point. There is practice, and there is practice. Reading over the plan and having a discussion during a meeting of high-level administrators is one level of practice. While this type of practice is better than nothing, you will be in a world of trouble if a true crisis presents itself. A true crisis is defined as a complex (Caponigro, 2000), fluid situation in which premium information comes in spurts amid widespread chaos, and no easy solutions exist. To say decision making is difficult under such circumstances is a vast understatement (Fink, 2002). Thus, simply talking about what you will do in the event of a crisis is not sufficient. Instead, you must construct your crisis management plan to mirror the circumstances created by an actual crisis and include full-blown practice exercises. Successful practice of each crisis level means that you are operating as if the crisis is actually occurring. Practice should mimic as closely as possible the feelings, behaviors, and thoughts you would experience during a real crisis. We want to caution you, though, against falling into the trap of using normal operating procedures to complete the practice exercise, since they may not be efficient or effective, especially during the survival stage. The bottom line is that practice allows you to test the effectiveness and reliability of the procedures you laid out in the crisis management plan and assimilate to the role you will play during an actual crisis.

As detailed in Table 6.1, there are several important aspects involved in planning a practice exercise. The selection of the type of exercise generally depends on the budget. A good rule of thumb is the more complex the exercise, the more expensive it is. But remember, you get what you pay for in terms of the quality of the exercise experience. It is also important to note that the higher the complexity of the exercise and the higher the budget, the better prepared the crisis management teams (CMTs) are to respond in the event of a real crisis.

We understand that justifying a budget for a scenario that may never happen can be an uphill battle. This situation is especially true for a crisis that has a low probability of actually occurring but a high rate of impact should it occur (Cornell, 2006). It is unlikely that your campus will experience a tragedy similar in scale to the shootings at Virginia Tech or Northern Illinois University. Yet violent events on university campuses do occur on a regular basis. Carr (2005) reported that approximately 25% of all college students were injured as a result of violence on campus, but only 60% of that number received any treatment for their injuries. According to Carr, weapons of some type (e.g., firearms, knives, clubs) were used in 34% of violent crimes on college campuses.

The most distressing figure is that 8% of men and 1% of women report having a working firearm on campus (Miller, Hemenway, & Wechsler, 2002). According to this research, if your campus has a student population of 10,000, about 900 will have working firearms at any given time. We understand that this number is just an average and your campus may not have as many students carrying firearms. At the same time, though, your campus may actually have more students carrying firearms than the

Table 6.1   Planning Practice Exercises

	Exercise	Drill Exercise	Full Scale Exercise
Define the scope of the exercise	The purpose of the exercise as well as objectives should be explained.	The purpose of the exercise as well as objectives should be explained.	The purpose of the exercise as well as objectives should be explained.
Scenario development	Narrative development.	Narrative development. Recruitment of people to play roles.	Narrative development. Recruitment of people to play roles.
Campus has been informed about the exercise	Not critical for tabletop exercises, unless staff or faculty members will be asked to participate.	Important in order not to cause alarm during the drill. Departments and units in which the drill will occur should be notified that normal operations may be disrupted.	Important in order not to cause alarm during the exercise as well as to allow departments and units to plan for possible disruption to normal operations.
First responders alerted to exercise	Only if the exercise requires input from these groups.	Vital if these groups will be asked to respond during the exercise.	Critical because these groups may be asked to participate in the exercise.
Other groups	Notified on an as-needed basis.	Groups may be alerted to the exercise based on the need for support services.	Groups may be alerted to the exercise based on the need for support services.
Performance evaluation	Procedures should be developed to assess the efficiency and effectiveness of administrators' and CMT's effectiveness. Attention should be given to relevant situational variables.	Procedures should be developed to assess the efficiency and effectiveness of administrators' and CMT's effectiveness. Attention should be given to relevant situational variables.	Procedures should be developed to assess the efficiency and effectiveness of administrators' and CMT's effectiveness. Attention should be given to relevant situational variables.
Plans to review effectiveness of crisis management plan	Time set aside to review plan based on weaknesses identified during exercise.	Time set aside to use evaluation of performance during exercise to revise crisis management plan. Also remainder of plan should be reviewed and revised based on any changes.	Time set aside to use evaluation of performance during exercise to revise crisis management plan.
Review of campus policies	If the crisis management plan is revised, a check of general campus policy should be made in order to avoid conflicts.	If the crisis management plan is revised, a check of general campus policy should be made in order to avoid conflicts.	If the crisis management plan is revised, a check of general campus policy should be made in order to avoid conflicts.

average predicts. The point is that violent acts can occur on your campus, and the potential for those to involve the use of weapons with deadly force is real. You may be damned if you do allocate resources to practice for high-impact but low-probability events, but you may be dead if you don't.

Recent research demonstrating that practice exercises increased the efficacy of groups faced with real-life crises bolsters the case for allocating resources to include complex exercises in crisis management plans (Caponigro, 2000; FEMA, 2006). Specifically, practice sessions better prepare you to engage in the three Cs of the recovery process: communication, coordination, and consultation. These key skills play an integral role in your ability to practice a crisis response across several different levels, each of which adds complexity and expense to the process. We have divided practice exercises into three levels: (a) tabletop, (b) drill, and (c) full scale. Each level has strengths and weaknesses, as well as practical and political reasons to want to use that method to prepare for a crisis. As we have previously stated, careful planning is needed for any exercise if you want to ensure optimal results.

Tabletop Exercise

One of the most time-honored methods of practice involves tabletop exercises, which can be practiced at various levels of complexity. The lowest level of complexity is to present the CMT with a crisis situation and discuss what actions are needed to resolve it. Discussion lasts only 1 to 2 hours and is guided to address the various facets of the situation. We recommend using this level as an orientation to the implementation of crisis management planning for administrators and newly formed CMTs. This level of the tabletop exercise is also useful in establishing an exercise starting point by assessing administrators' and CMTs' abilities to activate appropriate tacit knowledge sets and awareness of relevant situational variables during crisis situations.

The main advantage of tabletop exercises is that they require minimal time, resources, and budget commitment (FEMA, 2006). However, the major disadvantage is that they provide only a superficial test of a crisis management plan because the lifelike chaos that often emerges during a real crisis is missing (FEMA, 2006). Thus, you must be cognizant of the fact that tabletop exercises can deceive you into thinking the plan is effective when, in fact, during a true test, weaknesses may become apparent. These disadvantages can be overcome by introducing new information or changing variables that add to the complexity of the crisis at various points during the exercise. The focus of the discussion should always be on resolving the crisis as efficiently and effectively as possible by continuously asking yourself what communication, coordination, and consultation is needed to rectify the situation.

A way to add to the realistic quality of the exercise is to remove a member of the CMT from the discussion. The reason for this action is that everyone on the first response team may not be available when a crisis occurs. Take, for instance, 9/11, when terrorists launched their attacks on the World Trade Centers and Washington, D.C. The directors of the State Emergency Management Agencies (SEMA) were traveling to attend their annual conference and, therefore, extremely limited in their ability to engage in the response for the first several hours following the attack. Mirroring this situation in a tabletop exercise helps CMTs learn to be flexible and compensate for the absence of other team members. The disadvantage is that more time and therefore money is required.

Drill Exercises

The next level up from tabletop exercises involves drills that require actual field testing of your CMT on a limited basis. At this level, you select a particular department, unit, or building on campus and simulate a crisis by recruiting people to play various roles such as victimizers, victims, parents of victims, staff, faculty members, and so on. This level is much more time consuming and involves a greater number of people, but the advantage is that the practice more closely resembles a real crisis. We strongly encourage you to set aside time for an after-exercise review in order to identify the strengths and weaknesses of the plan.

The drills we are talking about go beyond simply timing how long it takes to evacuate a building. They actually involve walking through the logistics of moving people around and providing for both victims' and volunteers' needs in order to prevent logistical problems. As straightforward as moving resources to where they are needed sounds, the process may not be so easy amid the chaos of a crisis. For example, if victims who are injured are transported off campus, do you make support services available at that location? How do you keep track of where people were taken? What about if a group of students who are friends of the injured go to the hospital—do you make support available to them? If so, how do you get people there? What communication, coordination, and consultation are needed?

This type of practice exercise is limited to specific parts of the campus and/or possibly specific parts of the crisis management plan. For example, you might limit the practice to one building that may be at more risk of a crisis event taking place than others, such as a building housing chemicals that if spilled, could cause injury or even death. Such drills are most relevant in the impact phase, which is when a majority of crisis management plans tend to fall apart, but they can also be constructed for recovery phases.

As you might guess, planning for a drill is more involved than planning for a tabletop exercise since significantly more time and money are needed. The first issue is deciding on an appropriate scenario. This decision should be based on the part of the crisis management plan you want to practice. With respect to issues related to the human impact of a crisis, you might employ strategies to engage individuals who can provide psychological first aid at the locations where victims typically congregate. Another issue related to the realistic quality of the exercise involves securing the participation of first responders such as law enforcement agents, firefighters, and emergency medical personnel. Depending on the nature of the drill, it may be wise to involve other groups, such as local crisis intervention organizations. You will also need to inform university administrators and faculty, as well as the local news media, that a drill will be taking place to ensure that no one interprets the drill as a real crisis, such as happened during the radio broadcast of an adaptation of H. G. Wells's *War of the Worlds* in the 1930s.

Full-Scale Exercise

The final level of practice is the full-scale exercise. Obviously, engaging in a full-scale exercise involves significant time and planning to achieve the desired results. While these types of exercises are difficult to carry out, you can obtain extremely valuable feedback about the effectiveness of your crisis management plan. Conducting an exercise at this level is excellent for testing your plan during the impact and honeymoon phases of the recovery process. However, with a little modification, you can also use these exercises for the remaining three phases (avoidance, reconstruction, and reestablishment) of the recovery process. Once the full-scale exercise is completed, you can extend the exercise. Extending the exercise would involve assuming a specified amount of time has elapsed. You could ask administrators and CMTs to respond to a set of circumstances that evolve because of the passage of time. Extending the exercise in this manner helps to prepare for the fallout of a crisis.

At this level of practice, the entire crisis management plan is tested by developing a mock crisis involving most of the university, if not the entire campus. For example, you might simulate a riot on campus, a shooting incident in which several people were wounded, a hostage situation, a chemical spill, or a pandemic situation. This experience would involve all departments and units affected by the crisis. While the increase in expense and time is a disadvantage of the full-scale exercise, the benefit of getting the best insight into how the crisis management plan works in realistic situations is well worth the expense. Another benefit of the experience is that administrators and CMTs will be able to learn how to effectively work with one another to produce the desired results.

If it is your first time conducting a mock full-scale exercise, you may want to consider using a consultant to guide the experience. A seasoned consultant can not only help you develop and implement the exercise but also guide you through the evaluation and debriefing process. It is important to note that the debriefing process should focus on learning from weaknesses or mistakes, rather than placing blaming on individuals (Fink, 2002; Mitroff, 2004). A consultant can also make recommendations with respect to revisions that are needed in your crisis management plan. Depending on the consultant, he or she will probably want to conduct a preliminary review of the existing crisis management plan to identify strengths and weakness, as well as talk with several people on campus in order to identify perceived readiness and vulnerability to various crises. This information will allow the consultant to construct an exercise that will provide insight into necessary revisions to your plan.

CASE STUDY: CENTRAL UNIVERSITY

The following example is a worst-case scenario. Certainly, worst cases are the exception rather than the rule. The scenario highlights some of the common problems you are going to face in any crisis. Throughout each stage of the recovery process, we demonstrate the use of the eight-step model to develop well-thought-out and practical interventions. Undoubtedly, as with all ecosystemic or metastasizing crises, you may encounter other problems on your campus, but it will give you a pretty good yardstick to measure your responses and a general blueprint to follow.

The Appendix describes a crisis that took place at Central University, a campus of about 12,000 students. Five thousand of those are undergraduates, and the rest are enrolled in the graduate schools. Central University has a rich tradition and was established more than 100 years ago. The university enjoys a good relationship with the surrounding community and provides services throughout the area. About 600 full-time tenured or tenure track and 250 full-time one-year contract faculty are employed at the university. Approximately 850 support staff are employed by the university. The university offers a wide range of majors in five different colleges and schools: Liberal Arts and Sciences, College of Health Sciences, School of Education, Business School, and School of Leadership Adult Students (SLAS). In addition, Central University offers courses at two off-campus locations in nearby cities, as well as an extensive study-abroad program in Europe. These programs are currently growing at a fast pace and have outpaced the resources allotted to them.

About half of the undergraduate students and about 1,000 graduate students live on campus in several residence halls, none of which are higher than eight stories tall. The campus is located on the outskirts of a medium-size city. Student life offers a full range of activities, including intramurals held at the campus recreation center, concerts, movie nights, and dances sponsored by organizations housed at the university. Outside groups also are allowed to use campus facilities for a cost, providing no university events have been scheduled. The university fields several intercollegiate teams, and athletics have become an important part of university life. Two teams, the women's volleyball and men's basketball teams, have received national attention in recent years. This recognition has generated significant alumni support and increased the number of applications for admission. Academically, several departments in the College of Health Sciences and School of Education have received national recognition for being innovative. The innovations involve developing programs that have greatly benefited the surrounding community and have been recognized nationally as a model for other universities. The School of Business is also set to break into the national limelight because of the quality of its graduate programs. Graduates of these programs are being regularly hired by Fortune 500 businesses. Central University developed a crisis management plan 2 years prior to the crisis event. Up to this time, the crisis management plan had not been used, nor had the CMT ever met, except for once a year for a regular meeting mandated by its charge.

The CMT has 10 members. The leader of the team is the Emergency Management Preparedness Director Jason Mathews. He has been with the university for a little less than 2 years. The Provost/Academic Vice President Dr. Frazer has been at the university for 15 years but has served in her current position for only 2 years. Dr. Cliff Jones, the vice president of student life, came to the university a little over a year ago. The chief financial officer and vice president for business affairs is Mr. Bryce, who began his position a few months prior to the accident. Mr. Demetrius Keith has been the university counsel for 18 years and also serves on the CMT. The director of information service, Mr. Chon Lee, is also on the CMT. He has been at the university for about 3 years. Dr. Shelby has been the director of residence life for 8 years and is part of the CMT. Mr. Jerome Smith, who has been the facilities director for 25 years, is also part of the CMT, as is Captain Smith, head of the campus police for 24 years. The final member of the CMT is Roman Nouri who has been serving as director of information technology for 7 years. Dr. Eileen Richardson, liaison for President Tolliver, serves as an ex-officio member of the CMT and attends all the meetings.

SUMMARY

One of the problems of gaining entry into the system is the uphill battle. Part of the issue is that everyone agrees about the need for being prepared. We would dare to say that everyone on campus believes the university should be prepared to handle a crisis. No one in their right mind would disagree. The problem lies in getting the right person(s) or group(s) to take ownership of not just the need, but to commit resources to that end. Perseverance and patience is needed to obtain commitment, which hopefully will not come too late. Too often, universities wait until after a crisis to recognize the need for a comprehensive crisis management plan. Elements needed for this plan are described in the remainder of this book. This chapter should give you some ideas about how to make your case and get others to jump on the wagon with you.

REFERENCES

Brown, D., Pryzwansky, W. B., & Schulte, A. C. (1991). *Psychological consultation: Introduction to theory and practice* (2nd ed.). Needham Heights, MA: Allyn & Bacon.

Caplan, G. (1970). *The theory and practice of mental health consultation.* New York: Basic Books.

Caponigro, J. R. (2000). *The crisis counselor: A step-by-step guide to managing a business crisis.* Chicago: Contemporary Books.

Carr, J. L. (2005). *American College Health Association campus violence white paper.* Baltimore College Health Association.

Cherniss, C. (1993). Pre-entry issues revisited. In R. T. Golembiewski (Ed.), *Handbook of organizational consultation* (pp. 113–228). New York: Marcel Dekker.

Cornell, D. G. (2006). *School violence: Facts versus fears.* Mahwah, NJ: Lawrence Erlbaum Associates.

Dougherty, A. M. (2009). *Psychological consultation and collaboration in school and community settings* (5th ed.). Belmont, CA: Brooks/Cole–Cengage Learning.

FEMA. (2006). *Emergency planning.* Emmitsburg, MD: Emergency Management Institute.

Fink, S. (2002). *Crisis management: Planning for the inevitable.* Lincoln, NE: iUniverse.

Holtz, H., & Zahn, D. (2004). *How to succeed as an independent consultant* (4th ed.). Hoboken, NJ: John Wiley & Sons.

McLean, G. N. (2006). *Organizational development.* San Francisco, CA: Berrett-Koehler.

Meyers, J., Parsons, R. D., & Martin, R. (1979). *Mental health consultation in the schools.* San Francisco: Jossey-Bass.

Miller, M., Hemenway, D., & Wechsler, H. (2002). Guns and threats at college. *Journal of American College Health, 51,* 57–65.

Miller, W. R., & Rollnick, S. (2002). *Motivational interviewing* (2nd ed.). New York: Guilford Press.

Mitroff, I. I. (2004). *Crisis leadership: Planning for the unthinkable.* Hoboken, NJ: John Wiley & Sons.

Nicoletti, J., Spencer-Thomas, S., & Bollinger, C. (2001). *Violence goes to college.* Springfield, IL: Charles C Thomas.

Stroh, L. K., & Johnson, H. H. (2006). *The basic principles of effective consulting.* Mahwah, NJ: Erlbaum.

Appendix
Case Study: Crisis at Central University

EMERGENCY AND HONEYMOON PHASES: THE EXPLOSION

The crisis involves an explosion in the building housing the Departments of Biology, Chemistry, and Physics. The explosion happened without warning at 2:35 on a Tuesday afternoon late in the fall term. The class period had just ended 5 minutes before the explosion, which was powerful enough to break windows in buildings within 400 yards of the science building. Glass and bricks flew everywhere. Nine students, one staff member, and two faculty members lost their lives in the explosion, and several others died from injuries sustained because of the explosion. Numerous others students were hurt by the flying debris. One student was severely injured when a piece of glass partially severed her leg. Fortunately, several students and a staff member reacted quickly to stop the bleeding and probably saved her life. Hundreds of students saw this happen. People were running and screaming; many students became sick at the sight of a person whose armed was severed. The fire caused by the explosion also injured students, staff, and faculty members caught in the building at the time of the explosion. Hundreds of people witnessed a person on fire running from the building and screaming. Chaos reigned, with everyone running around.

Someone called 911, and first responders including emergency medical technicians, law enforcement, and firefighters were quick to respond. First responders were quick to provide medical assistance to the people who were injured. A perimeter was set up very quickly because of the amount of smoke from the explosion and the fire that resulted. The fear was that because the explosion happened in a science building, chemicals were burning that may let off toxic gases.

Many students and faculty members were transported to several local hospitals, some for minor cuts and bruises, and several for life-threatening injuries. After getting to the hospital, three more people died. Five people were almost immediately transported by helicopter to a neighboring city with a burn unit. The minor injuries included cuts, broken bones, and first- and second-degree burns.

Many people on campus complained of shortness of breath, watering eyes, and nausea. Because of the fear that toxic gases were causing these symptoms, some of these people were transported to the local hospital, but most were simply told to see their primary care physician if the symptoms did not go away in 24 hours.

Within 48 hours after the explosion, several rumors began circulating that someone had set the explosion. One of the rumors attributed the explosion to a graduate student who had threatened a professor because his graduate assistantship had not been renewed. The word around campus was that he had said he would make the professor sorry. Another rumor credited the explosion to an environmental group that had been protesting at several universities in the state. The reason for the protests was not clear, but probably the group thought it criminal that animals were being experimented on. A third rumor alleged the explosion had to do with someone making drugs to be sold and that a street gang had set it off. A final rumor supposed the explosion was set off by a terrorist group because the university had a grant from the Department of Defense.

AVOIDANCE PHASE: THE CLEANUP (OR COVER-UP, SOME WOULD SAY)

Three months have passed since the explosion in the science building. In the weeks following the explosion, an extensive investigation was carried out to determine the cause. The investigation found that the explosion was intentionally set. No group claimed responsibility. This has led to much speculation about who actually set off the explosion. The two most popular rumors seem to be that it was gang related and about drugs or that a disgruntled student caused the explosion, but there was no clear evidence. The most pressing concern at this time is the speculation that the lack of building maintenance contributed heavily to the amount of destruction.

The doggedness of the rumors is taking its toll around campus. To make matters worse, media attention and community support have faded to almost nothing. The grim reality of the recovery process is beginning to come into focus as the administration and CMT try to restore the campus to a precrisis level of functioning. The prolonged impact on students, staff, and faculty members continues to remain on the surface as the campus struggles to right itself and reestablish some semblance of normality.

A grassroots movement has been growing in the 3 months to tighten security for all campus buildings. The debate over the issue has spilled into many aspects of campus life. As with all debates, there seem to be three basic stances. One group wants security significantly tightened. Their argument is that the person or persons responsible have not been caught so it could happen again. A second group wants to leave things the way they have been and argue lightning does not strike the same place twice. The third group falls somewhere in the middle, seeing the need for better security but also recognizing the value of maintaining an open campus. The community is weighing in on this debate and offering to provide a neighborhood watch group to help keep the campus safe.

Six months after the explosion, the crisis has crept into unforeseen aspects of campus life. There is still no definitive answer to who set the explosion or even how the explosion was set. Admissions is being blamed by some people for having admitted gang members to the school, when these students were obviously not qualified. Pressure is mounting to form a faculty oversight committee that could deny admission to anyone with the slightest hint of a gang affiliation. Some staff and faculty members have been boisterous about calling for a dress code to forbid any semblance of gang-related apparel on campus. This issue has found its way to the local media, stirring up students and parents alike. The national media picked up the story, resulting in many inquiries from several civil rights groups as well as comments from celebrities.

RECONSTRUCTION AND REESTABLISHMENT PHASES: LIFE GOES ON BUT NOT THE SAME

Ten months after the explosion, fall-term classes are beginning at Central University. The science building has been cleaned up, but the scars from the explosion are still visible. Over the summer, law enforcement officials concluded the explosion was deliberately set, but no one was charged. Speculation is that one or more of the people who died may have set off the explosion. The investigation also found that the deteriorating condition of the building probably contributed to the deaths of at least two of the victims. An updated sprinkler system and better storage of hazardous substances could have prevented many of the injuries. The investigation into the cause is ongoing.

New policies have been put in place requiring students to swipe into certain buildings at specific times during the day. Two additional campus police have been hired. It is rumored that another campus police officer has been hired but that person is undercover. Other changes to help with security include a requirement that students, staff, faculty members, and administrators must have their ID visible at the end of a lanyard whenever they are on campus. Part of the reason for this policy is so that everyone can swipe into buildings and sometimes various parts of buildings.

An emotional speech at the matriculation ceremony held at the beginning of the term called on everyone to remember the students, staff, and faculty members who lost their lives in the explosion. Also mentioned were the people who were injured, some of whom are still recovering. During the ceremony, a loud murmuring could be heard because some people were offended, knowing that possibly one or more of the people killed were responsible for the explosion. Immediately after the ceremony, a spontaneous protest erupted against honoring the people who caused the deaths of so many friends.

The explosion and cleanup resulted in budgetary changes that are directly impacting several departments. One of the departments is the College of Health Sciences. Several well-known faculty members in that department have been very vocal, stating their displeasure that the ability to maintain their work is being severely hampered by the shifts in the budget and lack of space. The lack of space is because the departments housed in the science building have been given temporary quarters in the College of Health Sciences. Although the disgruntled express sympathy for the victims and state they recognize the need to help out, their work is critical if the university is to continue moving forward and receiving federal grants. Rumbles of discontent are beginning to surface from faculty members in the Departments of Biology, Chemistry, and Physics because they are feeling like second-class citizens. Rumors are also appearing that the move may become permanent as the university tries to cut its budget.

7

What You See Is What You Get . . . or Maybe Not: Assessment of the System

$\mathbf{W}$e understand that *assessment* is probably a four-letter word to many of you. You might be saying, "You want us to do what? I don't have the time." We understand time is a commodity that is precious. Because time is so valuable, we introduce you to a method for assessment that will save you time. This assessment is different from the types you do to complete reports for accrediting organizations or to justify programs for governing bodies. Assessment in crisis situations is designed to help you target resources to specific needs on campus. You avoid missteps and ultimately shorten recovery from the crisis. The case study involving Central University introduced earlier is used as an example throughout this chapter. Being aware of and having a plan to monitor the collective reactions across the campus is critical in each phase of the recovery process. Also in this chapter, we include information on practical issues such as the timing of assessment, who to assess in this process, and methods to conduct the assessment. Finally, we have recommendations about who should be involved in the assessment process.

The Office of Institutional Research is the first place to begin assessments that will help you understand the changes on a university campus following a crisis. Reinterpretation of this data is likely to be needed to apply it in a crisis situation. The reinterpretation of data would involve examining data through the lens of the crisis recovery process and attending to the characteristics described later in this chapter. We encourage you to consider augmenting this information with assessments specially designed to appraise organizational characteristics impacted by crises. Not using specific methods designed to look at collective reactions of the campus can prolong and possibly sabotage efforts by administration and crisis management teams (CMTs). These assessments help administrators and CMTs use resources in an efficient and effective way.

Assessment of the collective impact of a crisis should not and cannot be lost in the wake of helping individuals. Obviously, the first action should be to give medical attention to anyone in need (Fink, 2002; Mitroff & Anagnos, 2001). These actions are not only appropriate but the caring and humanitarian course of action. However, after the situation stabilizes, focus should turn to the well-being of the entire campus.

Even if very few students, faculty, and/or staff are involved, a crisis sends ripple effects throughout the university (Braverman, 1999; Mitroff, Diamond, & Alpasian, 2006; Tol, Jordans, Reis, & de Jong, 2009). In any organization, a crisis is not isolated to the unit in which it takes place (Mitroff & Anagnos, 2001; Myer & Moore, 2006; Pollard & Hotho, 2006). A disruptive student who physically assaults a staff member who is hospitalized can affect the entire campus. This incident might be a catalyst for demands from other employees for changes in policies regarding interactions with disruptive students. Staff and faculty members might demand assurances of being protected should a student become aggressive, believing they may get hurt. Also, they might ask for indemnification if they have to physically restrain someone. The faculty senate may join the fray, and unions may begin making noises that drastic changes are needed in workplace safety. Parents may become involved and want to know what is being done to safeguard their sons and daughters. A common demand by parents is that procedures be implemented to monitor every entrance to the campus to guarantee the safety of their sons and daughters. The surrounding community and news media could also begin asking questions as to why something happened and what is being done to prevent similar situations in the future.

Accurate up-to-date information is one approach to salve the concerns of these people and groups. Although administrators and CMTs may have some ideas about what is needed to improve the situation, they may have little to no information upon which to base their perceptions. Essential issues related to the crisis must be identified and acted on to facilitate the recovery process (Paton, Smith, & Violanti, 2000). Resources must be guided to areas in which they will be useful. Time cannot be wasted dispersing limited resources to areas where they will have little to no effect. Obtaining this information is best done by systematic assessment of organizational reactions to the crisis (Myer, Conte, & Peterson, 2007).

CHRONOSYSTEM SYSTEM

Understanding the life cycle of a crisis is critical in the assessment process. We have adapted the chronosystem system described by James (2008) by shifting the emphasis from stages of crisis to phases of recovery. (See Figure 7.1.) This shift is made to accommodate our focus on the recovery process rather than describe a crisis. The time frame associated with each phase of recovery is approximate. Too many factors influence the recovery process (e.g., the loss of lives, physical injuries, buildings destroyed, the number of people directly witnessing the event, resources available, experience with a specific crisis) for any exact timeline to be set. In addition, the recovery process is not a continuous unbroken progression to precrisis levels of functioning. Again, many factors will impact progress in recovery. You may experience starts and stops along the way. The campus may reach a plateau where recovery seems completely stalled for an extended period. Being aware of this possibility helps you avoid frustration throughout the entire recovery process.

Although each crisis generates its own set of issues for each phase of recovery, there are some concerns commonly encountered during each phase of recovery. These concerns are listed in Table 7.1. Be aware that this list is not exhaustive. However, attention to these issues can promote more efficient and effective recovery process.

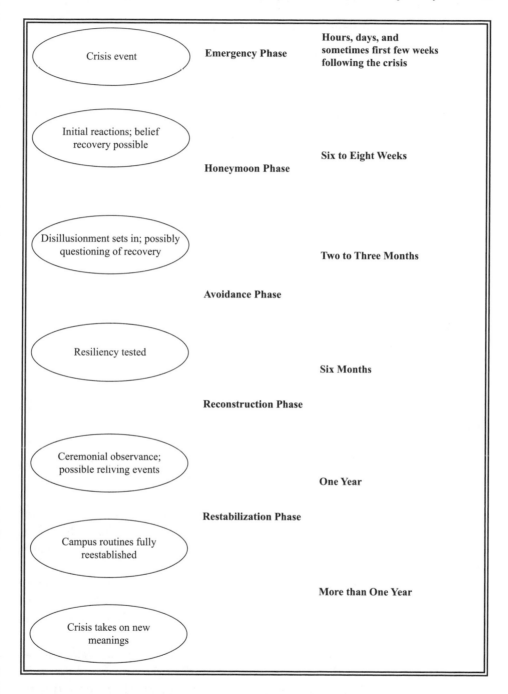

Figure 7.1 Chronosystem
Source: Adapted from James 2008.

Table 7.1   Common Concerns for Each Phase of Recovery

Impact Phase	1. Physical safety
	2. Psychological first aid
Honeymoon Phase	1. Shelter for anyone displaced by the crisis
	2. Shelter for volunteers
	3. Needs of the stakeholders
	4. Pop-up crises
Avoidance Phase	1. Continued monitoring of systemwide characteristics
	2. Belief the recovery process ends at the honeymoon stage
Reconstruction Phase	1. The need to switch from a pathogenic to a salutogenic approach
	2. Maintaining focus on communication, coordination, consultation
	3. Groupthink and tunnel vision
	4. Pop-up crises
Reestablishment Phase	1. Failure to institutionalize revision to policies and procedures
	2. Pockets of resistance

Emergency Phase

In the emergency phase, the awareness and experience of the crisis are acute. This phase takes place during the first hours or days and may sometimes extend into the first few weeks following a crisis. Often university crisis management plans are limited to this portion of the crisis (Mitroff et al., 2006). In the impact phase, there is little time to think. People simply react. A sense of emergency saturates the campus (James, 2008). Physical safety is often at risk at this time. The goal is to ensure everyone on campus is safe (Mitroff & Anagnos, 2001). Decisions must be made on the spot, much of the time without benefit of verifiable information. The furthest thing from the minds of administrators or CMTs is conducting a campuswide assessment in these first few hours. They simply want everyone to be safe and act accordingly. Many universities have emergency notification systems to speed communication during the initial minutes and hours of a crisis. While these systems are an excellent beginning point, much more is needed for campuses to be fully capable of responding to and recovering from a crisis.

Assessment in this phase of the recovery primarily involves gathering data from two sources. First, information should be obtained from anyone directly affected by a crisis. Every effort should be made to allow anyone, especially people in close proximity to the crisis, to provide information. Initially, this information is the best possible data to act on. Based on these reports, resources can be moved to where they are most needed. The second source of data is people who have the closest contact with anyone who might be experiencing problems caused by the tragedy. This group is in a unique position to pass along invaluable data to administrators and CMTs. Data from this group can be used to increase the understanding of the overall impact of the crisis across the campus. Generally speaking, such data are collected by talking with these people.

The key issue in this phase of recovery is the extreme fluidity of the situation. Drastic changes with respect to who needs support and where the support is needed occur on an hour-to-hour and day-to-day basis. Assessment in this phase may be ignored or done so quickly that the information is incomplete at best. At this moment, development of an assessment procedure is too time consuming, given the immediacy of the needs. We agree. The hours and days immediately following a crisis are not the time to create assessment procedures. Therefore, having an assessment plan in place prior to the crisis is important to collect reliable data. Assessment in this phase should be conducted to obtain data so that resources can be channeled to where they are most needed at that moment. Typically, this information will focus on ensuring physical and psychological health in the short term for anyone affected by the crisis. Part of this assessment should include reviewing the resources on campus and in the community that are available to give whatever support is needed. The following dialogue represents meetings in the first few hours after the explosion at Central University. The situation is fluid, making accurate information difficult to obtain. Obviously, the physical and mental health of everyone involved, both directly and indirectly, is important. As you read through the dialogue, watch the way the CMT tries to gather information needed to give initial support to students, staff, and faculty members directly affected by the explosion. The scenario is pretty typical of immediate postevent operations of a CMT. Chances are that some members of the CMT may be injured or unable to reach the emergency management center; therefore, having cross-trained people to serve as backup is a good idea. Note the way the team functions, even though all the members of the team are not able to participate in the meeting. Given the possibility that the original command center may be inoperable, a backup command center geographically distant from the original needs to be ready. A word of caution is called for. As in any crisis situation, politically correct language is not always used. Some of the language may be colorful as the CMT works to coordinate resources to give help to those in need.

The scenario: D-day 30 minutes after the explosion. The basement of the field house, approximately half a mile from the science building. The original CMT site in the administration building is not usable, with windows blown out and communications out.

Jason Mathews (Emergency Management Preparedness [EMP] Director) (With bandages on forehead and right arm from pieces of flying glass, speaking to the assembled CMT): My secretary, LaTonya Brown, has run the roll and we have these people unaccounted for: Lisa Frayser (provost), Eloise Smith (media), and Leslie Unseld (nurse practitioner). Does anyone know where these people are? They don't answer cell or landlines.

Don Smith (Police Chief): I saw Leslie working with the medics when I came in. There are a lot of people under shade trees in the quadrangle, because there is no place to put them. Lisa and Eloise were on the side of the administration building where the windows got blown out. We have a number of hurt people in there. Calls are pouring into 911, so we don't have a real good idea of how many or where they are.

EMP Director Mathews: Okay, we are going to need to get backup for them. What do we know about the science building and the people in it, Don?

Chief Smith: There was some sort of major explosion in the left wing. All the buildings facing it, administration, physical plant and planning, fine arts, and the old gym complex, were damaged, mainly from flying bricks and blown-out glass. The science building is on fire, and the left wing is a complete wreck. Central City Engine 2 is laying hose, but given where it is, it's a long run. The battalion chief immediately called in an extra alarm, and the other engine, snorkel, and ladder companies are on the way. He told me that we are going to need more than that to keep other buildings from getting involved. I have no idea what is going on with the people, it's too early to say. It's chaos right now. We have dozens of people laid out on the quadrangle. Some look pretty bad from what I can see.

EMP Director Mathews: Okay, I called Lester Kline (LEMA Director for Central City), and he is aware of the situation. This is the worst thing I have ever seen. We are going to need lots of help and in a hurry. I'll call him back and get him down here. We are going to need medical units and more fire units. What about police?

Chief Smith: All off-duty officers are being called in. We are probably going to need help from Central PD before news of this spreads.

EMP Director Mathews: What about communications? Raman and Chon?

Raman Nouri (Director of Information Technology): The main server is out from the explosion . . . oh yes, I think two technicians have been injured from window glass and shrapnel from the science building, but I am not sure. E-mail is down, so we can't send or receive messages. I don't know when it will be up and running. That depends a lot on when they get the fire in the science building under control. I think I heard something about it being hot and dangerous to get in there right now. Oh yes, a cell tower that was behind the science building is not working and our pickup for cell phones isn't working. (Shakes head.) Nor are the majority of landlines because the major trunk line went through the science building. We are pretty much screwed electronically. Police two-way radio and walkie-talkies are our means of communication on campus. We might be able to get through with some cell phone service, but the lines are jammed . . . damn students clogging the lines.

Chon Lee (Director of Information Services): We attempted to set our emergency communications in operations 10 minutes ago. But I don't think we were successful. Given what Raman said . . . maybe some twitters, but I just don't know. We are working to get communication links here and a briefing room for the press, parents, and students.

The EMP director's primary concern is with human safety and secondarily with building integrity. Critical to any recovery are communication systems. One of the hardest lessons learned in Hurricane Katrina is that when communication systems break down or are not compatible, rescue and recovery coordination becomes exponentially more difficult. Without reliable communications systems, implementing and coordinating different units will be chaotic. The EMP director is going to have to coordinate a lot of different units, and he is going to have to do that both horizontally (within the university system) and vertically (outside the university) with the local emergency management agency (LEMA) and the state emergency management agency (SEMA).

D-day 1 hour and 45 minutes after the explosion. Basement of the field house approximately half a mile from the science building.

EMP Director Mathews: Some of you may not know Lester Kline, Central City and Hall County LEMA director. What can you give us, Lester?

LEMA Director Kline: I have talked with Fire Chief O'Bannion. He doesn't think there will be any help for the science building. It is old and has natural convection systems for the fire that now have the center of the building and the right wing involved. Sorry to say the building is going to be a complete loss.

EMP Director Mathews: What about search and rescue? Hell, there may be people trapped in there.

LEMA Director Kline: (Sighs.) Two teams are in the right wing as we speak. They have gotten some people out. The left wing is fully involved, and the center hall will be soon. We can't put people in there, and Chief O'Bannion tells me they are going to have to work fast because the right wing is going up, too. They said that efforts and resources will concentrate on the adjacent buildings to save them. (Shakes head.) Pumper units are coming from O'Fallon, Griswold, and Clarendon, and another snorkel unit and ladder truck from Hazelton Air Force Base. Those trucks should be getting here within the next hour. But there is a problem. We need a dozer to knock down the concrete pylons so they can come across the parking lot and onto the quadrangle. We have to get access closer to the science building to do anything. We are laying hose too far, and it takes too long to get emergency vehicles in there for both the fire and the wounded. We are carrying people out on stretchers. About 300 yards to Walker Avenue, and that has got to change. Shit, who designed this place? Hall County Hospital is not going to be able to take care of all these people, so I have notified the SEMA director, and he has sent bulletins to other area hospitals to expect people and they are getting ready. So our first priority is to get open access to the area.

Information Services Director Lee: Our student community emergency response teams (CERTs) can probably act in some communication capacity as runners. They know a good bit about the system from their training. Right now, Leslie has them helping out on the quadrangle with the wounded.

Jerome Kelly (Director of Facilities): We also have them in the other buildings with our custodians going room by room looking for people.

EMP Director Mathews: Lester, what do we have in the way of assets for wounded and hurt people? Right now, I am aware of one nurse practitioner and one nurse and the student health center secretary out on the quadrangle with all kinds of wounded people out there.

LEMA Director Kline: I also have eight EMT units and their vehicles coming from those towns. Hazelton Air Force Base is sending a MASH unit and an EMT unit. I am in police radio communication with Dr. Overton, head of ER at Hall County Hospital. They are moving things around there and getting staff in to set up operations here. They said to triage people right here and move ones that are in bad shape and need emergency surgery to Hall immediately. Dr. Overton is going to send over an ER intern to help triage, but by the looks of things, the nurse practitioner is doing a good job. Any one not in immediate danger we'll transport to area hospitals. But some of the burn and blast victims are going to need to be medevaced to the area trauma center and burn units in Columbus, so we need to get a helipad set up pretty close to the triage area on the quad. This is going to become a busy place in a hurry. Not to mention the news media and the parents. Chief Smith, where do you stand on security?

Chief Smith: We will most definitely need help, and I think more than what Central PD can give. We may need a National Guard unit.

EMP Director Mathews: We have some severe communications problems right now. As you can see, this is our backup site. How do you think we can do that?

LEMA Director Kline: There is a Red Cross mobile communications center in Columbus. We can probably have it here and set up in 6 hours. If we can get lines into it, you should be okay.

EMP Director Mathews: Yes, media and parents. Is there any word on Eloise Smith?

Chief Smith: As of this minute, no.

EMP Director Mathews: Chon, you are the backup for Eloise. You need to get a prepared statement together. I understand that both Eileen, the president's liaison, and the president got cut up some with the flying glass, but both are okay, and they are out on the quadrangle right now. As soon as possible, I think the president needs to sit down and work out some prepared statements with you. If you can, run it by legal.

D-day 5 hours and 30 minutes after the explosion. Basement of the field house.

EMP Director Mathews: Jerome, it's getting dark. How are we for lighting, and how's access to the quadrangle?

Facilities Director Kelly: We have portable generators and lights up. The fire department has the fire knocked down and keeping water on it for the time being. Cinders started a couple of fires in administration when they blew through the blown-out windows, but they are out also and didn't cause a lot of damage. The barriers and posts are cleared. We are using the south end of the quadrangle as a heliport. They have transported five people to the trauma unit in Columbus and taken about a dozen people to other area hospitals. So far, we confirm that two students are dead that were outside the building and killed by shrapnel wounds and the explosion. As far as we know, 40 students, 5 faculty members, and a custodian cannot be accounted for. (Shakes head.) We do not know whether they are alive and somewhere else or died in the explosion and fire. The science building is gone. The fire chief says it won't be until later on tomorrow or the next day that they can start sorting through the rubble to look for bodies and try to determine the cause of the explosion. Chief O'Bannion says it was clearly an explosion that came from inside the left wing of the building. Probably from the basement the way the blast debris are laid out. He called the state fire marshal, and someone told me an arson team is coming from Columbus—and maybe the state bureau of investigation as well and the federal ATF. Anyway, he thinks something is up with the explosion. I heard out on the quad some rumors floating around, but they sounded pretty asinine. What if the FBI comes?

Information Services Director Lee: Eloise and I have talked about that. We need to check those out before the rumor mill gets going too good.

EPM Director Mathews: (Calling Leslie Unseld on walkie-talkie) Leslie, what's our injury status?

Nurse Practitioner Unseld: (reporting from quadrangle triage site) At this point in time, we have treated over 250 people. About 150 have been taken to various hospitals either by ambulance or medevac copter. We don't have an absolute count, but there are at least 75 people who are going to stay overnight for observation, but the count is sketchy since communication is spotty. We can use some student or faculty volunteers, maybe the CERT kids. We need to start getting information sheets set up and a clear list of casualties. We are still clearing injured people, but most of them are under cover now. We really can't give anybody anything definite yet. I mean this is a war zone. The MASH tent looks like something from TV, and one of the MDs in there said it looks like Iraq. If a call hasn't gone out for blood, it needs to happen. We have gone through a lot of it here, and I am sure the hospitals are going to run short.

EMP Director Mathews: We understand that Provost Frazer was seriously injured by shrapnel and is in ICU at Hall County.

Nurse Practitioner Unseld: That is right. Also, Eloise Smith was medevaced to Columbus with severe shrapnel wounds. She was critical when she left here.

EPM Director Mathews: Okay, Leslie, we'll get some help to you when we can, and get the call for blood out. Hang in there, you are doing a great job. (Turning to CMT.) After that initial statement by President Tolliver about an explosion of unknown origin, we have a swarm of people wanting information. The media has got national news coverage on this with all kinds of reporters running around trying to dig stuff up. We also are getting lots of frightened parents showing up and driving in from other towns. Why can't they just stay put? That is creating traffic problems and is hindering our operation, while state police are steering them away, but we have had some parents get extremely agitated. We have to figure out some place for them to park and gather. Parent calls are clogging up the phones, and they are now overwhelming Hall County 911. We need to get a handle on the media and get a message out to parents, relatives, faculty, and students about casualties, classes, what we are doing, and the need for parents to be patient and let us do our job and get students, faculty, and staff sorted out.

Information Services Director Lee: I have a press conference scheduled in an hour and a half at 9 p.m. Do you want me to move it up?

EMP Director Mathews: I think so, good idea. We need to get parents calmed down and off the lines and the streets. Chief Smith, can you and Cliff Jones [Vice President for Student Life] and Dave Shelby [Director of Residence Life] figure out a place to get students connected to parents?

Residence Life VP Jones: I think so. What if we tell them to move to the stadium lots? That's south of the school, and we can handle traffic there better. Any students in the residence halls can walk down there and meet them.

Chief Smith: Yes, that will work. Dave, if we get some RAs down there, we can walkie-talkie parents' names back to the residence halls and notify students to go down to the particular lot their folks are on. We could also let them in the south stands of the stadium and open up the portable food kiosk down there. They'd have restrooms, and we could brief them in the south end zone stands.

Edward Bryce (Chief Financial Officer [CFO] and Vice President of Business Affairs): Speaking of food, can we get some in here and some water, too. I haven't had anything to eat since noon. (Nods of agreement.)

EMP Director Mathews: Sorry about that. I had intended to get Jeremy Lions, the director for food service, on board. Chief, while they are getting the kiosk up, call the university union and see if we can get some hot packs and sandwiches and drinks down here.

EMP Director Mathews: (speaking to CMT) We are going to have to make some decision about classes tomorrow, Eileen, so I guess it's on your shoulders and the president's. You need to get that straightened out with Chon Lee before he goes on the air. So for right now, Chon, you're our go-to guy on media. You okay with that?

Information Services Director (and now Media Liaison) Lee: I guess I don't have much of a choice. I'm not with network news, but I'll handle it. Okay, we need to get going on classes, Eileen. What's President Tolliver want?

Eileen Richardson (Liaison to President): She wants to see Ed Bryce, Jerome Kelly, and Raman Nouri at 9 tonight and get a status report and then start making some decisions. She needs to appoint an acting provost. I think it is going to be me by the way she is talking. She'll have a statement for the press at 9:30, so Chon can say that at his briefing.

EMP Director Mathews: (Speaking to Leslie Holland, Director of the Counseling Center) It goes without saying we are going to have a lot of psychologically traumatized people. Where are you with this?

Counseling Center Director Holland: One hour ago, I put calls out to Hall Mental Health center and the mental health centers in the towns with hospitals that have our people. They will take care of our folks in the hospital. We have a memorandum of understanding with Hall Mental Health for mutual provision of services and an emergency plan we drew up with them that's modeled after Virginia Tech's. They will make contact with our hospitalized people and their families. We still don't exactly know who is where, but we have modeled Virginia Tech's electronic record system, so everybody we talk to is getting triaged on the TASSLE [see Chapter 9] and a DSM [*Diagnostic and Statistical Manual of Mental Disorders* of the American Psychiatric Association] evaluation the minute we finish with a first contact. All of our folks have laptops, and as soon as we get information systems back up, we can get that information downloaded and collated with our client list and check for students who might go hot on us. The other local mental health systems are interlocked with Hall County, and they in turn will feed us information. I have put Dr. Anseld Thorenson in charge of that coordination effort, and Imogene Crystal, the career counseling unit secretary, is now the direct receiver of that information. We are also assigning two graduate assistants and one of the interns to Anseld. The rest of the staff are going to be working in teams in the residence halls and for walk-ins in the center. Chon, that is information we need to get out with your briefing. We are also going to have some big-time grief and loss issues. Not just people who had friends killed or injured. This may seem insignificant, but it won't be to the people affected by it. It is my understanding that a number of doctoral students and professors tried to go back into the science building to get their research data. A lot of dissertations, master's theses, and research projects went up in smoke, too. I also sent a call out to the state college crisis consortium. Shawn Touhy at Upstate University is in charge of that, and he is assembling 20 counselors and psychologists to come here as soon as we have places for them.

LEMA Director Kline: Do you want me to call the Red Cross and get their calls out for mental health teams?

Counseling Center Director Holland: Not yet. Let's see how this goes. I don't want too many chickens running around here, and we wind up looking like we all have our heads cut off and don't know what we're doing and, worse yet, aggravate the situation by missing people who need our help. I want to be methodical about it, and I don't want to call up more than what we can handle logistically. We also are preparing some psych educational material on peritraumatic, acute stress and PTSD. We'll get that out through the fraternities, sororities, and residence halls face to face and put it out on the Net. We can follow up with clubs and student organizations later on, but that's hit or miss. I have called Dr. Kelly in school psych and Dr. Stromajor in counseling. All of their students take crisis intervention, and we have an agreement that if push came to shove, we could use them under faculty supervision to do assessment and intervention. They will be our second tier. We have all of our residence hall people trained in the TASSLE and basic listening skills, so if Anseld can get with you, Dave [David Shelby, Director of Residence Life], we'll start moving through the residence halls. Dr. Annie Smith, from the personal counseling unit, and our two other psych interns will be doing that and feeding information back to Imogene Crystal.

EMP Director Mathews: Okay, all well and good, but this is going to cost money. Where's it coming from, Ed?

CFO Bryce: I have been on the phone to the board of regents and the governor. They are going to apply for disaster funds and give us a draw on the rainy day fund. The building and everything in them are insured, but there are going to be a lot of other expenses from the heavy equipment to food services and housing for Leslie's incoming counselors. I am going to meet with my team here and have a teleconference with the board of regents president as soon as we get IT back up and running. Short term, we are looking at probably a million and a half, depending on how severe our steam line and electrical problems are.

D-day 15 hours after the explosion. Basement of the field house.

EMP Director Mathews: Okay, team, where do we stand?

Nurse Practitioner Unseld: (Now at the command center, disheveled, dirty, sweaty, with bloodstains on her clothes) We have all the wounded taken care of. There were 147 people that required hospitalization in five area hospitals and the trauma center in Columbus. We treated and released another 152 people for cuts, abrasions, bruises, and shock. Two people died, and one person was dead on arrival.

Interim Media Liaison Lee: We have issued three press releases so far and did a briefing with parents. All the residence halls got videotapes of the parent briefing, stating the facts as we know them. That there was an explosion of unknown origin. The number of people injured, contacts for hospitals, notification of relatives of the three dead persons. We have 14 people still unaccounted for that could have possibly been in the science building north wing. Attempts are being made to get hold of the 14 people we still can't account for. We have set up a reception center for parents under the south stadium and held a briefing for them. Any parents who want to contact their kids are being connected through the residence hall RAs. There are about 400 parents down there right now. We have food and drink available if they want it. After the press briefing and news release by the president, things seem to have calmed down considerably. There are still a load of calls coming into 911, but they are getting referred to the president's message and my briefing, which the local stations have on their web sites.

Acting Provost Richardson: School will not be held tomorrow. We will make a decision whether to have any school this week after tomorrow. The president was in a conference with the board of regents president in regard to working out a number of issues as far as academic decisions.

CFO Bryce: We are going to get some emergency funds to operate with. We are looking at utilizing Hall County High School and St. Elizabeth's High School for science classes on Saturday and weeknights. Our business manager is working on an agreement with them. We'll probably need to do some upgrading of those labs, and I have our biology, physics, and chemistry chairs going to look them over tomorrow.

Residence Life Director Shelby: We are having some trouble with food service because Bennett Hall took some blast damage and their food service is not operable right now. It will take a couple days to get things repaired in there. We are double-feeding students at Johnson Hall in shifts. There was some initial confusion tonight, but it went a lot better than expected. The students learned the ropes fast, so I think we'll be all right tomorrow. We have our residence hall staff and Dr. Holland's crew going through and talking to students. So far we have 157 students who are requesting some psychological help, and we have canvassed about a quarter of the students so far. Clearly, we are going to need mental health help in a big way.

Counseling Center Director Holland: We have 22 crisis counselors coming in from other universities in the state tomorrow. I am going to call up the school psych and counseling departments and activate their students to standby status.

LEMA Director Kline: Are you sure you don't want the Red Cross to activate their mental health folks?

Counseling Center Director Holland: Again, hold off on that. Let's see how many students, faculty, and staff are in bad shape. We ought to get through screening sometime tomorrow evening. I'll know better what we need then.

EMP Director Matthews: How about civil unrest?

Chief Smith: Things have been pretty quiet. We have the usual gawkers, and pushy news reporters, but between the Central City police, Hall County Sheriff's deputies, and the state police, we have things in control. The fire department has two pumpers on the scene that are still hosing down the building and watching for restarts, but the fire is out. The ATF will be here tomorrow, along with the state fire marshal, to investigate the cause. Right now, it is anybody's guess what blew up, but Chief O'Bannion is now real sure it went off in the northeast corner of the basement on the east wing. We are going to start interviewing people to find out who might have been down there tomorrow. They are also bringing cadaver dogs with them, although again, it was so hot we may have a smaller version of the twin trade towers here with remains pretty much cremated. We have no hope for survivors in the building.

Director of Facilities Kelly: You heard about Bennett Hall's kitchen. The north side of the administration building has about every window blown out, plus blast damage. It will take at least 3 days just to get that cleaned up and boarded up. The south side of the administration building is habitable, but it is not going to be pleasant working there. There is no air or heat at this time. The fine arts building took some damage, but I think we can get cleaning crews in there and get that back in business by the end of the week and ready to start classes Monday. The major problem is heat and communications. The steam tunnel under the science building is gone as the fiber optics and major electrical conduits. We are going to have to clean that out first and then start repairs, and we can't do that until the rubble cools down some more. We have no heat to three academic buildings and administration at this time. Raman can tell you about his problems.

Director of Institutional Technology Nouri: Along with the fiber optics and our damaged central computer and server, the phone lines are gone for the same buildings. Horizon Telecommunications is bringing crews in, and they will have a disaster mitigation specialist here tomorrow, but we are going to be out of service for some time. Hightower Communications is also coming to see if the tower can be salvaged. I looked at it, and I don't see how. They said if nothing else, they can put a portable tower up on the library roof. It wouldn't have the same power but it would keep our wireless mostly in service.

EMP Director Mathews: Anything else? Okay, it has been a tough day, but we have some semblance of control over a situation that surpasses anything we could have imagined. Our training has paid off, and I am proud of the way people have stepped in to fill the gap. Go on home and get cleaned up and get some sleep. We'll assemble here at 7 a.m. tomorrow. We will have some breakfast and something to drink here.

In the first hours after a major disaster such as this, there will be chaos as unforeseen problems occur. While the concrete poles and barriers to the parking lot keep drunk drivers and terrorists from dozing into the administration building or blowing it up, they also serve as a barrier to getting help where it is needed. It is critical then that someone knows who to get in contact with to get heavy equipment to the scene of a structure collapse. If no one in the university knows who or where to go to get some help or has the authority to okay it, then it is clearly important that the LEMA director be involved, because he or she will know. Other unforeseen problems the CMT had to deal with as well as work around included people from off campus wanting to see what happened and damage to the infrastructure of the campus (e.g., communication lines, the ability to provide heat to campus, and providing food and water for volunteers). Each problem must be addressed to give the support that is needed.

Care of the wounded in a disaster such as this reaches far beyond the scope of the university and even the midsize town in which it resides. There will have to be coordination between the university, EMP director, the LEMA director, and possibly SEMA. We cannot overemphasize the importance of working closely with the LEMA director and understanding his or her role and how that relates vertically to the state EMA.

Communication is also critical, both within the university and externally. Sometimes word of mouth is the only and best way to get information to those in need at the local level when electronic means go dead. We are not aware of a dedicated university student CERT team but see no reason in the world why they could not be established and trained. Citizens of every kind and every occupation volunteer and go through community emergency response team training. They are invaluable feet on the ground who can engage in basic search and rescue and provide basic first aid to the injured. The LEMA in your area can provide that training. Frankly, we think a lot of students would be interested in doing it. We can also imagine T-shirts, caps, and other badges of honor with the university logo or mascot CERT on it that signify that these students have gone through special training and are part of a university emergency response team.

External communication will also be critical in transmitting information within the university and with the world at large. It may seem callous to focus attention on getting contact established and prioritizing communication linkages with all the players in this disaster game. Many times to the layperson it appears that more should be happening, but to not put a priority on getting communication links reestablished would put even more lives in jeopardy.

D-Day 40 hours after the explosion. CMT field house command center.

EMP Director Mathews: Okay, everyone, let's see what is going on. Who wants to start?

Chief Smith: I guess I should. We had some problems late last night in Rawls residence hall. We almost had a mob scene two different times—one involving an Asian student who rumor has it was angry at the chemistry department so decided to blow it up. A number of students were assembling in his hall when an RA caught on to what was about to happen and got the police over there and broke it up. The other was wilder yet. Seems some students decided that another white kid from Arkansas who had a stars-and-bars flag in his room was part of the Aryan Nation and for some reason or other was part of a plot by them to blow up the science building. A bunch of African American students decided to make that a cause. They were going to take the guy out and tar and feather him or worse. Latavius Jackson, one of the top RAs over there—and he was the one that also dealt with the mob that was on that Asian kid, and deserves some kind of an award in my opinion—stood out in front of the white kid's room until we could get police over there. Then to top it all off, as I was coming over here after a quick breakfast at the university union, two professors got into it over there. Seems one of them believes one of the missing biology professors got unhappy because he probably wasn't going to make tenure and blew the place up. The other professor took some exception to that and was going to punch the first professor's lights out until I apprised them that would not be in either one of their interests if they were considering continued employment or advancement here. I think one was a physics professor and the other a biology professor. I can understand they are under a lot of stress and all, with the loss of their stuff, but that's over the top. It's getting pretty nuts, and when the ATF guys show up it's really going to get wild because with those big ATFs and state CSIs on their backs, there will be all kinds of conspiracy theories. We need to squelch those rumors ASAP.

Director of Residence Life Shelby: The problem for the two students is that they in fact are both known to the TAT. Their names are Sam Hull and George Giap. They got into a roommate pushing-and-shoving contest that got pretty heated. The Asian student is in fact an American Vietnamese from San Francisco who did have trouble with the chemistry department and sent a semithreatening e-mail to a professor. His roommate Sam Hull is a rural Arkansas kid. He has a number of friends here, but his accent, rural southern background, and the fact he's got a rebel flag up in his room doesn't endear him to the African American population. It'll be my guess as far out as this seems for both these freshman to be involved in the explosion, The ATF and state bureau guys are gonna want to talk to them.

EMP Director Mathews: Good Lord! We have a thousand things to do here, and all of a sudden we have conspiracy theories, and mad, crazy students and faculty bombers.

Demetrius Keith (Legal Counsel): I think that we need to get on this right now. I also think it is not Chon who goes on the air, but Chief Smith in his full uniform and tells everyone: (a) That as of right now there are no known terrorists or any other disaffected persons who are known to be responsible for the explosion. (b) The explosion is being investigated by the ATF, state fire marshal, and state bureau of investigation, and no stone will be left unturned until we find out what happened in the basement of the science building.

EMP Director Mathews: Let's set that up for 9 a.m. We need to squelch those rumors before somebody gets hurt and make it very clear that anyone who decides to be a judge and jury is going to get arrested and will be eligible for suspension or expulsion. I assume these two young men are being protected?

Chief Smith: Yes, but there is a longer-term problem. I am not sure they are going to be able to stay here. I don't know how, once they are under suspicion, they get that albatross off their necks.

EMP Director Mathews: Okay, Dr. Holland, Dr. Richardson, can we see to working something out with those two? Now can we get into the science basement? What about the other buildings?

Director of Facilities Kelly: Not yet. The forensic folks will probably want to go pretty slow. We will be busy boarding up the administration and fine arts buildings today and doing general cleanup. We have an emergency contract to get food service back up and running in Bennett Hall. We'll have a variety of contracts for window replacement and structural damage to the administration and fine arts buildings. The Horizon and High Tower crews came in early this morning, and communications systems repair is under way. The steam system is going to be a problem. We are going to have to build new steam lines or clean up the whole science building rubble. I don't believe we can do anything in the science building there until the forensic stuff is done. We probably need to think about laying new lines.

Interim Media Liaison Lee: We have positive identification on the people who were in the building and unaccounted for, the six missing and believed dead. Three professors, two doctoral students, and a master's student. One was a chemistry professor who was supposed to be in her office almost directly above the explosion. And the rest are all in the biology department. The biology folks seem to have been downstairs in the basement supply room getting set to go out and run a field biology experiment. We don't know what that was yet, but it doesn't seem like they would be doing anything that had to do with an explosion.

Counseling Center Director Holland: We are going to continue assessing students today. Once school was called off, a lot of them went home. That may be a blessing or a curse. I'd like to canvass all our students ASAP, but maybe if they're home, they get through the initial shock with a good support system. At least I hope so. We'll start on faculty after we get done with students, although we have put out a bulletin that faculty can call or just walk into the center if they feel distress. I have also been contacting department chairs and unit directors to see if they have noticed anyone who might need some help.

Acting Provost Richardson: We believe we can start school up Monday, at least on a limited basis. Getting coordinated with the two high schools and their science labs is our biggest logistics problem, although it is going to be difficult administering things for a while until we get the administration building put back together again.

LEMA Director Kline: We have Baker Construction on-site with backhoes, front end loaders, trucks, and the crews for cleanup. They are our specialists in disaster debris removal. They'll start on the other end of the science building and assign the delicate work to a crew who specializes in injury excavations to the forensics teams, although this time it will be evidence excavation. I think we can probably let the state police loose, but maybe keep city police and county sheriff's deputies out here until things cool down a bit. The MASH unit can fold up their tents too.

EMP Director Mathews: If there is nothing else, then let's go to work. Unless you get a call on the walkie-talkies, we'll meet back here at 4 today.

As you can see, the initial activities of recovery are beginning to occur. The CMT is working to continually evaluate the situation in order to have the most current data at hand to guide the recovery. However, even as progress is being made, other issues are surfacing. These issues are related crises that must be addressed. Addressing these smaller incidents and the growing numbers of rumors is a critical part of the recovery process (Ren, 2000). Decisions about handling the rumors must be made. Although some may be ignored, others must be managed through direct intervention.

Summary of D-Day + 2 Days

It should become very clear to you as this disaster unfolds over the first 2 days that the CMT is tasked with an enormous undertaking. The explosion affects every facet of life in the university, and every one of those facets will need to be dealt with to keep the university operational. How will students be served food? Where and when will classes meet? Who will replace the dead professors and hurt administrators? Will next week's football game go on? What kind of a memorial service should be planned, and whom should it include? What about the lost dissertations and theses?

If the national incident rate of PTSD (about a minimum of 20% if left on their own) emerges (Norris et al., 2002) from all the people who have been traumatized, the counseling center is going to be overwhelmed. Will the director's decision to hold off on the Red Cross be right? How will classes—and, indeed, graduation—be handled since there is essentially no facility to handle biology, physics, and chemistry, nor do surviving faculty have a place to teach or hold office hours or have any resources left? Morale will have a high likelihood of becoming a problem. What about graduate students who have seen their research go up in smoke and have to start over again? What about junior faculty members who are attempting to make tenure and also now have research that is in cinders? And what about the money? No disaster is ever cheap. In a time of budget crunches on universities, how will this affect not only staff and student morale but also the very infrastructure of the university? These are only a few of the questions and problems that are going to have to be dealt with by the CMT and the rest of the university. As the news media moves on to the next disaster, the university is left to fend for itself.

As this drama unfolds, we hope you see the complexity of the daunting tasks that are before a CMT after the initial impact of a disaster. These tasks include, among others, getting basic food and water to the team, organizing relief efforts that involve accessing help from across the state, obtaining mental health support, and getting bulldozers and forensic experts on-site.

Honeymoon Phase

Movement into this phase can be as soon as 48 hours or up to 3 weeks after the crisis. The honeymoon phase generally lasts approximately 3 months (Halpern & Tramontin, 2007). Optimism is high, and the belief that all will be well grows and generally remains strong in this phase of recovery (Faberow & Frederick, 1978). Media attention is widespread, and the public is quick to offer support. The urgency of the situation lessens, creating a feeling among administrators and CMTs that they have breathing room to make decisions. The feeling and belief of being able to manage the crisis is elevated as the university moves through this phase.

During this phase, systematic, carefully planned assessment becomes important (Myer et al., 2007). Data from the Office of Institutional Research may be helpful, but the usefulness of this information may be limited. The reason is that the recovery has not generally progressed to the point to make the best use of this information. We recommend conducting assessments specifically designed to gather data needed to steer resources, where these are needed. These assessments might involve doing individual interviews with people in a position to have a personal knowledge of where support is needed, as well as what efforts are being effective. Using several people from different departments or units to obtain this information helps to ensure the reliability of the data. For example, assessment of key people at Central University might include chairs of the departments housed in the science building, resident life assistants on floors where the students that were killed lived, and managers of custodial staff who worked in the science building. Remember that the crisis will have a ripple effect across campus, so other people may also be needed to provide perspective in this assessment. Talking with people outside those directly impacted by the explosion will give a cross-sectional perspective.

These early assessments are useful in monitoring the effectiveness of early interventions. Early monitoring of the effectiveness of the efforts to respond to the crisis in this recovery phase will allow administrators and CMTs to adjust the intervention to be more effective. Successful intervention soon after a crisis generally shortens the recovery process and prevents more long-term problems from developing. Assessment in this phase may also help university officials make projections about the nature of the recovery. Efficient and effective interventions indicate recovery is progressing in a satisfactory manner. This information is useful for responding to questions from supporters as well as from critics.

The following dialogue takes place 1 week after the explosion. We start this part of the dialogue with a debriefing of the CMT. This process is followed by another CMT meeting. As you will see, unexpected issues are emerging. If not dealt with swiftly and effectively, each has the potential to significantly sidetrack the initial recovery efforts.

Assessment is also becoming a key issue as the recovery process is moving forward. Also, please be aware the meetings we include are just a sample; other meetings have taken place.

Debriefing

Critical Incident Stress Debriefing (CISD) was developed by Jeffrey Mitchell, a firefighter and paramedic in Baltimore County, Maryland, because of his own experiences with traumatic events. It started with firefighters and EMTs who were first responders to fires, accidents, and other events and were exposed to horrible scenes filled with chaos, death, and human carnage (Morrissey, 1994). Debriefing is designed to lessen the psychological impact of a traumatic event, restore psychological equilibrium, prevent PTSD from developing, and identify people who will need further professional assistance to get through the traumatic wake of the event (Mitchell & Everly, 1995, p. 270). It has pretty much become standard operating procedure for emergency workers to be brought together immediately after they get through dealing with a traumatic event. The CISD has not been without controversy and has detractors as well as adherents (James, 2008, pp. 613–614). Whether the original CISD model that Mitchell and Everly (1995) developed is ultimate truth, beauty, and goodness or not, it is patently clear that *some* kind of debriefing process is necessary to help crisis workers steer clear of the vicarious trauma that almost necessarily goes along with doing this kind of work (Saakvitne & Pearlman, 1996) and maintain psychological equilibrium following their intensive intervention work in the aftermath of a chaotic crisis.

D-Day + 6 days after the explosion, 11:30 a.m. Debriefing session at CMT command center, field house.

> **EMP Director Mathews:** I have asked Dr. John Felton, a psychologist from the Columbus Veteran's Hospital, to be with us this afternoon. He is going to conduct a debriefing. I have worked with John before, and I have found his debriefing methods to be very helpful. The group is yours, John.
>
> **John Felton (Debriefing Specialist):** The last 2 days have been some of the toughest you've probably ever known if you are anything like most folks who don't do crisis management for a living. Jason told me in his call for me to come that it has been the toughest time for him in the 20 years he has been in this business, and my guess is it has been for you as well. Debriefings of emergency workers and particularly CMT teams such as yourselves serve two purposes. First and foremost to release some of the tension, anxieties, and stress that has naturally built up over the last 2 days. Second, to find out what lessons we have learned and how they can be put to use. This will be a variation on the standard Critical Incident Stress Debriefing format that has become pretty famous, or infamous, depending on the advocates and detractors you wish to believe. What CISD does is pretty formal and operates sorta by the numbers

by going through an introduction, then a behavior-thought-feeling sequence of what went on, and winds up with some psychoeducation. It is most commonly used with mud-and-blood first responders. What I want to do with you this afternoon is a variation on that theme. Indeed, I'd first like to hear from all of you about what went on from your own perspective. Then I would like to hear your thoughts and feelings about it. Finally, though, I'd like to hear what you learned and what needs to be changed. This is not a fault-finding mission. Understand that what will be said here will be held in confidence. What is said here stays here. There is no report going back to the president or the board of trustees. So what is said here stays here except for any recommendations that may need to be incorporated in future emergency preparedness plans. If there are no questions, I would like to start by asking each person what your particular perspective of this disaster was. What did you see, how did you react, what did you think and feel, and how did you respond, what went right and what needs to be fixed? There are no right or wrong answers here, just our perspectives. I am not going in any particular order around the room, so feel free to speak up. What I will do for the most part is listen and attempt to clarify what you are saying. I will not make any judgments or conclusions about what is said. (A period of silence ensues as people reflect on the questions and ponder whether they will speak.)

Acting Provost Richardson: I guess what I saw was some pretty darned good planning. Particularly from the standpoint of redundancy. I never imagined anything like this, but when it happened, we had a backup command center and people who could step up and step in. I sure didn't think I'd wind up being the interim provost and have to make the decisions I am now. Maybe I should have seen that coming, but I didn't. It scared the daylights out of me and still does to some extent. So maybe a bit more cross-training for me, although I would have probably tried to weasel out of it. (laughs)

Interim Media Liaison Lee: I agree. The redundancy thing is important. I never imagined Eloise would be out of action. At times going over her stuff to learn what she did seemed like a royal pain. It doesn't now. I did get frustrated with our inability to get communications out. We actually were using runners to get messages back and forth. It seems like we need to think about some way to back up communication systems, although I guess this was a perfect storm of electronic failures, so I don't see how it could get much worse.

Director of Residence Life Shelby: As this unfolded, I saw for the first time how we worked together as a team. Each person has a part to play, and I can't imagine how this could be done if every person here wasn't involved. Sometimes I needed to be in two places at once. Here and at the halls, and that was a little frustrating. If I had a do-over, I think I'd be getting some help in the halls so I could function better here. Maybe some student even like Latavius Jackson. Who really showed up through all this.

Chief Smith: Initially, it was a fur ball, and I was pretty frustrated because we were so shorthanded. I was glad when Lester showed up and got the Hall County LEMA involved. We needed help policing this mess, and he got three law enforcement agencies here, and they knew what to do. Communications was and is a problem. We didn't plan on the whole communication systems being down. Relying on walkie-talkies makes it a lot more difficult to get the word out or to link up folks fast.

Nurse Practitioner Unseld: Yesterday I was within 300 yards of ground zero. I am also amazed at how well we worked together. I did at times early on feel very, very alone. It was just me and the clinic's nurse and secretary and whatever students and faculty we could recruit to help the wounded. It was overwhelming and felt like I was back in my old army unit during the Gulf War only maybe worse. To tell you the truth, if I hadn't been a MASH unit nurse, I don't know whether I could have done what I did yesterday. There were so many people, and at times it was so overwhelming because of the wounds. Shrapnel and burns are the worst, and everybody I worked on yesterday had either one or the other.

CFO Bryce: I have an MBA and am a CPA. Those were both rigorous courses of academic endeavor. They did nothing to prepare me for these last 2 days. University financial decisions generally move slowly, with a lot of thought and consideration and input from various segments. Yesterday, those same decisions were moving at lightning speed. I am still kinda in shock at some of the decisions I made yesterday. Three days ago, I would have never done or imagined doing things that quickly. Yes! I am still sorta amazed.

As Dr. Fulton moves around the room, each person spontaneously speaks to their actions and some of their thoughts and feelings. When they are finished, Dr. Fulton tapes some butcher paper to the walls and asks each person to take a magic marker and write up a lesson learned and initial their name by it. He then goes over each one.

Dr. Fulton: Jerome Kelly said that we need hard copies of schematics and also have portable computers with memory sticks. So we can immediately get into buildings and know where to shut things off, start things, or have alternative means of access.

Facilities Director Kelly: We have those on computers, but when the power went out, they were of no use. And the only hard copies were in the physical plant safe, which I couldn't get to because of the fire.

Dr. Fulton: Leslie Unseld put down no battlefield help.

Nurse Practitioner Unseld: The EMTs and their wagons started showing up pretty quickly, but there was a lot of confusion on giving orders. I think they didn't know how to respond to me being an NP and not an MD. Or maybe they were hung up between their accustomed way of getting orders from an ER MD when they are faced with something beyond their skills. Either way, we need to figure out some better chain of command out in the field. There was a lot of initial confusion until I put my foot down. Some of the same stuff occurred with the Air Force MASH unit when they made the scene. I have all the respect in the world for those doctors and units. I served in one in Iraq. But they can't just come in and try to take over. Three hours into it, I and the EMTs were getting it pretty well organized, and then they show up and try to take over the show. I got pretty mad and sorta pulled rank on a young MD. Told him I'd been a major in Iraq long before he'd ever gotten his MD, and if this was his first deployment, he needed to listen to me. He didn't like it, but he did what I said. Maybe a memorandum of understanding or something like that to clarify working relationships. Or maybe we just need to sit down and talk to one another because that hadn't happened.

Dr. Fulton: Leslie Holland put down better linkages between student housing and organizations.

Counseling Center Director Holland: I'm not really sure how to approach this. Maybe there is no solution. We know there are some students and some professors here who are mentally fragile from our work with them at the center. We also know that some of those same folks were right smack in the middle of this. We have two examples that came to our attention today. One was the fight this morning between the two professors that Don broke up and another where a graduate student's wife dragged him in because a year and a half's research on his doctoral dissertation went up in smoke and he became suicidal. What we don't know yet is how they are reacting to it. And I don't want to find out by first reading about it in the *Hall Clarion*. Somehow we need to have a triage system that can catch those people early on.

Each person in turn brings up trouble spots and glitches in the plan. No attempt is made to correct these problems right now. They are recorded and will be discussed in after-action reports the EMP director will make after all the dust settles, unless the problem has immediate relevance to the situation at hand.

While a mandatory CISD attendance with its prescriptive processing can create passive-aggressive resentment and emphasize pathology over resiliency and trauma over strength in participants, we believe it is important to have some kind of regular debriefings—if not on a daily basis, then close to it—to deal with emerging tactical problems and to repair bruised psyches. A smorgasbord of different debriefing strategies that focus on the nuts and bolts of what the team has been doing, the emotional impact they have suffered, or both can be used (Armstrong, O'Callahan, & Marmar, 1991; Charlton & Thompson, 1996; Dyregrov, 1997; Myers & Zunin, 1994). Echterling, Presbury, and McKee (2005) believe that linking people in crisis, hearing one another's crisis stories, normalizing reactions, and facilitating the group's coping are positive outcomes that are critical to resolution. We agree. Debriefings should be a natural act during and following the disaster. They should be part of the CMT's standard operating procedure and should be no less expected than that of a fighter pilot after a combat mission.

D-Day + 8 days after the explosion, 9:30 a.m. CMT operations center, field house.

As you read through this dialogue, notice the shift in the emphasis from being in a state of emergency to the movement toward recovery. Note the continued importance of assessment during this phase of recovery, as well as handling the issue of rumors as they surface.

EMP Director Mathews: Okay, we are a week out; I'd like a report from everyone. Let's start with casualties.

Interim Media Liaison Lee: We have confirmed that the six missing persons are now dead: three professors, Dr. George Felsen, Chemistry, Dr. Leotia Talmadge, and Dr. Gene Sarazin, Biology; along with two of their doctoral students, Grace Sandrage and Malcom Brines; and one master's student, Jane Murrow. Dr. Felsen was in his office, and it appears he was killed outright by the explosion. The others were all in the basement getting an SUV loaded with field equipment. We also have another loss, Provost Lisa Frayser, our friend and colleague, died last night at Columbus Trauma from complications from surgery. (Collective sighs, muffled sobs, and gasps from CMT.) We have had two other students die at hospitals. The total dead including the three students that died on D-day stands at 12. We still have 8 students in ICUs and burn units and 19 others in the hospital in stable or satisfactory condition with broken bones, concussions, burns, and wound complications. On a positive note, Eloise Smith, our media relations team member, was released from the hospital yesterday and is at home and on the mend. (Collective hand clapping and cheers.)

Counseling Center Director Holland: So far, we have triaged over 2,000 students who were close to the physical epicenter of the explosion or were psychologically close to someone or had something to do with the explosion. Approximately 600 have peritraumatic symptoms that could move to acute stress disorder, but that is a wait-and-see deal. We are monitoring them, and they know what they need to do if things don't improve. We have organized and conducted 30 large-group psychoeducation information sessions on PTSD for students and faculty. We have had very good attendance with over 1,600 people. We have about 120 students and faculty we are seeing presently whose problems can be directly attributed or were exacerbated by the explosion. We have sent 12 of the state consortium counselors home but are rotating five new ones in because we can't handle the load we presently have. We are reserving one of those folks to deal with our staff and other personnel involved on campus with the explosion and cleanup because of the pressure they have been under. We are still in the heroic phase, so overall the mental health of the university is pretty good, and they are all pulling together, it seems.

Chief Smith: With one notable exclusion to the heroic business. We are still having problems with rumors floating around. That damn Aryan plot won't quit, and we have some Asian students reporting being harassed.

Counseling Center Director Holland: We also have some of that information. I asked Dr. Uggams from sociology and Dr. Nakajima from the counseling department to put together a cultural awareness, antidiscriminatory program that we could put up on PowerPoint and get some of their people to put on presentations. They are really good at that sort of thing. When can we expect to get Net service back up, because it will take them a long time to go around doing this on their own? Further, we have Asian students on the CERT teams. It might be a good idea to give them some publicity so as to let the rest of the students know that they are not some supposed enemy or terrorist group, but are right in there helping like other students. If we have any Southerners on the team, I'd give them some air time, too.

EMP Director Mathews: That's a great idea, Leslie Lieutenant Fleming is the advisor to those kids. See what she can come up with as far as giving them some publicity. We also may have information that will help on the source of the explosion. The ATF and state forensics folks think they have a cause for the explosion. It appears that two 50-gallon portable LPG tanks were down in the basement. We think that they were being loaded by the biology professors. It appears one or both had been leaking and gas accumulated and settled in the basement since it is heavier than air. Probably when they started the SUV a spark ignited it. It also appears that there was a sink full of naphtha that they were using to clean some equipment in and that immediately ignited, along with what was left in a 50-gallon drum of the stuff, which accelerated the fire. So the conspiracy theory and revenge motives are pretty much out the window. They should confirm that by tomorrow and when they do, Chon, I'd like to have an immediate press conference with them on that topic.

Director of Information Technology Nouri: If everything goes well and the new lines get laid, without problems, which is anybody's guess that will happen, I'd say in 3 days. The damage repair to the central computing center and server is about complete.

CFO Bryce: We have drawn about $1.5 million from the board of regents' rainy day fund and have applied for about another $1.5 million state disaster funds. Most of that money was for emergency services. We need the other money to instigate basic repairs on the administration, fine arts, and physical plant to make them serviceable.

Student Life Vice President Jones: We need to think about a memorial service. We have never dealt with anything remotely resembling this level of loss. I am getting a committee together of the campus clergy for a nondenominational service. I've put in calls to Virginia Tech and Texas A&M to see how they handled their tragedies. A lot of students are asking what we're going to do.

Acting Provost Richardson: We have started school back, as you all know, on Monday. Everybody seems to be adapting pretty well. Things are subdued, but we are educating students again. Of course, the biggest glitches are in science and coordinating with the high schools. But the chairs in biology, chemistry, and physics are all working closely with the two high schools, so I think those will iron out.

From a crisis stage development perspective, what is occurring in the 7 days since the explosion is known as the emergency or heroic phase. While a good deal of collective chaos occurs after the explosion, people reacted mainly in proactive ways, which is common when disasters occur. This phase of recovery from a crisis is characterized by perseverance, high energy, positive morale, and gaining relief by talking about their anxieties surrounding the crisis and their responses to it. It is also known as the inventory phase. As a way of attempting to regain control, people will aggressively seek information regarding loved ones, safety of home and possessions, and how places of employment have fared after the disaster. Typically, there is frustration with inability to find loved ones or anger at authorities for not letting the survivors back into their neighborhoods to find out about their homes (Myers & Wee, 2005, pp. 20–21). Because they are human, all of that foregoing behavior includes the CMT responses. Their sorrow and joy over the loss and survival of one of their own members will make an indelible mark on their memories. The same will occur for the counselors and other personnel working though this phase. Whether that will have a positive or negative effect depends a great deal on how the continued debriefing of the workers occurs. That's why Dr. Howard keeps one member of the visiting team available for staff who are working with survivors. The hallmarks of this early phase include immediate needs assessment of both the community and individuals (Speier, 2006), psychological first aid (Slaikeu, 1990; Young, 2006), and rapid deployment of early intervention models following a disaster like Central University's science building explosion (Ruzek, 2006). All of these interventions are characterized by the actions of Dr. Howard's response teams. The immediate goal is to strengthen coping strategies and improve resilience trajectories of survivors after a disaster (Watson, Ritchie, Demer, Bartone, & Pfefferbaum, 2006). It should become readily apparent that the staff of the counseling center will be called upon above and beyond the call of duty and most probably for some time after the disaster. It is imperative that these people receive training to do this work and that the administration appreciates the support they will need both to carry out their duties and to take care of themselves.

The Vice President for Student Life broaches the subject of a memorial service. By and large, we are not overly enthused about memorial services. While this may sound cold and uncaring, memorial services are problematic for a variety of reasons. First and foremost, who gets what kind of a service, and where does it occur under what conditions? This may seem straightforward, it is not. What happens when it is an auto accident involving students who had been drinking, as opposed to those who had not? How many student deaths does it take to have a school memorial service? What if the deaths happen off campus or during the summer when few students are present? Does it make a difference if it is an unknown student as opposed to a star football player? Does a tree get planted as a memorial as opposed to a bench seat by the fountain, or if the deceased's relatives have lots of money, a new building in the name of the deceased?

What if the death is a suicide? The experts in suicidology absolutely believe suicides should not be memorialized in any way so the suicide is not glamorized and creates a contagion risk of suicide (Poland & McCormick, 1999). But what if the parents are big contributors to the school, or a state legislator? That's easier said than done if they are insistent and have political or financial power in the university

Should there be a set number who have to die before a wide-scale memorial service is conducted, like Finland's rule that when 10 or more people die in a traumatic event, a day of national mourning is held (Nurmi, 1999)? Generally, consumable memorials such as scholarships are to be recommended over permit memorials such as fixtures. It is far better if living memorials are given that can be used for educational purposes such as education centers that provide continuing services for the university community in the name of the deceased. Over the years, a lot of bad things happen to faculty and students, and if all these students and faculty are given memorials, the campus will start to look like Elmwood Cemetery (Poland & McCormick, 1999, p. 209).

On the other hand, if a memorial service is not conducted, or black ribbons are not worn, or flowers and stuffed animals are not permitted at the disaster or trauma site, the administration will be seen as uncaring and heartless (Zinner, 1999). Therefore, the foregoing cautions being said, memorializing rituals that are culturally sensitive do provide a sense of group identity, provide mutual support, validate the person's life and the survivors, gives guidance for healing, and provides an outlet for grief and bonding (Nurmi, 1999).

The Oklahoma City Murrah Building bombing is one of the better examples of how a grieving community responded to a horrific loss that included numerous children. Key public leaders became very proactive and focused the community on shared values and common goals that united them in their sense of loss, grief, and bereavement. To make the foregoing happen, community leaders took the lead in speaking to survivors by providing accurate information, dispelling rumors, and providing calm and controlled role models. By meeting with bereaved families at the Compassion Center, they showed their humanness and sensitivity. They didn't do this extemporaneously but first met and were coached by mental health workers who had a great deal of experience in the business of grief and mourning (Sitterle & Gurwitch, 1999). From that standpoint, leadership should be very aware that notifications of death, messages of condolence, and presence and speeches at memorial services need to be well thought out. While we are not against extemporaneous responses of sympathy, most leaders would do well to take a short course in empathic responding from people who know something about the business of grief and bereavement. That goes double for any written statements given out to the media. Very careful thought should be given to what will be written.

The vice president's decision to call universities who have had previous experiences with mass disasters is a good one. While Northern Illinois University, Texas A&M, and Virginia Tech are not the same as Central University as far as type of disaster and the idiosyncratic needs that each disaster specifically generates, they also have generic commonalities, and their experiences in handling mourning and memorial services are lessons learned that can be passed on.

Over and above anything else, a memorial service on university grounds should create a sense of belongingness and community (Bolton, 1999). That traumatic experience threatens the whole community, and the loss of belongings imperils not only the individual but also the community's sense of security and purpose. Therefore, any memorial service should not serve just individual needs; it should be a unifying force that reaffirms the bond between the community and its alma mater.

While the heroic phase is characterized by a "we're all in this together" approach, the issue of the two culturally distinct students who have become the targets of rumors and possible violence are important issues. Augsburger (1992) and Shelby and Tredinnick (1995) found that new immigrants quickly reverted to old and original culture-specific ways of coping when they emerged from a disaster. We believe that can be said of almost everyone as they take inventory and attempt to gain control of their environment. Dr. Holland's creative attempts to quickly provide intervention strategies that are systemic and intended to pull all the community together (Norris & Alegria, 2006) are critical in not allowing tertiary effects of suspicions about others who are somehow different and easy to focus blame on for the crisis.

The week following the crisis has been hectic, horrific, and fraught with all kinds of challenges. Creative thinking and original solutions are needed. This is one of the most stress-prone times the CMT members have ever experienced. The original crisis is in control, but as the team moves along the postcrisis timeline, their work will not be done, and they will face other issues in the crisis chronosystem. Whether they know it or not, they are in the honeymoon phase of the crisis. The community pulls together. There is optimism for recovery, and the belief there will be full restitution of financial loss is high. There is a great deal of media coverage and high-level political attention. Public outpouring in the form of physical and financial donations give the community a sense of hope for rebuilding, and there is a strong sense of having shared a horrific experience but having prevailed over the worst of it (Farberow & Frederick, 1978). As in all honeymoons, this attitude will change.

Avoidance Phase

The avoidance phase comes next. In this phase, the university strives to achieve a period of temporary homeostasis (Rosenfeld, Caye, Ayalon, & Lahad, 2005). This phase may take place over several months and can last a year or more if the crisis had a particularly high impact on the campus. The resilience of a university becomes evident in the avoidance phase. Resilience is the capacity for flexibility within an organization and its ability to regulate itself during difficult situations (Martin, 2004). Although universities are bastions of bureaucracy, flexibility is critical in this phase of the recovery process. Assessment of strengths and limitations becomes increasingly important in this phase of recovery (Mitroff & Anagnos, 2001).

The shift from the honeymoon phase to the avoidance phase is obvious. Anxiety visibly decreases, and a sensation of composure emerges from the chaos experienced in the immediate aftermath of the crisis. However, the movement toward reestablishing equilibrium on campus is not without bumps. These bumps can be small or large and have the potential to significantly impede the recovery process. One bump that may arise involves some people or groups on campus pretending nothing happened or that everything is better. This issue is particularly problematic when these people throw up roadblocks to addressing needs resulting from the crisis (Knotek, 2006). Another concern is the development of disillusionment as media attention dies, community support fades, and recovery comes mired in bureaucracy (Halpern & Tramontin, 2007). Fatigue and even exhaustion are possible during the time this happens. A sense of abandonment is experienced, and people potentially become disillusioned to the point of losing hope in the recovery.

Assessment in the avoidance phase is useful to monitor the recovery process. The ideal situation is for assessment and interpretation of data to be scheduled on a regular basis. Periodic monitoring of issues related to the recovery ensures that important data will not be missed or ignored. The number and timing of assessments depend on the progress being made in the recovery. Any assessment at this point should also be attentive to variations that may be present across campus units. Just because one unit on campus has reestablished stability doesn't mean that another unit may not still be stuck in the recovery process.

Assessment will become more formalized, possibly involving several methods such as surveys, focus groups, and electronic methods to gather data. Data from the Office of Institutional Research become increasingly useful in this phase. For example, information about the use of health services and counseling services can be used to gauge students' continued reactions to a crisis. In addition, drops in the number of credit hours being taken and enrollment trends can help to assess the continued impact of the crisis across campus. With respect to staff and faculty members, the number of sick days used, the number accessing the employee assistance plan, resignations, disciplinary actions, and so on all can reflect the aftereffects of a crisis.

At the 4-month timeline, the CMT is entering another phase of recovery. Most of the university will be moving forward. However, problems resulting from the crisis remain to be resolved, while new ones keep surfacing. The CMT addresses some of these in this meeting. Note the tone of the meetings. At times, a positive attitude is being taken, yet a more pessimistic undertone seems to be present.

D-day +125 days, 3:30 p.m. Original command center, administration building.

EMP Director Mathews: This is our fourth follow-up meeting since D-day. I'd like Edward Bryce, our vice president for business affairs, to give us an update, and also Demetrius Keith about some legal issues that have arisen.

CFO Bryce: It will probably come as no surprise, but the insurance carrier is balking on paying off on damages. They claim since there appears to be negligence on our part in storing explosive and hazardous materials in the science building, that we, and not they, are liable for damages. Further, that our biology people were not certified to handle such materials. They have offered a settlement that will not begin to rebuild what we have lost.

Legal Counsel Keith: That is one problem we are currently working on. The other problem is that we have a number of lawsuits for wrongful death and negligence that are being lodged against us by students, parents, and faculty.

EMP Director Mathews: That's all the bad news, I hope. Any good news?

Acting Provost Richardson: We are making do with the high school science labs and have used the teachers there as adjunct professors to teach the basic courses. That seems to be working out pretty well. We have suffered a slight drop in enrollment second semester. That's hard to tell whether it is normal attrition or an artifact of the explosion. We have some professors who are anything but happy by being moved around. A couple of chemistry assistant professors are housed in consumer science. They gripe a lot about not having adequate access to research facilities and are worried about tenure because they can't get their research up and going again. However, it seems when the Consumer Science Department bakery unit is running, then they get all cozy with the consumer science professors. (Laughter from CMT.) That is a problem for all the research projects, both for professors and students, and it is causing morale issues. The faculty senate has started talking about those problems as they apply to tenure, promotion, graduation, and recruitment of new students. They don't have any answers either. Until we get a new science building under construction, I am not sure what we can do.

Director of Residence Life Shelby: The residence halls are pretty much back to normal. I think the job the sociology and counseling professors did really worked. Both Hull and Giap seem to be doing okay, although I'd like to see George make some more friends. He really appears lonely, and Latavius Jackson confirms that. On the other hand, Hull seems to be pretty good at blues guitar work, and amazingly enough, after Latavius stood his ground when that bunch of Black fraternity guys were gonna beat Hull up for being a rebel Southerner, he now seems to be getting involved with a Black blues band. I think Latavius had a hand in that. Wonders never cease! I think this committee needs to recognize Latavius Jackson in some way or another. I know he is a business major, but he has a real gift for student personnel work, and I think somebody needs to talk to him about a career change.

EMP Director Mathews: Well, besides a certificate of appreciation suitable for framing, we do have a paid summer internship. Do you suppose he'd want that? Any noes on the idea? (CMTs all nod heads vigorously and vote to offer LBJ a paid internship.)

Counseling Center Director Holland: Since D-day, we have referred 42 students and 9 faculty out to Hall County Mental Health or private practitioners that meet the criteria for PTSD. We are still seeing about 56 students on a regular basis who have some residual effects from the explosion that are exacerbating other conditions. Right now we are busy but functioning pretty well.

Director of Information Technology Nouri: As you all know, we got up and running in 3 weeks on a partial basis. As of last week, we completed renovation of the computing center and put a brand-new system in operation. If there is a silver lining in this thundercloud, it is that we have now one of the finest information systems and computing facilities of any school our size in the country. Given the damage that was done, that is indeed a miracle.

Facilities Director Kelly: We have everything else repaired, as you can see by sitting in the newly remodeled EMP room in the administration building.

Chief Smith: Nothing much to report except a student who was drunk on his motorbike and ran into the hole that was the science building. He broke a leg and almost suffocated in the mud. Nothing else.

EMP Director Matthews: Okay! It sounds overall pretty good except for our financial issues with insurance and lawsuits. May I introduce our renewed media relations person, Eloise Smith. Good to have you back. (Round of applause.) What's the plan on the science building?

Eloise Smith (Media Relations): Thank you, Jason. I can't begin to thank you for all your support while I was in the hospital and rehab. We are planning on mounting a funding campaign for the science building while Demetrius slugs it out with the insurance company. Several alums have asked about a fund drive. We are planning a $30 million drive. We have a campaign slogan "Brick the building." The idea is that if everyone buys a brick—or a thousand, we'd hope— that a little bit of money from our thousands of alums would get it built. Under the current budget crunch we don't have much hope of state funding for a good long while.

At about this time in recovery, an avoidance phase will emerge, and people will want to stop talking about the disaster and move on with their lives (Pennebaker & Harber, 1993). They may, in fact, start avoiding people who do continue to persevere on the event. For those who cannot, the result is probably manifested in the people Dr. Holland has referred out for specialized treatment for PTSD. Most people will enter an adaptation phase (Pennebaker & Harber, 1993). While the memories and images may be indelible that are imprinted on them of the disaster, they will adapt and move forward. So while the event begins to turn into a historical date and fade into the past, what happens now and in the coming months will dictate whether the university's attempts at recovery become salutogenic or pathogenic (Antonovsky, 1980, 1991). That is, will the university move toward a healthy model that is growing and vibrant or one that becomes riddled with malaise and disease? Certainly, there has been progress. Rumors have been squelched, the racial issues that surfaced briefly have died down, and a new and better computing and information facility is online and running. There are approximately 100 people still in need of psychological services, but that is a far cry from the thousands suffering from peritraumatic symptoms 4 months ago. All of the damaged buildings have been repaired, and the university is back in business.

However, troubling problems remain. The lawsuits for negligence have yet to play out. One way or another, they are going to exert an enormous toll in time, energy, and money on the institution, even if there is no guilt found. Its effects on morale, reputation, and recruitment of new students are only a few of the troubling questions that surround the lawsuit. A much larger problem is the science building. It has been key to the development of Central University's engineering, math, physics, chemistry, and biology. This grand old building was also an image of the university. There now exists a large muddy hole in the ground, and it appears there is no ready solution to start reconstruction. For all of the other issues that are being handled, if the university doesn't start to make strides on getting a new science building under construction, a variety of potentially bad things are going to start to happen, including loss of bright science students and faculty, loss of research funding, decreased faculty morale, and overall loss of prestige. If this issue is not handled well, its ramifications will be huge, and the whole university will be faced with a crisis even bigger than the one it faced when the science building blew up. And that crisis will have the potential to becoming a metastasizing crisis that spreads across the body of the whole university.

Reconstruction Phase

The recovery phase hopefully involves a shift to a salutogenic perspective (Stuhlmiller & Dunning, 2000) or strength-based viewpoint for some groups on campus. However, human nature being what it is, some people may remain stuck, viewing recovery from only a pathogenic perspective. A pathogenic approach focuses solely on problems and sees addressing these as the only way to facilitate recovery. We believe that a balance between the two perspectives is the best overall approach to recovery in this phase. In other words, neither a "pie in the sky" nor a "woe is me" attitude promotes the recovery process. You must recognize and use the strengths of the university to address the problems caused by the crisis.

Depending on the impact of the crisis to the campus as a whole, this phase can start as soon as a few weeks after a crisis to over a year afterwards (Myer & Moore, 2006). During this phase of recovery, procedures perceived as positive and constructive become institutionalized as the university adapts to the fallout from the crisis. For example, the use of metal detectors at university-sponsored events is perceived as ordinary. Threat assessment team monthly meetings are seen as just part of doing business. And the use of IDs to swipe into residence halls is no longer an irritation but viewed as expected if a campus wants to prevent violence.

Completion of this phase is related to the overall impact of crisis (Myer & Moore, 2006). Generally speaking, the more dramatic the crisis and severe the reaction, the more time needed to adapt to the resulting changes. During this phase, the university returns to business as usual, although business as usual may be quite different than previous to the crisis. As lessons are learned from the crisis, the university adapts in ways to militate against similar crises in the future.

Assessment during the reconstruction phase will become less frequent, yet still important in the recovery process. Data from the Office of Institutional Research become increasingly important. This data can be used to identify changes in trends in any number of areas. Examples include student dropout rate in specific departments, alumni gifts to the university, and enrollment numbers. These assessments provide a check for complications in the recovery process, assessment of the need for possible policy revisions, and other issues that may arise. These other issues will generally present themselves as changes from past trends. As these are identified, they can be addressed to prevent them from developing into a crisis themselves. Many times complications are experienced during anniversaries following the crisis (Echterling, Presbury, & McKee, 2005; Myer & Moore, 2006). In situations such as Central University, anniversaries include more than just the date 1 year after the crisis and involve all important dates, such as the first time classes begin after the crisis, a holiday break, commencement, and matriculation (Myer & Moore, 2006). Assessment during this phase can identify these opportunities as well as isolate possible roadblocks to the potential changes.

The following meeting takes place almost 1 year after the explosion at Central University. While some issues have been resolved, others continue to cause difficulties. Again this dialogue has been abbreviated, but it illustrates some of the ongoing issues that must be addressed.

D-day + 350, 3 p.m. Original command center, administration building.

EMP Director Mathews: We are about a year out from D-day, and what a year it has been. Anniversaries of disasters are always significant psychologically, so I want to be sure we are all up to speed on the coming anniversary of the science building explosion.

Eloise Smith (Media Relations): We are planning on having a memorial service for homecoming weekend. We are also going to break ground for the new state-of-the-art science building. We have 20 million bricks (dollars) so far, and our alumni are gearing up to raise 20 million more at the big kickoff weekend of "match the bricks bought." That'll be on Friday night. We have about 4,000 alums registered so far, and our alumni director is really gearing up for this event.

Counseling Center Director Holland: The residual effects from the science building are 25 students and 3 faculty still receiving services on an outpatient basis and about 25 students in-house. We are monitoring progress of about 200 other people with an as-needed checkup/check back that again we have modeled on the Virginia Tech plan.

Legal Counsel Keith: The insurance company is going to have to pay up. They are still dragging their feet, but the OSHA team found no culpability on our part or the biology professors and their students. There is no special certification to handle propane tanks unless you're selling the stuff, and the parts-cleaning area met OSHA standards. We'll get the money, but it certainly has been a drag on morale. We have 17 wrongful death and injury suits pending in court. This OSHA ruling will change that a good deal. I believe we will reach out-of-court settlements without admitting wrongdoing.

Acting Provost Richardson: The lack of a science building has hurt enrollment some, particularly in our science and engineering areas. We are still using the two high schools and have converted part of the old student center into labs and offices for science folks. Getting the new science building done is the number-one priority of the university. Between the faculty senate and administration, we have worked out tenure and promotion. Essentially, there will be a 2-year and possibly 3-year grace period for all science professors seeking tenure or promotion. At the end of that time, if they are granted tenure or promotion, they will be given tenure credit and back pay to the start of the grace period. We have gone forward with third-year reviews, and apparently that has caused at least one problem. I'll turn it over to Chief Smith.

Chief Smith: We have responded to a threat from a chemistry professor. This individual was up for third-year review, and his chances for tenure were slim due not only to a lack of publications but a lack of collegiality and some problems with students. He was the target of an Asian student's complaint of discrimination prior to the explosion, which was dropped. While there may have been some culpability on the student's part, we are not so sure now that that student might not have been justified in his accusations, based on the e-mail we now have. Here's the information we received and how we acted on it in regard to Dr. Haven Newport, assistant professor of chemistry. The chair of the chemistry department got the e-mail you have in your hand forwarded to him by a chemistry professor in Sweden that Newport had written. The professor was alarmed at the content of the e-mail from his old acquaintance, Dr. Newport. He forwarded it to the chemistry chair, who in turn gave it to Lt. Fleming, who is on the TAT [Threat Assessment Team]. After reading it and consulting with the committee, a search warrant was issued for Dr. Newport's apartment, where we found bomb-making materials and two fully assembled pipe bombs with the detonators attached. We arrested Dr. Newport. Dr. Thorenson of the counseling center did a psychiatric interview with him and found him to be highly suicidal/homicidal with a lot of paranoid ideation and persecutory beliefs. He couldn't contain himself emotionally and believes the third-year review committee has ruined his life and plans to get even with them. He had planned to set off a pipe bomb by remote control at the groundbreaking site. The press will find out about this when we arraign him, so we are going to have some queries, I am sure. Here are the assessments on him.

The following threat assessment worksheet (Figure 7.2) [see Chapter 9 for more information on the Threat Assessment Worksheet] was compiled by Lt. Fleming, Central University P.D. and Threat Assessment Team member. The letter (Figure 7.3) was deemed reasonable evidence to obtain a warrant and execute a search of Dr. Newport's residence, where bomb-making materials and fully assembled pipe bombs were discovered. Dr. Newport is now under arrest for manufacturing with intent to use weapons of mass destruction.

Dr. Holland: It doesn't take a forensic psychologist to be alarmed at this e-mail, but if we use Schneidman's, a famous suicidologist's (1985, pp. 121–149) characteristics of a suicide or expressive act homicide (where no material gain occurs, but emotional needs are met), this note takes on even more chilling and ominous aspect.

EMP Director Mathews: Whew! Well I said anniversaries had psychological significance. I wasn't quite thinking in those terms.

First are *situational characteristics:* (a) "The common *stimulus* in suicide/expressive homicide is unendurable psychological pain" (Shneidman, 1985, p. 124), and (b) "the common *stressor* in suicide/homicide is frustrated psychological needs" (Schneidman, 1985, p. 126). Newport's e-mail indicates that he has a long history of frustrated needs that have been unsatisfied.

Second are *motivational characteristics:* (a) "The common *purpose* of suicide is to seek solution" (p. 129), and (b) "the common *goal* of suicide is cessation of consciousness" (Schneidman, 1985, p. 129). What he is about is seeking a solution by killing his tormentors and finally finding peace.

Third are *affective characteristics:* "The common *emotions* in suicide are hopelessness and helplessness" (Schneidman, 1985, p. 131). Newport's powerlessness in the face of overwhelming forces arrayed against him depicts his helplessness and hopelessness of ever being a success in the academic field.

Fourth are *cognitive characteristics:* "The common perception is of constriction such that one's options become very narrowed and the world is seen through tunnel vision so that no alternative thoughts can emerge" (p. 138). Newport is out of options. He got "blown away and he will do unto others" the same.

Fifth are *relational characteristics:* (a) "The common *interpersonal act* in suicide is communication of intention" (letting another person know that one's decision makes sense) (Schneidman, 1985, p. 143), and (b) "the common *action* in suicide is egression" (the right to exit or go out as one wishes, or the right

THREAT ASSESSMENT WORKSHEET

Date: October 16, 2011   **Time:** 9:30 PM

Situation: Receipt of e-mail correspondence from Dr. Thurgood Aldevark, chemistry department, Stockholm University re. Dr. Haven Newport, Assistant Chemistry Professor, Central University, see attached e-mail of threats against university and professors of chemistry department angry over third-year review and thwarted attempts to do research to meet tenure expectations

Name of Person Making Threat: Dr. Haven Newport, Assistant Professor, Chemistry.

Factor	Report	Disposition
Method of Communication	Written	Refer to hall director and hall disciplinary committee
Credibility	High	File report with TAT
		Do not refer to judiciary committee at this time
Potential for Harm	Clear. Volatility high, knowledge and ability to institute means and methods	Contact police, obtain search warrant, put on psychiatric hold, psych assessment of subject
Dynamics of Threat	Impulsive/revenge	Substantive evidence from chair of chemistry
Type of threat (Transient, Continuous, Substantive)	Substantive	
Specificity of Threat	Target specific to department tenured faculty take Newport into protective custody	Warn faculty
Category of Threat (Direct, Conditional, Veiled)	Veiled to direct	
Other	See below	

Other Information: Note previous altercation with biology professor in university center reported 10-15-10 by police chief Smith. Also noted increasingly strident complaints of inadequate office space and research facilities since building explosion.

Figure 7.2   Threat Assessment Worksheet (© All Rights Reserved, CIP Solutions, June, 2009. Printed by permission from CIP Solutions.)

My dear and only friend Thurgood: I have struggled all my life in the shadow of others. I thought that Central University would be different but it is not. They set me up to fail here and now secretly laugh at me. My third year review was the pits and I was told to think about looking elsewhere. I am sick of this and will not stand for it anymore. Someone will pay and I will start with the chair who has constantly sabotaged my research by assigning me heavy teaching loads and other plebian duties. My mind is focused on research but they can't appreciate what I am doing; the narrow-minded monocular fools.

I hate the students and teaching them. They whine and are stupid. They expect handouts and easy grades for doing nothing. Particularly the Asian students whose English is atrocious. I even got in trouble because I was supposedly prejudiced against Asians. If I can't get tenure here there is no hope for me. I am powerless because the T&P (tenure and promotion) committee will decide and they are a good old boys club with the chairman on the throne. They leave me no choice but to take Draconian measures on them as they now do on me.

The dumb bastards here blew my research up and now it's their turn to get blown away. Do unto others . . . so if they would kill me professionally what should they expect in return? You have been my friend since graduate school, Thurgood. My only friend in this bleak and unforgiving, uncaring world. You'll get a package shortly. It will be my personal books and notes which you can use I think. Nobody else gives a damn about them anyways. Also there will be some pictures when we were in grad school. I remain, your lost friend but maybe at peace soon, Haven

Figure 7.3 E-Mail from Dr. Haven Newport to Dr. Thurgood Aldevark

to autonomously find a way out of one's pain) (p. 144). Newport's letter to his graduate school friend is a way of rationalizing the notion that a murder/suicide makes sense and that is ultimately the only way out.

Sixth is the *serial characteristic:* "The common *consistency* in suicide is with life-long coping patterns when deep perturbation, distress, threat, and psychological pain are present" (Shneidman, 1985, p. 147). This is not the first failure Newport has felt in life and may be characterized by all of the foregoing psychological dynamics that culminate in his lethal behavior. Even more dangerous and compelling are his responses in his interview with Dr. Thorenson. He has a clear motive, a clear and lethal plan, and the lethal means to act on his persecutory feelings.

Research examining the mental health status or potential lethality of faculty members under the pressure of the tenure review process is difficult to locate. Or for that matter, any other mental health, domestic tranquility, or job issues faculty may have are also unexplored. All of these problems and issues focus on students. Yet, we can assure you that professors have as many emotional upsets as students. Particularly in the high-pressure academic world of publish or perish, third-year and tenure and promotion peer reviews are pressure packed. Those reviews are not always the objective, data-driven peer analyses they are made out to be. Personalities and departmental politics enter into those decisions and are factors in decisions to retain or dismiss. Frankly, we are surprised that the murders of faculty in the Department of Biology at the University of Alabama–Huntsville didn't occur a long time before at some other tenure and promotion review. We also wonder how many faculty will be willing to sit on tenure and review committees and how those review practices may change after the University of Alabama–Huntsville shootings.

Anniversary

As time moves forward into the next year, the anniversary of the occurrence may become significant (Cohen et al., 2006). Depending on what the university does to proactively deal with the crisis, there will be a pathogenic or salutogenic shift. If the shift is pathogenic and becomes transcrisis in nature, it will take years for the university to recover. That's why it is critically important to immediately attack large-scale problems such as the rebuilding of the science building.

A continuing and contentious issue in the field of trauma therapy is how individuals attain and retain a salutogenic state and if they do or do not need assistance in doing it (Stuhmiller & Dunning, 2000). Antonovsky (1991) has demonstrated that the stronger the person's sense of coherence (to what extent is the stress manageable, coherent, and meaningful), the more able he or she is to cope with life's stressors. We believe that Antonovsky's research with individuals can be applied to university systems as well. The CMTs may be used as the glue that bonds together the fragmented parts of the university in crisis and demonstrates and models a sense of coherence through the crisis that can be emulated by the rest of the university. While no one that we are aware of has ever defined a CMT in this manner before, we believe that providing that sense of coherence is one of the most important missions of the CMT.

Unquestionably, during the long grind of putting the bricks and mortar of buildings and human psyches back together after a disaster, the potential is high to become disillusioned when everything goes wrong and no progress is made. There is good reason for a disillusionment phase in the crisis chronosystem (James, 2008). Thus, rebuilding is not just putting up a new science building after an explosion and fire. It is also about rebuilding and restabilizing one's emotional and social self and the university's as well. Therefore, our belief is that in the recovery process, one could do far worse than using the CMT as that agent.

Restabilization Phase

The restabilization phase of recovery occurs when rebuilding is complete and the campus has returned to a precrisis level of functioning. In this phase, policy and procedural changes become part of campus routine. This process may take several years before it is complete (Halpern & Tramontin, 2007). Setbacks during this phase of recovery are minimal and generally occur around anniversaries. The idea that time heals all wounds is not entirely true after a crisis. The passing of time results in the crisis taking on new meanings for those who were involved (Myer & Moore, 2006).

Assessment during this phase should be periodic to establish a baseline, should another crisis occur. Again, the majority of this data may already exist and be housed in various offices across the campus. Methods described later in the chapter can also be used to obtain this data. We encourage no more than 2 years to pass without an assessment of the well-being of the collective campus.

ORGANIZATIONAL FACTORS AFFECTED BY A CRISIS

No two crises are the same. Each crisis comes with its own impact on a university campus. Some crises are on a large scale, such as the devastation caused by Hurricanes Katrina and Rita to the universities on the Gulf Coast or the tragic events at Virginia Tech University or Northern Illinois University. Other crises are seemingly limited in scope, such as the suicide of a student, staff, or faculty member. The recovery process depends on administrators and CMTs making sense out of chaos. A crisis situation is fluid, changing moment to moment, while taking 90-degree turns without warning (Knotek, 2006). Information comes in a haphazard manner (Paton & Jackson, 2002). The information that is available can be confusing, contradictory, and even incomprehensible.

Myer, Conte, and Peterson (2007) offer a way to make sense out of the chaos that can follow a crisis. These authors identify nine characteristics of any organization—universities in this case—that will be influenced by a crisis: (a) rumors, (b) morale, (c) loyalty, (d) meeting agendas, (e) roles, (f) day-to-day operations, (g) decision-making protocols, (h) organizational goals, and (i) dynamics. Table 7.2 provides a short description for each of these characteristics. Not all of the characteristics are affected to the same degree, yet some interdependence exists among them. The culture of your campus as well as the specific crisis will influence which and to what degree individual characteristics are affected. Generally speaking, the higher the impact and the more pervasive the crisis, the more these characteristics are changed. The changes might be short-term or result in long-lasting changes on campus. Seeing the crisis from a holistic perspective and connecting the dots of a crisis on a specific campus is needed for the recovery process (Mitroff, 2004).

Rumors

Rumors are defined as unconfirmed bits of information that are important to people (DiFonzo & Bordia, 2000) that have the potential to compromise the recovery process in the aftermath of a crisis. Rumors are generated as a way to make sense of the chaos (Rosnow, 1980). One type of rumor is based on a misinterpretation or exaggeration of

Table 7.2   Campus Characteristics

Rumors	Unconfirmed pieces of information that have the potential to compromise the recovery process.
Morale	The courage, discipline, confidence, enthusiasm, and willingness to endure hardship within a group.
Loyalty	The degree to which a university uses a set of symbols and language that produces an effective conformity in the university.
Meeting Agendas	The first and generally most visible characteristic that can be used to assess a university's reactions to a crisis.
Roles	The part employees play in the university. Roles include sets of expected behavior patterns ascribed to individuals occupying a given position in the university.
Day-to-Day Operations	The ability to function at a certain level and maintain normal routine operations.
Decision-Making Protocols	The method by which a determination is made to allocate university resources.
Organization Goals	The mission, stated and unstated, of the university.
Dynamics	Refers to the relationship and interactions among groups internal and external to a university.

facts (Kimmel, 2004) and is an attempt to bring meaning to confusion people are experiencing (DiFonzo & Bordia, 2000). Other literature (Mitroff, Pearson, & Harrington, 1996) discusses rumors as a defense mechanism. Kimmel (2004) adds that this type of rumor may also be used by one group to gain advantage over another. In times of crisis, rumors multiply exponentially and have the power to create instability across the campus (Echterling et al., 2005; Wetlaufer, 2000). During a crisis, rumors may become supercharged and create a toxic atmosphere where distrust and discouragement suffocate the recovery process. Rumors can be about almost anything, ranging from the financial stability of the university to speculation about the safety of physical facilities. Each time the information is passed along, it becomes less and less accurate, whether it is simplified or made more complex (Rosnow, 1980).

Rumors can have a systemic impact on a university that ripples through the campus. For example, at Central University, one rumor said the explosion was caused because of a conflict about manufacturing illegal drugs. Imagine the potential for drops in enrollment when parents of prospective students heard this information. On the other hand, this sort of rumor might also attract an entirely different group of prospective students.

Therefore, assessing changes in the nature and number of rumors is critical in the recovery process.

Morale

Morale is defined as the courage, discipline, confidence, enthusiasm, and willingness to endure hardships with a group, and it is the second characteristic directly impacted by a crisis on a university campus. Morale is the basic tenet by which organizations gauge their emotional selves (Brenneman, 2000) and is vital in the recovery process. In the first few days to weeks after a crisis, morale can be expected to jump. A collective attitude that *we* are in this together will flood the campus (James, 2008). An all for one and one for all attitude is experienced by most people during this time. Having shared and prevailed over a horrific event is a catalyst for a renewed sense of community (Duffy & Schaeffer, 2002). Past conflicts are put on the back burner, and everyone is friends.

Yet, being lulled into a sense that everything is all right can be perilous (Knotek, 2006). After the initial circling of the wagons, old conflicts tend to resurface (Fink, 2002). Misunderstandings may become exaggerated, disagreements embellished, and dissent larger than life. Bickering intensifies, power struggles develop, and in general, the entire recovery process is held hostage. Possibly, the catalyst for these issues surfacing is the perception that some groups or units on campus are receiving favored treatment. A continuous monitoring of morale can warn of tensions resurfacing as the long-standing controversies resurface. Proactive steps can be taken before the situation gets out of control. On the other hand, if assessment finds that morale is steady or improving, this may indicate that the recovery is proceeding in a productive way.

Loyalty

Loyalty, the third characteristic, is the degree to which a university uses a set of symbols and language that produces conformity. These symbols and language create a sense of allegiance (Sagini, 2001). Everyone associated with the university (students, staff, faculty members, administrators, alumni, community members) will have some level of commitment to the well-being of the university. In universities, loyalty can be viewed as student retention, employees not seeking employment elsewhere, and alumni support, to name a few. Be aware that loyalties are more often than not split. Loyalty to the university must compete with commitment to families (Myer & Moore, 2006). Allegiance to departments or units may also interfere with loyalty to the university.

Monitoring loyalty in the aftermath of crisis becomes important because if loyalty is absent, an organization's strength can rapidly deteriorate (Sagini, 2001). Ideally, addressing loyalty issues is a process that should begin long before any crisis takes place. Waiting until a crisis to assess or build loyalty may be like spitting into the wind. That is, your efforts may be thrown back into your face because these are perceived as insincere at best or callow at worst. However, specific things that will help to maintain and even encourage loyalty after a crisis are attention to the emotional needs of everyone affected by the crisis, visibility of administration and CMTs over the entire campus (Mitroff, 2004), and clear, consistent messages regarding the recovery process.

Note that a low level of loyalty creates increased potential for violence (Bravermann, 1999). Civility takes a back seat as people express their frustration in various ways. Behaviors from verbal disagreements to physical attacks indicate hostility is erupting across campus. The fighting can range from minor verbal confrontations to all-out brawls. Everyone is on edge; nerves are raw, tempers become short, and people are not willing to turn the other cheek. Everyone begins looking out for number one. Anyone associated with the university may get involved. Students, staff, faculty members, and even administrators engage in aggressive behaviors in order to protect themselves. The result is an increased disruption of the university's ability to respond efficiently and effectively to the crisis. Keeping tabs on loyalty following a crisis allows administrators and CMTs to take steps to prevent these problems. Seen in this context, loyalty is a vital characteristic of an organization's affective response to crisis.

Meeting Agendas

Meeting agendas are the first and generally most visible characteristic that can be used to assess a university's reaction to a crisis. The degree of the university's preoccupation with the crisis can be argued as being a direct correlation with the impact of the crisis (Myer & Moore, 2006). The more time spent discussing a crisis in a meeting, the more severe the crisis. Basically, it boils down to how much time in meetings is spent talking about the crisis.

In the days, weeks, and months following a crisis, discussion in meetings will intentionally and sometimes unintentionally focus on the crisis. Initially, discussion focuses on doing whatever is necessary to address the immediate crisis situation. Imagine intentional and unintentional changes in meetings in the hours and days following the discovery of a threat in 2007 by Olutosin Oduwole, a student attending Southern Illinois University–Edwardsville, to cause another tragedy like Virginia Tech (Farrell, 2007; Meyer, 2008). While there is no way to know for sure what was discussed, it is likely that once the threat became public, the topic dominated meetings.

As the recovery process progresses, meeting agendas should be expected to return to a more normal state (Myer et al., 2007). A good measure of the effectiveness of the efforts to restore routine functions on campus is discussion at meetings. If the crisis remains a distraction in a majority of meetings, this distraction is a signal the recovery efforts may not be working and the collective reaction of the campus is still at a high to severe level. Assessment at this time should focus on gathering data about why the crisis continues to dominate discussion. Possible reasons for meeting agendas continuing to focus on the crisis include unsuccessful recovery efforts, ineffective communications from administrators and CMTs, the inability of some people to adjust following the crisis, inability to address all the problems resulting from the crisis, and the failure to appreciate the hardships some departments or units are experiencing because of the crisis.

Three general questions to ask to assess changes in meeting agendas are: Have special meetings been called with the sole purpose of addressing issues related to the crisis? How many meetings are called? Does discussion in other meetings drift to talking about the crisis? Specific questions based on the specific crisis should also be generated. These questions should concentrate on the unique aspects of the crisis. Responses to these questions are an indicator of the severity of the crisis.

Roles

Roles are sets of expected behavior patterns ascribed to individuals and groups occupying a given position in the organization (Robbins, 1993). The shift in roles to one degree or another is felt in each phase of the recovery process. Functioning based on these roles is vital to maintain the smooth day-to-day operations of any organization (Moorhead & Griffin, 1989). However, when a crisis occurs, everything seems to be turned upside down. Students, staff, faculty members, and administrators suddenly are thrust into positions in which they must deviate from their expected role (Paton et al., 2000). Shifts in roles depend on many factors, such as the size of the university, resources available, the extent and severity of the crisis, relationships within and between various campus units, the personalities involved, and experience with crises (Rollo & Zdziarski, 2007).

Think about changes in roles at Central University following the explosion. Immediately following the crisis, anyone close by became first responders. People were thrust into a position of giving the initial support and rescuing some people trapped by the explosion. Obviously, this situation is expected, yet it illustrates the change in roles that takes place in a crisis situation. In the few days following the explosion, administrators felt the need to make decisions regarding emotional needs rather than allowing professionals trained in this area to handle the situation.

As enticing as it is and as much as administrators may want to act as if operations are running as usual as soon as possible, roles will remain disrupted to a certain degree until the recovery process has run its course. This situation can lead to frustration as staff and faculty members are trying to reestablish normal routines while helping in the process of recovery. The result is that a person feels torn, not knowing what to do, when to do it, or who to listen to. Assessing changes in roles helps administrators and CMTs to address problem areas, especially those involving people not having enough time to do their jobs yet still being held accountable for their typical responsibilities.

Day-to-Day Operations

Day-to-day operations are the ability of the university to function at an acceptable level and also to maintain normal routine operations. University life has a rhythm that is disrupted immediately following a crisis as well as in the recovery process. Obviously, chaos is expected immediately following a crisis with respect to day-to-day operations (Fink, 2002; Mitroff, 2004). Normal routine operations, such as the traditional ideas of teaching, scholarship, and service, can be disrupted. In addition, disruptions in day-to-day operations may include the provision of housing for many universities, providing food services, keeping up intercollegiate sports, Greek life, general maintenance of campus, monitoring investments and endowments, and many more. Assessing the impact on the day-to-day operations on academic and student life is a good gauge of the severity of the crisis.

The disturbance of routine operation may spread throughout the recovery process. Monitoring the level of disruption and pinpointing the departments and units in which this is occurring helps administrators and CMTs target interventions. You must ask yourself in what way normal operations are being interrupted or changed (Sagini, 2001). Are buildings being cleaned and maintained and research being conducted? What about the impact on recruiting potential students, maintaining scheduled student life functions, and continuing athletic events? Special observances during events on campus such as athletic events and class time are signs of the disruption of normal university operations (Johnson, 2004). No activity, no matter how innocuous, is immune to some amount of interruption. The amount of disruption is a sign of the impact the crisis had on campus (Myer & Moore, 2006).

One indicator that day-to-day operations are affected is change in the number of students requesting health services, both physical and mental. The number of students needing to use health services will almost certainly increase because of the stress they feel. The already overwhelmed campus mental health services will likely see more students asking for help after a crisis (Kadison & DiGeronimo, 2004). These services are already overwhelmed with requests prior to the crisis (Mowbry et al., 2006). The upsurge in people asking for help can stretch the ability to meet those needs to the breaking point (Tol, Jordans, Reis, & de Jong, 2009). Resident life programs also may be affected by a crisis.

Another issue with respect to normal functioning involves loss of work due to taking time off. The university's day-to-day functioning is directly affected by employees' tendency to take excessive time off work after crises (Mitroff et al., 1996). The reason for taking time off varies for each employee. Some people may need time to address the emotional impact of the trauma. They are not able to handle being in close proximity to where the traumatic event took place. If the crisis also caused damage or had some effect on the community, some people may be taking time off to assist family or neighbors. Regardless of the reason, absenteeism can create problems for the university.

Decision-Making Protocols

Decision-making protocols refer to the method by which a determination is made to allocate resources. During normal times, decisions are generally orderly and based on careful examination of all the available information. Research must be done on pricing and product quality, paper work must be completed, bids solicited and obtained, and proper modus operandi followed. Although standard procedures promote continuity, these do not necessarily lend themselves to crisis situations (Paton & Jackson, 2002). When a crisis happens, standard decision-making procedures are severely tested, and more often than not, these procedures come up short (Fink, 2002; Greenstone & Leviton, 2002; Paraskevas, 2006). Decision making in a crisis must not be locked into an inflexible, rigid process. Decision-making procedures should reflect the needs of the situation (Pollard & Hotho, 2006; Paton & Jackson, 2002). Just as the crisis situation is fluid, so should be the way decisions are made (Fink, 2002).

As the recovery process moves forward, the decision-making protocols will resemble a more normal process. This return to normalcy signals the recovery process is on track. However, caution must be exercised to avoid assuming normal operations too quickly. When this situation occurs, blunders are made and oversights occur because the decision-making process fails to consider all issues. Consultation during these stages cannot be underestimated (Knotek, 2006). We believe consultation helps a university avoid missing or misinterpreting data.

Assessment of decision making helps administrators and CMTs identify possible hot spots for why the recovery process is and is not moving forward. Assessment should focus on problems related to decisions concerning the allocation of resources. Data are needed to understand if decision making has either helped or hindered the allocation of resources. Assessment of decision making provides a snapshot of ways the recovery process might be obstructed. At the same time, this assessment can indicate that the recovery process is going well and that what is being done is effective.

Note that a major issue that impacts decision making in a crisis is ego. People who are used to being in charge and making decisions do not want to lose that power. During a crisis, when everything seems out of control, this situation is especially true. Some people believe the issue is solely a question of leadership. Leadership is involved, but leadership during a crisis is not the same as during noncrisis times (Mitroff, 2004). Leadership during a crisis recognizes that some decisions are best made by people who are on the front line, in a manner of speaking. Leadership in a crisis must understand that reliance on standard decision-making procedures may block recovery. However, guidelines need to be built into your crisis management plan to guard against people making sweeping decisions for which they have no experience, authority, or credentials. These guidelines should outline limitations in this area.

Organizational Goals

Organizational goals are the mission, stated and unstated, of the university. In general, these statements usually involve helping students develop into competent, responsible adults. To some degree, a crisis disrupts a university's ability to fulfill its mission. The degree of disruption to the university's mission is one way to gauge the severity of the crisis. For example, in what ways do you imagine the mission of Central University was disturbed by the explosion? If the mission of the university was to provide an education with a strong grounding in the sciences, it would be disrupted. Possibly resources that would have been used to bolster the mission of the university had to be diverted to support recovery efforts. Grant monies generally received by the university may decrease for several years because faculty members are not as productive due to the lack of space, and top students choose to pursue their education elsewhere. As you can see, a crisis can have a widespread impact on the mission of the university.

Factors contributing to the degree of disruption to the mission of a university following a crisis include location, type, and size of campus (Rollo & Zdziarski, 2007). Being located in an urban area as opposed to a smaller city many miles from a metropolitan area is significant with respect to the impact of a crisis on the university's mission. If your campus is situated in a smaller city, the disruption of the mission is potentially higher since the surrounding community may not have the resources to assist in recovery. Being situated in a larger urban area means the community is more likely to have resources to support the recovery process. The type of university—meaning private or public, for profit or nonprofit—is a factor in the alteration of the mission in the aftermath of a crisis. For example, private universities may not have access to the same resources as a public university. The size of a university also has a bearing on the impact of a crisis on its mission. Larger universities typically have more resources and are better positioned to weather the recovery process after a crisis (Rollo & Zdziarski, 2007). Smaller universities may experience difficulties in maintaining their mission due to factors such as limited resources, smaller enrollment, and lesser endowment, to name a few. A poignant example is the disruption caused by Hurricane Katrina to universities and colleges in the region around New Orleans. Several smaller universities and colleges (i.e., Southern University at New Orleans, Lady of the Lakes College, and Our Lady of the Holy Cross) closed their doors for an extended period of time and eliminated programs. Although these schools reopened, there was a time in which each was not filling its mission.

As with any organization, changes in the mission are seen throughout the recovery process (Mitroff, Pearson, & Harrington , 1996). As time passes, a shift back to the university mission will take place (Myer & Moore, 2006). The focus will gradually swing back to the original mission. Monitoring the shift is important to gauge the success of interventions. Immediately following a major crisis, the shift away from the mission is expected. But for up to a year, you may not fully shift back to the focus being primarily on the university mission.

Assessment of the disruption to organizational goals should be based on the mission of the university. A basic question that can be asked is how and to what degree the fulfillment of the university mission has been interrupted by a crisis. Assessing this characteristic involves taking a holistic as well as a departmental or unit perspective. Conducting an assessment with understanding appreciates the collective impact of the

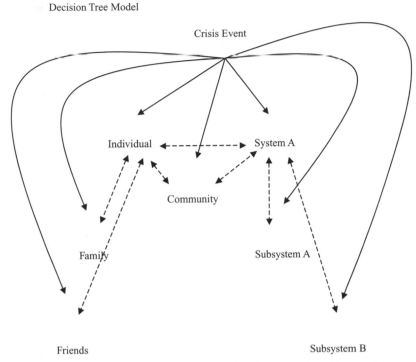

Decision Tree Model

Figure 7.4   Contextual Systemic Model (Used by permission, Myer & Moore, 2006).

crisis across the entire campus while recognizing that departments and units may be affected in individualistic ways not experienced by others on campus.

Dynamics

Dynamics refer to the relationship and interactions among groups internal and external to a university. The dynamics within the system are the working relationships various departments and units have with one another. Assessing this disturbance provides administrators and CMTs insight into some of the difficulties encountered during the recovery process. Higher levels of disturbance generally mean a more severe collective reaction to the crisis and often result in an increased number of obstacles to overcome during recovery.

Myer and Moore (2006) introduced a method to understand the dynamics in a system that is experiencing a crisis. Figure 7.4 depicts this model. These authors describe dynamics using the idea of layers. The solid lines denote a direct relationship of the crisis to individuals and groups. The lines that are dashed signify the interaction of the individuals and groups impacted by the crisis. For example, the explosion at Central University affects not just the people who were injured or saw the explosion but other people and groups connected to the university. In turn, these people and groups exert influence on each other.

These layers in a university setting involve groups internal and external to the campus that will influence recovery directly and indirectly. Understanding internal dynamics on campus involves the culture of the university. Specifically, does the culture at the university allow and even encourage departments and/or units to share resources? Does the culture encourage or discourage communication and coordination across departments or units? These questions become very important in the recovery process. If the culture is that departments and units guard and allocate resources internally, recovery may be obstructed. Take, for example, a campus in which student affairs rigidly refuses to allow personnel assigned to that unit to help out in academic areas. Or the opposite, academic departments refuse to permit their personnel to help in other units on campus. This situation can impede recovery.

External dynamics are also disturbed by a crisis on campus. A good example involves the relationship your university has with the local media. If you have engendered a cordial relationship with this group, they are more likely to be supportive during a crisis. However, if you have developed an adversarial relationship, you can imagine the kind of press you will receive after a crisis occurs on campus. The relationship you have with the surrounding community is another example. If your university has cultivated a supportive relationship with the community, when a crisis occurs, the community is more likely to reciprocate. If the relationships are poor and distant, the community might be helpful but not as much as it could because of the prior history.

Assessment of dynamics should start long before a crisis occurs. We encourage you to assess dynamics before a crisis to determine what dynamics will facilitate or hinder recovery. Identifying these relationships prior to a crisis can help make recovery a more trouble-free process. This information can be used by administrators and CMTs to guide the development of interventions throughout the recovery process. Assessment of dynamics should continue throughout recovery. The data obtained from this assessment will help you refine interventions to meet the needs that emerge during recovery.

These nine characteristics are interconnected. For example, dynamics are directly influenced by decision-making protocols and a university's mission. Roles can be influenced by morale and loyalty. Rumors influence the dynamics and meeting agendas. Changes in one characteristic will produce waves of alterations in the others. Attention through careful periodic monitoring of these characteristics is needed to increase the efficiency and effectiveness of universities' responses to crises.

TIMELINE FOR ASSESSMENT

You must understand that time is needed to recover from a crisis. Just because the immediacy of the situation has passed does not necessarily mean the crisis is over (Myer & Moore, 2006). Many times it is at this point the crisis really begins. As in the case of Central University, many months were needed to recover from the impact of the crisis.

Days, weeks, and sometimes months may be needed before the process is complete (James, 2008). Assessment throughout recovery is needed to help ensure that the needs resulting from a crisis are being addressed.

It is also important to understand that crisis situations change quickly with little or no notice (Barton, 2001). One minute everything may be fine, but in the next minute chaos erupts across campus. Again, Central University provides a poignant illustration. Several people were transported to local emergency rooms and were expected to survive. However, what if that did not work out, and a few of these people also lost their lives? The initial relief students, staff, and faculty members felt because the victims were expected to recover abruptly changes into disbelief that their classmates are gone, and information emerges connecting the tragedy to a drug deal that went bad. Dramatic changes in morale, rumors, and roles will likely occur because the situation changed and new information surfaces.

Baseline Assessment

A baseline assessment is helpful in monitoring the overall organizational health of the university (Barton, 2001). The best practice is to conduct baseline assessments on a regular basis so that up-to-date information is maintained. Similar to Mitroff and Anagnos's (2001) concept of signal detection, these assessments can alert staff to problem areas needing special attention in the case of a crisis. Establishing a baseline also provides a way to understand and interpret changes during a crisis and in the recovery process (Langford, 2004). The Office of Institutional Research may be of assistance in this process. This office collects data on a routine basis from all parts of campus that can be used to understand many of the organizational characteristics affected by a crisis. An example is the turnover rate with respect to the number of staff and faculty members leaving the university. This information can be used to understand the way a crisis can affect loyalty. Retention rates of students can be used in a similar fashion. Data on faculty productivity obtained from annual reports with respect to scholarship might be interpreted to understand morale, day-to-day operations, and the organizational goals or mission of the university. Data regarding the number of complaints filed with human resources or other departments on campus might help in grasping the idea of dynamics. Changes in the numbers of complaints after crisis could signal that dynamics among departments and units are strained.

Assessment During Recovery

The purpose of assessment during recovery is to monitor the effectiveness of interventions and identify new problems, should they develop. As we have said previously, monitoring efforts to respond to the crisis are used to adjust interventions to make them more effective. Not everything that is done to facilitate recovery will work as well as administrators and CMTs plan. Assessment can be used to gauge the effectiveness of efforts, and if they are not being successful, adjustments can be made. Identifying emerging problems during recovery is also important. Rest assured that problems will surface during the recovery process. These problems will be in some way related to the characteristics described earlier in this chapter. Attending to these issues will help to decrease the time needed for a full recovery to the crisis.

A secondary advantage of assessment during this phase of recovery is that the data can be used to justify your actions to groups such as governance bodies. Sooner or later, you will be asked to defend the decisions that were made and your use of resources. Saying decisions were made because you thought it seemed prudent will only go so far. Rationalizing the use of resources because you thought it sounded like a good idea will probably not work that well either. Without having the data to back the actions taken, administrators and CMTs will be hard-pressed to argue the decisions were appropriate and the resources used were needed.

Assessment during the recovery period should be conducted periodically. However, identifying specific times and/or intervals to monitor the progress being made in recovery is impractical. Decisions about when to assess should be based on two factors. The first factor is the impact of the crisis on your campus. Crises that have a high impact on your campus will typically require more frequent assessment and for a longer period of time. High-impact crises are unique for each campus. What may be a high impact for one university may barely be noticed by others. However, high-impact crises characteristically involve shootings resulting in multiple injuries or deaths and major disasters affecting a significant part of the campus. Recovery from these crises can be more complex, with the potential of encountering problems that are more persistent. Crises that have a lower impact require less monitoring for a shorter time period. Recovery from these types of crises is not as involved because the overall impact is not as invasive. Experience is the second factor that influences the timing of assessment during recovery. Administrators and CMTs who are battle-tested by having already guided the university through a recovery from a crisis may be able to recognize problems caused by a crisis with minimal assessment. Yet do not be lulled into complacency; each crisis presents its unique set of problems, making some assessment vital even for experienced administrators and CMTs.

Postcrisis Assessment

Postcrisis assessment is used in two ways. First, postcrisis assessment should be conducted to reestablish a baseline. Establishing a new baseline is critical should another crisis occur. While no one wants to think another crisis will happen, that is not realistic. Sooner or later, another crisis will happen. New baseline data are needed to understand the recovery process. Second, assessment at this time is used to review the effectiveness of the overall recovery process. Reviewing procedures provides valuable information for responding to future crises. This assessment can involve reviewing documents, conducting individual interviews, having focus groups, and meeting with departments and units. Each of these methods provides information that can be used to understand the efficiency and effectiveness of the university response to the crisis. In most situations, this assessment is best conducted approximately 1 year after the crisis. This timing allows most people involved in the crisis to discuss the recovery process from a more objective perspective. However, the timing of this assessment depends on the overall impact of the crisis.

ASSESSMENT PROCEDURES

Access to reliable and valid data is critical in the recovery process. Nothing is worse than wishing you had some way to make a decision about directing resources to where they are needed and ways to do that. Having assessment procedures in place or, better, having practiced those strategies will help you make decisions and develop intervention strategies that target areas in need.

Key concepts to consider when selecting procedures to use for assessment are (a) intensity, (b) duration, and (c) pervasiveness. Intensity refers the strength or degree of impact of a crisis. The higher the intensity, the more debilitating the problems can be. Obviously, duration refers to the period of time the issue has been going on. The longer the problems have been around, the more difficult it will be to effectively resolve them. Pervasiveness concerns extent of the problem across campus. Pervasive signals that the recovery process will need to be comprehensive, involving more than just the groups directly affected by the crisis. Whenever making a decision about an assessment procedure, these concepts can be considered separately or in combination.

Identifying an office or someone who has the responsibility of collecting data is very important. The office or person will vary from campus to campus. Crisis management plans include information about who will be responsible for collecting the data. Crisis management plans should also give some form of guidance to whoever is charged with data collection.

Types of Data

The first decision to make with respect to assessment procedures involves using existing and/or generating new data. Existing data is the information universities have collected for any number of reasons, including tracking enrollment (e.g., applications made, retention rate), monitoring use of health services, personnel records (e.g., absenteeism rate), and credit hours taken. These data are particularly helpful to understand the long-term impact of a crisis on the overall well-being of the university. New data are useful in monitoring the recovery process with respect to the effectiveness of interventions, as well as detecting problems as they emerge during recovery.

We recommend a review of the various types of data already available on your campus to start the process of assessment. Consider what offices already have data that can be used to understand the collective and extended impact of crisis. We have named a few, including the Office of Institutional Research, Department of Admissions, Human

Resources, and Alumni Relations. Records from Campus Security, Residence Life, Business Affairs Office, and utilization of Health Services might also be used to assess and, if warranted, provide support to areas in need. Your campus probably has many other offices that could be used to mine data that could help in the recovery process. Ingenuity is important to identify possible sources of data.

Data collected specifically to understand the crisis situation is not so easily accomplished but still possible. For example, measuring rumors, morale, and roles with quantitative methods is possible but may also be accomplished with qualitative strategies. Putting a number on decision-making protocols also poses psychometric issues. Gauging other characteristics such as university goals, dynamics with the university, and roles can also be accomplished through both quantitative and qualitative approaches.

Electronic Methods for Gathering Data

Another decision to make regarding assessment procedures concerns the use of electronic methods to gather data. The Internet is fast becoming an important method to gather data. Three basic strategies can be used to obtain data in this manner. The first is to post surveys or open-ended questionnaires and send these out to groups who can provide information to help the recovery process. The advantage of this strategy is that data can easily be analyzed and reported. This advantage is invaluable when time is of the essence. We do recommend that templates for these surveys be developed prior to the crisis. The template would outline the areas that could be assessed, depending on the situation and point in the recovery process. A second method for using the Internet for assessment is the creation of blogs to allow people to have conversations about the recovery. Discussion starters can be used as a catalyst to start conversations about specific topics. These topics might include any or all of the nine characteristics described earlier in the chapter. Consideration should be given to the group or person who starts a blog. For example, a blog started by the president of the student government might encourage a different type of discussion than a blog begun by the president of the university. Each blog will give valuable but different types of information. A third more novel use of the Internet for gathering data would be to glean social network sites for information. This strategy is likely the most unreliable but might be useful to identify trends or issues that merit additional attention in the overall assessment process.

Whom to Assess

Decisions must also be made about whom to assess as well as the number of people to include in the assessment. Assessment should involve as many people as possible. All units should be represented in the assessment process. Myer and Moore (2006) can be used to design this aspect of assessment. These authors introduce the idea that the impact of crisis can be understood in part by proximity. We suggest assessment use proximity to decide the groups to assess during recovery. Obviously, assessment of groups closest to the epicenter of the crisis should initially be part of the assessment. This group most likely includes students, staff, faculty members, and administrators. Each has a different perspective valuable in the recovery process. The next level of assessment should involve people who may not have been directly affected by the crisis but who are close to those that were. These groups might include floors in resident halls, fraternity and sorority members, student organizations, and departments or units. These groups can be considered at risk because of the relationship they have with the people directly impacted by the crisis. The level of assessment is often overlooked in the recovery process. This group includes family members of employees and students of the university. Although family members' perspective is not unbiased, their point of view offers insight to the recovery of the university from the crisis. The final level of assessment might include others who are connected with the university and have a stake in the recovery process. These people include community members, alumni, parents of students, local officials, and vendors. These groups provide a different perspective on the recovery of the university from the crisis. The value of this information cannot be underestimated. While these groups do have biases, they are generally less influenced by campus politics. An impartial perspective can provide data otherwise inaccessible by any other means. Together, these groups give a well-rounded perspective of the progress being made in the recovery from the crisis situation.

METHODS FOR ASSESSMENT

Assessment methods during the recovery process must consider time and costs. Time is of the essence. Information is needed now, not after a long period of developing interview questions or the validation of a survey instrument. Time-consuming methods have limited usefulness in a crisis. Again, administrators and CMTs need the information yesterday, not in 2 to 3 weeks. Having assessment procedures developed prior to the crisis is critical if administrators and CMTs are to obtain data in a timely fashion. Costs are always important for any evaluative process. However, undue focus on this aspect can slow the recovery process. Reasonable costs are to be expected and may be outside the usual budgetary line. Guidelines for spending monies should be in place to address the extra costs associated with a crisis. Relying on institutional protocols for budget requests is likely to not be effective immediately following a crisis and will slow and possibly prevent the recovery process. The effort needed to analyze data is also a principal concern. Decisions about the distribution of resources must be made to smooth the progress of recovery from the crisis. Waiting for even a day, much less a week or two, can be too long in some circumstances. Decisions cannot be put on the back burner while waiting for analysis of data to be put into spiral-bound notebooks.

Interviews

Interview methods of gathering and interpreting data can be done through both structured and unstructured approaches. A strength of interviews is that data gathered can be rich in detail, providing insight that otherwise would be missed. Another benefit of these methods is that data can be obtained with relative ease and minimal costs. The ease of gathering data is important in the aftermath of a crisis. Efficiency is important during a crisis.

The primary problem with using interviews is the time needed to analyze data. Identifying themes and relationships in the data takes time when done in isolation. As a result, we recommend that interviews always be used in conjunction with more standardized strategies in crisis situations. This strategy allows decisions to be made and interventions introduced that recognize the idiosyncratic issues present in any recovery process.

It is important to have a general idea of the types of questions that will be asked in interviews and focus groups. A sample of questions that can be used during interviews and focus groups can be found in Table 7.3. You will want to generate other questions based on the specific crisis and the uniqueness of your university.

Table 7.3 Sample Interview Questions	
Individual Interviews	• What issues do you face on a day-to-day basis because of the crisis? • How is the crisis causing you stress in getting your work done? • What would be the most help to you to do your work? • What is causing you the most problems because of the crisis?
Key Informants	• What resources would be the most helpful? • What can't you do because of the crisis? • What or who is interfering with fulfilling your responsibilities? • What kinds of pressure do you and the people who report to you experience because of the crisis?
Focus Groups	• What keeps you from accomplishing your work? • What has helped you do your part in the recovery process? • What has changed about the relationship of your department or unit with other areas on campus as a result of the crisis? • What suggestions would you give to administrators and CMTs to help in the recovery from the crisis?
Department/ Unit Town Hall Meeting	• What are the most pressing issues you face? • What resources are you lacking to recover from the crisis? • What has caused your department or unit the most problems? • How can the administration or CMT help you the most?
Exit Interviews	• What caused you to make the decision to leave the university? • How did the crisis influence your desire to seek employment elsewhere?

Interviewing individuals can be done at any of the phases in the recovery process. However, in the impact phase, we believe this should not be until after the sense of emergency has faded. Interviews should be designed ahead of time but also be flexible enough to gather data relevant to the uniqueness of the crisis. Questions should not be set in stone; rather, they should be fluid in order to tailor them to the situation. A model such as the triage assessment system (Myer, 2001) can be used as a guide in the development of interviews. A model provides a framework for the basic information that is needed and helps avoid the problem of asking irrelevant questions based heavily on interviewers' biases (Myer, Williams, Ottens, & Schmidt, 1992). Questions are asked in order to fill out the framework. Interviewers should ask questions regarding experience of the crisis across campus and, as appropriate, in individual units. Questions should also be posed regarding the current status of the recovery process. The nine characteristics described earlier in the chapter can serve as a model of understanding the data from interviews. Other issues may also arise, but generally speaking, a vast majority can be understood within the framework provided by these characteristics since they are hot spots in the recovery process.

Key Informants

Interviewing key informants is one strategy particularly useful in the recovery from a crisis. Key informants include anyone with a stake in the recovery process. Students, staff, faculty members, and administrators are the first to come to mind when thinking about key informants. Key informants may be leaders of these groups and willing to be honest about their experience (Heppner, Wampold, & Kivlighan, 2008). However, others such as alumni, community members, and vendors should be included in these interviews. Each of these groups has a stake in the recovery process. Interviews can be formal with a planned set of questions. Using a planned set of questions allows data to be collected in a systematic manner. Everyone involved in the interview process would have the same experience. Interviewers would be asking the same questions, and subsequently interviewees would be responding to the same stimuli. However, the structured nature of the interview may miss extremely valuable information. We recommend the use of semistructured interviews that allow the people being interviewed to expand their responses. This method blends the advantages of asking questions in a systematic manner with the capacity of interviewers to follow up on interesting information.

Informal interviews can also be used with key informants to obtain data for the recovery process. One way to conduct informal interviews is to visit various parts of the campus and just talk with people. Discussion in these informal meetings should, as in formal interviews, revolve around a model in order to gather data relevant to the recovery process. As with formal strategies, informal approaches have benefits and drawbacks. A major benefit to informal interviews is that interviewees may be more open. The people being interviewed will feel less anxious and freer to express their perceptions. Less than flattering information that could be seen as critical yet also constructive may be volunteered that would otherwise be withheld in more formal settings. Another benefit of gathering data in this manner is that it shows concern. If administrators or CMTs are seen out and about talking with people, morale may be improved. Students, staff, faculty members, and others will see the interest of administrators and CMTs in wanting to make things better.

The low cost of informal interviews makes this approach attractive. Cost for this strategy will be minimal since it is likely people outside the university will not be used, thereby saving money. One drawback is the data may not be representative of the entire campus. Important units and groups of people may be missed because these were not visited. In addition, data may be biased since not everyone was represented. Decisions based on this information may not reflect the needs of the entire campus.

Focus Groups

Using focus groups is a practical and efficient strategy to gather data to understand a university's reactions to a crisis and performance in the recovery process. Although usually homogeneous (Heppner, Wampold, & Kivlighan, 2008), heterogeneous groups may also be beneficial. Heterogeneous groups allow people with different involvement in the crisis and recovery process to interact and fill in information that the others are not aware of. Time is the primary benefit of focus groups. Interviewing individuals takes time that may be a luxury in a crisis. Focus groups allow more people to give their input in the same amount of time. Focus groups preserve the advantage of data rich with detail. The drawback for this method is analyzing this information. In crisis situations, time is of the essence, and rapid analysis is needed. As with analyzing data from individual interviews, analysis of data obtained in focus groups can be time consuming. We recommend using focus groups particularly in the later phases of the recovery. Focus groups should also be representative of everyone on campus. Leaving out even one group can result in limited and possibly faulty conclusions. The question arises of how to select people to participate in a focus group. Asking for volunteers is one method; another would be to have the leadership of the units and departments nominate possible participants. Both methods have strengths and drawbacks. A hybrid method in which individuals volunteer and are also nominated by the leadership of their unit or department can overcome these issues. The final selection should be made either randomly or by the CMT, with an equal number of each in the focus group.

Department or Unit Town Hall Meetings

Department or unit town hall meetings are similar to focus groups except that the group only represents itself. This method involves someone attending a department or unit meeting with the expressed purpose of gathering information. Obviously, the advantage of this method is that you collect data specific to one department or unit. However, if this method is used, we encourage you not to attend just meetings of one department or unit. Doing so may communicate the wrong message to other departments or units. A secondary gain of using this method is that you can communicate the progress being made toward recovery. This information can itself be worth the effort to gather information with this method.

Exit Interviews

Exit interviews of staff and faculty are another method to obtain information that can be helpful in crisis situations. These interviews should include questions regarding the reason for leaving the university. In the year following a university crisis, a question asking about the influence of that event on leaving could be asked. The information could be fed back to the administration and CMT for analyses. The results of the analyses could be used to help CMTs gauge the effectiveness and efficiency of the intervention on the recovery process.

Existing Records

Existing records include such data as turnover rates and absenteeism of employees. Productivity is also an indicator of the impact of crises. A drop in the number of scholarly activities, grants submitted, and so on is an indication that faculty members are preoccupied with the recovery process rather than scholarly activities. Changes in ratings for teaching can also suggest that faculty members have been distracted by the crisis.

The admission department is a veritable golden bucket of information. Drops in the number of inquiries, applications, and admissions suggest the need to follow up to determine why this is occurring. Also, the registrar's office may provide information about the impact of a crisis at a university. For example, a drop in credit hour production overall or in specific academic units hints that a crisis has had an influence. Lower retention of current students also signals problems following a crisis. Granted, more information is needed, but we recommend that changes in these numbers following a crisis should be considered as valuable in understanding the effect of the crisis on the university.

Surveys

Surveys can be used to gather quantitative data about the impact of a crisis, as well as monitor the recovery process. Surveys can be designed for use with a specific crisis event (e.g., multiple deaths, environmental crises, disease outbreaks, fires, major crimes). The university can also develop a survey designed to be used specifically on its campus. The advantage of creating a survey is that the idiosyncratic aspects of the crisis and the campus can be taken into account. For example, if the crisis involved the outbreak of a communicable illness, items can be asked regarding health services and possible dining services if it is suspected that tainted food caused the illness. However, taking on the development of a survey designed specifically for one event or even to be used at one university is time consuming and costly. In addition, someone experienced in developing a survey of this nature may not be available.

Using previously developed surveys is an excellent alternative. However, given the fact that crisis management is only 20 years old (Mitroff et al., 2006), surveys of this kind are almost nonexistent. The Triage Assessment Form: Organizations (TAS:O) is an instrument developed for use in any organization. It was designed to measure an organization's reaction following a crisis and to monitor the recovery process (Myer et al., 2007). The TAS:O can be used with all types of crises regardless of the severity. It is divided into affective, behavioral, and cognitive subscales. Scores on these scales can be used to direct resources where they are needed. Scales on which the scores are highest indicate that resources are needed most in that area. For example, if scores on the affective scale are the highest, administrators and CMTs should direct resources to intervene in those characteristics (i.e., rumors, morale, and loyalty). As scores in the affective area decrease, behavioral and cognitive areas should be addressed. Full-scale scores can be used to determine the severity of a crisis. Crises in universities can be divided into mild, moderate, marked, and severe. The full scale suggests how direct the intervention should be; the severer the reaction, the more direct the intervention. This information is useful for administrators, CMTs, and consultants as they develop plans for the recovery process. Take, for example, the tragedies that occurred at Northern Illinois University. The day following the shooting, consultants experienced in that type of tragedy were brought to campus to help set up the university's response (Personal communication, Rick Long, February 18, 2008). Research on the TAS:O concluded it is both reliable and valid (Conte, 2005; Conte, Myer, Miller, & D'Andrea, 2007). Reliability was tested using internal consistency and was measured at higher than 80%. Validity was tested using confirmatory analysis. This analysis found that the TAS:O has three distinct scales, each measuring a different aspect of an organization's reaction to a crisis. Another aspect of validity involves effectiveness of the TAS:O in determining the severity of an organization's reaction to a crisis. Probably the best aspect of TAS:O is using it to monitor the recovery process. A decrease in scores on subscales and the full scale suggests the recovery process is progressing in a positive direction.

Behavioral Observations

A final method is using behavioral observations. A simple stroll around campus and impromptu conversations with students, staff, and faculty can give indispensable information about life on campus following a crisis. Be prepared to hear information that does not always affirm what is being done. Literature on crisis leadership recommends that leaders be visible in the recovery process (Mitroff, 2004). Staying sequestered behind closed doors too often leads to erroneous ideas and rumors. Be visible and listen to what people have to say.

Each of the assessment approaches offers valuable information to understand the reactions of the campus to the crisis as well as a method to check the progress of the recovery. We recommend the use of multiple strategies to assess the situation. Reliance on the results from one strategy may present a partial picture of the situation.

SUMMARY

Crisis intervention and prevention on college campuses must extend beyond offering services and support to individuals. The intervention process must extend to the university as a whole as well as the units and departments on campus. At times, expanding services to other stakeholders is warranted, especially in situations that are considered dramatic and extensive. Stakeholders might include families of students and employees, along with the surrounding community. Failure to consider this issue can severely impede the recovery process. Administration and CMTs must be guided by more than gut instinct; objective information is needed to distribute resources. Gathering objective information rather than reliance on the squeaky wheel is critical. Although the squeaky wheel draws attention to specific needs, providing resources to those who cry the loudest may mean more quiet but may also not be the best use of resources. Systematic assessment is the overarching process to ensure that resources are shunted to the areas with the greatest need. Creativity in assessment is important and we encourage you to use as many as possible given the restrictions of the situation. Assessment should be conducted periodically throughout all phases of the recovery process. Each phase calls for different strategies for assessment and the provision of service and support.

REFERENCES

Antonovsky, A. (1980). *Health, stress, and coping.* San Francisco: Jossey-Bass.

Antonovsky, A. (1991). The structural sources of salutogenic strengths. In C. Cooper & R. Payne (Eds.), *Personality and stress: Individual differences in the stress process* (pp. 67–104). London: John Wiley & Sons.

Armstrong, K., O'Callahan, W., & Marmar, C. (1991). Debriefing Red Cross disaster personnel: The multiple stressor debriefing model. *Journal of Traumatic Stress, 4,* 581–593.

Augsburger, D. W. (1992). *Conflict mediation across cultures.* Louisville, KY: Westminster/John Knox Press.

Barton, L. (2001). *Crisis in organizations II* (2nd ed.). Mason, OH: South-Western.

Bolton, D. (1999). The threat to belonging in Enniskillen: Reflections on the Rememberance Day bombing. In E. S. Zinner & M. B. Williams (Eds.), *When a community weeps: Case studies in group survivorship* (pp. 193–210). Philadelphia, PA: Bruner-Mazel.

Braverman, M. (1999). *Preventing workplace violence.* Thousand Oaks, CA: Sage.

Brenneman, G. (2000). Right away and all at once: How we saved continental. In *Harvard Business Review on crisis management* (pp. 87–118). Boston: Harvard Business School Press.

Charlton, P. F. C., & Thompson, J. A. (1996). Ways of coping with psychological distress after trauma. *British Journal of Psychology, 35,* 517–530.

Cohen, P., Kasen, S., Chen, H., Gordon, K., Bereson, K., Brook, J., & White, T. (2006). Current affairs and the public psyche: American anxiety post 9/11 world. *Social Psychiatry and Psychiatric Epidemiology, 41*, 251–260.

Conte (2005). *Examination of the reliability and validity of the Triage Assessment Survery: Organizations.* Unpublished doctoral dissertation: Duquesne University.

Conte, C., Myer, R. A., Miller, J. A., & D'Andrea, L. M. (2007). Assessing human impact in organizational crises: Reliability and validity of the Triage Assessment Scale for organization (TAS:O). *Journal of Contingencies and Crisis Management, 15*, 134–142.

DiFonzo, N., & Bordia, P. (2000). How top PR professionals handle hearsay: Corporate rumors, their effects, and strategies to manage them. *Public Relations Review, 26*, 173–190.

Duffy, J., & Schaeffer, M. S. (2002). *Triumph over tragedy: September 11 and the rebirth of a business.* Hoboken, NJ: John Wiley & Sons.

Dyregrov, A. (1997). The process in psychological debriefings. *Journal of Traumatic Stress, 10*, 589–605.

Echterling, L. G., Presbury, J. H., & McKee, J. E. (2005). *Crisis intervention: Promoting resilience and resolution in troubled times.* Upper Saddle River, NJ: Pearson.

Faberow, N. L., & Frederick, C. J. (1978). *Training for human service workers in major disasters.* Rockville, MD: National Institute of Mental Health.

Farrell, E. F. (2007, October 3). Southern Ill. Student Threatens Rampage. *Chronicle of Higher Education.* Retrieved from http://business.highbeam.com/434953/article-1G1-166994085/southern-ill-student-threatens-rampage.

Fink, S. (2002). *Crisis management: Planning for the inevitable.* Lincoln, NE: iUniverse.

Greenstone, J. L., & Leviton, S. C. (2002). *Elements of crisis intervention: Crises and how to respond to them.* Pacific Grove, CA: Brooks/Cole.

Halpern, J., & Tramontin, M. (2007). *Disaster mental health: Theory and practice.* Belmont, CA: Brooks/Cole.

Heppner, P. P., Wampold, B. E., & Kivlighan, D. M. (2008). *Research and design in counseling* (3rd ed.). Belmont, CA: Thomson.

James, R. K. (2008). *Crisis intervention strategies* (6th ed.). Belmont, CA: Brooks/Cole.

Johnson, K. (2004). The effects of trauma on post-secondary learning. In R. Lee & D. Casey (Eds.), *Crisis and trauma: In colleges and universities* (pp. 45–58). Ellicott City, MD: Chevron Publishing.

Kadison, R., & DiGeronimo, T. F. (2004). *College of the overwhelmed: The campus mental health crisis and what to do about it.* San Francisco: Jossey Bass.

Kimmel, A. J. (2004). *Rumors and rumor control: A manager's guide to understanding and combating rumors.* Mahwah, NJ: Erlbaum.

Knotek, S. (2006). Administrative consultation after 9/11: A university's systems response. *Consulting Psychology Journal: Practice and Research, 58*, 162–173.

Langford, L. (2004). *Preventing violence and promoting safety in higher education settings: Overview of a comprehensive approach.* Washington, DC: U.S. Department of Education.

Martin, T. E. (2004). A model for business resiliency. *Continuity Insights, 2*(6), 30–33.

Meyer, H. (2008, October 30). Ex SIUE student back in jail after trying to buy gun: Threatened rampage last year. *Belleville News Democrat,* np.

Mitchell, J. T., & Everly, G. S., Jr. (1995). *Advanced critical incidents stress debriefing.* Ellicott City, MD: International Critical Incidents Stress Foundation.

Mitroff, I. I. (2004). *Crisis leadership: Planning for the unthinkable.* Hoboken, NJ: John Wiley & Sons.

Mitroff, I. I, & Anagnos, G. (2001). *Managing crises before they happen.* New York: American Management Association.

Mitroff, I. I., Diamond, M. A., & Alpasian, C. M. (2006). How prepared are America's colleges and universities for major crises? *Change: The Magazine of Higher Education Learning, 38*, 61–67.

Mitroff, I. I., Pearson, C. M., & Harrington, L. K. (1996). *The essential guide to managing corporate crises: A step-by-step handbook for surviving major catastrophes.* New York: Oxford University Press.

Moorhead, G., & Griffin, R. W. (1989). *Organizational behavior.* Boston: Houghton Mifflin.

Morrissey, M. (1994). ACA, Red Cross to work together to help disaster victims. *Guidepost, 36,* 1, 6.

Mowbry, C. T., Megivern, D., Mandiberg, J. M., Strauss, S., Stein, C. H., Collins, K., . . . Lett, R. (2006). Campus mental health services: Recommendations for change. *American Journal of Orthopsychiatry, 76,* 226–237.

Myer, R. A. (2001). *Assessment for crisis intervention: A triage assessment model.* Belmont, CA: Brooks/Cole.

Myer, R. A., Conte, C., & Peterson, S. E. (2007). Human impact issues for crisis management in organizations. *Disaster Prevention and Management, 16,* 761–770.

Myer, R. A., & Moore, H. (2006). Crisis in context: An ecological model. *Journal of Counseling and Development, 84,* 139–147.

Myer, R. A., Williams, R. C., Ottens, A. J., & Schmidt, A. E. (1992). Crisis assessment: A three dimensional model for triage. *Journal of Mental Health Counseling, 14,* 137–148.

Myers, D., & Wee, D. F. (2005). *Disaster mental health services.* New York: Bruner-Routledge.

Myers, D., & Zunin, L. (1994). Debriefing and grief: Easing the pain. *Today's Supervisor, 6*(12), 14–15.

Norris, F., Friedman, M., Watson, P., Byrne, C., Diaz, E., & Kaniasty, K. (2002). 60,000 disaster victims speak: Part I. An empirical review of the literature, 1981–2001. *Psychiatry: Interpersonal & Biological Process, 65*(3), 207–243.

Norris, F. H., & Alegria, M. (2006). Promoting disaster recovery in ethnic-minority individuals and communities. In E. C. Ritchie, P. J. Watson, & M. J. Friedman (Eds.), *Interventions following mass violence and disasters: Strategies for mental health practice* (pp. 319–342). New York: Guilford Press.

Nurmi, L. (1999). The Estonia disaster: National intervention, outcomes, and personal impacts. In E. S. Zinner & M. B. Williams (Eds.), *When a community weeps: Case studies in group survivorship* (pp. 49–72). Philadelphia: Bruner-Mazel.

Paraskevas, A. (2006). Crisis management or crisis response system: A complexity science approach to organizational crises. *Management Decision, 44,* 892–907.

Paton, D., & Jackson, D. (2002). Developing disaster management capability: An assessment centre approach. *Disaster Prevention and Management, 11,* 115–122.

Paton, D., Smith, L., & Violanti, J. (2000). Disaster response: Risk vulnerability and resilience. *Disaster Prevention and Management, 9,* 173–179.

Pennebaker, J. W., & Harber, K. D. (1993). A social stage model of collective coping: The Loma Prieta earthquake and the Persian Gulf War. *Journal of Social Issues, 49,* 125–146.

Poland, S., & McCormick, J. A. (1999). *Coping with crisis: Lessons learned.* Longmont, CO: Sorpris West.

Pollard, D., & Hotho, S. (2006). Crisis, scenarios, and the strategic management process. *Management Decision, 44,* 721–736.

Ren, C. H. (2000). Understanding and managing the dynamics of linked crisis events. *Disaster Prevention and Management, 9,* 12–17.

Robbins, S. P. (1993). *Organizational behavior: Concepts, controversies, and publications* (6th ed.). Englewood Cliffs, NJ: Prentice Hall.

Rollo, J. M., & Zdziarski, E. L. (2007). The impact of crisis. In E. L. Zdziarski, W. D. Dunkel, J. M. Rollo, & associates (Eds). *Campus crisis management: A comprehensive guide to planning, prevention, response, and recovery* (pp. 3–33). San Francisco: Jossey-Bass.

Rosenfeld, L. B., Caye, J. S., Ayalon, O., & Lahad, M. (2005). *When their world falls apart: Helping families and children manage the effects of disasters.* Washington, DC: NASW Press.

Rosnow, R. L. (1980). Psychology of rumor reconsidered. *Psychological Bulletin, 87,* 578–591.

Ruzek, J. I. (2006). Models of early intervention following mass violence and other trauma. In E. C. Ritchie, P. J. Watson, & M. J. Friedman (Eds.), *Interventions following mass violence and disasters: Strategies for mental health practice* (pp. 16–36). New York: Guilford Press.

Saakvitne, K. W., & Pearlman, L. A. (1996). *Transforming the pain: A workbook on vicarious traumatization.* New York: W. W. Norton.

Sagini, M. M. (2001). *Organizational behavior: The challenges of the new millennium.* Lanham, MD: University Press of America.

Shneidman, E. S. (1985). *Definition of suicide.* New York: John Wiley & Sons.

Shelby, J. S., & Tredinnick, M. G. (1995). Crisis intervention with survivors of natural disaster: Lessons from Hurricane Andrew. *Journal of Counseling and Development, 73,* 491–497.

Sitterle, K. A., & Gurwitch, R. H. (1999). The terrorist bombing in Oklahoma City. In *When a community weeps: Cases studies in group survivorship* (pp. 161–188). Philadelphia, PA: Bruner-Mazel.

Slaikeu, K. A. (1990). *Crisis intervention: A handbook for practice and research* (2nd ed.). Needham Heights, MA: Allyn & Bacon.

Speier, A. H. (2006). Immediate needs assessment following catastrophic disaster incidents. In E. C. Ritchie, P. J. Watson, & M. J. Friedman (Eds.), *Interventions following mass violence and disasters: Strategies for mental health practice* (pp. 80–102). New York: Guilford Press.

Stuhlmiller, C., & Dunning, C. (2000). Challenging the mainstream: From pathogenic to salutogenic models of posttrauma intervention. In J. M. Violanti, D. Paton, & C. Dunning (Eds.), *Posttraumatic stress intervention: Challenges, issues, and perspectives* (pp. 10–42). Springfield, IL: Charles C Thomas.

Tol, W. A., Jordans, M. D., Reis, R., & de Jong, D. J. (2009). Ecological resilience: Working with child related psychosocial resources in war-affected communities. In D. Brom, R. Pat-Horenczyk, & J. D. Ford (Eds). *Treating traumatized children* (pp. 164–182). New York: Routledge.

Watson, P. J., Ritchie, E. C., Demer, J., Bartone, P., & Pfefferbaum, B. J. (2006). Improving resilience trajectories following mass violence and disaster. In E. C. Ritchie, P. J. Watson, & M. J. Friedman (Eds.), *Interventions following mass violence and disasters: Strategies for mental health practice* (pp. 37–53). New York: Guilford Press.

Wetlaufer, S. (2000). After the layoffs, what next? In *Harvard Business Review* on Crisis Management. Boston: Harvard Business School Press.

Wiger, D. E. (2003). *Essentials of crisis counseling and intervention.* Hoboken, NJ: John Wiley & Sons.

Young, B. H. (2006). The immediate response to disaster: Guidelines for adult psychological first aid. In E. C. Ritchie, P. J. Watson, & M. J. Friedman (Eds.), *Interventions following mass violence and disasters: Strategies for mental health practice* (pp. 134–154). New York: Guilford Press.

Zinner, E. S. (1999). The *Challenger* disaster: Group survivorship on a national landscape. In E. S. Zinner & M. B. Williams (Eds.), *When a community weeps: Case studies in group survivorship* (pp. 23–48). Philadelphia: Bruner-Mazel.

8

No Rest for the Weary:
System Recovery After a Crisis

The line "it ain't over 'til the fat lady sings" is fitting to begin this chapter. Too often administrators and crisis management teams (CMTs) are too quick to close the book on recovery from a crisis. Many times just when they think recovery is complete, it is really just beginning. This chapter introduces you to a model adapted from Gilliland (1982) that can be used to make recovery possible on your campus. Although developed as a method for crisis intervention workers to understand ways to intervene with individuals, the model is easily modified for groups. After describing the model, we discuss its implementation throughout the stages of the recovery process. This discussion focuses on complications that may arise because universities are complex organizations. We close the chapter with a discussion of nine strategies that can be used to develop interventions to facilitate the recovery process.

A general time frame for a campus returning to what appears to be a normal routine is approximately 2 months. This time frame has been accepted as a guiding principle in crisis intervention (Caplan, 1961). Think about campus life 2 months after the explosion at Central University. Except for the construction around the science building, campus life appears normal to the casual observer. Classes are being held, students are hanging out after classes, day-to-day operations are being taken care of, and all the other customary activities that take place on university campuses are happening. The groups that came to campus offering support in the hours, days, and weeks following the crisis have gone home. The pavilion tents that were pitched on campus for the volunteers have been packed up, and the emergency response teams, media, and curiosity seekers are gone. However, during the next few months, many problems will bubble to the surface. The real work of recovering from a crisis has just begun.

EIGHT-STEP MODEL FOR ORGANIZATIONS

Figure 8.1 depicts a revised version of a model developed by Gilliland (1982). Although we present the model as linear, recovering from a crisis is anything but linear. As new information comes to light or problems arise, you may need to move to earlier steps in the model. In the real world of crisis intervention, steps 2 through 7 often blend together as the interventionist adapts to changing conditions. Step 1 (Predisposition)

EIGHT-STEP MODEL

(For Campus Intervention)

CONTINUOUS AND DYNAMIC ASSESSMENT

1. PREDISPOSITION – Conduct risk analysis to determine if campus is crisis prone.

2. DEFINE THE PROBLEM – Explore and define problem from employee perspective.

3. ENSURE SAFETY – Address employee and other stakeholders' real and perceived safety concerns.

4. PROVIDE SUPPORT – Locate support systems, internal and external, depending on severity of reaction.

5. EXAMINE ALTERNATIVES – Investigate immediate choices and coping mechanisms, internal and external, depending on severity.

6. MAKE PLANS – Develop realistic short-term plan, identify additional resources and coping mechanisms, and make definite action steps that employees can own and comprehend.

7. OBTAIN COMMITMENT – Communicate plan and initiate definite short-term positive action steps that employees can realistically accept and implement.

8. FOLLOW-UP – Review of the effectiveness of plan. Revise crisis management plan and appropriate campus policies.

Figure 8.1 Eight-Step Model

involves a systematic examination of situational and environmental conditions on your campus prior to a crisis occurring. Steps 2, 3, and 4 (Define the Problem, Ensure Safety, Provide Support) focus on developing an understanding of the problems associated with the crisis, as well as demonstrating a commitment to work through the recovery process. Steps 5, 6, and 7 (Examine Alternatives, Make Action Plans, and Obtain Commitment) are more action oriented and focus on developing and implementing interventions. As you move through the model, new problems may arise, or you may find that the problem has not been accurately defined. If this situation occurs, you will need to move back to earlier steps to develop efficient and effective interventions. The final step (Follow-up) involves follow-up after the recovery process has run its course.

As you can see in Figure 8.1, assessment as discussed in the previous chapter is an overarching process. Assessment should be continuous and dynamic as you work through each step of the process. Continuous assessment throughout the recovery process allows administrators and CMTs to identify the hot spots on campus. Each stage of the process brings new challenges, making it important to be attentive to changes on campus. The assessment process may look different with respect to when, how, what, and who to assess in each stage. Assessment also allows administrators and CMTs to monitor the effectiveness of the intervention. By monitoring the nine characteristics described in Chapter 7 through the eight-step model, the recovery will avoid missteps and smooth the process.

Step One: Predispositioning

Technically, this step is a continuous practice involving two issues: (a) assessing risks on your campus and (b) building resiliency. Assessment of these two issues is important to position your campus for both preventing and recovering from a crisis. Predispositioning involves intentionality. A deliberate effort to assess risks and strengths must be made if your campus is to be prepared for a crisis. This process should be woven into the fabric of day-to-day activities for it to be the most effective.

Risk Analysis

Similar to the idea of the practice of risk analysis (Barton, 2000; Haddow & Bullock, 2006), predispositioning first involves conducting a risk analysis with respect to the human impact of a crisis. This involves canvassing your campus for hazards that unless addressed have the potential to generate a crisis. Although all crises cannot be predicted 100% of the time, in many situations, crises give signals or possibly begin as smaller, almost innocuous, and seemingly trivial situations that go creeping along until they explode into a full-fledged crisis. Predispositioning involves a systematic examination of situational and environmental conditions that may either cause a crisis or prevent a satisfactory response to a crisis. Predispositioning assumes that situational and environmental characteristics may be a flash point for a crisis that can be identified. By identifying the vulnerable areas with respect to the human impact of a crisis, you create an opportunity to work to alleviate them (Mitroff & Anagnos, 2001). The result is that you position your campus to prevent and/or diminish the likelihood of some crisis occurring.

Building Resiliency

The second aspect of predispositioning involves assessing and building your campus resiliency. Resiliency is all about sustaining campus life and having continuity of day-to-day operations. Both internal and external resiliencies are involved in this step of the model. Each is important as you prepare for a crisis on your campus.

Internal resiliency means creating an infrastructure that facilitates your response to a crisis (Jackson, 2007). An infrastructure based on resiliency positions your campus to respond to crisis and limit its impact. Knowing your campus's resources to respond to crises and its ability to bounce back following a crisis can significantly lessen the overall impact of a crisis. This information allows you to use the unique strengths that are specific to your campus and to also tap resources to facilitate recovery. Thinking about resiliency ahead of time increases your campus's capacity to restore normal day-to-day activities as quickly as possible.

Reliance on internal resources alone may not adequately address a crisis situation. Assistance from agencies off campus may be vital to each stage of the recovery from a crisis. Predispositioning can be a springboard to establish relationships with first responders and to identify agencies and organizations that may be needed in the recovery from a crisis. Establishing relationships with first responders means meeting with these groups and having an understanding of their general operating procedures (Nicoletti, Spencer-Thomas, & Bollinger, 2001). Although you may not think that a shooting or a hostage incident can happen on your campus, having local law enforcement officers who know the procedures for handling these incidents and have thoroughly familiarized themselves with your building layouts is important. This is true even on small campuses in rural settings. Having procedures helps students, staff, and faculty understand their roles in situations such as this. A practice exercise with first responders is one way for everyone to understand the others' perspectives in crisis situations.

Development of working relationships with human service agencies outside the university is also part of erecting an infrastructure based on resiliency (Mancini, 2009). Obvious agencies include general hospitals, crisis intervention response centers, agencies providing both inpatient and outpatient mental health services, sexual assault response centers, and domestic violence shelters. Initiating and maintaining relationships with these agencies can help students, staff, and faculty access the support they need in the wake of a crisis. When we speak of creating a relationship, we are not just talking about having a phone number. We are talking about the university intentionally identifying specific persons, inviting them to campus, talking with them, and establishing personal working relationships so that when a crisis does occur, these outside agencies can be seamlessly integrated into the crisis response.

Step Two: Defining the Problem

Although this step may seem obvious, it is critical to understand the breadth and depth of the issues your campus faces during the recovery process. Defining the problem is developing a three-dimensional understanding that includes severity, pervasiveness, and duration. This three-dimensional perspective helps administrators and the CMT develop interventions to address the specifics of the situation. *Severity* refers to the power the problem has to influence campus life. *Pervasiveness* is how much of the campus is being impacted by the problems. *Duration* is the length of time the problem has existed. Each phase of the recovery process presents unique challenges. For example, in the emergency and honeymoon phases, defining the problem must be done quickly, whereas in the later phases of recovery, time is not as critical. However, care must be taken not to become bogged down in what seems to be a never-ending process of gathering information that delays decision making. Getting stalled in information gathering is frustrating to everyone, especially those departments and units waiting for much-needed resources. Seeing blue roofs on buildings 2 years after the fact or working in a temporary office will not make people feel loyal or show high morale; ongoing inconvenience does not make a "Can Do!" statement about the university's ability to respond to the long-term effects of a crisis.

The question arises about knowing when to move to other steps in the model. When will you know that enough information has been gathered? Our response to this question is simply that it is important to gain and utilize all the information you can in making decisions, while balancing the need to be responsive to the immediacy required by the situation. However, if you have done a diligent job, making the decision to move to the next step will be apparent. Keep in mind that assessment is continuous, and if you find that you have not correctly defined the problem or problems, you can always recycle back to this step at any point in the model.

Step Three: Ensuring Safety

At first glance, this step in the model seems to apply only to the emergency stage primarily because of the threat to people's physical and psychological safety on campus. For example, at Central University, physical safety was a major concern not just immediately following the explosion but for the next few days. Concerns during the few days following the explosion centered on possible exposure to toxic gases because of the fire. Psychological safety was also a concern at Central. Providing psychological first aid and mental health services as people try to come to terms with a crisis situation is critical in staving off long-term psychological maladjustment. What kinds of questions do you think should be asked about physical and psychological safety in the first meetings of administrators and the CMT? Who should take the lead in asking these questions in the CMT? We believe these questions should address the issues of communication, coordination, and consultation: What and how to communicate information? Who should be involved in coordination of services? And if and when should consultation be sought?

Although this step is concerned with the physical and psychological safety of individuals who were at the epicenter of the disaster, safety issues also extends to anyone giving support especially in the emergency phase and care should be exercised to esnure the safety of people trying to help victims of a crisis. Law enforcement and fire fighters are trained to understand and avoid unnecessary danger to themselves. However, well-meaning bystanders may want to rush into dangerous situations that could result in serious injury to them. Crisis management plans should include guidelines for ensuring the safety of people who are simply trying to be of assistance. These guidelines might involve getting a person in authority to the scene of a crisis or disaster who understands potential dangers and has the power to prevent people from placing themselves in danger. An obvious example of such a person is campus police officers.

Saftey issues also continues to the later phases of recovery. The concern shifts from the immediacy of crisis to the overall well-being of the collective campus during the recovery process. The well-being of campus life involves assuring students, staff, and faculty that they are safe on campus and throughout the recovery process.

Depending on the scope of the crisis and ensuing chaos, your campus will experience, to one degree or another, a feeling of vulnerability. Ensuring safety in this situation involves the need to make meaning of the crisis. In this way, the campus gains psychological control over the crisis. The event is placed in the proper perspective as a tragic event that is now finished business, which allows the campus as a collective group to move forward (Neimeyer, 2001). Failure to gain an understanding of the crisis can result in a collective sense of despair that might plague the campus. Despair may be seen through poor morale, increased conflict, and increases in faculty leaving for other positions, student flight, and the virulence and number of rumors. Institutionalizing the positive changes that have been made resulting from a crisis is one way to help make meaning of a crisis. This involves reframing the crisis as an opportunity to make changes that will help prevent future crises.

Campuses can experience growth during this phase, possibly through becoming more caring, appreciative of the opportunity to learn, willing to change priorities, and resilient (Tedeshi & Calhoun, 1996). Everyone's confidence must be solidified. Students, staff, and faculty must trust that procedures and policies have been set in place to avert a similar crisis—and not just that procedures and policies exist on paper but that these are being followed. Everyone on campus also needs to know that the lessons learned from a specific incident have also been generalized to other possible crises.

Step Four: Providing Support

Providing support means getting your hands dirty. Administrators and CMTs who remain sequestered in their offices will have a difficult time managing the recovery process. Students, staff, and faculty may see them as aloof and not in touch with the reality of what is happening. Getting out among the people who lived the crisis demonstrates a sense of involvement and caring (Caponigro, 2000). Being seen lends credibility to the actions that will be implemented during the following three steps of the model. We cannot overemphasize the value of being viewed as involved and in touch with your campus. While sending messages via e-mail and other means is helpful, sole reliance on these methods is not adequate. In the aftermath of a crisis, students, staff, and faculty want to see the people who are leading them through the recovery process.

Obviously, showing care and support to anyone who has been physically injured by a crisis is a given. The value of visiting a person physically hurt in a crisis cannot be overestimated. Taking the time to also visit displaced faculty who have lost their office space and students who have lost thesis and dissertation research communicates a comprehensive sense of interest and caring. An example is a faculty member whose teaching schedule is disrupted by the crisis and now must teach off campus at a satellite location. The disruption is causing havoc with child care for the faculty member's two elementary-age children. While this may seem trivial in the greater scheme of things, it is most definitely not trivial to the faculty member. Attending to details like this sends a clear message that the CMT is aware of and sensitive to faculty disruptions and is attending to them. What do you think this does for morale and loyalty as word spreads that the CMT has responded by setting up a temporary child care center staffed by the College of Education's Early Childhood Department students?

Support must also be shown for those who were psychologically traumatized by a crisis. It is important to recognize that trauma is not isolated to those who were a direct part of or witnessed a crisis (Myer & Moore, 2006). To one degree or another, the impact of a crisis will extend to the entire campus (Fink, 2002). Thinking in these terms helps administrators and CMTs provide the necessary support. For some, a message of assurance is all that is needed; for others, more direct contact is warranted. Which administrators and members of a CMT are best suited for conveying this support? Be honest about this assessment. Arbitrarily deciding that the dean of student affairs or the director of the counseling center should assume these responsibilities because they have a title or position is a bad idea.

In the tragic situation that lives were lost, support to those closest to the victims becomes paramount. Dealing with survivors of those who died is not done in a spur-of-the-moment or spontaneous way. Determining ahead of time how sudden death or injury is to be handled and by whom is a critical issue. Although each crisis is unique, thinking about general guidelines to communicate support to students, staff, faculty, and family members is important. Understand that this process may involve attending viewings at funeral homes as well as funerals. Thinking about this process prior to actually having to engage in showing support allows you to avoid some terrible blunders in this step. What message do you want to send? The president of your university attending a viewing or funeral sends a very different message than sending the associate dean of the physical sciences college. You must also consider who is the best to show that support in a given situation. Not everyone is suited for this responsibility. Working through these questions prior to a crisis can help you move through this step effectively. Whoever is tasked with this responsibility should have a background in grief and loss. If your university does not have a person with this knowledge and ability, you need to think very seriously about obtaining consultative help to train people or using the consultant as the official spokesperson. Nothing we know of can ruin credibility, create angry constituencies, destroy morale, and extinguish loyalty more than poor responses to loss.

This step may involve attending various meetings to discuss the current state of the recovery process (Cohen, 2004). Listening to complaints, worries, and problems during these meetings can help you understand the parts of the intervention process that are lacking as well as those that seem to be working. It is important that both successes and failures be discussed in these meetings. Being truthful is important to build the confidence of the campus that recovery will be successful. However, remember that while you need to share the truth, not everyone needs to hear everything (Caponigro, 2000). Careful consideration should be given to the amount and kind of information that will be shared. Don't make the assumption that everyone is on the same page. Before ever walking into such a meeting, the CMT should discuss what information will be shared and what will be withheld. This process has nothing to do with covering up material and everything to do with being consistent across the campus and putting out the same clear, factual message. People in the meetings are likely to want more information than you are prepared to disclose. Thinking about the situation and practicing ahead of time can help you avoid saying something that you wish you had not.

Attending meetings across campus also serves an assessment purpose. You will be able to gather important information on problems that have not yet been addressed. Early identification of these issues can prevent them from evolving into major potholes for the recovery process. So while you are providing support, you are also engaging in assessment and problem definition. You will be best served in this capacity if you read and practice the basic listening skills in Chapter 10.

Step Five: Examining Alternatives

Examining alternatives is the first of three steps within the recovery model that focus on implementing the intervention. In this step, possible solutions are generated to address all the problems associated with recovery. The generation of these ideas can build on the strategies developed by Myer and James (2005) listed in Table 8.1. These nine strategies can be used as a springboard to develop interventions to facilitate the recovery process. As you can see in the table, some strategies are particularly helpful with specific problems. However, all nine may be used for any problem arising from a crisis. Their use is dependent on the needs of the situation and your creativity. We discuss these strategies more completely at the end of this chapter.

Examining alternatives means generating as many ideas as possible to address the problems identified in "Step Two: Define the Problem." Situational awareness is needed to successfully complete this step (Paton & Jackson, 2002). As we have stated

Table 8.1	Basic Intervention Strategies
Catharsis	Allows students, staff, faculty members, and others to voice concerns. Particularly useful to address problems associated with issues related to rumors and the relationships individuals and groups have in the university.
Awareness	Offers the opportunity to develop knowledge and understanding of issues. Useful with concerns related to role confusion, goals related to the mission of the university, meeting agendas, and morale.
Validation	Permits the opportunity to confirm and support the experience of students, staff, and faculty members. Useful to address morale, problems with loyalty, dynamics of the system, roles, and issues related to the university mission.
Expansion	Promotes a wider vision of the potential solutions to the crisis throughout the recovery process. Particularly useful with decision-making processes, the ability to function on a day-to-day basis, problems associated with roles, and loyalty issues.
Focus	Encourages development of methods to facilitate recovery, especially in the middle phases of recovery. Useful for issues related to decision making, dispelling rumors, promoting loyalty, and overcoming problems associated with dynamics.
Guidance	Supports a more direct intervention process that connects departments and units with resources. Mainly useful with addressing issues with roles, meeting agendas, and decision-making protocols.
Mobilization	Provides support to encourage taking positive steps to resolve problems associated with the crisis. Used with decision-making protocols, concerns related to morale, and promoting attainment of university goals.
Ordering	Helps develop priorities with respect to problems for all issues. Particularly helpful with loyalty issues and decision-making protocols.
Protection	Focuses on safeguarding departments and units from problems associated with the crisis. Useful for all problems but specifically with those related to day-to-day operations, dynamics, roles, and rumors.

previously, situational awareness means being able to make sense out of chaos. That is the ability to sift through the jetsam and flotsam to find those issues that require attention. At Central University, what are the situational variables that may need attention? Immediately after the explosion, the situational variables primarily involve safety concerns. Among the variables are issues related to injuries caused by the explosion as well as the fire afterwards, making sure everyone is kept out of the building until safety problems have been resolved, and also providing psychological support for anyone experiencing psychological trauma. Later in recovery, other situational variables may become important. These variables will be unique, based on the crisis and your campus. Examples include alumni support, service relationships with the community, students whose education was disrupted, an increase of the use of health services, and lack of classroom space. This list will vary, depending on the crisis, your campus, and the phase of recovery.

Getting as many ideas as possible on the table is important. Some might appear outrageous and deviant, but then the crisis itself is outrageous and deviant, so considering and encouraging creative thinking is the watchword. Generation of ideas should be done without fear of ridicule. Methods to generate ideas include but are not limited to the time-honored brainstorming activities, suggestion boxes that allow input from many people, focus groups designed to get ideas, online surveys or suggestion forums and blogs, and town hall types of meetings. A decision about which method is best depends on the crisis and your comfort level with each method. Whatever you use, we recommend following Gerald Egan's (2006, 2007) and Richard James's (2008) three rules for brainstorming alternatives:

1. Generate as many solutions as possible. There are no bad ideas at this point, only possible alternatives.
2. Creativity and novelty are at a premium. Right-brain thinking is for problems you have never dealt with before and don't have ready solutions for in your file drawer.
3. Piggyback one idea on another. If we hooked these two up, it might look pretty screwy, but would it work, and would the whole be greater than the sum of the parts? Get input from the constituency. A focus group of engineering, art, and counseling students may have ideas about providing infrastructure support and psychological assistance that you never dreamed of doing. Consider what has worked in the past that may have been forgotten or considered outmoded but will do for the time being. If the power is out, kerosene lamps will let you see in the dark.

Each method has benefits as well as drawbacks. Regardless of which one or more of these formats is chosen, you should get publicity and enthusiastic backing from the administration that essentially says, "We need your views on this. You are important!" The CMT can then filter these ideas and select the workable ones.

This step is complicated because you will be generating ways to intervene for multiple problems associated with the crisis. Coordination is therefore important as you generate solutions. Although each problem should be viewed individually, you must recognize that all are related (Ren, 2000). Interventions developed for a specific problem in a specific department or unit should be viewed as having a symbiotic relationship with other interventions. Care must be taken to think about the systemic impact of every intervention. We recommend that you develop a method that compels you to consider the impact of any intervention on the entire campus. One method would be to ask someone on the CMT to play the role of devil's advocate. This person's responsibility is to challenge decisions and keep CMTs from falling into a groupthink mentality. These challenges are likely to be in the form of questions regarding the decisions about actions to be taken. A consultant can also function in this manner. A consultant should be able to ensure you are not forgetting issues needing attention and also function as a third-party peacekeeper (Golembiewski & Rauschenberg, 1993). Sooner or later, tempers are going to get frayed, not only across campus, but within the CMT itself. Whether the individual assigned to this task is an external consultant or internal to the system, that person needs to have good conflict resolution techniques (Fisher, Ury, & Patton, 1991). As time passes and the university moves into the disillusionment and possible reconstruction phase, conflict will most definitely arise when decisions have to be made about scarce resources.

Step Six: Making Action Plans

Step six takes the ideas from the previous step and turns them into workable plans. These plans must be realistic and promote the recovery process. Again the nine strategies in Table 8.1 can be used as a springboard for developing workable plans. These strategies give you a basic idea of how to implement a plan. For example, expansion might be used if what you have been doing has not been effective. This strategy can be used to open discussion about other ways to see and resolve the problem. Ordering might be used in disorganization if you are spinning your wheels and not getting anywhere. This strategy will help you prioritize the problems, as well as lay out specific tasks that need to be accomplished. However, realize that interventions typically involve a couple of related activities that must be done. You may be combining several strategies to address a particular problem. You might combine ordering and mobilization to outline what needs to happen to give the people in charge encouragement. Validation of the experience and catharsis might also be combined to allow groups to express their views and then reinforce this expression. Plans should always have a measure of flexibility and be based on the continuous assessment process. Obviously, staying with a plan that is not producing the expected results is counterproductive. You must be willing to switch in midstream if the need arises. That is the reason for continuous assessment throughout the entire model.

Plans that are too ambitious are doomed to fail and will derail the recovery process. The eight-step model provides a strategy for staying targeted on the crisis. A critical aspect of this step is developing plans that students, staff, and faculty can own and comprehend. Other stakeholders such as the community, board of directors, trustees, and other governing bodies will also need to be on board with the plan. Although these latter groups may not be directly involved, they are groups that are sure to question the soundness of any intervention. Following are five basic questions (Gutkin & Curtis, 1999) that the CMT needs to ask itself as it seeks to implement the plan:

1. Is the intervention in agreement with what the constituency thinks needs to be done?
2. Can it be accomplished with relative ease and without disrupting too much of the constituency's routine, as opposed to being so complex and intrusive that no one will do it?
3. Do the participants see it as part of their duties, and are they committed to it?
4. Can it be seamed into their everyday world of work quickly and become part of their daily routine?
5. Do you believe it will work?

As you move through the recovery process, consideration can be given to entertaining long-term changes. These changes might involve procedural and policy changes. For example, at Central University, policy changes might include issues related to access to buildings. Building access might become more restricted or involve other security issues, such as the installation of surveillance cameras. Yet care must be exercised not to let the crisis act as a catalyst to make sweeping changes that may not be related to the situation.

Although you should try to anticipate everything with the interventions you are implementing, unforeseen situations will arise. We know of no crystal ball that will anticipate everything that might go wrong—or right, for that matter—with the intervention. Continuous assessment of some type is critical in this step. Assessment allows you to monitor the effectiveness of a plan and make needed adjustments or dump it if it isn't working. Contemporary educational policy and mental health approaches have placed a great deal of emphasis on evidence-based outcomes of intervention. Crisis intervention is no different. This is not a forever business. If it isn't working, change it. Each method has benefits as well as drawbacks.

Step Seven: Obtaining Commitment

Step seven should flow naturally from the previous step. It requires getting a buy-in from the campus as a whole, as well as from individual departments and units. Students, staff, and faculty members collectively must have a commitment to the plan. However, this step is not about getting 100% agreement, especially in the later stages of the recovery process. Communication and coordination are needed to obtain commitment. Considerable effort should be exercised to make sure everyone knows what is going to happen. This process helps curb rumors and can be used to minimize resistance. Obtaining commitment also helps to discourage issues related to roles in the recovery process and makes use of the dynamics on your campus.

We don't have to tell you that getting 100% agreement is not possible in a university. Not everyone will be on the same page with respect to all aspects of the recovery process (Knotek, 2006). Expect individuals to voice concerns about the plan and even outright dissent. What this step involves is getting pledges that everyone will work toward full recovery in the best possible way (Caponigro, 2000). A commitment is needed from everyone impacted by the crisis that as a group they will work toward restoring the campus to its precrisis level of functioning and do what is needed to improve the day-to-day functioning of the university.

Obtaining buy-in from a group involves consensus building. There are many activities to build consensus, but the key concern is to ensure everyone understands the overall goal. This process should start with administrators and CMTs. If they are unsure of the goal, how can they expect anyone else to understand? Should the goal be to merely restore the campus to what it was like before the explosion or to consider this crisis as an opportunity to make changes? If changes are going to be made, what are those changes? These are decisions that must be made to obtain buy-in.

The use of continuous communication throughout the entire model can help make completing this step much easier. As we have repeatedly discussed, communication must be two-way, from the bottom up as well as the top down. Everyone wants to be valued, and listening to them demonstrates that. If people have their say, they will be more willing to compromise and support the plan. The complication comes when messages are conflicting. One department or unit seems to think a strategy to help recovery will be effective, while another believes that strategy will result in more problems. You have to work toward obtaining commitment from as many departments and units as possible. At these times, you need leadership from administrators and CMTs (Mitroff, 2004). You must work to find a way to compromise and minimize the conflict.

Ongoing coordination also helps to smooth the process of obtaining commitment (Knotek, 2006). Coordination in this step can mean ensuring that no one feels left out of the recovery process. Creating discontent because you have inadvertently failed to include a department or unit in this step is a problem that is easily avoided. We recommend that a list of departments and units be used as a means of coordination; it is too easy to forget a department or unit when making decisions and developing interventions under stress (Fink, 2002).

Step Eight: Follow-Up

Follow-up should be conducted after each phase in the recovery process. You can use information gained in this step to learn from the experience to help prepare for the next crisis, as well as adjust your approach as you move into the next phase of recovery. Be careful not to start pointing fingers (Mitroff & Anagnos, 2001). In crisis management planning, singling out people at this point in the recovery process is counterproductive. Meetings should focus on the plan or intervention, not the performance of specific people. When there is chaos, there will be mistakes; it is part of the process. Performance can be evaluated at another time. If people know ahead of time that this step will focus on strategies used in the recovery, you are likely to obtain more accurate data. In addition, the people involved will be more receptive to hearing feedback. Falling into the trap of blaming individuals will not improve the crisis management plan when and if another crisis occurs. Another trap that derails this step is the desire to move on too soon. We believe that immediately following a crisis is the perfect time to evaluate the efficiency and effectiveness of the crisis management plan and the interventions used in the recovery.

The first goal of this step is to determine how well your crisis management plan functioned, not what specific people could have done differently. Review of your crisis management plan should focus on logistics. For example, did the emergency notification system work? Were the resources where they needed to be at the right time? What other resources, specifically those related to addressing the human impact of the crisis, would have been helpful to speed the recovery process?

The second goal of this step is to determine the effectiveness of specific interventions in the recovery process. Potentially several interventions will be used to address problems in individual departments or units on campus, and these specific interventions should also be evaluated to determine if they were successful. Minimal attention is usually given to follow-up with specific interventions. It may be felt that they can be included in the overall follow-up. While this process can be used, you risk missing valuable information that can be used as you move to different phases of the recovery.

Feedback about the overall crisis management plan as well as specific interventions should be constructive. A balanced perspective is much more helpful than one-sided feedback, positive or negative. A common mistake is to think that only the parts of the plan or intervention that were not successful should be evaluated. To a point, this belief is accurate. Revisions are needed for the parts of the crisis management plan or intervention that did not work. This allows you to avoid making the same mistake twice. However, we strongly recommend that you also use an assessment process that allows gathering data on the strengths of the plan or interventions. Identifying the strengths of your overall plan or specific interventions permits you to use those strengths as building blocks to revise other areas as well as overcome weaknesses.

The best way to do follow-up is to build ways to obtain feedback into an intervention plan (Caponigro, 2000). Every action plan developed in step six of this model should include methods to receive feedback. You do not want to say you wish you had that data after it is too late. Formal and informal methods can be used to gather this information. As you develop your crisis management plan and specific interventions, make sure you integrate an evaluation plan. The evaluation plan should be communicated to everyone involved in implementing the plan or specific intervention, as well as those being assisted by the plan.

The use of multiple methods to obtain feedback is also extremely useful (Caponigro, 2000). Do not make the mistake of listening to only the squeaky wheels. The intervention plans that were used to facilitate recovery will, almost undoubtedly, cause some department or unit to feel slighted in one way or another. Using multiple methods to gather feedback will help these groups feel they are being heard, while at the same time ensuring that you get a balanced perspective. Chapter 7 describes several methods that can be used in this step: interviews, focus groups, existing data (e.g., turnover rate, absenteeism, and student applications), surveys, and several more.

Consultation may be needed to accomplish step eight. Administrators and CMTs may be too close to the situation to take the proverbial step back and evaluate their actions in a fair, impartial manner. We encourage you to consider bringing in a consultant to lead the follow-up process. The consultant can be internal or external to the campus. The advantage of an internal consultant is that this person will be familiar with the campus. Yet this person should be selected carefully. He or she should have a high degree of credibility across campus. A disadvantage of using an internal consultant is that he or she may lack the distance to accurately conduct an evaluation of the crisis management plan and specific interventions with departments and units. A key issue in using an internal consultant is whether he or she will have the freedom to submit an honest report with no fear of repercussions if the report contains unfavorable information. An external consultant, on the other hand, has the advantage of fewer restrictions with respect to submitting a report that may be viewed unfavorably. The disadvantage is that an external consultant may not have the credibility nor as full an understanding of the history of the crisis or campus.

USING THE EIGHT-STEP MODEL

As much as we would like to think that moving through the eight-step model will be a smooth process, we would be misleading you to say that. You will encounter problems, setbacks, and delays in implementing your plans. Each phase (i.e., emergency, honeymoon, avoidance, reconstruction, and restabilization) of the recovery process poses its own unique set of challenges. In the following section, we make you aware of some complications that if known ahead of time, can help you navigate and minimize the impact of some problems. This list is not meant to be exhaustive; rather, it covers generic issues most often encountered in the recovery process.

Using the eight-step model as a guide to move through the recovery process for the entire campus is similar to using it with individuals but with one major difference. The similarity lies in the implementation of the model. Just as you would use the model with an individual to resolve a crisis, you would do the same with the entire campus to help the collective whole recover from the crisis. You move through the model in a careful way, continually assessing to attend to emerging issues on your campus. The primary difference is that systemic crisis intervention on your campus will generally involve addressing several problems at the same time. With individuals, intervention focuses on one issue at a time. For example, intervention might involve supporting a student as he or she recovers from being a victim of violence or helping a student with suicidal ideations form a purpose to live.

Phases of Recovery

Each phase of recovery presents unique challenges for implementing the eight-stage model. We have identified some of the more common difficulties, tasks, and opportunities encountered in each phase of the recovery. You may also encounter additional problems, responsibilities, and opportunities unique to your campus and the specific crisis. It is important to use the eight-step model as you work through the issues related to the crisis

Emergency Phase

In the emergency phase of recovery, the eight-step model provides a step-by-step process to ensure that you have addressed each problem. You might be thinking that, of course, each problem will be addressed and that you are well equipped to handle whatever happens. Of course, you are correct, except when the campus is in crisis, all bets are off. Recovering from a crisis is different from handling day-to-day routine operations. Depending on the severity of the reactions, administrators and CMTs may have difficulty making what on the surface seem to be simple decisions. The eight-step model can assist administrators and CMTs to make those decisions in a constructive, thoughtful manner. The eight-step model, while it may seem very simple, helps you focus on critical issues related to the human impact of a crisis on your campus. The model can also help you maintain a perspective that allows you to see the larger picture instead of just reacting to immediate concerns.

Honeymoon Phase

The honeymoon phase presents a unique challenge because of all the help that is being given. Adding to the difficulty is that the immediate chaos has dissipated, and a relative calm has probably spread across campus. A hopeful attitude may result in administrators and CMTs being lulled into a sense of complacency. The net result is interventions to promote recovery are not thought through, while other issues related to the crisis are missed. The eight-step model helps to make certain that an attentive attitude is maintained as administrators and CMTs come up with interventions to address the crisis across campus. The rumors surfacing as a result of the explosion at Central University are a good example. During the honeymoon phase of recovery, these would be easy to ignore, yet administrators and the CMT should realize that the rumors could become a significant obstacle in the recovery process. Dissemination of accurate and consistent information is a powerful tool in lessening the damage.

Avoidance Phase

A major issue in this phase of recovery is the desire to make everything seem normal. And in general, we agree with that attitude. Making the day-to-day activities on campus resemble standard operations is important for the recovery process. However, too often administrators fail to make the connection between emerging problems and the crisis. Assessment becomes critical in identifying problems resulting from the crisis. The eight-step model helps to ensure that appropriate deliberation has been given to addressing each concern as it is identified. Among the issues that tend to surface in this phase are decision making, roles, morale, and rumors. Issues related to decision making and roles are particularly troublesome during this phase of recovery. The rub comes with trying to find a balance between operating in a typical way as opposed to a crisis mode. Understanding the impact on specific departments and units is critical to determine whether a standard or crisis style of management is needed.

Reconstruction Phase/Restabilization Phase

In the final two phases, day-to-day operations will resemble typical operations across campus. Again the issue is failure to recognize that some problems related to the human impact of the crisis may persist through these phases. Many times these issues relate to loyalty, morale, and dynamics on campus. These issues may be experienced for several years after a crisis. For example, tenure and promotion may be affected for several years. This situation could possibly be encountered at Central University because the scholarly activity of some faculty may be adversely impacted by the explosion. Another example involves the shootings at Virginia Tech and Northern Illinois University. The issue of quickly addressing concerns related to disruptive students and security may be experienced for several years. Staff and faculty members may demand action be taken with students whose behavior is the least bit troublesome. If action is not taken quickly, they may leave the university. The eight-step model provides a process that can be used to address these issues as they arise.

CMT Meetings

Solving all the problems associated with the crisis in one meeting is impossible. Meetings will be spaced throughout the recovery process. Initially, the meetings will be spaced close together but further apart as recovery unfolds. They will probably begin as separate meetings from other daily operations and regular business continuity. They will require full attention to recovery in the beginning. Later, they are likely to meld into conducting business at regular meetings as recovery lessens in terms of needs of immediacy and weaves into campus operations. A list of the problems identified in the assessment process can help administrators and CMTs focus on the critical problems. We suggest that you have an agenda and goals for what is to be accomplished in your current meeting. Spell these out and stick to addressing those recovery issues. Otherwise, it is possible that you will become distracted by trying to put out fires.

We know that sometimes current needs takes precedence in meetings; some issues simply cannot wait. In the recovery process from a crisis, there are always pressing concerns. However, neglecting the issues for which the meeting was called can cause significant disruptions in the recovery process. A chart that tracks each problem you have identified and where you are in the eight-step model can be invaluable to maintain up-to-date knowledge of your progress. See Table 8.2 for an example of a chart that can be used to track the intervention progress. The eight-step model is a vehicle you can use to structure your meeting so that you know what to discuss and what has yet to be done for specific collective concerns. New issues seemingly materialize out of nowhere, problems grow and/or shrink for what appears to be no reason at all, and concerns evaporate just as quickly as they develop. Continuous vigilance helps you avoid being blindsided by a problem you did not even know existed.

Complexity of Campus Life

The complexity of the campus tremendously complicates implementation of the eight-step model (Mitroff, Diamond, & Alpasian, 2006). Administrators and CMTs will be trying, directly and indirectly, to support and intervene with multiple groups and problems related to the crisis event. Each group on your campus will have their perspective on the problem. One group may see the overall issue as the lack of resources; another group may see the problem as the lack of clear leadership. The specific problems experienced in various departments or units may also not be the same. Another department may be experiencing poor morale and conflict with another group on campus. And yet another unit's morale is high because they have finally been given much-needed resources, and the crisis has resulted in their meetings being purposeful and productive. All three groups are correct from their own perspective. Development of interventions requires seeing the issue from a particular department's or unit's point of view while

Table 8.2 Tracking Chart

Description of Problem	Step 1	Step 2	Step 3	Step 4	Step 5	Step 6	Step 7	Step 8
Problem 1								
Problem 2								
Problem 3								
Problem 4								
Problem 5								
Problem 6								

respecting the perspective of the other departments and units. Interventions need to be designed to help each address the issues that have arisen in their area while not suppressing the recovery of the other units.

Thinking in terms of layers can help you understand the complexity of this step. For college campuses, academic layers move from the individuals to departments to colleges or schools to the university as whole. Student affairs department layers include residence life, extracurricular activities, and off-campus life. There are also layers outside the campus, including the surrounding community, state-level governing bodies, and boards of directors, to name a few. Each layer may require a separate problem definition and intervention. Consideration should be given to identify and characterize problems from each layer. While this task may seem overwhelming, you may find that in the long run, you save time by working with these groups in the recovery process.

Leadership

Implementation of the eight-step model is more effective if latitude is given to departments and units to make some decisions internally (Mitroff, 2004). Allowing others to make decisions may go against your instincts at that moment. The appeal of controlling everything can be overwhelming in times of crisis. It is normal to want to manage everything, but depending on the breadth and severity of the crisis, it may not be realistic. Trying to make all the decisions will slow the recovery (Schoenberg, 2005). At Central University, who should be making decisions about health concerns? What about the psychological needs of everyone on campus? Who is best suited for making those decisions? Should the president of the university, or possibly the vice president of student affairs, be making the decisions? In addition, who makes the decisions about the deployment and use of resources? It is very easy to slip into the need to control everyone and everything. Avoiding this problem takes a frank examination of ego, along with some effort and much practice.

Allowing others to make decisions empowers the people who know what is happening to determine what is needed in a given moment. Granted, some decisions should be made by administrators and CMTs, yet not every decision has to be made at the highest level. Some decisions can and should be made by those closest to the recovery process (Schoenberg, 2005). Allowing the decisions to be made at this level demonstrates a sense of trust and support.

Any limitations on decisions should be communicated to departments and units to avoid redundant efforts. Allowing departments and units to make even limited decisions is likely to be a sensitive and scary issue for administrators and CMTs. The need is to regain a sense of control after the crisis event. A crisis management plan can help you avoid this problem by giving guidelines for the decision-making process. Sharing some of the decision-making authority conveys a message of confidence to everyone involved. Let the system work for you during recovery. A related issue is the time-honored tradition of passing the buck. While we advocate a limited and specified amount of sharing decision making during a crisis, passing on your responsibility or blaming someone else is counterproductive in the recovery process. Crisis management plans should be developed in a way that clearly outlines the decision-making process and lines of authority.

Volunteers

Depending on the number of volunteers, you may consider requiring them to participate in a workshop prior to being allowed to provide services (Paton, 1996). The content of the workshop depends partly on the nature of the crisis. Some basic information should be included, such as an accurate account of what took place, the current state of the intervention, your expectations and limitations of the service and support they are to offer, and the time limits for offering these services. Another concern that should be addressed at this time is informing the volunteers of where they are expected to be and when they are expected to be there. In addition, this workshop should include information regarding any plans for providing meals or a place to stay. You might also distribute armbands to volunteers that they are expected to wear to identify themselves to the campus. Finally, any paperwork you expect them to complete should be done at this time. This paperwork might include waivers of liability, confidentiality agreements, and an agreement not to recruit clients or proselytize while on campus. We recommend that you consider these issues and develop procedures prior to the crisis.

NINE INTERVENTION STRATEGIES

Myer and James (2005) can be a starting point to develop a tool bag of common strategies to use during recovery; these can be used throughout the eight-step model. These nine strategies provide administrators and CMTs a way of thinking and of planning concrete ways to address problems resulting from the crisis: (a) catharsis, (b) awareness, (c) validation, (d) expansion, (e) focus, (f) guidance, (g) mobilization, (h) ordering, and (i) protection. Most of the time, the strategies are used in combinations, not separately. Using the strategies in combination allows the creation of powerful methods to promote the recovery process. Administrators or members of the CMT can use these strategies as appropriate in meetings to address a crisis. During the meetings, whether it be the CMT or with other groups, the strategies should be used to support the development of action plans to address issues related to the crisis. Throughout this section, we give examples of what you might say when using specific strategies. These are meant as suggestions and should be adapted for the specific situation.

Catharsis

Catharsis involves creating a safe environment in which students, staff, and faculty members can express feelings and thoughts regarding the crisis and recovery process.

Catharsis for organizations serves two purposes. The first is as a safety valve that allows steam to be vented. As feelings build and thoughts race across campus, venting is necessary. The second purpose of catharsis is that the expression of feelings and thoughts establishes trust in administrators and CMTs throughout the recovery process.

Establishment of a forum that permits frank expression may not be as easily accomplished. The culture on your campus prior to the crisis plays a significant role in developing ways to use this strategy. If the culture is replete with the fear of retribution for anyone criticizing or questioning decisions, the use of catharsis will be difficult at best. If this is the situation on your campus, we suggest you find a way to allow the expression of ideas while protecting the identity of those who are willing to share. Suggestion boxes are one way to do this. An outside consultant might also be used to listen to anyone wanting to express an opinion, with the understanding that no one will be identified in any report made to administrators or CMTs. Another method to allow catharsis is to have representatives from departments and units serve as mediators to administrators and CMTs. Again, this method requires assurance that no one will be identified in any report. On the other hand, if a culture has been cultivated in which administrators are willing to listen to ideas that may differ from theirs, setting up venues that allows catharsis will be less difficult. Venues can include town meetings, attending departmental and unit meetings, and meetings with individuals. More than likely, your campus falls somewhere between the extremes of being open and closed to discussion of this nature. Administrators and CMTs should be honest with themselves when using this strategy. If not, the use of catharsis will not be effective.

If meetings are being used for catharsis, we suggest guidelines be in place prior to the start of the meeting. These guidelines function as a safety valve that can be opened and closed. A moderator who structures the meeting is the person who enforces the guidelines. This person must not only lead the meeting but also maintain control so that all groups are heard. Participants in the meeting must understand the structure and guidelines for the meeting. These guidelines should be stated at the beginning of the meeting and possibly be distributed in written form. Guidelines might include that everyone will have an opportunity to speak, interruptions will not be tolerated, and a time limit will be set for each person to express his or her feelings. These must be strictly enforced so that all opinions, both positive and negative, are represented.

Not everyone will be good at leading meetings in which catharsis takes place. Someone who can listen without becoming defensive will be the best person to lead this meeting. The leader should also be capable of keeping the meeting focused and under control. Being focused means that discussion will focus on the problem for which the meeting is being held. Inevitably, some people in the meeting will want to discuss a specific issue not related to the meeting. The leader might say, "I feel like I am trying to hold 12 basketballs underwater, let's keep our discussion on [the reason for the meeting]." Keeping the meeting under control means not allowing individuals or groups to dominate the meeting. Maintaining control is partially accomplished by enforcing the guidelines for the meeting but can also be achieved by saying, "Let's slow down for a minute. Let me recap what has been stated to this point." These are meant as suggestions; we encourage you to find other ways that fit for your specific situation.

Awareness

Awareness for a campus involves creating a wide perspective designed to focus attention on the holistic impact of the crisis. This strategy is used to help groups become aware of the problems they are facing, as well as how much they have accomplished to this point. Summarizing what has been done, what is being done, and what will be done in the recovery process promotes awareness. When questioned about the progress being made in recovery, a statement that simply outlines specific accomplishments and the plans for future attempts to resolve the crisis helps to create awareness. "Let me summarize how far we have gone and what is yet to be done . . ." is one way to help groups see the larger picture of the recovery process.

This strategy is particularly useful in steps two, three, and four (i.e., Define the Problem, Ensure Safety, and Provide Support) of the eight-step model. Administrators and CMTs can use this strategy to help the campus understand the complexity of the recovery process. Too often the crisis and recovery are viewed only through the lens of the impact on individual departments and units. Students, staff, and faculty do not have all the information. They need to be made aware of the range and number of demands being made on resources.

Methods for using awareness include active and passive communication. Active communication involves face-to-face meetings. These meetings might involve individuals, but a more efficient use of time is to attend department and unit meetings. Passive communication involves such things as the distribution of flyers and having e-mail blasts that update everyone regarding the current situation with respect to the recovery process. You don't want people to hear information on the radio or television first. Whether active or passive communication is used, you should help everyone maintain an up-to-date awareness of the recovery process.

Validation

This strategy involves creation of a work environment that respects each department or unit's collective reaction to the crisis. Marginalizing any department or unit because its reaction does not seem to fit into the accepted or expected reaction has the potential to generate animosity and sabotage the recovery process. Validation is needed to legitimatize the unique impact of a crisis to start the recovery process. For example, what message would be sent to the faculty members who are in conflict about sharing lab space at Central University if administrators and the CMT made a statement a few months after the explosion that all is well and the campus is back to normal? We imagine that the faculty members who are in conflict would feel discounted. The statement might result in faculty leaving the university, in morale dropping, and so on. An honest statement recognizes that recovery is not complete, although some progress has been made.

Validation is needed for not just the negative reactions but also positive reactions. Acknowledging positive reactions helps departments and units activate resiliency. Resiliency can be contagious and serve as a shot in the arm, with departments and units building on what others have already done. However, care must be used to promote the recovery process in this manner. Be aware that when you validate the efforts of a department for positive action, other departments should also be recognized. This awareness should not limit your ability to emphasize those going above and beyond— if they have earned the recognition, give it! You can avoid groups feeling left out by making sure everyone is reinforced and validated for their efforts in recovery process. Letters, e-mail, and personal visits are all excellent ways to give groups a pat on the back.

We encourage the use of proactive strategies to validate the experience of departments and units. Don't wait: Go out and find ways to validate the reactions, whether positive or negative.

Expansion

Expansion is a strategy used to broaden the focus of an organization. This strategy involves reframing a crisis from a narrow to a more realistic point of view that allows new and more productive attempts for recovery to be considered. If administrators and the CMT at Central University only saw the crisis as the need to rebuild the science building, they will miss seeing the larger issues that have impacted the entire campus. Also, the strategy of expansion is used to break the cycle of continuing to use variations of the same method by encouraging a different perspective, which allows them to entertain different avenues to improve morale.

Throughout the recovery process, expansion can be used to break out of groupthink. Many times groupthink occurs when administrators and CMTs get caught up in viewing a crisis as simply rebuilding a building, increasing security, providing only psychological aid, and so on. An example would be limiting the recovery process to rebuilding resident halls destroyed at Union University by the tornado that ripped through Jackson, Tennessee, in spring 2008. Instead, this campus used the crisis to expand and improve the university. Expansion promotes the critical examination and evaluation of all the problems associated with the crisis.

Expansion helps to counteract an "all is lost" attitude. When you encounter a department or unit that is in the throes of despair, expansion can be used to instill hope. In meetings with these groups, you can help them see what choices are open to them. We recognize that at times options may be limited, but we believe options exist. Encouraging a group to stop and think beyond the immediacy of the situation can be used for this strategy. In some situations, you may have to start the process of expansion by offering what you see as options. Members of the group should be persuaded to join in the discussion through gentle encouragement and prompting. Positive reinforcement can be used to convince group members to expand their perspective and search for solutions to the problems associated with the crisis.

Focus

Focus in many ways is the opposite of expansion. When the impact of the crisis seems overwhelming with no hope of recovery, focus can be used to help administrators and CMTs break the recovery process into manageable pieces. This strategy is useful to avoid becoming bogged down in what seems to be the never-ending process of recovery. A specific method to promote a sharper focus during meetings is asking the group to slow down and concentrate attention on the problem at hand. Another way to do the same thing is to ask for a time-out or break during the meeting. A break creates an interruption in the discussion and allows the person leading the meeting to take control of the meeting and direct discussion to more productive areas. If you are so inclined, humor is also an effective method to focus the meeting. If humor is used, we suggest you make light of your ability to understand everything all at once. You can follow with a statement to point the group in a more constructive direction.

This strategy is useful to focus the recovery process. At times, the recovery process either becomes disjointed or seems to be the monster that took over a university. When this situation takes place, the focus strategy helps to sort through the important issues. A common experience for organizations recovering from a crisis is being pulled in many different directions. Not only must the routine operations be restored and maintained but now problems resulting from the crisis need attention. Following a crisis, universities must attend to the typical functions of teaching, scholarship, and service, while also addressing problems associated with the crisis. Prioritizing involves helping administrators make decisions regarding what needs to be done first, second, third, and so on. When administrators and CMTs seem stuck and unable to clearly select a course of action because they are being asked to make so many decisions, focusing can be used to break out of this indecisiveness.

Guidance

Guidance is used throughout the recovery process. In the emergency phase of recovery, guidance is used to help departments and units identify and make use of resources that will promote recovery. In the later phases of recovery, guidance is used to help departments and units locate and obtain resources that support efforts to return to precrisis functioning. When meeting with groups, you might say something like "Have you thought about [a specific action or resource that might be helpful]?"A less directive way to offer guidance would be to say something like "I wonder if this [specific action or resource] might be helpful."

Two approaches can be used for this strategy that involves helping departments and units access resources to support the recovery process. The first approach involves referring departments and units to resources needed to help them recover from the crisis. This approach empowers the department or unit to take responsibility for their recovery. A message is communicated that you have confidence in their ability to work through the recovery process on their own, albeit with a little assistance. This type of guidance pays dividends after recovery since it builds and reinforces resiliency. Often guidance used in this manner requires employment of the next strategy, mobilization.

The second approach involves bringing the resources directly to departments or units and is particularly useful for high-impact crises. High-impact crises generally involve violence of some type in which significant injury or loss of life has occurred. These crises are relatively rare but are dramatic and directly impact departments and units in which the violence occurs. Typically the reaction is considerable in these crises, resulting in the need to bring resources directly to the department or unit. Often, a mistake is made by assuming that only psychological first aid is needed. Many times other resources are needed to help the department meet obligations in research, teaching, and scholarship. For example, academic departments may need resources to put courses online if that is required. Other units may need resources to manage and maintain day-to-day responsibilities if staff members are being used in areas of the university as part of the recovery process.

Mobilization

Mobilization is used to activate resiliency throughout the campus. This strategy empowers departments and units to activate internal resources and obtain external assistance as needed. It is used to overcome the "woe is us" attitude that sometimes sets in after a crisis. Administrators and CMTs can use this to instill hope and a renewed sense of direction. Mobilization can be used to reframe the crisis from a tragic experience to an opportunity for growth and renewal. This situation happened at Gustavus Adolphus College and Union University following the partial destruction of their campuses. The crises were used as rallying points around which the campuses were expanded and a new sense of purpose grew. Mobilization might also be used to guide departmental or unit recovery attempts to productive rather than destructive actions. Anything from a gentle nudge to a directive may be used in this strategy.

In the eight-step model, mobilization is useful in step two, "Problem Definition"; step five, "Generating Alternatives"; step six, "Making Plans"; and step seven, "Obtaining Commitment." It is also useful when departments and units seem stuck and seem to have no direction. In this situation, these groups may need encouragement to keep going even though the work seems hard and needs are so great. Visits by administrators and members of the CMT can be used as an opportunity to activate resiliency. You can think of this as a pep talk at half time when your team is behind. Following a crisis, departments and units might experience a similar feeling. Mobilization is a way to drum up their willingness to see that they can recover from the crisis.

Reinforcement is an effective way to mobilize groups during the recovery process. Administrators and members of CMTs should find ways to support efforts that groups are making to recover from the crisis. Publicly recognizing efforts goes a long way to further recovery. However, caution must be used so as not to ostracize other groups. We suggest finding a way to give tribute to the efforts of all groups involved in recovery. Ceremonies, certificates of appreciation, and plaques recognizing hard work can mobilize additional efforts for groups as they work to help the recovery process.

Ordering

This strategy involves helping departments and units prioritize their needs and actions. Ordering is used to help these groups slow down and organize efforts to address the problems associated with the crisis. This strategy helps to maintain continuity in the functioning of the university. It allows a systematic plan to be developed that concentrates on returning the campus to a precrisis state. Ordering is used throughout the recovery process. Its use is especially needed when emotions during meetings seem to be taking over. Administrators or members of the CMT leading those meetings might want to appeal to the logic of systematic problem solving in these situations. Taking control in this way can be done by communicating a sense of calm yourself. If you are in control and being logical, that will help the group regain a sense of control. One way a group regains a sense of order is by being asked to review what has been discussed to this point in the meeting. This method can defuse the emotions and help the group get back on track with resolving the problem. However, you must be aware that ordering is a fluid process and not static. Administrators and CMTs should not get locked into a specific list of priorities or actions. As different needs are identified during the assessment process, these must be incorporated into the list of needs.

A typical experience immediately following a crisis is being out of control. Everything is jumbled and upside down. Standard operating procedures are not effective at best and at times are an obstacle to accomplishing the tasks that must be done. Ordering is most effective as a proactive strategy to assist departments and units to take control after a crisis. Waiting until turmoil becomes entrenched means that the recovery process will be prolonged. The earlier in the recovery that needs are categorized and efforts methodically planned, the smoother the process will be.

Ordering can help you move beyond routine procedures in these early phases of recovery. As recovery progresses, prioritizing needs becomes critical. Often the most important problem that should be addressed is not the first issue that must be handled. Ordering can help departments and units sort through the myriad issues facing them as they work toward a full recovery. This strategy ensures that the issues related to the crisis are not overlooked as you move back to normal operations. An example of ordering is when departments or units list the issues related to the crisis. This list needs to be as inclusive as possible and include the order in which these issues will be addressed.

Protection

Protection is used with departments and units that are experiencing vulnerability because of the crisis. This strategy is particularly helpful for high-impact crises that significantly disrupt routine operations for a prolonged period. Initially, protection may be taking direct action to help departments and units. An example of protection is when administrators or the CMT takes over some of the responsibilities of the department or unit in the early phases of recovery. It might also mean providing additional help or budget support to assist with the extra work that is a result of the crisis. Another example of protection is providing counseling services with additional staff to protect them from being overwhelmed.

This strategy involves shielding and defending groups that are vulnerable as a result of the crisis. Shielding means taking a proactive stance to guard groups from being victimized after a crisis. Defending is a reactive position when groups are being discriminated against after a crisis. Both involve helping vulnerable groups receive fair treatment after a crisis. An example is the departments housed in the building that was partially destroyed by the explosion at Central University. These departments are likely to need some level of protection. The exposure of these departments may extend to several years, as individual faculty members attempt to resume scholarly activity. Protection as a strategy can guard these groups from being expected to produce at the same level during recovery as they work to restore precrisis functioning.

This intervention strategy is used throughout the recovery process. As recovery progresses, protection might come in the form of new policies or special provisions with respect to performance evaluations. You cannot expect the faculty members who were displaced as well as imposed upon at Central University to maintain a consistent level of scholarly activity. In most universities, the tenure and promotion process takes place in faculty members' sixth year. At Central University, a new policy extending that time temporarily for affected faculty members is a way of protecting them. Protection can also be used to develop policies to address issues related to disruptive students by making it easier for the university to minimize the risk of violent behaviors that would endanger others. The strategy of protection is used with departments and units that are at risk following a crisis.

As we said at the beginning of this section, these strategies are not used in isolation. They are used in conjunction with and to complement each other. Used in this manner, they become a powerful way to guide the recovery process. Although it would almost seem common sense, remember that in a crisis a model that can used to guide discussion about taking actions is extremely valuable. Throughout this section, we have also suggested ways to use the strategies in meetings. These methods were not meant as an exhaustive list but as samples to help you begin to personalize them.

SUMMARY

Full recovery from a crisis on your campus is a formidable task. The higher the impact of the crisis, the more daunting the recovery process. The eight-step model described in this chapter can help you navigate the recovery process in a way that will make recovery more efficient and effective. The nine strategies listed can be used in any part of the model as a way to support and sustain the recovery. There is a light at the end of the tunnel, and this model and these strategies can help you get there.

REFERENCES

Barton, L. (2000). *Crisis in organizations*. Florence, KY: South-Western College Publishing.

Caplan, G. (1961). *An approach to community mental health*. New York: Basic Books.

Caponigro, J. R. (2000). *The crisis counselor: A step-by-step guide to managing a business crisis*. Chicago: Contemporary Books.

Cohen, S. (2004). Social relationships and health. *American Psychologists, 59,* 676–684.

Egan, G. (2006). *Essentials of skilled helping*. Belmont, CA: Thomson Brooks/Cole.

Egan, G. (2007). *The skilled helper* (8th ed.), Belmont, CA: Thomson Brooks/Cole.

Fink, S. (2002). *Crisis management: Planning for the inevitable*. Lincoln, NE: iUniversitys.

Fisher, R., Ury, W., & Patton, B. (1991). *Getting to yes: Negotiating without giving in* (2nd ed.). New York: Penguin.

Gilliland, B. E. (1982). *Steps in crisis counseling*. Memphis: Memphis State University, Department of Counseling and Personnel Services. [Mimeographed handout for crisis intervention courses and workshops on crisis intervention].

Golembiewski, R. T., & Rauschenberg, F. (1993). Third party consultation: Basic features and one misapplication. In R. T. Golembiewski (Ed.), *The Handbook of organizational consultation* (pp. 393–398). New York: Marcel Dekker.

Gutkin, T. B., & Curtis, M. J. (1999). School-based consultation theory and practice: The art and science of indirect service delivery. In C. R. Reynolds & T. B. Gutkin (Eds.), *The handbook of school psychology* (3rd ed, pp. 598–637). New York: John Wiley & Sons.

Haddow, G. D., & Bullock, J. A. (2006). *Introduction to emergency management* (2nd ed.). Boston: Elsevier Butterworth-Heinemann.

James, R. K. (2008). *Crisis intervention strategies* (6th ed). Belmont, CA: Brooks/Cole-Cengage.

Jackson, J. (2007, March–April). Continuity trends: The migration to resiliency. *Business Continuity*. Retrieved September 4, from http://www.continuityinsights.com/Magazine/Issue_Archives/2007/03-04/CTmigration.html.

Knotek, S. (2006). Administrative crisis consultation after 9/11: A university's system's response. *Consulting Psychology Journal: Practice and Research, 58,* 162–173.

Mancini, F. (2009, December). *The key to effective student mental health crisis management: On and off-campus strategic alliance*. Presented at the 1st Annual National Behavioral Intervention Team Association in San Antonio, TX.

Mitroff, I. I. (2004). *Crisis leadership: Planning for the unthinkable*. Hoboken, NJ: John Wiley & Sons.

Mitroff, I. I. & Anagnos, G. (2001). *Managing crises before they happen*. New York: American Management Association.

Mitroff, I. I. Diamond, M. A., & Alpasian, M. C. (2006). How prepared are America's colleges and universities for a major crisis? *Change: The Magazine of Higher Learning, 38*, 60–67.

Myer, R. A., & James, R. K. (2005). *CD ROM and workbook for crisis intervention.* Belmont, CA: Brooks/Cole–Cengage.

Myer, R. A., & Moore, H. (2006). Crisis in context: An ecological model. *Journal of Counseling and Development, 84*, 139–147.

Neimeyer, R. A. (2001). *Meaning reconstruction and the experience of loss.* Washington, DC: American Psychological Association.

Nicoletti, J., Spencer-Thomas, S., & Bollinger, C. (2001). *Violence goes to college: The authoritative guide to prevention and intervention.* Springfield, IL: Charles C Thomas.

Paton, D. (1996). Training disaster workers: Promoting wellbeing and operational effectiveness. *Disaster Prevention and Management, 5*(5), 11–18.

Paton, D., & Jackson, D. (2002). Developing disaster management capability: An assessment centre approach. *Disaster Prevention and Management, 11*, 115–122.

Ren, C. H. (2000). Understanding and managing the dynamics of linked crisis events. *Disaster Prevention and Management, 9*(1), 12–17.

Schoenberg, A. (2005). Do crisis plans matter? A new perspective on leading during a crisis. *Public Relations Quarterly, 50*, 1–7.

Tedeshi, R. G., & Calhoun, L. G. (1996). The posttraumatic growth inventory: Measuring the positive legacy of trauma. *Journal of Traumatic Stress, 9*, 455–471.

9

Not Buying a Pig in a Poke

Identifying individuals who may become disruptive to the learning environment by engaging in undesirable, dangerous behaviors has skyrocketed to the forefront of higher education since the shootings at Virginia Tech in 2006 and Northern Illinois in 2008. In this chapter, we describe a model to recognize individuals who may become injurious or lethal to themselves or others, the Triage Assessment Scale for Students in Learning Environments (TASSLE) (Myer, Moulton, Rice, & James, 2006), a modification of the triage assessment system for assessing persons in crisis that was developed by Myer, Williams, Ottens, and Schmidt (1992). The chapter begins by looking at the idea of threat assessment, discusses using the threat assessment system on your campus, and ends with a discussion on creating and using threat assessment teams on college campuses with a case example involving Latavius Jefferson, George Giap, and Sam Hull, whom you've met in previously chapters.

Before we begin, we want to share a word of warning. Buying a pig in a poke refers to a con game dating back to the Middle Ages that involved people buying what they thought was a piglet but in truth was a small cat in a bag. We cannot encourage you enough to make sure the item or services you are purchasing is what you imagined and can perform the way you hope. Within weeks of the tragic shootings at Virginia Tech, the number of sales pitches extolling the ability of this product or that product to prevent similar incidents and facilitate the recovery process increased geometrically. Mass mailings were sent out, advertisements in journals and professional magazines abounded, and the number of commercial e-mail messages praising easy and instantaneous methods for assessing and controlling potentially violent individuals of every kind, type, and variety flooded the ether. These hucksters attempted to spread a climate of fear across campuses (Flynn & Heitzmann, 2008). While some of these products were probably capable of performing at the level promised, most showed little reliability or validity to support them. Unfortunately, in the effort to prevent the occurrence of a high-impact event, some universities, fearful of their own potential shooting rampages, moved quickly to purchase these products and services without fully examining the claims being made. The real question is whether what you bought was worth it. Is your school at risk for buying a pig in a poke?

UNDERSTANDING THREATS

Some of the most feared words on any campus are "There is an active shooter on campus." Those words mean that whatever efforts have been taken to prevent such a crisis were not successful. Violence prevention programs are unsuccessful for many reasons. One reason for failure is the lack of a model to sort through the meaning of a specific threat. Using a model to understand the potential lethality of a threat is the first step in taking action when a threat is made. This chapter outlines the Triage Assessment Scale for Students in Learning Environments (TASSLE), which we believe fits a model that can be used to make appropriate intervention decisions.

All threats should be taken seriously. Yet some threats should be viewed more seriously than others because not all threats are created equal. Some threats are valid or legitimate; others involve an individual merely blowing off steam and are empty of any real intent to do harm. The problem is that each must be treated as real until proven otherwise. The principal point we want to make is that all threats should be considered genuine until proven otherwise. Even off-the-cuff comments made in a fit of anger, jealousy, or embarrassment in the heat of the moment must initially be considered a legitimate threat until evidence shows they are not. On the other end of the threat continuum, just as many problems can occur when a wary and paranoid administration overreacts to a potential threat. A zero tolerance policy that throws sound judgment out the window in a one-size-fits-all threat reaction has negative and potentially severe ramifications for the university as well as for the individual. Sound judgment, based on a model to understand specific threats, is needed before sounding the alarm and taking action that might not be prudent (Braverman, 1999) and winds up with the university suffering bad public relations while getting sued for maligning and falsely labeling a now traumatized individual who has been ostracized because of fears that he is the next Freddie Krueger.

Making a decision about the veracity of a threat is no easy task. Make the wrong decision and someone might die, but if you cry wolf too often, everyone stops listening and then the potential for making a wrong decision becomes more likely. Knowing that making the wrong decision may lead to people getting hurt or dying only adds to the pressure of making the correct decision. This section outlines several perspectives that can be used to analyze threats. These perspectives allow you to sort through the situation and make the best decision possible given the circumstances. Breaking down threats into clear components makes decisions less subjective (Borum, 2000). Notice we say *less* subjective. You need to recognize that all decisions will be in part subjective, but a model based on observable criteria that allows the evaluator to dissect the characteristics of a specific threat allows you to make better decisions that are based in fact and not conjecture (Braverman, 1999).

Method of Communication

Threats can be made verbally, nonverbally, in written form, or through electronic means. No specific way of communicating a threat makes it more likely to happen. Regardless of the means to communicate a threat, it can be convincing and scary to the person or persons on the receiving end. Each must be treated as having the potential to be carried out. Although all threats should be taken seriously, logic suggests those made via two or more means of communication seem to be more creditable. Using two or more methods implies that the person making the threat has taken more time thinking and possibly planning what he or she intends to do. Written threats on paper or in electronic form should be preserved, regardless of the decision and actions taken because of it (Nicoletti, Spencer-Thomas, & Bollinger, 2001). If the threat is made verbally, the words of the person making the threat should be recorded as close as possible to what was said. If the threat is nonverbal, such as a person pretending to have a gun pointed at someone and then pulling the trigger, a written description of the behavior should be made and kept in a file. Keeping a record allows you to justify the action taken when the situation warrants. To that end, an incident report, such as the one in this chapter, would seem mandatory when an incident escalates to the point that it comes to your attention and is interfering with the rights of others.

Credibility

An extremely important consideration is credibility. Credibility involves whether the means are not only available, but readily at hand. Saying something like "if I had a gun, I would shoot you" is very different from "I am going to get my gun and shoot you now." In the first statement, the means do not appear to be immediately available, whereas in the second statement, the means appear to be readily available, and the time frame is clear. Although both threats must be taken seriously, obviously the second threat should be viewed as more dangerous with respect to taking immediate action. Another issue with respect to credibility concerns whether the person making the threat has a history of violence (Halikias, 2004). A history of past violence is the best indicator of potential for violence (Collins & Collins, 2005; James, 2008). If an individual has a file filled with incidents of aggressive and/or violent acts, the likelihood that the individual will carry out a threat of violence significantly jumps. Keeping a record of violent incidents is extremely important because it shows trends. Violence research over and over shows that escalation of violence, both in number and intensity, moves individuals ever closer to crossing a lethality line (James, 2008, pp. 466–469).

Potential for Harm

The potential for harm with respect to method is also another consideration in understanding threats. Consideration of the means of lethality has a long history in determining the actions to be taken by police officers and mental health professionals who are confronted with potentially assaultive, suicidal, or homicidal clients (Hoff, Hallisey, & Hoff, 2009; James, 2008; Slatkin, 2005). Using any type of instrument or method to harm another person is not acceptable under any circumstances, but some methods are clearly more lethal than others. Indiana Jones, in *Raiders of the Lost Ark,* clearly understood this when he shot his scimitar-twirling assailant and remarked, tongue in cheek, about bringing a knife to a gunfight. The second part of the significance of the means to carry out the threat is the ability to use a weapon. A member of the ROTC who has spent three summers in military training has a great deal more knowledge of firearms than a coed who knows where her boyfriend keeps his shotgun. Both may be dangerous, but the ROTC student's ability to use weapons is clearly more profound and thus more lethal than the girlfriend's.

Dynamics

Another perspective useful in understanding threats is examining the dynamics of the situation that instigates the threat (Greenberg, 2007). The dynamics of a threat involve understanding the intentions of the threat. A threat is a way of trying to accomplish something by getting someone else to accede to the threatener's wishes. Understanding motive is critical to determining the person's commitment to carry out the threat. For example, someone may demand that the university stop using animals for research. This is a coercive threat that is couched in terms of holding some perceived higher moral ground. Therefore, the background and history of the person or persons making the threat becomes important. Is the person the president of the local animal rights organization, or is he or she a bystander who had nothing better to do on Monday morning than stage a sit-in at the science building?

A second category of threat focuses on revenge for some real or imagined injustice (Nicoletti et al., 2001). Many times this threat involves an attempt to right some real or imagined wrong. These threats can be very dangerous because the person is no longer just an adherent of the cause but on a mission for it. "You did 'blank' to me so now I am going to get even." The shootings at Virginia Tech and Northern Illinois University seem to fall into this category. In both situations, the shooter appears to have thought he was avenging some wrong done to him.

Threats can also be thought of as impulsive (Greenberg, 2007). The shootings at Duquesne University involving five basketball players after a dance fall into this category. There was no premeditated plan to shoot five basketball players. They happened to be in the wrong place at the wrong time and were involved with the wrong woman, a scene that has played out in thousands of bars. That certainly does not make the threat less valid, the injuries less severe, or the fear it spreads across campus less intense.

In each of these categories, the threat does not have to involve the use of deadly force. The threat may involve other acts, such as vandalism, overt or covert harassment, bullying, and stalking. However, such threats do not make such behavior less problematic. If the threats are not effective and are not stopped, they are more than likely going to escalate. Thus, the nature and kind of dynamics of a threat can be helpful in providing university officials with information needed to respond appropriately and not underreact or overreact (Nicoletti et al., 2001).

Type of Threat

Another perspective to use in trying to understand a threat is whether it is *transient* or *substantive* (Cornell et al., 2004). We would add to this way of understanding threats the idea of *sustained threats*. Transient threats are statements that don't communicate or express an enduring desire to do harm. These threats tend to dissipate as quickly as they appear. In legal terms, these threats may be termed an "excited utterance." These statements are made in the context of a burst of anger or excitement and may be recanted once an individual has calmed down. Be aware, though, that these statements can be used as hearsay evidence (Byrom, n.d.).

Substantive threats represent a sustained intent to harm someone or something beyond the immediate situation. "Just wait until the next time I see you and the RA is not around" also suggests an intention to harm another person at a later time. Sustained threats are the same ones that occur multiple times over an extended period of time. These threats suggest that the person making them has maintained a need to do harm that goes well beyond an isolated incident. Understanding the purpose of these different types of threats is important for the threat assessment team (TAT) decision-making process. Although each type must be taken seriously, the sustained threat is generally of more concern since it seems to represent an obsession with the idea of doing harm to someone or something.

Specificity

Degree of specificity adds another layer of insight to a threat (James, 2008, pp. 94–95). Specificity refers to target, place, time, and means. Some threats are very specific while others are vague. Specific threats permit university officials to take action to prevent it. Vague or nonspecific threats make taking action more difficult. For example, if a specific target is identified, and time and mode of operation are given, steps can be taken to protect the individual, group, or building. However, not knowing the target makes preventing a threat from being carried out extremely difficult. Each level of specificity adds to the university's ability to take actions designed to prevent the threat from being carried out. Thus, one task of a TAT is attempting to clarify and ascertain the degree of specificity of a threat.

Category of Threat

The category of threat provides a final method to analyze a threat. According to Nicoletti, Spencer-Thomas, and Bollinger (2001), threats can be broken into three general categories: (a) direct, (b) conditional, and (c) veiled. Using a continuum with respect to the level of ambiguity is the best way to understand the types of threats. Direct threats are statements that indicate action; something is going to happen. There is no ambiguity that the person making the threat is going to take action. This type of threat is the easiest to handle because it is punishable by law (Nicoletti et al., 2001). Conditional threats add some ambiguity. This threat sets an "if-then" scenario: "Do this or I will take things into my own hands." A concern with this type of threat is the potential for it escalating as frustration builds (James, 2008, pp. 187–188). As frustration builds, the likelihood of following through on the threat increases. The most ambiguous type is the veiled threat. Veiled threats are circuitous, making it very difficult to take any action (Braverman, 1999). If confronted about a threat of this kind, the person making the threat may laugh it off, saying he or she was just misunderstood. Therefore, maintaining a record of this type of threat is important in order to take any action.

Table 9.1 combines the type of threat with specificity. Understanding the degree of ambiguity is important in making decisions and taking actions with respect to threats. Yet the means of communication, credibility, dynamics, and potential lethalness must also be considered. We cannot state strongly enough that all threats should be taken seriously. However, policies and procedures must allow for flexibility in making decisions and taking actions based on the threat.

We recommend that the TAT use a Threat Assessment Worksheet. See Appendix A to this chapter for this form. Using the worksheet ensures that all factors related to understanding a threat are considered. Completed threat assessment worksheets can be found later on (Figures 9.1 and 9.2) when we revisit Sam and George, our two freshmen

Table 9.1   Examples of Statements

	Direct	**Veiled**	**Conditional**
Specific	I am going to blow up the science building.	You drive a red Ford Focus, don't you? You park in the lot for faculty, right? I hear they are having trouble with break-ins in that lot.	If things don't change, I will take care of the guys in the room above.
	I'll get that professor for giving me that bad grade.	There are a lot of ways to get even, some nice and some not so nice.	If he doesn't say he is sorry, he will be sorry, that's for sure.
Non-specific	I don't care who gets hurt, but someone will get hurt if this doesn't stop.	Everyone will be sorry for what they did. Bad things can happen when least expected.	If something doesn't happen soon I will be forced to take care of it myself.
	Whatever happens they will know not to mess with me.	I heard someone got mugged in the science annex parking lot. Kinda dark there. A person really needs to keep his eyes and ears on out there at night.	They better stop using animals for experiments, otherwise they will be surprised.

introduced earlier. This form can be easily modified to fit the needs of your campus. Basic information needed on the form includes the date, time, and location of the threat. Date, time, and location are useful to determine if a pattern emerges regarding people making multiple threats in specific locales or at specific times or dates. A description of the situation is also useful in developing a comprehensive understanding of the nature of the threat.

The name of the person, persons, or group making the threat is critical. However, there will be times when a name is not known. Anonymous threats cause TATs headaches. Is the threat real or a hoax? We encourage you to regard anonymous threats seriously and take appropriate action. The table on the form is divided into three columns. The first column lists the factors for understanding threats, as discussed previously. We suggest including a blank or "other" row for specific circumstances that may be unique to the threat. Column two involves the report of the threat using the factor listed on that row. A brief analysis of the threat should be included in the appropriate boxes. Enough information should be included to allow TATs to make decisions as well as to track multiple threats from the same person, persons, or group. The final column involves relating the disposition and thinking of TATs regarding this factor of the threat. Below the table is a final section for reporting other issues and circumstances that might be considered relevant, given a specific threat.

TRIAGE ASSESSMENT SCALE FOR STUDENTS IN LEARNING ENVIRONMENTS (TASSLE)

Accurate and consistent assessment of individuals who are disrupting the campus is the most critical aspect for making decisions and taking action to prevent a crisis. Taking actions based on capricious, inaccurate information will come back to haunt the person making the decision. This concern is especially true when assessing individuals who are acting in ways that might escalate into dangerous, life-threatening behaviors. These situations often involve taking drastic actions, such as barring an individual from campus, initiating the process to force a psychiatric evaluation, or contacting local law enforcement agencies in order to have the individual taken into custody. These situations often involve multiple episodes of disruptive behaviors rather than single incidents. Single occurrences of disruptive behaviors may not rise to the level to warrant drastic actions such as barring an individual from campus. Several episodes are needed before such a sweeping decision is made. Assessments based on a structured assessment model that have been shown to be reliable and valid are a key element in taking action to help the individual and to also protect the campus (Borum, 2000).

The need for such tools is clearly evident in the National Behavior Intervention Team Association's (NBITA) decision to develop its own holistic threat assessment because standard law enforcement and mental health assessment tools fall short of addressing a comprehensive assessment of the various types of violence that may occur on a college campus (Sokolow & Lewis, 2009; Sokolow, Lewis, Wolf, VanBrunt, & Byrnes, 2009). The NBITA assessment tool includes measures for generalized risk to the institution, such as harm to facilities, institutional reputation, or finances. It also assesses mental and behavioral health in regard to both risk to oneself and aggression toward others. Mental health and related risk are measured by a D scale that has specific definitions for distress, disturbance, dysregulation, and medical disability categories. There are five levels of generalized risk that range from mild to severe and have definitive rubrics attached to each risk level. There is also an aggression management model built on a three-phase model of an initial trigger phase, an escalation phase, and the crisis phase. These phases are overlaid by nine levels of primal and cognitive aggression. Primal aggression may be considered the adrenaline-driven, red-in-the-face, temper-boiling-over, neck-vein-bulging type of aggression, whereas cognitive aggression is the cooler, detached, revenge-is-best-served-cold aggression. This is not a simple model and takes people with skill and knowledge to understand and use it. *Understanding* and *skill* are operative words and should guide the team you are going to develop.

We believe the foregoing system is elegant and has merit as a postaction reporting system. We also believe it is important to have a system that is simple to use, can be taught in a short time to any employee of a university, and has immediate, on-the-spot use in determining how volatile an individual is. This need was articulated to us initially by Director of Residence Life, Danny Armitage, at University of Memphis, who knew of our development of a triage assessment system for mental health workers dealing with out-of-control clients and wondered if we could adapt it for use by his resident hall assistants. This request gave birth to the Triage Assessment System for Students in Learning Environments (TASSLE).

It was developed using the triage assessment system for crisis intervention, a structured model based on the idea that people react with a restricted range of feelings, limited number of behaviors, and narrow range of thoughts in crisis situations. TASSLE uses this idea to assess individuals' disruptive behaviors. Limiting the assessment of disruptive behaviors in this manner promotes greater accuracy in the evaluation of individuals. While this model appears simplistic, the system has elegance.

A copy of TASSLE is in Appendix B of this chapter and is used later with Sam Hull and George Giap, the freshmen you met earlier. The form can be purchased from CIP-Solutions, Inc. and cannot be reproduced in full or part without permission. The form is one page printed on both sides. Side one of TASSLE has three separate sections. The first section asks for basic demographic information and a description of the situation. The second section has three columns and involves making observations about individuals' behaviors. The first column lists characteristics associated with mental illness. Included in this column are hallucinations, thought processes, flashbacks, and bizarre behaviors. All behaviors that apply should be checked in this column. The second column contains items associated with violence toward self and others, from harassment to clear homicidal or suicidal plans. These observations are critical in determining the disposition of individuals engaging in any of these behaviors. The third column has items commonly associated with a person who is either vulnerable or not cooperative in some way. Examples include inability to recall personal information, confusion, inability to control emotions, and unresponsiveness. Items address the issue of individuals' ability or willingness to work toward resolving the situation. The last section on the front side of TASSLE is used to assess the severity of the disruptive behaviors. Assessment of the severity is based on the severity scales on the back side of the form.

Five independent research studies have been conducted on the triage assessment system format (Blancett, 2008; Conte, 2005; Pazar, 2005; Slagel, 2009; Watters, 1997). Each study found variations of the basic model reliable and valid for quickly assessing reactions in crisis situations. The study most relevant to dealing with individuals was conducted by Blancett (2008). In his study, Blancett examined the reliability and validity of the TASSLE. In his research, Blancett collected data from approximately 100 individuals who were trained to use the TASSLE in college settings. The people trained included office assistants, professional staff of resident halls, instructors, campus security, and personnel from college counseling centers. The participants in Blancett's research were asked to rate five videos of individuals engaging in different levels of disruptive behaviors. These ratings were compared with the ratings of five experts in the triage assessment system and were found to be consistent with those ratings. A specific strength of the research is that the training was conducted by seven different people, sometimes working alone and at other times conducting the training in teams of two. The fact that reliability coefficients consistently remained above .70 indicates the reliability of TASSLE. The criterion validity of the model was supported because newly trained individuals consistently rated individuals' disruptive behaviors the same as crisis intervention experts' ratings.

Severity Scales

The TASSLE is made operational through the use of individual severity scales that assess feelings, behaviors, and thoughts. The severity scales are used to assess the degree of each reaction. Each severity scale (i.e., feeling, behaviors, and thoughts) is organized in the same manner, rating the reactions on a scale of 1 to 10. An example of the general scale is provided in Table 9.2. The scale has six basic levels of severity. Except for the anchors of the scale (no impairment = 1 and severe impairment = 10), each level has two numbers allowing you to rate an individual as either low or high in that level. That approach allows a finer differentiation in these levels of impairment.

Severity scales rate individuals' ability to *control* the reaction, the *intensity* of the reaction, and the *duration* of the reaction. Generally speaking, the less control individuals have, the more intense the expression, and/or the longer in duration of the disruptive behaviors, the higher the rating on the severity scales. However, each dimension (i.e.,

Table 9.2 Severity Scale

1	2	3	4	5	6	7	8	9	10
No Impairment	Minimal Impairment	Low Impairment			Moderate Impairment		Marked Impairment		Severe Impairment

control, intensity, and duration) is independent of the other and should be viewed in that way. All three do not have to be at elevated levels to assess an individual high on the severity scale. For example, an individual might be able to control a reaction, but the intensity is such that a high rating is warranted. Or the duration of the reaction may be extended over a significant amount of time, thus a higher rating is warranted even though the intensity and ability to control the reaction are only average. Using these three ideas to assess feelings, behaviors, and thoughts gives you a powerful method to determine the appropriateness of individuals' ability to function on college campuses.

After rating an individual on each scale, the scores are combined, resulting in a lowest possible score of 3 and a highest possible score of 30. It is the final score that guides decision making with regard to accessing support systems and/or taking action in the form of sanctions or suspensions. Final scores may fall in one of four categories: (a) single digit, (b) teens, (c) twenties, and (d) high single scale score. Table 9.3 summarizes this information.

Single Digit

Individuals rated in the single digits are not likely to be causing disturbances of any kind. They may merely need a sounding board to activate problem-solving skills. By talking

Table 9.3   TASSLE Score Categories

	Characteristics	Support
Single Digits	• Feelings—parallel with incident • Behavior—purposeful • Thoughts—rational	Released on their own or with assurances support system in place
Teens	• Feelings—bursts of feelings • Behavior—erratic and potentially dangerous • Thoughts—clear thinking significantly diminished	Ranges from medium to high, support services recommended
Twenties	• Feelings—Flooded to limited • Behavior—No thought to consequences • Thoughts—Highly distorted and irrational	Referral to support services, implementation of campus sanctions likely, evaluation for hospitalization recommended
Single Scale High Score	• Feelings—Hysterical to nonexistent • Behavior—Dangerous to self and others • Thoughts—Decision making absent	Implementation of campus sanctions, hospitalization probable

through the problem, they can acknowledge the problem and its severity but show control over the situation by not brooding on it to the exclusion of everything else in their lives. The intensity of the feelings, behaviors, and thoughts matches the situation. The expression of the feelings, behaviors, and thoughts is limited with respect to duration. Individuals' behaviors and thoughts are generally purposeful. Decisions are focused on avoiding, monitoring, or resolving the crisis. Individuals' feelings are relatively parallel with what is going on. That does not mean they will necessarily be calm, cool, and completely collected! Certainly, depending on the crisis, emotions such as fear, anger, and sadness are reasonable, proper, and warranted. In fact, if little emotion is expressed, a higher rating might be more appropriate. For example, an individual who has just received a phone call that his family has been in a horrific car accident would be expected to express an intense level of fear and anxiety. If the individual expresses no emotion, a higher rating might also be given.

As ratings move toward the teens, control, intensity, and duration become altered. The debilitating emotions, inappropriate behavior, and faulty thinking start to gain intensity and duration while control begins to diminish. In other words, there is more of it and it lasts longer.

Teens

Individuals with a total score in the teens are the most problematic in regard to disposition. Their ability to function is limited, with an increasing degree of incompetence. For incidents involving persons with mental health problems, they may be off their medication, under more stress than usual, using alcohol or drugs to medicate themselves, or experiencing new symptoms. At this level of impairment, the possibility exists that these individuals are threatening others or are so incapacitated by the situation that they have difficulty behaving in socially acceptable ways. Not all individuals at this level of severity constitute a clear threat of harm to themselves or others, but their thinking is compromised to the point of being irrational, their feelings are becoming more labile or subdued, and their behavior is becoming increasingly erratic and less purposeful. These individuals are rapidly moving beyond a momentary burst of anger, crying spell, or touch of panic. Their behaviors will most likely become increasingly disruptive to campus life if not addressed.

People assessed at this level definitely need a support system. Support might be given by a family member or close friend, or the support might be from a staff person who is in regular contact with the individual. The situation may also dictate that the person doing the assessment become the support system on a temporary basis if no one else is available. Support can range from medium to high involvement. Support for these individuals should be available for as long as needed. The amount of time may range from a few minutes to several hours.

Feelings are either exaggerated or severely damped down. Besides the increase in the amount of the emotion, there will also be an increase in the time the emotion is present. If emotion is brought under control, it will be difficult to retain that control. Mood swings will become more pronounced and rapid. It is most likely that at this level individuals will feel some threat—either externally from the environment or internally as they sense themselves spiraling out of control. Behavior is erratic enough to require some serious effort on their part and probably a fair amount of effort from you to keep it in control. Behavior has increasing potential to deteriorate to the point of significantly disrupting specific areas of campus life. As total ratings move into the upper teens (i.e., 18 and 19), individuals may act in ways not typical for them. A real concern is that these individuals may believe they need to take some sort of action, which may end up being dangerous to themselves or others.

Clear thinking and problem solving start to disintegrate for these individuals. As individuals reach the upper teens, thought processes with respect to coping and problem solving will begin to collapse. They start to have trouble making sense of what is going on around them and focus on the crisis so much that they may have trouble communicating or understanding communications from other people. As a result, instructions should be stated slowly and may have to be repeated. As the scores increase, duration lengthens, intensity increases, and control decreases.

Twenties

Individuals falling into this category require immediate intervention that may involve close professional supervision, in-depth support, suspension from campus, and/or possibly confinement (e.g., hospitalization). Individuals with a full-scale score in the 20s may need to be removed from campus. At this level, individuals have only limited ability to think through the consequences of anything they feel, do, or think. Minimally, individuals with full-scale scores in the 20s should not be left on their own. Some type of support system (e.g., family, friends, and university staff, if no one else is available) must be activated to assist individuals scoring in this range. As scores increase to mid and high 20s, hospitalization becomes a realistic option. Campus security may be called in situations involving individuals who are either threatening others or simply unruly to the point no one other than trained personnel should get near them. Campus policies should be checked for clarity to ensure that procedures are clearly spelled out for the actions to be taken in these situations.

Generally speaking, individuals with scores in the 20s are generally easy to rate and hard to control! Their scores are indicative of people who are putting themselves or others in harm's way. Their thinking is severely distorted and highly irrational and may even include hallucinations, messages, commands, or mandates from higher powers or demons. For persons suffering from hallucinations, their ability to keep the hallucinations at bay may become difficult, and the hallucinations will start to take over more and more of their decision making and behavioral actions. In other situations, individuals may express significant confusion, be unable to recall personal information such as phone numbers and addresses, and be incapable of following simple directions. When asked to comply with commands, they might just look at you with a blank expression or do the opposite of what you ask. Individuals falling into this rating are flooded by waves of feelings that wash over them. Alternately they may appear absolutely feelingless or catatonic. Individuals will have a great deal of difficulty responding to requests for compliance.

People's behavior becomes erratic and out of control and likely to make the situation worse rather than better. Their threat level will be high, and they present a clear and present danger to themselves or others. As an example, while individuals who threaten suicide or homicide who are rated in the teens may state that they want to kill themselves or somebody else, their plans and actions are ill defined, their means less lethal, access to those means is poor, and their motivation may be lacking. Suicidal and/or homicidal individuals who get ratings in the mid-20s and up have very clearly defined plans, more lethal means, access to those means, and the motivation to go forward.

High Single Scale Scores

When the total of scores on the three scales exceeds 20, the removal of an individual from the campus becomes more likely. However, when an individual has a score of 10 on any *one* scale, temporary removal from campus is a given. Removal of the individual is warranted not just for the safety of others, but for the individual. If the assessment on a scale is an 8 or a 9, serious consideration should be given to removing the individual from the situation. Temporary removal is warranted in such cases until the individual is able to resume normal day-to-day campus activities. The reason is simple. Any score ranging from 8 to 10 on a single scale indicates that the potential for ultimately harming oneself or others is high.

Feeling Reactions

Crisis situations cause people to draw on their most basic emotions. They do not stop and think about the situation; they just feel. There are three basic negative emotions that present during a crisis; (a) *anger*, (b) *fear*, and (c) *sadness*. Many feeling reactions of individuals begin with a growing frustration. The situation might involve frustration over medication that is not working, voices that won't go away, physically disabling conditions, broken love lives, failing grades, obnoxious roommates, or a host of other conditions for which an individual's problem-solving ability and resources are inadequate. As frustration builds and an individual's tolerance decreases, disruptive behaviors increase. In the end, frustration gives way to anger, fear, or sadness, which results in a full-blown crisis situation.

Anger

The expression of anger can range from annoyance to rage. People who are physically combative, agitated, rapidly pacing, and uncooperative are obviously angry. Subtler signs of anger include talking faster than normal or talking at a higher pitch. The color of people's faces, such as flushing or red blotchy skin, is also an indication of anger. Additionally, nonverbal responses such as a need for increased personal space and a rigid, combative stance are indicators of anger. Certainly, we associate anger as closely allied with potential violence. Individuals expressing anger should be handled with care. Individuals who are highly agitated have an extended personal space. What may appear to be a normal conversational distance to you may appear to them to be right in their face. We suggest maintaining a safe distance from agitated people as you assess and attempt to help them, and that means keeping a good arm's length away from them (so they can't hit you), not cornering them so they have an exit (so they don't run over you), and having a ready exit that does not cross through their space (you can get out while the getting is still good) (James, 2008, pp. 474–475).

Fear

Fear comes in many forms, ranging from uncomfortable nervousness to complete and absolute mind-numbing terror. People react with fear when they are uncertain what is going to happen or they do not know how to behave. You may experience individuals screaming and flailing their arms or huddled in the corner. Physical expressions of fear range from a queasy stomach to cold sweats to trembling. Fear is also closely allied with potential violence. The desire for the protection of oneself, someone else, or some cherished idea is most often the purpose of violence based on fear.

Sadness

The range of expression of sadness is from mild unhappiness to extreme despair to the point of being unresponsive. Sadness is often accompanied by a loss of hope. The loss of hope may cause individuals to act in unexpected and dangerous ways. These individuals can lull you into a false sense of safety. Be aware that individuals may appear quite calm and seemingly cooperative when they are extremely sad, but a word or gesture on your part may be misinterpreted and provoke a violent outburst.

Feeling Severity Scale

The Feeling Severity Scale is shown in Table 9.4. At first, using this severity scale may seem complicated. However, note that the Feeling Severity Scale differentiates emotions using four descriptors. Each descriptor considers individuals' ability to control the feeling, the intensity of the feeling, and/or the amount of time the feeling has been present. As descriptors become familiar to you with usage, you can assess individuals' emotional reactions quickly and accurately.

As shown earlier in the general severity scale, emotions are rated on a scale of 1 to 10, with 1 being no impairment and 10 being severe impairment. To determine a rating, start with a score of 10 (severe impairment) and work your way down. While this seems backward, it is the most efficient way to assess the severity of individuals' feelings. Starting with minimal ratings results in confusion in trying to determine what individuals are not feeling rather than what they are feeling. If none of the feeling characteristics that are described under a 10 rating fits, move down the scale to a score of 8 or 9 (marked

Table 9.4 Feeling Severity Scale

1 No Impairment	2 3 Minimal Impairment	4 5 Low Impairment	6 7 Moderate Impairment	8 9 Marked Impairment	10 Severe Impairment
• Stable mood, control of feelings.	• Affect elevated but generally appropriate.	• Evidence of negative feelings pronounced and are increasingly inappropriate.	• Feelings are primarily negative and are exaggerated or increasingly diminished.	• Feelings are negative and highly volatile or may be nonexistent.	• Feelings are extremely pronounced to being devoid of feeling.
• Feelings are appropriate.	• Brief periods of slightly elevated negative mood.	• Duration of feeling intensity longer than situation warrants.	• Efforts to control emotions are not always successful.	• Extremely limited control of emotions.	• No ability to control feelings regardless of potential danger to self or others.
• Emotions are under control.	• Emotions are substantially under control.	• Emotions are controlled but focused on crisis event.	• Emotions not under control but remain focused on crisis.	• Emotions start to generalize from crisis event to other people and situations.	• Emotions of the crisis are generalized to other people and situations.
• Responses to questions/requests are calm and composed.	• Responses to questions/requests are emotional but composed.	• Responses to questions/requests vary from rapid and agitated to slow and subdued.	• Responses to questions/requests are emotionally volatile or beginning to shut down.	• Responses to questions/requests noncompliant due to interference of emotions.	• Cannot respond to questions/requests because of interference of emotions.

impairment). Continue going down the scale until you identify a rating where at least one characteristic fits the individual's emotional response. You will notice that four categories (minimal, low, moderate, and marked) have two ratings. Choose the higher number in the category if half or more of the characteristics in the category fit; choose the lower number in the category if fewer than half of the characteristics in the category fit.

Behavioral Reactions

The behavior of individuals engaging in disruptive behaviors generally operates in three ways. People will *approach* the situation trying to work out a solution, run from or ignore the situation in *avoidance* of it, or just be stuck and *immobile*, unable to do anything that can resolve the situation. Depending on the setting and the specifics of the incident, each of these reactions may be either constructive or destructive. A simple guideline to determine if an approach is constructive or destructive is to consider the possible outcomes of the action. If the behavior is likely to improve the situation, it is probably constructive. On the other hand, if the behavior has a high probability of making things worse, it is probably destructive.

Approach

Actively trying to resolve the situation is an approach tactic. The problems are that while the individual sees approach as a proactive means to solve the problem, in the objective and rational view of others, it may do anything but that. An example of an approach tactic that is destructive might involve an individual ambushing another individual who had previously assaulted him or her. The approach response in this case is a poor choice because it not only may be illegal and physically harmful but also causes further problems that will invariably involve a host of other people devoting time and effort to solving the issue.

Avoidance

Acting as if nothing is wrong is an avoidance tactic. The person may discount the gravity of the situation or pretend as if nothing is going on. Again, avoidance may be constructive or destructive, depending on the situation. The example of the individual who was assaulted can be used again. Constructive use of avoidance might involve sidestepping direct contact with the individual who committed the assault, but if the person is constantly bullied by the other, then it is clearly a bad choice.

Immobility

Immobility is a tactic of remaining in the debilitating situation but doing nothing. At times, remaining immobile and giving oneself time to size up the situation before engaging in what could be precipitous behavior may be a wise tactic. In other instances, individuals may be working to find a solution but behave in ways that cancel out the action. Finally, individuals may be powerless and simply do not know what to do. An example of a destructive immobile reaction is an individual who is so frightened of future violence or abuse that he or she does not seek assistance when dating violence occurs.

Behavior Severity Scale

As with the Feeling Severity Scale, you rate individuals' behavior on a scale of 1 to 10. Again, four descriptors are used to assess individuals' behaviors (Table 9.5). As assessment increases to higher levels, individuals are increasingly unable to control their behaviors, the intensity elevates, and possibly the longer the behaviors are used. As with the Feeling Severity Scale, starting at 10 and working down is the best strategy. Once at least one descriptor is met, that is the rating for the individual on behavior.

Cognitive (Thought) Reactions

The cognitive scale is the most complex of the three scales. Emotions and behaviors can be seen, but thoughts cannot. At the heart of individuals' disruptive behaviors is perception. Perception of what "has been," "is," or "will be" drives disruptive behavior. As severity on this scale increases, so does the unpredictable behavior. Thinking becomes increasingly illogical. Frustration and desperation in problem solving quickly follow, and severe behavior problems are usually not far behind. Problem solving all but shuts down at the higher severity levels, causing individuals to act before thinking.

Thinking involves three principal areas: (a) *transgression*, (b) *threat*, or (c) *loss*. Usually, the focal point of individuals' perception will be one of these, yet when things really get bad, individuals may be operating under all three at the same time! Adding to the complexity of thoughts is the idea that these are experienced in four life dimensions and three time dimensions. Assessment of life dimensions is explained following the description of the time dimensions.

Transgression

Transgression involves what is going on right now. Individuals experience transgression as happening to them in the here and now. They believe that they are in harm's way at this moment. A typical perception of these individuals is that of being victimized. The perception is that the experience is happening right now but is unending, with no hope of it discontinuing.

Threat

Individuals who are dealing with threat believe that the future, either in the immediate or long term, holds potential harm. Individuals operating out of a threat framework use

Table 9.5 Behavior Severity Scale

1	2 3	4 5	6 7	8 9	10
No Impairment	**Minimal Impairment**	**Low Impairment**	**Moderate Impairment**	**Marked Impairment**	**Severe Impairment**
• Behaviors are socially appropriate.	• Behaviors mostly effective, outbursts if present are inconsequential.	• Behaviors are somewhat ineffective, yet not dangerous.	• Behaviors are maladaptive but not immediately destructive.	• Behaviors are likely to intensify crisis situation.	• Behaviors are totally ineffective and accelerate the crisis.
• Daily functioning unimpeded.	• Can perform tasks needed for daily functioning with minimal effort.	• Performing tasks needed for daily living minimally compromised.	• Performance of tasks needed for daily living is noticeably compromised.	• Ability to perform tasks needed for daily functioning seriously impaired.	• Unable to perform even simple tasks needed for daily functioning.
• Threat or danger nonexistent.	• Behavior demonstrates frustration but is nonthreatening.	• Behaviors minimal threat to self or others.	• Behavior is a potential threat to self or others.	• Impulsivity has the potential to be harmful to self or others.	• Behaviors are highly destructive, possibly to cause injury/ death to self or others.
• Behavior is stable and nonoffensive.	• Behaviors mostly stable and nonoffensive.	• Behavior becoming unstable and offensive.	• Upon request, behaviors can be controlled with effort.	• Behaviors are very difficult to control even with repeated requests.	• Behavior is out of control and nonresponsive to requests.

the future tense as they talk. They may talk about being worried or say they don't know what is going to happen.

Loss

Individuals who are dealing with loss have already experienced the traumatic event. There is no hope of regaining what was lost. Individuals experiencing loss often feel hopelessness. Perceiving the situation as hopeless often leads to disruptive behaviors that are dangerous to themselves and others. Self-medication with alcohol, over-the-counter medications, prescription medications, or drugs may be used to dull the sense of loss. Individuals may throw caution to the wind, thinking they have nothing else to lose. Suicide is a possibility with these individuals, as is homicide of those who may have been responsible for the loss.

Cognitive Severity Scale

Descriptors for this scale are found in Table 9.6. Descriptors for thoughts focus on problem solving and using appropriate coping mechanisms, as seen through making healthy decisions. Just as with the feeling and behavior severity scales, begin your rating by examining the severe impairment characteristics and move down the scale until you find characteristics that describe the individual's cognitive responses. Once you find a characteristic that fits in a category, choose that rating.

Life Dimensions

Cognitive reactions to a crisis manifest themselves in four areas: (a) physical, (b) psychological, (c) social relationships, and (d) moral/spiritual issues. Think of these areas as a sort of stairstep scale having to do with needs satisfaction. Cognitive issues relating to the physical area have to do with basic survival needs like food, water, clothing, shelter, and safety. Issues relating to psychological needs may include self-concept, emotional stability, and personal integrity. Cognitive issues relating to social relationships can involve family, friends, coworkers, business partners, marriage partners, and boyfriends or girlfriends. Cognitive issues relating to higher-order moral and spiritual needs may manifest themselves as distorted thinking and confusion with personal values and/or God. For example, at this level it is not an uncommon response in individuals who have experienced loss of a loved one to believe that God has forsaken them. Repeated content is extremely important in the assessment process with respect to life dimensions (Myer, 2001). The more often individuals discuss a specific life dimension, the more distress they are experiencing in that area.

THREAT ASSESSMENT TEAMS

The use of TATs to identify individuals who are disruptive to the learning environment is not new. The practice has been used informally for quite some time, and only

Table 9.6 Cognitive Severity Scale

1	2	3	4	5	6	7	8	9	10
No Impairment		Minimal Impairment		Low Impairment		Moderate Impairment		Marked Impairment	Severe Impairment
• Decisions are considerate of others.		• Decisions may not be considerate of others.		• Decisions are inconsiderate of others.		• Decisions are offensive and antagonistic of others.		• Decisions have the potential to be harmful to self or others.	• Decisions are a clear and present danger to self and others.
• Decisions are logical and reasonable.		• Decisions becoming indecisive but only with respect to crisis.		• Decisions becoming illogical, unreasonable, and generalized beyond crisis.		• Decisions about crisis beginning to interfere with general functioning.		• Decisions are illogical, have little basis in reality, and general functioning is compromised.	• Decision making frenetic or frozen and not based in reality and shuts down general functioning.
• Perception of crisis event substantially matches reality.		• Thinking influenced by crisis, but under control.		• Thinking focused on crisis but not all-consuming.		• Thoughts are limited to crisis situation and are becoming all-consuming.		• Thoughts about crisis have become pervasive.	• Thoughts are chaotic and completely controlled by crisis.
• Able to carry on reasonable dialogue and understand and acknowledge views of others.		• Able to carry on reasonable dialogue understand and acknowledge views of others.		• Ability to carry on reasonable dialogue restricted and problems in understanding and acknowledging views of others.		• Responses to questions/requests are restricted or inappropriate and denies understanding views of others.		• Defiant to requests and questions and/or inappropriate and antagonistic of others.	• Request and questions are believed as threat and responded to aggressively.
• Problem solving intact.		• Problem solving minimally compromised.		• Problem solving limited.		• Problem-solving ability impacted by lack of concentration.		• Problem-solving ability absent due to inability to concentrate.	• Problem solving not observable with no ability to concentrate.

recently have universities begun to formalize the functions of these groups (Flynn & Heiztmann, 2008). Development of TATs gained popularity following the Virginia Tech incident (Flynn & Heiztmann, 2008). However, as early as 1986, literature addressing the increasing numbers of disruptive individuals can be found in professional journals (Gerald, 1986). Much interest was generated in developing programs to identify potentially violent individuals after the shooting at Columbine High School (Cornell et al., 2004). Although not in a university setting, the tragedy of this high school mass murder captivated the public's attention, with everyone demanding something be done to prevent future incidents such as this one. Early efforts seemed to have focused on prevention through the use of profiling strategies borrowed from law enforcement agencies (Cornell et al., 2004). According to these authors, even though the profiling strategies were modified for use with adolescents and in school settings, success varied in identifying individuals who posed a real threat. Therefore, numerous attempts began to develop around the concept of specific behavioral indicators of potential violence and the development of teams to determine the degree of threat those behaviors entailed (James, 2008, pp. 413–423)

TATs and CMTs Working Together

The relationship of TATs to crisis management teams (CMTs) should be clarified in creating a system in which both function. We recommend TATs and CMTs function as independent committees, although membership may overlap to a limited degree. The reason for the independence is simple. The general purpose of TATs is to prevent violence on campus, while CMTs are charged with overall governance of a crisis, from prevention to intervention to postvention. Although this distinction seems obvious, it is easy for the university community to confuse the two committees.

Obstacles to Development of TATs

Development of TATs faces a number of obstacles in university settings (Nicoletti et al., 2001). The first issue to address is membership. Membership on TATs depends heavily on the specific university. The culture of every university is unique with respect to which departments and divisions are needed. Generally, we recommend that the team have both official members and ex-officio members who attend on an as-needed basis. Care must be exercised not to make the team too large or too small. We recommend a team of at least five official members. At a minimum, these should include representatives from residence life, judicial affairs, counseling center, police/security, administration, and academic affairs (Flynn & Heitzmann, 2008). Other members might include a representative from college athletics, student activities, health services, and outreach and off-campus services. We believe it should be mandatory that at least two members of the TAT be on the CMT so there is a clear and redundant communication link between the two teams.

A TAT must be trained to work together as a group (Greenberg, 2007), and this should certainly include training in the use of the TASSLE or other threat assessment system employed by the university. TATs should meet on a regular basis. While there may not be pressing cases, updates and upgrades to information and warning systems, notifications of minor problems by police or security, and continuing education in the form of role plays and tabletop exercises keep the team sharp and functional. Deliberate and purposeful ongoing training and interaction are the hallmarks of highly effective TATs.

TATs and University Policy

Another issue to be addressed in the development of TATs is how the TAT operations fit with university policy (Flynn & Heitzmann, 2008). A careful review of campus policies must be made when implementing any procedures involving TATs. Policies must be consistent across campus and also be readily applied without prejudice to all individuals (Nicoletti et al., 2001). A common concern involves the Students' Disability Act and ensuring that individuals are not discriminated against. However, our research and understanding of case law is that sanctions can be taken against individuals, including being barred from campus, regardless of disability status, if the procedures are applied evenly to all individuals.

Policies must walk the tightrope of balancing individuals' rights and the maintenance of a safe learning environment. Braverman (1999) discusses this quandary in his book on workplace violence. Citing federal law, Braverman concludes that the need to maintain a safe workplace takes precedence over individuals' rights (disabled or not) when safety issues are at stake. For our purposes, we are applying these ideas to the safety of a university campus. The critical issue is that policies must be consistent and applied to everyone evenly if TATs are to function appropriately.

Legal matters go hand in hand with policies. We recommend that legal counsel be consulted before implementing any policy and activating a TAT. The tendency for legal counsel is to be cautious. Legal counsel may suggest not putting anything in writing. The logic seems to be that if it is not written, liability is less. This argument has merit and has been used in the past (Bickel & Lake, 1999). However, according to Bickel and Lake, the idea of the "bystander" policy has taken a back seat. Universities are now seen as responsible to ensure well-being as well as safety of students.

Morally, it should be an expectation and an obligation of the university to have procedures and policies in place to make the campus safe and to allow all individuals the optimum opportunity to learn, and we believe this supersedes any passivity and failure to set and enforce standards out of some imagined fear of legal consequences. We further believe that if universities do not take proactive stances in establishing TATs, they may be even more liable legally for their failure to act, given the current amount of information available to set such policies in place. As more and more universities formalize TATs, this process may become the expected level of care, in other words, the due standard of care.

Political issues are always in play on university campuses. With respect to TATs, specific people with specific expertise need to be appointed. Expertise in human behavior and not politics is what is needed on a TAT. Areas to consider when identifying someone with experience and expertise include the psychology and sociology departments, counselor education departments, criminal justice, and nursing programs. While an administrative liaison is a highly important team member, placement of an administrator to keep an eye on things is a hindrance and impedes the TAT's work. However, just because a person is licensed as a psychologist, professional counselor, or nurse does not make the person an expert at identifying individuals who may become violent. Putting a professional in the helping service area on the team just for the sake of having such a person to give the team some imagined face validity is also a bad idea.

TAT Logistics

Logistics is the final issue TATs must address. Departments and other units at universities have a history of being fiercely independent. This independence must be dealt with if TATs are to be successful in carrying out their charge. Autonomous silos generally sabotage the efforts of TATs. A system must be created that not only permits but rewards communication, coordination, and consultation. Communication, coordination, and consultation are the three Cs of crisis intervention and prevention in a university setting.

Communication should be bidirectional: from the top down and from the bottom up. Crisis management teams as well as TATs must be willing to listen to the first responders and those directly involved in the crisis. This communication up the ladder helps to make for efficient and effective resolution from the crisis. Therefore, a system must be developed that allows people to take a leadership role in a specific crisis. This leadership should not be without limits, but people on the front line need to have the leeway to make some types of decisions. For example, someone on the front line may need to have the authority to shift resources to areas in more need but not necessarily spend thousands of dollars to purchase resources. Note that crises disrupt normal communication processes. Absolute reliance on routine communication methods can, and probably will, hamper efforts to address and resolve crises. Development of procedures for communication in crisis situations is therefore important. For example, having something other than cell phones with which to communicate during a crisis is important. Handheld walkie-talkies may be invaluable if other communication methods are not available or fail.

Coordination is also very important for TATs. A systematic method for TATs to receive information must be created. Clear procedures that follow written policy must be developed. An e-mail simply giving this information is unlikely to be effective. Likewise, just distributing a brochure describing the role of and how to communicate with the campus TAT will also have limited effectiveness. We recommend a formal effort to educate everyone on campus about these procedures.

In addition, we encourage the inclusion of how to contact TATs in all orientation procedures, including students and new employees. Periodic reminders and training can be conducted on an as-needed basis. Finally, consultation is needed if TATs are to fulfill their mission. TATs need access to consultation through training and professionals who are considered experts as specific situations arise.

Role and Responsibilities

The role and responsibilities of TATs must be clearly delineated prior to its development. Failure to provide a clear charge to TATs will result in uncertainty on the part of the committee. This uncertainty will lead to ineffectiveness in the attempt to prevent campus violence. Policies regarding the role and responsibilities of TATs must be unambiguous for two reasons. The first involves the ability of TATs to function. If the members of this group are uncertain about their purpose, the decisions made by the group will reflect this dilemma. Decisions may become so vague that no actions can be taken. A second reason to have clear roles and responsibilities is to encourage referrals to the TAT. If members of the campus community understand the purpose of TAT, they will be more willing to make referrals to this group. Clearly defining the role and responsibilities of the TAT to the university community creates a positive expectation and environment for the entire campus.

A careful study should be conducted that considers the idiosyncratic needs of a campus prior to setting the role of TATs. Several issues must be considered. First, does the TAT make decisions or recommendations? While this may seem clear, the issue concerns power. Power involves the ability to take action based on the information presented to the team. There are benefits and drawbacks to the TAT having that power as well as not having it. Giving TATs the ability to take action based on information means that quick responses to prevent violence can be made. At the same time, giving the TAT this power takes it out of the hands of administrators who are used to making these decisions. Another benefit of allowing TATs to make decisions regarding the disposition of individuals is that it shows trust and empowers this group. Not giving the TAT the capacity to make decisions may result in the team not taking its role seriously, especially if the TAT's recommendations are often discounted and overturned.

The responsibilities of the TAT must also be carefully considered. This issue is especially true with respect to the TAT being the receiver of information or the seeker of information. Is the expectation of the TAT to wait for someone to refer a disruptive individual, or should the team actively seek out these individuals? The answer to this question is critical for the TAT to understand its limitations and boundaries. On the one hand, passivity can lead to missing opportunities to intervene and prevent violent acts. On the other hand, a zealous, proactive TAT may create problems by acting too quickly and decisively. Finding a balance between the two extremes is what we recommend. Will the TAT on your campus make recommendations or decisions about the disposition of individuals? The response to this question will guide the agenda of meetings.

Development of clear guidelines around these issues is essential for TATs to operate at an optimum level.

Training

Awareness is not enough (Greenberg, 2007). If TATs are to be effective, training is needed. Expecting a TAT to function at an optimum level without training is a TAT that is designed to fail. Training should involve understanding threats, approaches to assessing threats, issues related to legal rights of individuals, and the disposition of individuals making threats. Training involves practice. This practice should focus on difficult, ambiguous situations. As we have said, making decisions in mild and severe situations is easy. Making decisions in situations in which the information is contradictory and not clear-cut may cause debate, polarization, and general conflict. Developing ways to work through these disagreements takes trust and experience. Short of actually making decisions, practice is the best way to develop confidence in the team. The same levels of practice (i.e., tabletop exercises, drill exercises, and full-scale exercises) discussed in Chapter 6 can be used to help TATs learn to work together.

Building practice cases based on the threat assessment worksheet is a good place to start. We suggest that cases be developed by someone other than the local TAT. This process gives a realistic flavor to the exercises and also does not allow the TAT the ability to forecast outcomes. These cases should involve realistic, complex threats that are not clear-cut. The outcome of the threat—that is, whether it was carried out—must be decided ahead of time. Practice cases should be presented to the TAT, which is then asked to work through the process of assessing the veracity of the threat as well as making a decision about the recommended disposition. Practice should also include time to discuss the decision-making process after the final disposition is decided. This discussion should include constructive feedback with respect to positive actions the TAT took as well as talking about what the team missed in the scenario.

Central University's TAT in Action

The following scenario depicts what might occur when a potentially violent student is spotted. It should be clearly understood that the way this scenario plays out is not chiseled in stone. It is an example of how one of many possible outcomes might occur. Given the particular policies of each university, the potential outcomes may be very different. Thus, we are much more concerned that you get a small sample of the dynamics of a TAT rather than the idea that what you are about to read is a prescriptive solution that covers all situations in all universities.

Membership

The members of the Central University TAT are Director of Residence Life David Selby; Dr. Jason Semens, personal counselor from the counseling center who has

THREAT ASSESSMENT WORKSHEET

Date: October 5, 2010   **Time:** 9:30 PM

Situation: Altercation with roommate over loud music. Stated he would beat roommate over the head if he didn't stop playing country rock. Derogatory comments to roommate in English and Vietnamese. Picked guitar up and then tussle with roommate occurred, interrupted by and broken up by hall RA. Individual extreme labile, screaming in English, French, and Vietnamese.

Name of Person Making Threat: George Giap

Factor	Report	Disposition
Method of Communication	Verbal	Refer to hall director and hall disciplinary committee
Credibility	Low-to-medium	File report with TAT. Do not refer to judiciary committee at this time
Potential for Harm	Unclear. Volatility high, but no clear means methods	Change room assignments as soon as available. Refer to counseling center for unspecified problems, potential academic difficulties refer to Educational Support Program
Dynamics of Threat	Impulsive/revenge	
Type of threat (Transient, Continuous, Substantive)	Transient	
Specificity of Threat	Target specific to roommate	
Category of Threat (Direct, Conditional, Veiled)	Veiled	
Other		

Other Information: Note e-mail sent to chemistry professor complaining of racial bias. Related to poor grades in chemistry professor's course.

Figure 9.1 Threat Assessment Worksheet, George Giap

THREAT ASSESSMENT WORKSHEET

Date: October 5, 2010   **Time:** 9:30 PM

Situation: Altercation with roommate over playing loud music with his guitar. Subject appeared to be intoxicated. Admitted have "two beers at Lowball Cue." Shoved roommate into wall and dresser after roommate picked his guitar up and threatened to break it over his head for his playing while roommate was trying to study. Retaliated and said nobody touched his guitar and particularly no "Gook." Pushing and shoving and numerous verbal "I'll get you good" threats.

Name of Person Making Threat: Sam Hull

Factor	Report	Disposition
Method of Communication	Verbal	Refer to hall director and hall disciplinary committee. File incident with TAT
Credibility	Medium	Change room assignments when available
Potential for Harm		Do not refer to judicial affairs at this time. Apprise subject of alcohol problems and refer to counseling center
Dynamics of Threat	Impulsive/revenge	
Type of threat (Transient, Continuous, Substantive)	Transient	
Specificity of Threat	Target specific to roommate	
Category of Threat (Direct, Conditional, Veiled)	Direct	
Other		

Other Information: Subject has been advised twice before to maintain quiet hours by RA. Both times subject appears to have been mildly intoxicated. Complied with RA's requests both times. Note subject hunts and knows firearms, use, although no direct threat of firearm use in the incident was noted.

Figure 9.2   Threat Assessment Worksheet, Sam Hull

special training in crisis intervnetion; Lieutenant Flemming, Central University Police Department and trained crisis intervention team officer; Assistant Dean of Academic Affairs, Dr. Braxton Jones, head of Judicial Affairs and chair of the Student Conduct Committee; and Dr. Alton Hamel, associate professor in the Department of Psychology. Ex-officio members on call are Demetrius Keith, university counsel, and Dr. Eileen Richardson, liaison to the president. Selby, Keith, and Richardson are also members of the CMT. All of the members have been trained and are knowledgeable in the use of the TASSLE system. See Figures 9.3 and 9.4 for the completed TASSLE forms.

Dr. Jason Semens (chair of the TAT): We have one event to consider. It involves two individuals in a residence hall altercation. Usually this would be handled by David's people and maybe go over to the residence life disciplinary committee, but there are some other issues here, and it was felt that it ought to move forward to us. Is that about right, Dave?

David Selby: That's correct. Two days ago, we had an altercation between two roommates. You have their TASSLE scores in front of you that were filled out by their RA and a follow-up TASSLE from the on-call center counselor. It appears that this had been simmering for a while. We've got two freshmen who are about as different as you can get for roommates. One's from rural Arkansas, a Caucasian by the name of Sam Hull, and a Vietnamese American from San Francisco by the name of George Giap. Both are engineering students, but that's about the end of the resemblance. We would have moved them, but we are full and don't have any spare room. I have the RA Latavius Jefferson outside, who was the first responder. It's his floor and wing, and he got there in about 30 seconds after some other individuals heard the ruckus and got him. Do you want me to call him in?

Dr. Semens: In a moment. We do have one other incident report on one of the participants, don't we, Lieutenant Flemming?

Lt. Flemming: There is a report filed from the chemistry department on George Giap. It appears he isn't doing well in a chemistry course and became angry at the professor and accused him of discriminating against him because he is an Asian. He got angry in front of the rest of the class and then wrote an e-mail involving the accusations. No specific threats were made, and the professor decided to drop it, particularly after the student's grade came up some, but then the chair of the department talked to the emergency preparedness director, Mr. Mathews, and thought enough of it to write Mr. Giap up and send it to the TAT.

Dean Jones: We've since checked with his other professors, and it appears he is struggling. He does have a presidential scholarship and also has a performance scholarship in music. He has a heavy schedule with difficult courses.

Dr. Semens: Okay. Please bring Mr. Jefferson in and let him tell us what occurred.

The committee would normally not meet for a roommate problem. But the fact that there were threats of violence and actual hands-on contact to the point the police were called puts the incident on the radar screen for the committee. A crosscheck of problems of the two perpetrators reveals that Giap is already on file. That warrants a TAT meeting.

Latavius Jefferson, RA Rawls Hall East Wing: I made the scene after it had escalated and been going on about 5 minutes until some other individuals heard the noise coming out of the room and came down and alerted me. When I made the scene, they were really going at it. More of a wrestling match than anything, but they both got banged up some against the furniture. They were both hot under the collar. It appeared that Giap yanked the

---

Staff Member: ___Lativius Jefferson___

Date: _10/5/10_____ Location: _Rawls Hall left wing rm209_ Times: Contacted: _9:42–10:40 PM_____

Complaint Information ___Individual fighting with roommate George Giap. Mainly pushing and shoving. Individual had_ abraded lip. Refused medical treatment. Both made threats of harm against each other with lots of swearing and name_ calling, volatile enough to call police. Once police came, both calmed down under threat fo transport. Put Hull in guest_ room for the night. Individual had been drinking. Stated he had three beers at Lowball Cue._

Individual _____Hull_____ ___Sam_____ _Lehigh_____
                     (Last)   (First)   (Middle)

Observations (Check as many that apply)

__ off medication	_x_ harassment	_x_ uncooperative
__ hallucinating *** (__ smells __ sights	___ coercion/intimidation	___ absence of emotion/affect *
__ sounds __ touch)	_x_ aggressive gestures	_x_ impulsivity
__ bizarre behavior/appearance	___ reckless behavior	___ hysterical
__ poor hygiene	___ self-injurious behavior	___ confusion
__ absurd, illogical, nonsensical speech	_x_ physically violent ***	_x_ unable to follow simple
__ paranoid/suspicious thoughts	_x_ verbal threats to self or others	directions
__ flashbacks, loss of reality contact	___ suicidal/homicidal *	_x_ unable to control
__ intoxicated/drugged	thinking/verbalizing	emotions *
	___ suicidal/homicidal *	___ cannot recall personal
	gestures/behaviors ***	information (phone,
	___ suicidal/homicidal plan clear ***	address) *
		___ situation perceived as
		unreal (spectator)
		___ nonresponsive *

*** *removal from learning environment recommended   *additional evaluation recommended*

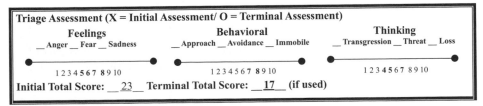

Triage Assessment (X = Initial Assessment/ O = Terminal Assessment)

Feelings	**Behavioral**	**Thinking**
__ Anger __ Fear __ Sadness	__ Approach __ Avoidance __ Immobile	__ Transgression __ Threat __ Loss
1 2 3 4 5 6 7 8 9 10	1 2 3 4 5 6 7 8 9 10	1 2 3 4 5 6 7 8 9 10

Initial Total Score: __23__ **Terminal Total Score:** __17__ (if used)

Figure 9.3   TASSLE for Sam L. Hull

Staff Member: ___Latavius Jefferson, RA___

Date: 10/5/10____   Location: ___Rawls Hall Left wing rm209_ Times: Contacted: _9:42–10;30PM_

Complaint Information _____Individual fighting with roommate Sam Hull. Mainly pushing and shoving. Individual__ had swollen eye. Refused medical treatment. Both made threats of harm against each other. Appeared to be incoherent at times and lapsed between English, French, and what is believed to be Vietnamese. Volatile enough to call police, Once police came both calmed down under threat of transport. Put Giap back in his room after on-call counselor, Lee Halstand, pscyh intern from Counseling center talked with him and he de-escalated. Appeared very remorseful. Kept saying "What have I done." Was crying. Individual had not been drinking or judged to be on any drugs.

Individual Name: ___ Giap _____   George _____   Nyguen _____
                        (Last)   (First)   (Middle)

Observations (Check as many that apply)

__ off medication	__ harassment	_x_ uncooperative
__ hallucinating *** (__ smells __ sights	__ coercion/intimidation	__ absence of emotion/affect *
__ sounds __ touch)	_x_ aggressive gestures	__ impulsivity
__ bizarre behavior/appearance	_x_ reckless behavior	_x_ hysterical
__ poor hygiene	__ self-injurious behavior	_x_ confusion
_x_ absurd, illogical, nonsensical speech	_x_ physically violent ***	_x_ unable to follow simple
__ paranoid/suspicious thoughts	_x_ verbal threats to self or others	directions
__ flashbacks, loss of reality contact	__ suicidal/homicidal *	_x_ unable to control
__ intoxicated/drugged	thinking/verbalizing	emotions *
	__ suicidal/homicidal *	__ cannot recall personal
	gestures/behaviors ***	information (phone,
	__ suicidal/homicidal plan clear ***	address) *
		__ situation perceived as
		unreal (spectator)
		__ nonresponsive *

*** *removal from learning environment recommended *additional evaluation recommended*

Triage Assessment (X = Initial Assessment/ O = Terminal Assessment)

Feelings	**Behavioral**	**Thinking**
__ Anger __ Fear __ Sadness	__ Approach __ Avoidance __ Immobile	__ Transgression __ Threat __ Loss
1 2 3 4 5 6 7 8 9 10	1 2 3 4 5 6 7 8 9 10	1 2 3 4 5 6 7 8 9 10

Initial Total Score: _ 27 ___   **Terminal Total Score: 15** __ (if used)

Figure 9.4   TASSLE for George N. Giap

power supply out of Hull's guitar that he was tuning because he was attempting to study and it disrupted his concentration. Hull retaliated by attempting to get Giap's viola out of the case and smash it. There was a lot of nasty name calling with both of them calling each other pejorative names full of racial epithets. Stuff like "slant-eyed gook" and "red-necked hillbilly." Although Giap kinda lost it and kept hopping around from English to I think French and probably Vietnamese, he wasn't making a lot of sense for the first part of this when he was trying to explain it to me and was pretty hysterical. I got them separated, and then they started in again. At that time, two police officers arrived, and after stating that if they didn't calm down, they'd be transported to jail, they both got hold of themselves somewhat. Hull calmed down pretty quickly, but was claiming Giap had wrecked his guitar. Giap was clearly agitated, so I made a call to the on-call counselor at the counseling center. In the meantime, I had them both start writing down their complaints. It seems Giap blew up when he was studying and Hull started to tune his guitar. It got on his nerves although Hull maintains that he wasn't really playing it but just tuning it for a session for a band tryout, and Giap didn't say anything to him beforehand about it being a bother. Writing it all down got them busy and focused, so they both calmed down a good bit. The on-call arrived in about 15 minutes and was able to calm Giap down even further in about another 15 minutes so that I felt I could leave him in his room with her. The hall director was away from the building so at about 10:30 Mr. Selby made the scene, and the decision was made to move Hull down to the guest room for the night. The counseling intern stayed with Giap until he calmed down enough to get ready for bed, and when I got back there, she checked him out and we tucked him in. We have since moved Hull into the guest room semipermanently until we get a vacancy. Things have been calm, and they have avoided each other for the last 3 days.

Lt. Flemming: Those initial TASSLE scores were pretty high, 23 and 27 with 27 being in the low end of the lethal range. I don't want to sound like I am questioning your judgment, Mr. Jefferson, but I wonder if you could say a bit more about the 27?

Lieutenant Fleming's query to Jefferson is not so much a questioning of his judgment but rather seeks more data to get a fuller picture of his assessment of the affect, behavior, and cognitions of Giap, since he scored him as lethal. Jefferson's report includes not only behavioral observations but will now detail his rationale for acting based on his TASSLE ratings.

Jefferson: Well, I may indeed be high on that. It is mainly that he couldn't keep a straight train of thought in English. He kept losing it and hopscotched in three different languages. His thoughts were chaotic and really controlled by the crisis. He couldn't problem solve much at all, and in the beginning he was pretty unresponsive, at least in English. So he got a 10. His behavior was accelerating when I got there and was likely to intensify the situation. And again because of the language problems, he couldn't seem to comply with my requests to chill out. His feeling state was highly volatile, and he had limited control over his emotions, so I'd put him at an 8 or 9 on both the behavior and feelings scales. For a full scale of 27 or 28. It was more his thinking and language skills than anything else, and I guess it could have influenced my behavioral and feeling scores. I finally chilled him by getting him to go over and sit down at the desk and write out for me what was going on. He got his act together, and his behavior calmed way down to a 3. I'd say his feelings and thinking were at a 6 because he kept perseverating on his remorsefulness, saying he shouldn't have acted like that, and had tears in his eyes while he was writing. So he got a 15. I think the counseling center intern did a good job of staying with him and keeping him calm, although he shifted from being hysterical to remorseful and did seem down on himself. Hull got a 22 to 24, most likely 23. I mean he was giving as good as he was getting. He had something to drink, so maybe the alcohol gave him some liquid courage. His feelings were pretty high like a 9 after he got the plug pulled on his guitar. He was highly volatile and pretty noncompliant due to my requests. He kept trying to tell me how Giap had violated his guitar. That guitar is his baby, almost human, and it set him off, so he was running a 9 on emotions and didn't get it together until the cops came. He was still pretty hot, even though he calmed down some. Emotions were still pretty much focused on the event, and still pretty heated to any requests, so he got a 6 to 7 on feelings. While he was actively involved both physically and verbally, I felt like he had a bit more control and was running between a 7 and 8 on both behaving and thinking. I gave him an 8 because he was impulsive and his behaviors were going to escalate the crisis and he wouldn't calm down. I just felt like he wasn't quite running amok, though, and the anger was more controlled. I think Sam has been in fights before and knew about how far to carry it. That goes to his emotional involvement and irrational thinking about his guitar, although maybe I'd feel the same way if somebody messed with my stuff. I would say his problem solving was limited, but he felt like his personal property had been violated and was able to rationalize what he did. So I put him at a 6. His thoughts were certainly on the crisis, but weren't all-consuming. His thinking was blocked, but he could get his point across in some linear manner and was pretty logical when I listened to him. Overall, by the end of it his behavior was minimally threatening, and he was able to go down to the guest room without griping. He realized it was a good compromise so his behavior really calmed down to a 4 or 5. I'd say the same for his thinking. He was able to carry on a reasonable dialogue and could see the sense in ending that way. His feelings were still fairly hot, and he got pretty agitated when he started talking about nobody hurting "Cindy," his guitar, but he could think well enough to put his feelings somewhat in place about the rest of the fracas, so he got a 6 to 7 for a full scale of 15 to 17. Putting him two floors and a wing away next to the director suite helped put a lid on it, and I would say he was down around a 10 to 12 by the time I checked him out for bed.

Jefferson, like the rest of the RAs at Central, received training in the use of the TASSLE when he first became an RA, so his report is in sync with the language and assessment techniques of the TAT. His responses are based in behavioral anchors that clearly indicate the individuals' state of being at the time the incident occurred. The chair seeks to confirm Jefferson's terminal rating of Giap.

Dr. Semens: One of the psych interns was on call. What was her rating on Giap? She had TASSLE training, didn't she?

Mr. Selby: It was Leslie Simmons, a first-year psychology intern. All the interns got trained in August. When Leslie left, she had him a little lower at a 10 to 11 and 2s on thinking and behavior with a 6 to 7 on affect, although she confirms Jefferson's summary that he was remorseful instead of angry. She also indicated that he was very anxious about his grades and afraid he would fail, which would be unacceptably shameful and dishonor his family. She noted that cognitively he felt transgressed on by his roomie because he feels threatened about failing and losing his scholarship, which would be a severe loss of face for him and his family. She felt that because he was dealing with loss, threat, and transgression, this incident might be a warning sign. If his academic life doesn't take a turn for the better, he was headed for a breakdown emotionally.

The threat assessment team uses the intern's terminal rating on George as independent verification to determine how safe he is. Such redundancy is characteristic and in no way disparages Jefferson's rating. The TAT also seeks to compare present to past behavior, even though George's and Sam's histories at Central University are very brief.

Professor Hamel: Mr. Jefferson, how have these two freshmen adapted to life in the residence hall? Any problems? Friends? Social ability? Any opinions?

Latavius Jefferson, RA: Sam Hull seems to be doing okay: He is pretty gregarious and has made some friends in his wing. I see him eating dinner and breakfast with a group of guys from Alpha Beta Omicron fraternity, and he also is picking some guitar with some other guys that have a band. He's gotten boisterous a couple of times coming in from shooting pool and drinking some beer, but he immediately calmed down, when asked. George Giap has been no problem at all. In fact, he is really quiet and does stay to himself. He seems awfully harried and I don't see him smile much—always serious and purposeful with a backpack on. Generally he eats alone. I talk to all of the new individuals on my wing, trying to get an idea of just who they are. I encouraged him to go over to the Far East Asian Association meeting for newcomers, but he told me he wasn't a foreigner, so I don't think that happened. I don't know if there are many Vietnamese kids in it, and there aren't many here that I know of. So I don't think he has much of a social life and seems pretty driven and probably lonely.

Professor Hamel: Thank you Mr. Jefferson, your input was really helpful and we appreciate how well you handled this situation. (Latavius is thanked by the team and dismissed.)

Dr. Selby: It sounds like Sam Hull gets a date with the residence life discipline committee and some strong suggestions about his drinking, and that's it for the present. Are we in agreement on him? (General agreement acknowledged.) It appears that George Giap may need some monitoring and support and that we need to get involved in the monitoring and make some support recommendations.

Professor Hamel: So what do we have on George Giap as far as academics are concerned? Is he at risk?

Dean Jones: All we have is a progress report in Qualitative Analysis in chemistry. No other bad grades presently. He is presently in Calculus II, Mechanics in Physics, English Comp II, French III, and Orchestra. Clearly a heavy load for a first-semester freshman.

Professor Hamel: I think we need to see how he is doing in all his courses and give his advisor in mechanical engineering a heads up on this and see how close he is to George. What about counseling and ESP (Educational Support Program)? In fact, what about a psychological evaluation?

Dr. Selby: We can have Leslie Simmons, the intern who did the on call, stop by and see him. She seems to have developed a relationship with him. She's in her 40s, so may be a kind of a mother figure, which wouldn't hurt him, being a thousand miles from home. She's really warm and outgoing. And see if he won't stop by and talk some with her. I'll prep her some on not making it come off as if he is mentally ill or inadequate, although I am pretty sure she is culturally sensitive to not doing that. Rather, set it up as a way of getting to know some people and things about how the world works in the Midwest, coaching, if you will. Right now, I don't think there is any way we can mandate that he goes to counseling. I suppose we could take the verbal threats at the start and the scores he received and get a psych workup based on that, but he was able to calm down, and his emotions changed from anger to contrition.

The discussion that follows supports Dr. Selby's view, and it is decided that Ms. Simmons will stop by to see George before the week is out and invite him to come to the counseling center or possibly meet her at the university center for tea. It is also decided that the Student Ambassadors will be contacted, and if an Asian American individual is available, that he or she be put in contact with George.

Dean Jones: We could mandate him to judicial affairs and prescribe anger management group at the counseling center. In fact, we can do that for both these guys, given that their infraction actually did result in some physical injury.

A discussion follows on the usefulness of mandating anger management group. It is decided that since this is a first infraction, and given that the conditions were such that there was some basis for the fracas, such action isn't warranted and might even add to George's problems because it will say he cannot control himself.

Professor Hamel: Do we notify his parents he is having problems?

Another general discussion ensues, and it is decided that at this point there is not enough evidence to indicate that George is a threat to himself or others. However, it is also decided that Latavius Jefferson, RA, and Leslie Simmons, the counseling center intern, will meet with the academic advisor for freshman engineering individuals and see if they can come up with a plan to integrate George into the fabric of the university a good deal more than he is now. They will also act as his behavioral weathervane and be tasked with reporting any problems George is having that seem to be putting him at greater academic or personal risk.

Dr. Semens: So we agree that Sam Hull will be given a warning by Dave Selby that his behavior was unacceptable and that a second offense will put him in front of the disciplinary committee and be cause for removal from the residence hall. George Giap will be monitored in the residence hall and in his academic department. Any other instances will call for an appearance in front of the disciplinary committee and possible referral for anger management at the counseling center.

This scenario is a general representation of what a TAT might do. There is no formula that we know of for such decisions, certainly no formula that guarantees that individuals who make the radar screen of this committee will not get into trouble or experience continued problems. However, the collective wisdom of this campus cross-cultural group brings a great deal of expertise and professionalism to the situation and ensures that it will not be swept under the rug or dealt with summarily. From that standpoint, the TAT not only provides for the general safety of the university but also does act in the best interests of the individual student.

SUMMARY

Understanding threat and its various typologies is a primary key in containing and controlling campus violence. Threats may be direct, veiled, or conditional and either specific or nonspecific as to their intent, means, and timing. Furthermore, threats may be transient, continuous, or substantive. Transient threats typically are made in a moment of emotional volatility. Continuous threats occur over and over for long periods of time, and substantive threats have clear and present malevolence and danger in their concrete, specific means as to what and when it will be done. Veiled and conditional threats are more difficult to determine as to the degree of lethal intent, but they can be even more unsettling and intimidating to the receiver.

As a result of increased lethality on college campuses and the perceived threat to the university community's safety, TATs are becoming increasingly common. Their stated mission is to receive, collate, analyze, recommend, and disseminate information about potential threats and potentially violent individuals. The TAT is generally composed of five or more members who represent typical divisions of the university, such as housing, academics, student affairs, administration, counseling, police, and judicial affairs.

One of the critical components of creating a common language of threat assessment among all the constituencies of the university is creation of a commonly understood assessment tool to determine degree of violence potential and possible lethality. One such tool is the Triage Assessment Scale for Students in Learning Environments (TASSLE). It has a numerical rating scale that ranges from 3 to 30 that rates students across feeling, behavior, and thinking criteria in regard to the degree of disorganization and disruption they are experiencing while in crisis. Scores in the 20s are indicative of high potential for continued and increasing problematic behavior and possible lethality. Scores in the teens indicate that at the least, support systems and some supervision of the individual are warranted and necessary while students attempt to return to a precrisis state of psychological equilibrium. Single-digit scores typically mean the problem is transient in nature and easily resolved within a short period of time.

A short scenario demonstrating a typical TAT in action illustrated some of the dynamics of how a TAT would operate when presented with a somewhat unclear case of a student in psychological trouble.

REFERENCES

Bickel, R. D., & Lake, P. F. (1999). *The rights and responsibilities of the modern university: Who assumes the risks of college life?* Durham, NC: Carolina Press.

Blancett, J. (2008). *A reliability and validity study of the Triage Assessment System for Students in Learning Environments.* University of Memphis, Memphis, TN.

Borum, R. (2000). Assessing violence risks among adolescents. *Journal of Clinical Psychology, 56,* 1263–1288.

Braverman, M. (1999). *Preventing workplace violence: A guide to employers and practitioners.* Thousand Oaks, CA: Sage.

Byrom, C. E. (n.d.). *The use of the excited utterance hearsay exception in the prosecution of domestic violence cases after* Crawford v. Washington [Abstract]. Retrieved October 15, 2009, from http://www.utexas.edu/law/journals/trol/volume_24/Byrom%20Abstract.pdf.

Collins, B. G., & Collins, T. M. (2005). *Crisis and trauma: Development-ecological intervention.* Boston: Lahaska Press.

Conte, C. (2005). *Examination of the reliability and validity of the Triage Assessment Survey: Organizations.* Duquesne University, Pittsburgh, PA.

Cornell, D. G., Sheras, P. L., Kaplan, S., McGonville, D., Douglass, J., Elton, A., . . . Cole, J. (2004). Guidelines for individual threat assessment: Field test findings. *School Psychology Review, 33,* 527–546.

Flynn, C., & Heitzmann, D. (2008). Tragedy at Virginia Tech: Trauma and its aftermath. *Counseling Psychologist, 36,* 479–489.

Gerald, A. (1986). Dealing with disruptive college students: Some theoretical and practical considerations. *Journal of American College Health, 34,* 221–225.

Greenberg, S. F. (2007). Active shooters on college campuses: Conflicting advice, role of the individual and first responder, and the need to maintain perspective. *Disaster Medicine and Public Health Preparedness, 1,* 57–61.

Halikias, W. (2004). School-based risk assessment: A conceptual framework and model for professional practice. *Professional Psychology: Research and Practice, 35,* 598–607.

Hoff, L. A., Hallisey, B. J., & Hoff, M. (2009). *People in crisis: Clinical and diversity perspectives* (6th ed.). New York: Routledge.

James, R. K. (2008). *Crisis intervention strategies* (6th ed.). Belmont, CA: Brooks-Cole/Thomson.

Myer, R. A. (2001). *Assessment for crisis intervention: Triage assessment model.* Pacific Grove, CA: Brooks/Cole.

Myer, R. A., Moulton, P., Rice, N. D., & James, R. K. (2006). *Triage assessment scale for students in learning environments.* Pittsburgh, PA: CIPS.

Myer, R. A., Williams, R. C., Ottens, A. J., & Schmidt, A. E. (1992). Crisis assessment: A three dimensional model for triage. *Journal of Mental Health Counseling, 14,* 137–148.

Nicoletti, J., Spencer-Thomas, S., & Bollinger, C. (2001). *Violence goes to college: The authoritative guide to prevention and intervention.* Springfield, IL: Charles C Thomas.

Pazar, J. P. (2005). *A reliability study of the Triage Assessment Scale.* University of Memphis, Memphis, TN.

Slagel, L. (2009). *Examination of the reliability and validity of the Triage Assessment Survey: Families* Duquesne University, Pittsburgh, PA.

Slatkin, A. A. (2005). *Communication in crisis and hostage negotiations.* Springfield, IL: Charles C Thomas.

Sokolow, B. A., & Lewis, W. S. (2009). *2nd Generation behavioral intervention best practices.* Retrieved September 28, 2009, from http://www.nabita.org/docs/2009NCHERMwhitepaper.pdf.

Sokolow, B. A., Lewis, W. S., Wolf, C. R., VanBrunt, B. V., & Byrnes, J. D. (2009). *Threat assessment in the campus setting.* NaBITA 2009 white paper. Retrieved September 28, 2009, from http://www.nabita.org/docs/2009NABITAwhitepaper.pdf.

Watters, D. S. (1997). *A study of the reliability of the Triage Severity Scale.* University of Memphis, Memphis, TN.

Zdziarski, E. L., Dunkel, W. D., & Rollo, J. M. (2007). *Campus crisis management: A comprehensive guide to planning, prevention, response, and recovery.* San Francisco: Jossey-Bass.

10

Basic Training

This chapter is not about making you a world-class psychotherapist. It is about making you competent to diffuse and de-escalate an individual who is in crisis, and if you can do that, you are doing something most of the world-class therapists can't do. The basic training in this chapter covers a variety of concepts and skills that go a long way toward getting a student back into psychological and behavioral equilibrium. The problem is that we can't give you a formula to do this. Trainees often become frustrated when they ask us, "When do I move to alternatives in the eight-step model?" "Should I use an open-ended lead after a reflection when the student gets cynical?" "Which one of the nine intentional strategies should I use when the student is depressed?" There are no formulas in this business. It is truly a stand-up act. Throughout the chapter, we will refer to using these skills with students. However, understand that the same skills can be used with staff, faculty members, or anyone else on campus.

Trainees also make a mistake when they try to emulate us. You can no more be Dr. James or Dr. Moulton than Dr. James can be Sigmund Freud or Dr. Moulton can be Anna Freud. What you can do is really learn this stuff like your life depended on it, and the fact is that it just might! You also need to practice the stuff under supervision. The idea is that you are going to make mistakes, and somebody who has been there, done that, is going to watch you, critique you, and teach you how to put the stuff together in your own style so that it works for you. Some of the very best crisis interveners that we have seen never took a college psychology course in their lives. They are crisis intervention team (CIT) police officers, and they use their street smarts and personal creativity, along with the model, strategies, and techniques in this chapter, to indeed become world-class. They didn't know a molecule more about this than you do right now. Thus, this chapter is basic training in crisis intervention. Don't be afraid to take risks when you practice the techniques. Learn from the criticism and practice, practice, practice. Now let's start!

THE EIGHT-STEP MODEL OF CRISIS INTERVENTION IN COLLEGE ENVIRONMENTS (INDIVIDUALS)

There are a variety of models for crisis intervention (Aguilera, 1998; Hoff, Hallisey, & Hoff, 2009; Roberts, 2005; Slaikeu, 1990; Zdziarski, Dunkel, & Rollo, 2007) that range from what is optimistically and somewhat simplistically called psychologist first aid to some very sophisticated flowcharts and multidimensional representations of what goes on in a crisis intervention plan.

Our eight-step model of crisis intervention emphasizes listening and acting to systematically help the student regain as much of the precrisis equilibrium, mobility, and autonomy as possible. Two of those terms, *equilibrium* and *mobility*, and their antonyms, *disequilibrium* and *immobility*, are commonly used by crisis interveners to identify personal states of being and coping. To make that happen, we operate in an active, assertive, intentional manner while assessing what is occurring with the student in an attempt to get him or her back to a state of equilibrium and mobility. We have chosen to use Burl Gilliland's (Gilliland, 1982; James, 2008) six-step model, modified to eight steps (see Figure 10.1). We have added an initial step called *predispositioning* and a terminal step called *follow-up* that we believe works better in a closed system like a college environment. We use this modified Gilliland model for a variety of reasons. First and foremost, it is simple, straightforward, and easy to use and understand. Second, assessment overarches the model from start to finish, and by now, you should realize that we are very big on assessment. Third, it serves both the student and the system by considering safety as a preeminent part of the model. Fourth, it is fluid and dynamic, just as crisis situations are. This eight-step model is the axis around which the crisis intervention strategies in this book revolve, and the steps are designed to operate as a fluid, dynamic, and integrated problem-solving process that brings the individual crisis interventionist and the crisis response system into a congruent whole.

Assessing

Assessment using the Triage Assessment Scale for Students in Learning Environments (TASSLE) system is a pervasive strategy that arches over and permeates crisis intervention from start to finish and is the keystone to the eight-step model. It gives the interventionist three major pieces of information that are critical to the process. First, assessment lets the interventionist know how the student is doing in regard to de-escalating emotionally and behaviorally and regaining psychological equilibrium, autonomy, self-control, and mobility. Second, and perhaps more importantly, assessment tells you, the interventionist, how you are doing as far as de-escalating and defusing the crisis, which can be very important to your health and well-being and future retirement plans! Third, real-time assessment using the TASSLE allows threat assessment teams (TATs) to have an after-the-fact common ground on which to assess the student and plan their strategic intervention.

A major difference between crisis intervention and counseling and psychotherapy is that the crisis intervener generally doesn't have time to gather or analyze all the background and other assessment data that might normally be available under less stressful conditions. A key component of a high-functioning crisis intervener is the ability to take the confusing, chaotic information that's available and make some meaningful sense out of it. This notion of real-time, interocular analysis (literally, "eyeball assessment") may be

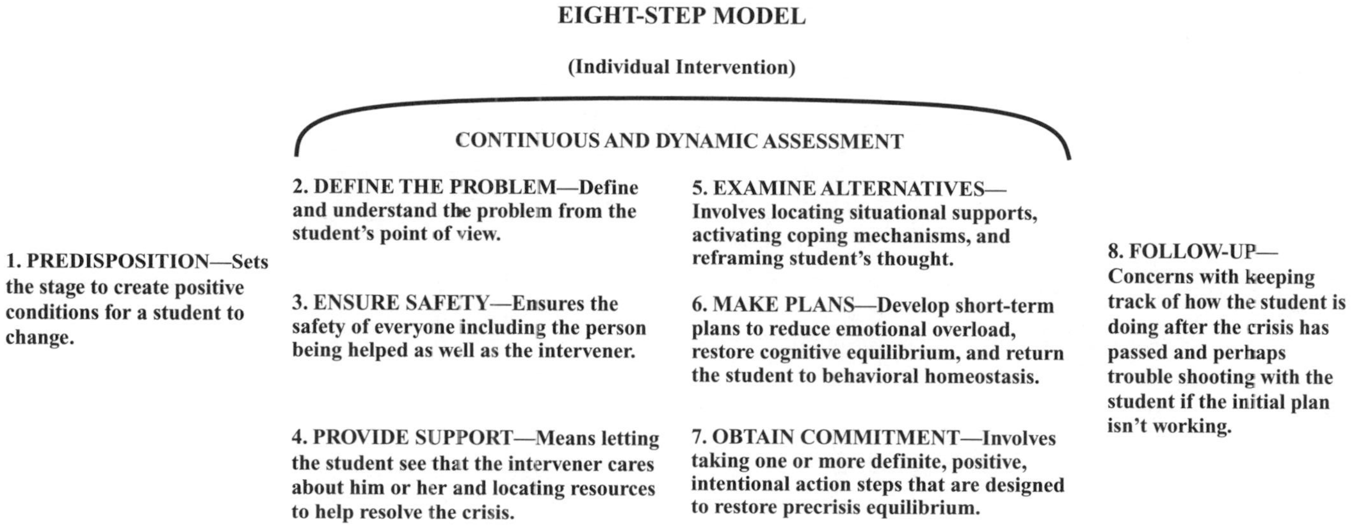

EIGHT-STEP MODEL

(Individual Intervention)

CONTINUOUS AND DYNAMIC ASSESSMENT

1. PREDISPOSITION—Sets the stage to create positive conditions for a student to change.

2. DEFINE THE PROBLEM—Define and understand the problem from the student's point of view.

3. ENSURE SAFETY—Ensures the safety of everyone including the person being helped as well as the intervener.

4. PROVIDE SUPPORT—Means letting the student see that the intervener cares about him or her and locating resources to help resolve the crisis.

5. EXAMINE ALTERNATIVES—Involves locating situational supports, activating coping mechanisms, and reframing student's thought.

6. MAKE PLANS—Develop short-term plans to reduce emotional overload, restore cognitive equilibrium, and return the student to behavioral homeostasis.

7. OBTAIN COMMITMENT—Involves taking one or more definite, positive, intentional action steps that are designed to restore precrisis equilibrium.

8. FOLLOW-UP—Concerns with keeping track of how the student is doing after the crisis has passed and perhaps trouble shooting with the student if the initial plan isn't working.

Figure 10.1 Eight-Step Model

problematic to those human services workers who are accustomed to having complete social and psychological workups available to them before proceeding with intervention. However, the ability to quickly evaluate the degree of student disequilibrium and immobility—and to be flexible enough to change one's evaluation as changing conditions warrant—is a priority skill that crisis interveners must seek to cultivate. This situation is true whether that interventionist is a PhD in clinical psychology or a sophomore residence hall assistant.

From beginning to end of the crisis, assessment is a central, continuous process. The crisis intervener must not assume that because the crisis appears to have been resolved, assessment is no longer needed. Assessing the student's crisis in terms of severity, longevity, current emotional status, alternatives, situational supports, coping mechanisms, resources, and level of lethality is never complete until the student has gotten back his or her precrisis level of mobility, equilibrium, self-control, and autonomy.

Gilliland's (1982) original model had "defining the problem," "ensuring student safety," and "providing support" as the first three steps in the model. These first three steps are as much involved in listening and observing as acting. While it may seem paradoxical in the midst of a chaotic crisis, the skills of first listening, observing, and assessing as the crisis situation unfolds and the intervener attempts to understand what is occurring are as important, if not more so, as acting. To this side of the model, we have added "predispositioning" as the initial step in intervention.

Step One: Predispositioning

Predispositioning derives in part from the motivational interviewing model of Miller and Rollnick (2002) and the transtheoretical model of Prochaska and DiClemente (1982, 1984). These models were developed to help persons with one of the biggest crises going—addictions. We believe that predispositioning is particularly helpful in a college setting for two reasons. First, from a system perspective, the college setting is a closed system, and unlike the wide open systems in which most crisis intervention occurs, it is an ideal place for dissemination of information, education, training, and motivating all the stakeholders in the college community to share in the responsibility for, and believe in the utility of, a safe learning environment. Second, predispositioning means setting the stage to create positive conditions for a student to change. Predispositioning in crisis intervention starts with creating a positive bond with the student. This bond says the intolerable dilemma can be solved and that the student now has help and support. Predispositioning starts with learning how to introduce yourself to a student in crisis. A number of other basic skills that set the stage to enhance the potential to motivate students to take control over the crisis and retake control over their lives are also included.

Step Two: Defining the Problem

After establishing contact with the student, the next step is to define and understand the problem from the student's point of view. Unless the intervener can perceive the crisis situation from the affective, behavioral, and cognitive viewpoint as the student perceives it, all the intervention strategies and techniques the intervener has in his or her intervention arsenal will have little effect. The core listening skills of empathy, genuineness, and acceptance or positive regard that Carl Rogers (1951) made famous are at work in defining the problem. The skills described later in this chapter should greatly enhance your competency in this basic initiating step of crisis intervention.

Step Three: Ensuring Safety

Safety is paramount in crisis intervention: safety for the student as well as safety for others in the campus community, and last, but not least, safety for the intervener! Because the potential for injury and lethality is at the forefront of all crisis intervention when dealing with volatile and out-of-control students, safety is paramount and needs to become a natural component of the intervener's repertoire. While safety is positioned as the second step in the model, this step is applied in a fluid way, meaning that safety is a constant consideration throughout crisis intervention. Assessing and ensuring the student's and others' safety, whether explicitly or implicitly stated and acted on, is always part of the intervention process. Even though we like "Amazing Grace," particularly when it is rendered with bagpipes, attending a memorial service for any of you as a result of not staying safe when doing crisis intervention is not something in which we want to participate. We will have a great deal more to say about safety later in this chapter.

Step Four: Providing Support

The fourth step in crisis intervention focuses on providing support. Support occurs in two ways. First and foremost, support means letting the student see that the intervener cares about him or her and not just in a shallow, superficial, "This is just my job!" way. Interveners must be able to genuinely convey unconditional and positive acceptance to all recipients of service, whether the recipients feel the same way about them or not. This is easily said and not so easily done when students don't act, talk, look, or even smell nice.

Second, support means finding the resources, most typically other humans, that can give the student the support that he or she needs to get through the crisis. In most crisis situations, students get there because their social support system went bankrupt. As a result, they feel little valued or cared for and see themselves as helpless because of the crisis events. With no social supports to anchor to as the crisis carries them along, they spiral out of control in a crisis whirlpool.

In a more general sense, support may not only need to be emotional, but instrumental and informational as well (Cohen, 2004). At times, the student may not have basic necessities for living or staying in school. As vividly illustrated in the TASSLE cognitive scale, the basic necessities of living and surviving come first before psychological needs. In other instances, students do not have adequate information to make good decisions, especially when they are in the new, strange, and unfamiliar environment of college. The need for obtaining informational support is often critical in the next step, "examining alternatives."

Step Five: Examining Alternatives

The next four steps in the model are more involved with acting. That being said, listening, observing, and assessing are still continuous and let the intervener know whether the alternatives, plans, and commitment that are made are viable and functional.

In the heat of the moment, both recipients and interveners often fail to look at alternatives. In the black-and-white, all-or-none thinking that is prevalent in crises, students become immobilized and forget they have options. Often students in crisis believe that, in fact, there are no options, and they become immobilized because they believe they are helpless to do anything about their predicament. They forget alternatives that had previously worked for them in the past or don't believe those will work for them in the present. To that end, generating viable and workable alternatives generally requires the intervener to put three change agents in operation.

First, is finding *situational supports,* as described in step four. Situational supports are other persons who can provide specific aid and assistance to the crisis. This assistance may range from emotional to financial support. These are people the student knows who care about what happens, although the student might not at present think so or be too embarrassed or ashamed to ask them for help. Most often these situational supports are friends and family. However, given the college setting, new support systems may need to be put in place. The student may be unaware that these supports even exist. The job of the intervener then becomes to find those resources. Engaging these situational supports give the student both the social and problem-solving human resources necessary to ride out the storm and get through the situation.

Second is developing *coping mechanisms.* Coping mechanisms are actions, behaviors, or environmental resources the student has used in the past that could help get him or her through the present crisis. Or when the student has exhausted those resources, the intervener may start providing information and guidance to generate new coping mechanisms. Many times when the person in crisis is in a new environment such as a college setting, it will be incumbent on the intervener to help marshal those resources.

Third is helping to *reframe thinking patterns* that change the student's view of the problem. Lessening the student's level of stress and anxiety is critical in resolving the extreme cognitive dissonance that often goes with a crisis. One of the main premises of solution-focused brief therapy (de Shazer, 1985) operates here. The point is to get the person in crisis to view the present dilemma as an unpleasant and undesirable exception to the generally positive and fruitful way they live their lives and then have them to start thinking in those terms.

Throughout the intervention process, the crisis intervener builds a repertory of options and constantly evaluates their appropriateness for the student as conditions rapidly change. In assessing alternatives available to the student, the intervener must first consider the student's viewpoint, mobility, and capability of generating alternatives and plans as much as safety and the tolerances to keep the campus system functional will allow.

Alternatives include knowing the referral resources available to the student, both on and off campus, or at least having the ability to get the student to someone who does. Even though the student may be looking for only one or two concrete action steps or options, the intervener brainstorms, in collaboration with the student, to develop a list of possibilities that can be evaluated. Most will be discarded before the student can own and commit to a definite course of action.

The intervener ponders questions such as What actions or choices does the student have now that would restore the student to a precrisis state of autonomy? What realistic actions (coping mechanisms) can the student take? What institutional, social, vocational, or personal (student's) strengths or support systems are available? (Note that "support systems" refers to all the people within the system, even professors!) Who would care about and be open to assisting the student? What are the financial, social, vocational, and personal impediments to student progress? By asking these questions, the intervener forces the student to start making value judgments as to the plausibility of the options. In terms of reality/control/choice theory (Glasser, 1965, 1998), making such value judgments means students start to take back control over their behavior and stabilize it.

The key in generating alternatives is not providing a smorgasbord of options, but settling on a few simple alternatives that can be put into immediate operation. Therefore, getting out of bed and washing one's face may not pull a person out of acute depression but it is a viable and doable alternative to being frozen in bed with the shades pulled, and is a start that the student can make happen, retake some self-control, and clearly mark and own behavior change.

Step Six: Making Plans

The sixth step in crisis intervention, making plans, flows from generating alternatives. When we are speaking of "plans," we are talking in the short term. Planning in crisis intervention is not what students are going to do for the rest of their lives. A plan is about getting the student through the crisis and is measured in minutes, hours, and days, not weeks, months, or years. A plan is about reducing emotional overload, returning the student to behavioral homeostasis, and restoring cognitive equilibrium. A plan should identify persons and other referral resources that can be contacted for immediate support and provide short-term, concrete, and positive behavioral goals. These should have a good chance of succeeding in the near term, and the student should be able to do these immediately. Any plan should be realistic in terms of the student's psychological, social, and financial resources. Planning is best done in collaboration with students so they feel a sense of ownership of the plan. Any imposed plan is less likely to work than one that is collaboratively generated and agreed upon. Even though the intervener may be very directive at times, it is critical that students feel empowered and have at least some modicum of control back in their lives as they attempt to plan how to overcome the crisis.

Step Seven: Obtaining Commitment

The seventh step, obtaining commitment, comes directly from the short-term crisis plan. If the planning step is done effectively, the commitment step will fall into place. Most of the time, the commitment step is brief and simple: asking the student to verbally summarize the plan, straightening out any misunderstandings or glitches, and getting a handshake to seal the deal. Where lethality is involved, the commitment may be written down and signed by both parties so there is concrete evidence that lethal behavior is not a current option. Commitment is all about taking one or more definite, positive, intentional action steps that are designed to restore precrisis equilibrium. No commitment should be imposed or coerced by the intervener. Commitments should be voluntarily made and seen as doable by the student. Any hesitation on the part of the individual to commit to the plan of action should be reflected and queried by the intervener. No crisis intervention should ever end without a commitment to do something, no matter how small, about dealing with the crisis.

Step Eight: Follow-Up

Long-term or even short-term follow-up many times is not an option in one-shot crisis intervention. However, by the very nature of the closed system of a college campus, it is far more likely that the student will not disappear but reappear either at the original point of contact or in some other part of the system. Thus, follow-up is not only necessary but mandated if the potential for increased violence is present. Many of the students you will encounter may be much like what crisis intervention team police officers call the chronic mentally ill whom they see over and over again in their patrols. They are called "Pete" and Repete" for the number of times they answer repeated service calls about them. The problems experienced by these chronic mentally ill leave them in what we term a *transcrisis* state (James, 2008).

A transcrisis state occurs when the individual has suffered some previous traumatic event and has unfinished business with it. Much like a chronic sinus infection, the pathology remains in the individual and is best coped with by using over-the-counter decongestants. However, when unplanned and unforeseen events, such as getting soaking wet when caught in a downpour, turn the sinus condition into pneumonia, a trip to the ER, antibiotics, and bed rest are in order. Thus, when unforeseen events that seem small to others rock the world of people in transcrisis, they fall into disequilibrium. Given what we know about the state of mental health on today's college campuses and the many stressors that blindside students, it is highly likely you will meet students who admirably fit the definition of *transcrisis*.

Thus, follow-up is essentially concerned with keeping track of how the student is doing after the crisis has passed. This step also troubleshoots with the student if his or her initial plan isn't working well. Follow-up is particularly important on a college campus because of decisions threat assessment teams need to make. The very concept of a threat assessment team that reviews and makes decisions about what to do after a crisis dictates that follow-up by the system is an integral part of the model.

Follow-up also tells students that the intervener is still interested in their welfare, and for newcomers to a college campus, this may be critical in keeping them from falling back into crisis. Finally, if follow-up is done in a sincere, concerned, and genuine manner, it brings the eight-step model full circle, because it predisposes the student to be more amiable and accepting of the intervener if and when another crisis occurs.

MOVING ON THE DIRECTIVE, COLLABORATIVE, NONDIRECTIVE CONTINUUM

The process of applying these skills and steps is fluid rather than mechanistic. It would be really neat and tidy if we could walk through the model in a stepwise, linear manner, doing a checkoff list as we went. The problem is that crises are almost never neat and tidy. Thus, when we employ this model, it sometimes appears we are doing so in a hopscotch manner, bouncing from safety concerns to plans and back to problem exploration. Nothing could be further from the truth. The step of the model we are using is dictated by what is happening in front of us. Resiliency and fluid reaction ability are key components to making the model work. In that regard, crisis intervention typically operates on a directive, collaborative, and nondirective continuum (James, 2008).

The crisis intervener's level of action and involvement in the student's world is based on the student's level of mobility-immobility, which may be anywhere on a continuum ranging from nondirective through collaborative to directive. The appropriateness of alternative coping mechanisms hinges on the student's degree of mobility. Thus, assessment of student mobility is a key concept governing the degree of the crisis intervener's involvement.

Directive Intervention

Most traditional counseling approaches (Rogers, 1951) believe that allowing individuals to come up with their own solutions with as little direction and guidance from the therapist as possible is the best way to facilitate independence and autonomy, not to mention reducing dependence on the therapist. In therapy, that approach is generally known as being nondirective or client-centered (Rogers, 1951). However, that is *not* the case in the initial stages of most crises. The affective chaos, behavior immobility, and cognitive disequilibrium clearly indicate the person is not equal to the task of getting out of the crisis on his or her own. Therefore, a much more directive approach is called for when the student is assessed as being too immobile to cope with the current crisis.

As discussed in Chapter 9, a TASSLE score in the high teens or 20s typically calls for a good deal of directiveness from the intervener. The crisis intervener temporarily takes control of the problem, proposes alternatives, and is the primary developer of a short-term plan to get mobility and homeostasis back into the student's life. Directive intervention has little to do with "you" or "we." It is an "I" approach. By using a very directive stance, the intervener takes temporary control, authority, and responsibility for the situation and instructs, leads, or guides the student in the action.

There are many kinds of immobile students, ranging from those who need immediate hospitalization because of drug use to students who are suffering from such severe depression that they cannot function. Some students who are immobile may have just received a severe shock from news over the sudden loss of a parent or be experiencing anxiety levels over school so high that they cannot function academically. Other students, for any of a variety of reasons, are out of touch with reality and may be a danger to themselves or others, and they are also immobile.

However, if the intervener makes an error of judgment (i.e., believing a student to be unequal to taking action when in fact he or she is not), no harm is usually done because the student may simply respond by refusing to accept the intervener's direction. That, of course, is contingent on students not being a threat to themselves or others; in that case, not only will the intervener become more directive, but so will a lot of other people from the college who are involved in the crisis response.

Hopefully, in most cases the intervener can shift out of a directive mode into a collaborative mode, which is our preferred mode of operation because it starts to give back control to the student. Many times an intervener will begin in a directive mode and then shift into a collaborative mode during the session.

Collaborative Intervention

Collaboration moves from an "I" to a "we" approach as the student gains more ability to marshal resources and govern behavior. A partnership is forged with the student in evaluating the problem, generating acceptable alternatives, and implementing realistic action steps. When a student has a TASSLE score that is in the high single digits to middle teens, we can typically operate in a collaborative mode. Many crisis interventions operate in this mode. The collaborative student is a full partner in identifying the precipitating problem, examining realistic alternatives, planning action steps, and making a commitment to carrying out a realistic plan. The collaborative student is not as self-reliant and autonomous as the fully mobile student but does have enough resources and mobility to participate in resolving the problem. The intervener serves as a temporary catalyst, coach, consultant, facilitator, and support person.

Nondirective Intervention

Nondirective intervention seldom if ever occurs early on in crisis intervention, but rather when the student is in control emotionally, behaviorally mobile, and cognitively stable. Most generally, a nondirective approach is taken when a student's TASSLE rating is in the single digits or very low teens. The intervener does not manage, manipulate, prescribe, dominate, or control. It is the student who owns the problem, the coping mechanisms, the plan, the action, the commitment, and the outcomes.

The intervener is a support person who may be a sounding board, encourage actions, reflect thoughts and feelings about alternative and plans, reinforce taking action steps, summarize and clarify plans, and become a cheerleader and troubleshooter as the student attempts to put plans into action. Nondirective intervention is certainly the desired end goal in that it assists students in mobilizing their intellectual capacities, physical abilities, and emotional coping strengths to solve their own problems and return self-control to them.

TOOLS OF THE TRADE

The four basic building blocks of active listening to facilitate exploration are restatement and summary clarification of the content of the crisis, reflection of the person's feelings and thoughts, open leads that expand and clarify the dilemma, and owning statements about the intervener's state of being as he or she wades into the crisis. These are standard facilitation techniques that would be found in almost any counseling model. However, in crisis intervention, a great deal more emphasis is placed on owning techniques that set limits, make assertions, reinforce behavior, and deal in real time in regard to both intervener and student thinking, feeling, and behavior. Also in crisis intervention, a lot more closed questions are asked. Closed questions are used when clear, direct answers are needed, particularly when safety issues are involved.

Open Leads

Typically when we want people to talk, starting with an open-ended question works best. Open-ended questions usually begin with *what* or *how* or ask for clarification or details. Open-ended questions encourage students to respond with fuller explanations and with deeper levels of meaning. Remember that open-ended questions are used to elicit from students something about their feelings, behaviors, and thoughts. These questions are particularly helpful in the problem exploration step in the eight-step model. Here are some guidelines for forming open-ended questions.

1. *Getting the big picture:* "Start wherever you'd like and tell me how this happened." "What got this all started?"

2. *Seek expansion:* "So tell me more." "Then what happened?" "Who else was there?" "How did things change then?"
3. *Request description:* "Expand on that some." "Tell me about. . . ." "Show me." "In what ways does. . . ?" "Could you add some more details?"
4. *Generate plans and alternatives:* "What will you do if. . . ?" "How will you make it happen?" "How will that help you to. . . ?" "Where do you want to wind up?"

Close-Ended Questions

Closed questions usually begin with verbs such as *do, did, does, can, have, had, will, are, is,* and *was. How, when, who, where,* and *what* questions may also be closed when they request specific pieces of information. Thus, closed questions seek specific, concrete information from the person. They are designed to elicit specific yes or no or factual responses. Closed-end questions are used throughout the eight-step model, from determining safety needs to getting commitments. Closed questions obtain specific information that ranges from getting a student's age, class, school, or home address to determining if the student is lethal. Closed questions help the crisis intervener make a fast assessment of what is occurring, particularly when lethality (i.e., suicide or homicide) is an issue. Close-ended questions are particularly suited to obtaining commitments to take action.

Here are four guidelines for forming close-ended questions.

1. *Request specific information:* "When was the last time this occurred?" "When are you going to go?" "Have you decided to stop doing it?"
2. *Determine lethality:* "Are you thinking of hurting her?" "Have you gone back there when you were told to stay away?" "Does this mean you are going to kill yourself?" "Do you have a gun?" "Do you know how to use it?" "Do you have a plan?"
3. *Detail alternatives and plans:* "Can you get up and get on the bus at 6 a.m.?" "Which option are you going to choose if you do stay in the residence hall system: moving to another floor or moving to another hall?"
4. *Obtain a commitment:* "Will you go to counseling?" "Will you confront him about this?" "Do you agree to. . . ?" "When will you do this?"

Restatement and Summary Clarification

Restatement and summary clarification are critical ingredients in crisis intervention. Three good things happen when restatement is used. First, the intervener attempts to get clarification in regard to what is happening by restating the student's content message. Second, it gives the student in crisis a chance to correct the intervener's interpretation of the event. Third, restatement and clarification slow things down. Restatement can serve as an effective governor for a student who has to stop cognitive and emotive racing and listen and then affirm or correct the intervener's recap. Since universities have different titles for people who work in resident halls, we select the Resident Hall Professional (RHP) to designate the intervener for the following examples.

> **RHP:** So right now, Jeremy, you are concerned that the guys upstairs are beaming homosexual thoughts down through the ceiling. That's why you put the aluminum foil up there. But it isn't working, and now you want me to stop them.

Restatement sounds simple. It is simple if the crisis intervener focuses totally on the student's world. Restatement is not simple if the crisis intervener is distracted by environmental stimuli or gets hung up in his or her agendas, biases, or stereotypes about what the student is saying and then tacks some value judgments on for good measure. The following illustrates this:

> **RHP:** Alpha waves! Aluminum foil on the ceiling! Come on, now, get a grip! Those guys upstairs aren't interested in your body. I happen to know they are big time into chicks. I think for your own good you need to consider getting some counseling, and pretty quickly at that. I mean, come on, aluminum foil on the ceiling!

Restatement can also be used in the commitment stage to check out a plan and be sure everybody is on the same page. Often the person in crisis is the one who makes the summary clarification.

> **RHP:** Okay, so we have talked this over, and right now you don't want to go to counseling, but you do want them to quit. Tell me what we have come up with!
> **Jeremy:** I am going to call my parents and get a doctor's appointment and see if I am stressing too much because of school. You and I are going to meet with the guys in Room 303 and talk this through tomorrow afternoon. If I start to get stressed out and think there are alpha waves coming through the ceiling, I am to go down to the resident hall director, John, and talk to him.

Reflection of Thoughts and Feelings

Communicating Empathic Understanding

Empathy is the attempt to see what persons in crisis see from their perspective, to hear what they hear with the same resonance, to smell and taste with their olfactory senses, to feel their sense of touch with the same tactile sensitivity, and to feel the cognitive chaos and confusion as thinking disintegrates and spirals out of control. By accurately hearing and understanding the core feelings and thoughts going on inside the student and accurately and caringly communicating that understanding to the student, you are demonstrating effective listening. One of the very best ways of doing so is by using a counseling technique called *reflection*. The intervener deals *directly* with the student's concerns and does not veer off into talking *about* the student's concerns or some tangential student or event. That distinction is important. Here is an example of the intervener veering off:

Chandra: I'm afraid they'll never understand if I decide to pledge another sorority. They think I was a traitor, and I couldn't tell them Psi Phi Omega didn't want me.
RHP: (*Talking about the situation and tangentially focusing on Chandra.*) Well, you need to realize that sororities don't accept women for lots of reasons. If your mom and sister think that, they seem pretty narrow-minded to me and don't appreciate what you have gone through. Indeed, more for them than you. I think that's pretty darn selfish of them.
RHP: (*Deeply reflecting feelings and thoughts of the dilemma.*) You're feeling torn. On the one hand, you want to have their respect, but aren't sure how to go ahead and make your own choices without hurting them on the other.

The latter response stays on target by reflecting Chandra's feelings and concerns in the present moment. It does not get into making value judgments about relatives that may lead to a protracted discussion and defensiveness by Chandra. Chandra may start defending her mom and sister, which is tangential to dealing with the present moment of a young woman actively contemplating suicide. Reflection as a crisis intervention technique is different than restatement and summary recapitulation that attempts to capture only the content of the message. Reflection attempts to capture the undergirding feelings and thoughts that go with the content.

RHP: So beneath all the hurt by not getting into the sorority, it sounds like there's shame that you let your family down.

Reflection of feelings attempts to probe the student at a deeper level and bring closed affect to the light of day.

Chandra: I don't ever seem to live up to their expectations.
RHP: So for a long time now, you've tried to be the ideal of what they expected, and here you seem to have failed again. Failed at not only something your sister succeeded at doing but your mom as well.

Reflection of cognitions attempts to do the same by picking the cognitive needles out of the jumbled haystack of thinking that is present in most crises.

RHP: I am guessing the billboard that goes though your mind reads something like, "I must finally succeed at college because I have been a failure in their eyes up until now." And now with this rejection not only from their sorority but also a boyfriend that meets their standards, I am betting that has now changed to words like "Absolutely an abysmal failure."

Reflections do not make judgments about the merits of the feeling or the thought, nor do they seek to interpret the meaning. Reflections are typically formed as working hypotheses that are tested out with the individual as opposed to making pronounced judgments. Thus, reflections are put forth in a conditional, tentative sense that allows the student to accept or reject them without fear of losing face or feeling put down, as the RHP does above by putting in the conditional words of *guessing* and *betting*.

When students are trained in conventional therapeutic techniques, reflection of feelings as a major counseling technique is heavily emphasized. The notion is that most people ignore, deny, and repress feelings. Those feelings need to come to the surface and be dealt with because they keep the individual emotionally stuck and frozen. However, that is not always the case when an individual is in crisis and the intervener who makes a feeling-based reflection to an already emotionally volatile person may be exacerbating the situation.

> **RHP:** So, Jeremy, it seems like your feelings have been getting more and more threatened by the homosexual come-ons that these guys are beaming down to you, and as a result you are becoming angrier and angrier and frustrated that nobody else seems to care what they are doing to you.
>
> **Jeremy:** That's right. You can't imagine what it's like with those bad things coming into my head they beam down through the ceiling. It's getting worse, and the foil can't seem to stop it anymore. It's like I can't think anymore. It makes me so angry at them—so I'll have to stop it. Stop them!

Although that reflection may be right on target, it has the potential to pour psychological gasoline on an already burning fire. While reflecting feelings with Chandra and allowing her to cathart may be exactly the right strategy for her, it probably is most likely the wrong strategy for highly agitated individuals like Jeremy and generally should be avoided. For students in crisis like Jeremy, whose affect and cognitive TASSLE scales are high, the focus should be on controlling and cooling his hot cognitions and emotions rather than attempting to tap into them.

> **RHP:** No, I can't imagine what that's like, but I wonder if you couldn't put some other thoughts in place. I'm no counselor, but it seems like you need to get something in your head like music to drown them out.

Owning Statements

Owning, or "I," statements are directive, straightforward, declarative sentences about the intervener's own state of being in regard to what is going on. They are extremely important in crisis intervention because of the directive stance the crisis intervener often has to take with students who are immobile and in disequilibrium. These statements are employed in a variety of ways to do a variety of things. Therefore, we have illustrated a number of different types of owning statements the crisis intervener may find useful for particular problems that occur during intervention.

Owning statements are also important because when you are the intervener, what happens is between you and the person in crisis and no one else. It is tempting to "third person" or "third thing" the dialogue as a way of distancing responsibility. It would be ever so convenient to offload the problem onto the president of the university, the housing director, God, the biology professor, English class, residence hall food, or any other person, deity, or thing the intervener can think of to get the onus of responsibility off his or her back. That is a very bad idea! The student does not have much of a chance against those authority figures, nor can any effective dialogue or solution occur against such amorphous entities as residence hall food, the biology department, or an unreachable university president. While it may appear to offer the intervener escape from responsibility to work the problem through, what actually results is an attempt to externalize the problem rather than confront it in real time. At worst, it immediately accelerates the problem because it discounts the possibility of any immediate steps toward solution, and at its best, it makes the intervener appear incompetent, as may be seen in the following response.

> **RHP:** The residence hall director is very concerned about you and says if you can't snap out of this funk you're in, Chandra, she is going to call your parents because she believes you are a physical danger to yourself. I am sorry, but it is out of my hands now. So I don't think you'd want your parents to see you in this shape, so you need to get out of bed before I have to report back to the director. The counseling center staff thinks you are probably depressed and need to be evaluated to see if you need medication, so you need to see them, too.

Compare the foregoing disowned statements with the RHP's clear owning statements about her state of being as she engages Chandra here:

> **RHP:** I am concerned about you, Chandra. Let me put a big *very* in front of *concerned.* I don't know you at all, but I believe anybody who has been in bed 3 days crying their eyes out has spent a tremendous amount of emotional energy trying to get rid of the hurt, and it hasn't worked. I want to try and get you out of this terrible pit you seem to be in. I want to help you help yourself, and I hope that you and I can do this together.

Owning State of Being

One of the toughest jobs is owning up to our own frailties. We don't want to appear stupid, incompetent, or otherwise unequal to the task. However, if we pretend we understand when in fact we are confused, the student who is listening to one of us is going to be doubly confused. Being willing to own our confusion or frustration and to attempt to eliminate it does three things: (a) both student and intervener can reduce the need to pretend or fake understanding of one another and begin to see more clearly where communications are getting crossed, (b) the student sees the intervener as a real human being who does not have all the answers and paradoxically can generate respect for the intervener, and (c) the student can begin to become actively involved with the intervener in an attempt to work together on moving toward a solution.

> **RHP:** (*Unsure and nervous as she attempts to get Chandra to communicate*). Chandra, I have never dealt with someone as distraught as you, and I am not sure what to do to get you to talk to me. But I do think getting out of this bed and washing your face and getting some clothes on and maybe eating a little and talking to me about what is going on is a start. So if I am wrong, let me know what you think.

Conveying Understanding

Students in crisis often feel that no one understands what they are going through. The "I understand" statement is an owning statement that clearly conveys to the student that you do understand that what is happening in the here and now of the moment is causing the student severe problems. The intervener cannot understand what it is like to be blackballed by her mother and older sister's sorority and then have her boyfriend tell her he can't date her because she is not in a sorority. However, the intervener can understand and acknowledge the fear and anguish that the student is demonstrating. The "I understand" statement may have to be combined with what is commonly called a broken-CD (repeated) response because the individual may be so agitated or out of touch with reality that he or she does not hear what is being said the first time.

> **RHP:** I can't understand how getting dumped by your boyfriend over not getting a bid into the right sorority must feel, but I do understand right now that it's so awful and overwhelming the only thing that seems to work is penning yourself up in this room and waiting to die.
> **Chandra:** You couldn't begin to understand. I won't be ever able to face my mother or sister. I am so ashamed. How I have let them down.
> **RHP:** You are absolutely right. I have never been through anything like that, but if it has put you in bed for 3 days, I get a pretty good idea of how devastating it must be.

Value Judgments

Most of the time in standard counseling, value judgments are to be avoided like the plague. All too often, value judgments are based in the intervener's own biases, stereotypes, and prejudices about what truth, beauty, and goodness are. However, in times of crisis, the intervener has to make judgment calls about the student's behavior, particularly when the student is in danger of doing something hurtful to himself or herself or to others. Owning statements specifically speak to the intervener's judgment about the situation and what he or she will do about it. Owning statements are not about the personhood of the individual but rather about the specific behavior that the individual is eliciting at the present time that is disrupting the individual's life and those around him or her.

> RHP: (*Making a judgment.*) The way you say that really concerns me. If I leave, you seem so down right now you might go ahead and take those pills. If you can't get up and come to my office, I'll have to call the police to see that you are kept safe.

However, using owning statements does not generally mean making value judgments about the student's character, because such judgments are put-downs and do nothing to change behavior.

> RHP: (*Sarcastically.*) Yeah, you're in a world of hurt because that snobby sorority didn't give you a bid and your loser boyfriend dumped you. Get real!

Positive Reinforcement

There are a number of ways to couple positive reinforcement with owning statements, and a number of reasons for doing so. To be genuine in crisis work is to say what we feel at times. When a student has done well and the intervener is happy and feels good about it, he or she says so. However, such positively reinforcing statements should always be used in regard to a behavior, as opposed to some personal characteristic.

> RHP: Excellent, Jeremy! See, you can get control back, even though you feel like everybody's against you for moving down on the first floor. I really appreciate you being able to sit down to talk this over.

Positive reinforcement is used a great deal in crisis intervention to gain compliance. Many times, taking ministeps to get a student to calm down or stop engaging in a dangerous behavior is tied to positive reinforcement.

> RHP: (*Jeremy is standing up and pounding his fist on the table swearing.*) I need for you to take a deep breath and let it out gently. (*With difficulty, Jeremy complies.*) Great! That shows me you can get control of your emotions.

We often use positive reinforcement to successively approximate a student toward a total goal we are seeking to achieve.

> RHP: Good! You were able to take a deep breath. So you can sit down here and start to talk reasonably about your eviction. That's great. I respect your ability to

get yourself back in control. If you can keep that up, I think we can go talk to the area director about a move back after a probationary period.

Be careful with positive reinforcement and use it judiciously. Continuously reinforcing someone reduces its effectiveness and may not come across as sincere. So be careful about what and how many times behavior gets reinforced. Sticking with here-and-now behavior that moves toward compliance is your safest bet.

Personal Integrity and Limit Setting

You are not a psychological rug to be trod on. An irate student who starts to swear, browbeat, threaten, or otherwise pin us physically or psychologically in a corner steps over a boundary. At this point, it does little good to try to hide our fear, anger, disappointment, or hurt feelings. It is further important to set clear limits with students who are starting to get out of control or are trying to manipulate the crisis intervener.

> **Jeremy:** (*Sneeringly.*) What do you know, you're nothing but a crappy dorm director who'll never go anywhere! I don't have to take this shit! Who are you to tell me whether there are alpha beams or not. Are you a physicist? Huh? (*Steps toward the hall director with a menacing look.*)
>
> **RHP:** (*Calmly, owning feelings and setting limits.*) I don't appreciate the demeaning comments, the language, or your attitude toward me. I'd like an apology, and I'd also like you to be civil. If you can't, I'll assume you'd rather explain your problems to a police officer, and we'll terminate this conversation right now. I'm willing to back up and try this again if you are willing to discuss the issue with me without insults. I'm here to help you, man, if you will let me.

Assertion Statements

Assertion statements clearly and specifically ask for a specific action from the student. They are not long-winded sermons about right or wrong, and they are not made up of compound, complex sentences. They are composed of a subject, verb, and object and get right to the action that needs to be taken. Finally, because crisis intervention often calls for the crisis intervener to take control of the situation, requests for compliance in the form of owning statements are often very directive.

> **Police Officer:** I understand you feel that everybody here is against you, but you threw things around the lounge and wrecked some furniture. I need you to sit down and explain what happened.
>
> **Jeremy:** What if I don't want to sit down?
>
> **Police Officer:** If you don't sit down, I will take you into custody right now. I'd prefer not to do that. So I need for you to sit down now. And if we can

sort this out, then you chill out in the residence hall, studying, playing videos, listening to your iPod, or whatever you'd like to do. Or if you don't want to discuss this reasonably with me, I will take you down to the justice center, and you get to spend the night with some drunks who have puked all over themselves.

As George Thompson puts it, even if the person is crazy, enraged, or just bent on raising hell for the fun of it, a personal appeal to cease and desist when coupled with what they have to gain or lose in concrete terms presents peaceful options that most people will find hard to resist (Thompson & Jenkins, 2004, pp. 124–125).

DON'TS

There are a few communicative "Don'ts!" when you are doing crisis intervention. Most of these don'ts will not send you or someone else to the emergency room. Well, a few might! However, they will most likely shut down communication and make your job more difficult. So heed the following and stay away from them like the plague.

Personal Value Judgments Are Not Good PR

Personal value statements discount the person, which is at the top of the "you don't want to do that" list. No matter how poorly the person is functioning and how badly they are behaving, they are indeed trying to problem solve. Your read on Jeremy so far is that he admirably fits the out-of-date and pejorative label of lunatic. Indeed, most likely he is a candidate for a diagnosis of paranoid schizophrenia. However, to discount him is to belittle his problem-solving ability. That is about the last thing he needs to happen. Making value judgments about presenting behavior and what kind of trouble that is causing is not needed. Making value judgments and generalizations about a person's character put not only you but also others at risk (James, 2008).

> **Untrained Security Officer:** Whoa, boy! You don't settle down and get those looney tunes out of your head, you're gonna be in a heap of trouble. What kinda dope you on, anyways? Geez, is that LSD crap back again! Is that what you been doing? You don't want me to have to Taser you now, so calm down.
> **Crisis Intervention Team (CIT) Campus Police Officer:** It sounds like you were scared enough to go into defensive mode big time and try to attack those guys because they were scaring the hell out of you. That's what I'm here for. If you have a reason to be scared, call for me. You can't attack those guys, period! No questions! If you're scared or threatened you get help.

"It's for Your Own Good" Does Not Make You a Better Intervener

That's what your mother said when she gave you that awful cough medicine in the middle of the night. Did you believe that? It did come from your sainted mother, you know? Implying that whatever is going to be done is for someone's own good is not going to endear you to them. Their mom probably gave them the same stuff, so they already know better! If it is for the person's own good, show them the reasons (Thompson & Jenkins, 2004, pp. 53–54).

> **CIT Campus Police Officer:** I am going to get you out of here for the night. We have a room over in the police building. It's not a jail cell, just a time-out room, with TV, computer, minifrig, I think it's got some sodas in it. You aren't gonna be charged with anything. But I can't risk you staying here. I don't want a riot, and I don't want you hurt. There are some pretty pissed off folks here right now.

"Why" Questions Are for the Tabloids

The tabloids in the rack by the checkout stand at your local grocery store believe that inquiring minds want to know why Elvis was abducted by aliens and is not dead but singing on Mars. Crises, particularly those on college campuses, invariably are often exotic and unusual in how they got to be, and beginning interventionists are curious about why students get themselves in such convoluted predicaments. As a result, beginning interveners feel a compulsion to find out why a student does those really crazy things. "Why" questions are generally poor choices for obtaining more information. Even though they may provide the student with an opening to talk more, they also make the student defend his or her actions. Most of the time, students have no idea why they did what they did. Asking them only forces them to rationalize or intellectualize their actions or externalize blame to somebody or something, which provides little help and may even exacerbate the crisis (James, 2008).

> **Judicial Board Officer:** Jeremy, why did you threaten those students in 303?
> **Jeremy:** I didn't threaten anybody. I was only attempting to reason with them to stop beaming stuff down to my room. You need to ask them; they're the ones doing it.

As the example demonstrates, what generally happens is that students become defensive and attempt to intellectualize about the problem or externalize it to somebody or something else without taking responsibility or ownership of the problem.

"Be Reasonable" Almost Guarantees Unreasonableness

Everybody thinks Jeremy is very, very unreasonable with the aluminum foil and alpha beams and all. Do you suppose Jeremy thinks he is being unreasonable when those beams seem to be burning holes in his head? You only invite conflict by asking, "Why don't you be reasonable about this and take the aluminum foil down, quit hassling the guys upstairs, and get on with your life?" It is far better to allow them to become reasonable by reasoning with them. The easiest way to do that is by using a summary clarification statement to reassure them you hear what they are saying and understand what's going on (Thompson & Jenkins, 2004, p. 54).

"Negative Interrogative" Is Not Just a Grammatical Term

A negative interrogative is a closed question that is often a camouflaged way of getting the listener to agree with the speaker (James, 2008). *Don't, doesn't, isn't, aren't,* and *wouldn't* all tend to seek or imply agreement. The negative interrogative statement "Don't you think that's right?" really is a camouflaged exclamatory statement saying, "I believe that's right, and if you don't, you are a jackass!"

> **RHP:** Don't you think it'd be a good idea if you were to get a little of that stress off by going over to the counseling center?

Such statements generally don't get agreement and do get a lot of oppositional defiance. It is generally better to make a negative interrogative question into a clear, declarative assertion statement.

> **RHP:** The way you say they are beaming those alpha waves down here, and how much it bothers you to have those beams continuously intruding into your thoughts, I believe you might get some relief if you went to the counseling center.

Calm Down! *Not!*

Often when people are in doubt about what can be done to diffuse volatile, out-of-control individuals, they say, "Stay calm!" or "You need to calm down now!" If people were able to problem solve and find a solution, and weren't at their wits' end now because they couldn't work the problem out, they would be calm. Because all of those things and more are happening, about the last thing they are going to do is stay calm, and telling them to do so is likely to make things a whole lot less calm. Thompson and Jenkins (2004, pp. 156–158) believe that the best way to get people to calm down is to get them fruitfully occupied by writing down their issues (and calming down while doing it). Substituting proactive behavior is a far faster way of regaining peace, tranquility, and a return to reasoning than calming down. Thompson and Jenkins further state (pp. 157–158) that for people who have English as a second language—and there are clearly many students on college campuses for which this is true—a crisis exacerbates their language problems. Handing students a piece of paper and pencil and telling them the following slowly and clearly goes a long way toward calming down.

> **CIT Campus Police Officer:** Okay, I can see you are pretty excited and upset. I am not getting all of this about alpha waves and who is beaming them down and how. I want to get this straight, so take this notebook and write down what's going on that got you hot enough for me to get a call to come over and break a fight up. Take your time because I want to get it very clear in my mind.

The police officer acknowledges the feelings of the student and indicates his concern by wanting to get the facts of what is happening. He also conveys his concern and patience by giving the student time to think through the issue. He then puts the student to work, and the student has to concentrate on stating his case as opposed to angrily bouncing off the ceiling.

Those Are the Rules

There are rules, and if you are an administrator, it's your job to enforce those rules when need be. However, you better be able to back up those rules by stating why those rules apply in this particular situation (Thompson & Jenkins, 2004, pp. 48–49). If you can't or won't, you will lose credibility immediately, and that will cause you problems.

> **Jeremy:** Why are you hassling me, man. It's them!
> **CIT Campus Police Officer:** It may be. We'll sort that out. But your contract with the residence hall says you can't tear the place up, and that's what you were in the process of doing. So you need to sit down and chill out plain and simple.

In summary, the don'ts seem simple enough to avoid, but in the heat of the moment, it is easy to regress back into familiar and pat responses. You don't want to do that because a whole lot of people who are really good at diffusing and de-escalating out-of-control behavior have found it's the new stuff we are teaching you that works.

BASIC STRATEGIES OF CRISIS INTERVENTION

Myer and James (2005) have formulated nine strategies used in crisis intervention. The basic core listening and responding skills you have already read about in this chapter are tactical skills necessary to put your grand strategic crisis intervention plan in operation. No formula exists for using these strategies. They may be used singularly or in combination. Their use depends a great deal on the context of the setting events, the triage level of the student, and within what step of the eight-step model the crisis intervener is operating. While the foregoing may sound like a cop-out, it isn't. As you get familiar with these strategies, they will start to fall into place. Here are the nine strategies.

Creating Awareness

The crisis intervener attempts to bring to conscious awareness feelings, thoughts, and behaviors. Although this may sound patently ludicrous, given that people in crisis would seem to be pretty aware of the crisis that is tearing up their world, the fact is they are often not. They get caught in a psychological whirlpool that turns ever more tightly and paralyzes their ability to act in response to the crisis. Creating awareness is particularly important in step one, defining the problem.

> **RHP:** What would all this mess look like if it were sitting out there on the table like a bag of groceries? What labels would you stick on them? Instead of vegetable, meat, and dairy products, you have feelings, thoughts, and behaviors. Take each one of those bags, mom and sister, boyfriend, sorority, and the biggest shopping bag of all, you. Let's take those products out and label them so we can start to put them in the pantry and get this pile of stuff off the table.

Here the intervener uses a very basic counseling technique of making concrete a host of jumbled feelings, behaviors, and thoughts that involve a variety of systems. The student needs to separate individual trees from the forest of emotions she is lost in. By doing so, she can choose and focus on one or two realistic short-term goals.

Allowing Catharsis

At times, bringing shunted-off and submerged feelings and thoughts to the surface may be one of the best ways of taking the pressure off boiling emotional pots. To do this, the crisis intervener needs to provide a safe and accepting environment that says, "It's okay to say and feel these things." By so doing, the crisis intervener clearly says he or she can accept those feelings and thoughts, no matter how bad they may seem to be. Note that allowing catharsis has direction and purpose to it. Chandra has been crying for 3 days. While that may appear to be catharsis in the extreme, it is not. It is merely an emotional response to a perceived overwhelming situation. Catharsis has to do with well-timed and targeted reflections of feelings and thoughts that allow the student to emote on a particular subject and gain relief. Once the reflection is made, the use of silence may be the best course of action as the student ventilates. In other words, reflect the feeling or thought, and then be quiet and see what happens.

A word of caution here! Allowing angry feelings to ventilate may allow them to continue to build and escalate. That may not be the wisest course of action. This strategy is most often used with students who *can't* get in touch with their feelings and thoughts, as opposed to those whose feelings are already volcanic. This strategy is most likely to be used in step one, defining the problem, and step three, providing support.

> **RHP:** I think maybe it might be tough to talk about the real core issues here. After all, it involves the people you love the most, and those people don't seem to be hooked up to any positive emotions at all right now. Rather, what I seem to be getting are tied to things like shame, embarrassment, guilt, anxiety, and maybe even a little anger down beneath all those other emotions that somehow you got put in this horrible situation trying to meet their expectations. I am kinda wondering if those aren't some things that need to see the light of day. (*Becomes silent and give Chandra time to ponder what she has said.*)

By making a simple reflective statement that ties Chandra's loved ones to these yellow-, red-, black-, and blue-light emotions she is experiencing, the intervener sets the stage for purposive catharsis to occur. If Chandra can get some of these emotions purged from her system, she can start to focus on what she is going to do about getting out of the crisis as opposed to wallowing in her emotions.

Providing Support

Although this strategy may seem redundant because one step of our model is "providing support," it is not, and here's why. Often the crisis intervener is the *sole, immediate* support available to the student, whose other support systems are either geographically or psychologically 500 miles away. While one of our students in the examples in this chapter is losing contact with reality, most students we encounter are not. That doesn't mean they don't think they aren't. Therefore, in providing support, the crisis intervener supports the behavior as being as reasonable as could be expected, given the situation, and most likely a common response to it. Many times interventionists try to assure trauma survivors that what they are experiencing is normal. We think *normal* is a bad choice of words. There is nothing normal in the student's view about the situation or the behavior that follows it. This kind of affirmation is particularly critical to students who feel they have no support system available to them. That being said, the crisis intervener *never* supports injurious or lethal feelings, thoughts, or actions toward oneself or others.

> **RHP:** I don't want to minimize what has occurred here for you in your first few days of college, Chandra. It's really hard to take. Your reaction is common, though. I have seen it before in other women who didn't get bids from a sorority.

I am also not going to tell you it doesn't seem like the end of the world, given where your family is in all of this. You have certainly lost something, and like all losses, you are mourning it, and that is perfectly reasonable.

Providing support is utilized throughout the eight-step model, but it is particularly important when the student is attempting to make his or her first tentative move into action. A great deal of debate takes place in standard psychotherapy about not breeding dependence in the client. In crisis intervention, we hold that to be a useless discussion. You would not watch a drowning man to see if he could swim over to the boat and grab a life jacket. You throw it to him or swim out and get him if you can. The same is true in crisis. In a new, strange, and hostile environment when the student is immobilized and drowning, you give Chandra a life jacket or go in and pull her out.

Chandra: I can't take this. I am a total washout and screw-up. A human zero. I hate myself. How can I ever tell them? I would be better off dead.

RHP: Right now you may feel that the only solution is to kill yourself rather than face your family, but you aren't alone. I am here with you. I am going to stay in it until we get some control and direction back for you.

Chandra: I don't know how I can ever get any control back, and why should you care? You don't even know me . . . (*Starts sobbing again.*)

RHP: (*Puts her arm gently around Chandra and gently massages her head.*) No, I don't know you, but I am in charge on this floor, and what you don't yet know is that we take care of one another on my floor, and one of the ways that happens is that I and some other women you are going to meet pretty quickly are going to give you the support you need to get back in control.

Increasing Expansion

Crises often cause students to have tunnel vision about their dilemma. They focus exclusively on the crisis to the exclusion of everything else. However, while we might chart them on the TASSLE behavior scale as proactively trying to deal with the crisis to the exclusion of everything else, they are, in fact, immobilized by their perseveration and repetitive failed attempts to work through the crisis. Increased expansion means that the intervener takes the blinders off students and opens up their field of vision to allow them to consider other perspectives. This strategy is particularly effective in reframing students' all-or-none thinking and getting them to start thinking about the numerous choices and options they have.

RHP: I want you to think about this. Just you, not your sis or mom or anybody else in there but you. When you were going through rush, were there any other sororities that you liked? That you felt really comfortable with the women? That you felt part of, that seemed to hold the same values you do? I noticed some other bids on the desk, so somebody out there apparently thinks you fit with them.

Emphasizing Focus

In the extreme opposite direction of too much focus on the crisis, at times individuals are all over the map in their attempt to extinguish a thousand brush fires the crisis has created and watch their fruitless efforts as the forest burns down. One of the most effective strategies in crisis intervention is to downsize the problem and break it into manageable parts. Getting the individual to take one piece of what appears to be an onrushing, unending wall of problems and focus exclusively on one part of it often changes catastrophic interpretations and perceptions of the crisis event into more manageable pieces and provides doable alternatives. This strategy has particular utility in attempting to break the frenetic behavior and generate a small, doable plan that has immediate, observable outcomes.

> **RHP:** What is the one thing, if you could do it right now, you would want to happen?
>
> **Chandra:** Call home and tell them what happened and what a disgrace I am, but I just can't do that.
>
> **RHP:** That's right. Not only you can't but you won't. One look in the mirror will tell you that. What you need to do is first get yourself together. So first things first. Take a shower and get some food in you. I am going to help you get out of bed. I want you to take a shower, do your face, and then we are going to get something to eat, and if you want, we can talk about what you are going to say to them. I believe you can do that. How about you?

Note how the RHP affirms the student both in agreeing with her that such a huge chore is not possible at present and then in encouraging her to start moving. While the intervener is very directive in suggesting a small plan because Chandra is so immobilized, the idea is to get the person focused on taking one small step that successively approximates and reinforces her to begin to plan on tackling the big problem. It is also noteworthy that the intervener does not leave her to her own devices here but provides continuing support, which we believe is absolutely critical.

Providing Guidance

Guidance is not about becoming someone's parent, teacher, or guidance counselor. Guidance is about providing information to people who do not have the knowledge or resources available to make good decisions. It is an understatement to say that newcomers and even veteran students on a college campus aren't always privy to or can't find the sources for the information they need to make good decisions. Thus, the crisis inter-vener provides information, referral sources, and direction in getting students in crisis to the external resources and support systems they need to solve the dilemma. In the eight-step model, the strategy is used primarily in steps five and six but is also utilized at times in steps three and four when students cannot access support systems or are engag-ing in unsafe behavior.

> **Chandra:** (*Nibbling on a tuna sandwich in the cafeteria.*) I have no idea how to make that phone call. I want to throw up every time I think about it.
> **RHP:** Well, I could get Crissy, she lives down the hall from you. She's a graduate student in counseling. She loves doing role plays. Always wants to try stuff out on me. I know I could get her to role-play that call and coach you through it. If you don't want to do that and think you are putting your dirty laundry out on the street, I know people at the counseling center, and if you wouldn't think you were nuts for going over there, I'm pretty sure they could give you some help. I'd be willing to walk you over there if you want.

Promoting Mobilization

Plain and simple mobilization means getting the person moving. The RSA provides two options in the foregoing dialogue. By using options, the intervener puts decision mak-ing and control back on the student and attempts to reactivate the individual's ability to take action. The intervener also uses her knowledge of external support systems to help the student start moving and planning.

> **RHP:** So what do you think? Want me to give Crissy a call or want to walk over to the counseling center?

The intervener pushes a directive, forced choice to Chandra. Chandra may tell her that neither option is viable or choose one or the other. Either way, in terms of Glasser's reality/control/choice theory (1965, 1998), she will have to make a value judgment and a choice. In doing so, she is taking back control and decision making in her life.

Implementing Order

The crisis intervener puts cognitive and behavioral linearity back into the student's life. She helps the student rank priorities; categorize separate issues into big, medium, small, and trivial compartments; and sequentially attack the crisis in a logical and linear manner.

> **RHP:** I am going to suggest something. You talked to me about the Sigma Tau Rhos and Tri Gammas and really liking them. I know both of those sororities

pretty well, and I think either one of them would be a good fit. There's late rush, and you could still take their bid. So what if you did? Your mom and sister might have a cow, but you practiced talking to them with Crissy so I wonder if you couldn't make that the main point. Like you are now your own woman, and these are just a better fit for you. They might not like it, but they would have to respect it because they made their own choices, so why can't you do the same.

Providing Protection

Providing protection is overarching in crisis intervention and so important it is given its own step in the eight-step model. The crisis intervener monitors for injurious or lethal behaviors to themselves or others and keeps students from engaging in them. In the section on suicide and homicide in this chapter, you will see the resident hall director and the RHP go immediately into action to provide protection to students in crisis.

These nine strategies combine with the TASSLE, eight-step model, and crisis intervention verbal techniques to form the structure of how we use crisis intervention.

LISTENING AND RESPONDING IN CRISIS INTERVENTION

Accurate and well-honed listening skills are necessary and indeed sometimes sufficient skills that all therapists and particularly crisis interventionists must have. For that reason, listening skills are a major component of the eight-step intervention model, and a lot of these tools of the trade have to do with what we call active listening. Our preferred conceptual model for effective listening and responding in crisis intervention comes from a variety of therapeutic models and includes person-centered counseling (Egan, 1990; Rogers, 1951), reality/choice/control theory (Glasser, 1965, 1998), rational emotive behavior therapy (Dryden, 1984; Ellis, 1962), Adlerian therapy (Adler, 1958; Dinkmeyer & Sperry, 2000), behavioral modification theory (Skinner, 1953; Wolpe, 1990), assertiveness training (Alberti & Emmons, 2008), and even some hostage and crisis negotiation (Slatkin, 2005; Strentz, 2006) and policing (Memphis Police Department, 2008; Thompson & Jenkins, 2004). Dialogues from two students named Chandra and Jeremy, who are in a lot of psychological hot water for very different reasons and who are both having exceedingly bad hair days that are rapidly moving toward lethal behavior, illustrate the basic tactics and skills you will need to get in the game.

FACILITATIVE LISTENING IN CRISIS INTERVENTION

Listening is critical in crisis intervention. Listening is more than using your ears. It means focusing all your energy on understanding both the verbal and nonverbal messages the student is sending. Listening is attending.

Attending

Attentiveness is equal parts attitude and skill. Attending is an attitude in that the intervener focuses fully on the student right here and now. It is a skill in that conveying attending takes practice. Attending means that you focus your total mental energy on the student to the exclusion of everyone and anything else. Picture the last seconds of a Super Bowl. The ball is on the 35-yard line. A long, 52-yard field goal will win the game. The kicker comes on the field in front of a crowd of 75,000 screaming fans. Those fans, the TV audience, and everything else disappear. There is nothing else but seeing the snap of the ball, ball planted, moving to it, planting the pivot foot, kicking, and following through to the exclusion of everything else. The field goal kicker did not just walk out on the field and do that. It took practice to develop that skill, and you will need that same amount of practice if you are going to be a pro at doing this.

You focus on the individual and nothing else. The world, the state of the union, whether you'll have pepperoni pizza tonight, what the finish on that term paper will be, the need to text your boyfriend, and the thought of calling your mom all disappear. You are monitoring the student's voice tone, intonation, decibel level, and body language, because all those get connected with the words pouring out to help you make sense of what's going on (Cormier & Cormier, 1991; Gilliland & James, 1998).

However, it is not just attending to the student's verbal and nonverbal behavior, but attending to your own as well.

Thompson and Walker (2007, p. 65) state that 93% of your effectiveness in defusing an intense situation lies in your delivery style. They further note that rarely do police officers draw complaints on what they do, as opposed to how they sounded when they did it. You are no different. Voice tone, pace, pitch, decibel level, word choice, clarity, and smoothness of delivery tell students a great deal about the attentiveness of the crisis intervener (Cormier & Cormier, 1991; Gilliland & James, 1998). Pace refers to how fast you are talking. It is easy to get caught up in a rapidly escalating situation by talking too fast and trying to talk over the person. Keep it slow and steady. Keep your pitch even.

There is also a tendency to increase your decibel level when somebody is hostile and screaming. It is a very large temptation to want to yell right back as if somehow our decibel level will overcome the other person's angry exhortations. How you modulate your voice is also important. By modulation, we are talking about the rhythm and inflection you use. Take, for example, "No! I didn't say they thought you were crazy." Emphasizing the "No!" indicates that I had nothing at all whatsoever to do with it. Emphasizing "I" means you didn't say it, but someone else clearly did. Stressing "they" clearly implies they are the guilty culprits. Stressing "crazy" tells the recipient that his or her mental competence is indeed in considerable question. We have time and a need to take the time to put all of this together. This is not a NASCAR sprint to the finish. Speed does not win this race. Take your time! We have plenty of time to get it right. Indeed! At times you need to shut up!

Silence

Silence is often golden. Beginning crisis interveners often feel compelled to initiate talk to fill any void or lapse in the dialogue because they believe they would not be doing their job otherwise. Nothing could be further from the truth. Students need time to think. To throw out a barrage of questions or engage in a monologue says more about the crisis intervener's insecurity in the situation than it does about resolving the crisis. Silence gives the student thinking time—and the crisis intervener, too.

Indeed, at such times, verbiage from the crisis intervener may be intrusive and even unwelcome. Remaining silent but attending closely to the student can convey deep, empathic understanding. Nonverbally, the message comes across: "I understand your struggle trying to put those feelings into words, and it's okay. I know it's tough, but I believe you can handle it. However, I'm right here if you need me" (James, 2008).

What has been said here about the intervener applies equally to the respondent. Being sensitive to and taking the time to dissect the client's pitch, pace, modulation, diction, and verbiage is critical in assessing how the de-escalation process is coming along.

Nonverbal Communication

While you may have all the verbal qualities of tone, pace, pitch, decibel level, word choice, and smoothness of delivery to put Billy Graham to shame, if your nonverbals aren't congruent with what you are saying, you are not going to get very far. What individuals in crisis are hopefully going to see is an individual who has good eye contact but is not staring them down and who has a fairly intense and earnest facial expression but one that also changes as the emotional content of the student changes. The effective crisis intervener is smiling, nodding, showing appropriate seriousness of expression, leaning forward, staying in close physical proximity to the student without invading the student's space, and keeping arms and legs in an open, accepting posture. By using these attending skills, the crisis intervener conveys a sense of concern and commitment and continuously builds trust (Thompson & Walker, 2007, pp. 64–66). You are the Rock of Gibraltar here. Your slow, steady pitch and modulation not only says that, it models it in your open stance, eye contact, and body movements.

Nonverbal communication is also about the flip side of the dialogue. It involves accurately sensing and reflecting all the unspoken cues, messages, and behaviors the student emits. Nonverbal messages may be transmitted in many ways. The intervener should carefully observe body posture, body movement, gestures, grimaces, vocal pitch, eye movements, movement of arms and legs, and other body indicators. Students may transmit emotions such as anger, fear, puzzlement, doubt, rejection, emotional stress, and hopelessness by different body messages. Crisis interveners should be keenly aware of whether nonverbal messages are consistent with the student's verbal messages. A part of empathic understanding is the communication of such inconsistency to the student, who may not be consciously aware of the difference.

To that end, the TASSLE is not only useful for rating the person in crisis but also useful for rating the crisis intervener. If the TASSLE scale is not decreasing, then it is highly likely that little empathic bonding has been established, and the interventionist needs to take a time-out, change tactics, and monitor his or her attending skills.

Making Contact

Listening is first making contact and predisposing the student in crisis to establish contact with you. One of the first ways we do that is by personalizing the initial encounter by giving our name and being polite (Memphis Police Department, 2008; Thompson & Jenkins, 2004, p. 141). By being polite and attempting to establish a positive relationship immediately, the intervener sets the stage for a collaborative rather than adversarial relationship. Compare the two initial contacts of the RHP.

> **RHP:** (Knocking on the door and then opening it with pass key.) I'm the resident hall assistant for the third floor Fowler east. Your roommate said you hadn't been out of bed for 3 days and are crying. What's the problem?
>
> **RHP:** (Knocking on the door.) Chandra, this is Renee Antoine, I'm your RHA. I need to talk to you. Your roomie is really concerned. She says that you haven't been out of your room for 3 days. I'm going to open the door and come in, okay?

In the first example, the RHA does not give her name but her title. In making contact with a person in crisis, it is tempting to emphasize one's position or authority role, but that generally sets the stage to escalate an already volatile situation. By giving her name first and then her title, the RHA is seeking to establish contact and not control. By asking permission to come into the room before entering, her politeness indicates respect. She also indicates a problem with owning statements that convey her concern without confronting the student (Memphis Police Department, 2008). One important aspect of listening is for the intervener to make initial owning statements that express exactly what he or she is going to do.

> **RHP:** Chandra, I can see you're really hurting. Your roommate said you had been in bed for 3 days crying. I'm not sure what has caused you to be hurt so, but I understand you are hurting badly. To fully understand what's going on and what needs to be done, I'm going to focus as hard as I can on what you're saying and how you're saying it, so please talk to me and tell me what happened.

Accuracy

A second major component of listening is to respond in ways that let the student know that the crisis intervener is accurately hearing both the facts and the emotional and cognitive state from which the student's message comes. Here we are searching for both the fact and feeling—thinking dimensions of the problem. The crisis intervener combines the problems, feelings, and thinking by using restatement and reflection.

> **RHP:** So what you're saying is that between the sorority not giving you a bid and your boyfriend dumping you, you've given up on school and life. It seems hopeless. You can't think of any solution other than the only way out of this misery is to kill yourself.

The third component in effective listening is facilitative responding. It is generally a summative statement that provides students in crisis with a clearer understanding of their feelings, thoughts, and behavioral choices. Facilitative responses gently push students to start to realize they do have choices and begin to make judgments about how to get out of the dilemma. Here the crisis intervener targets a specific action and tries to get the student to remember and employ past resources she has used. She creates an exaggerated analogy that attempts to portray the ridiculousness of attempting to try to handle a host of problems at one time.

> **RHP:** So, given the five emotional bowling balls you are juggling, plus the one you are balancing on your nose, which one do you want to deal with first and set the others down? Look back on how you handled things when you juggled those emotional balls when you felt rejected. What worked then that might work now? Using that as an example, can we sort each one of these out and get the one bowling ball you want to use rolling down the lane for a strike, or just say that particular ball isn't important right now and just set it back on the rack, until you are ready to use it.

Expansion

The fourth dimension of effective listening is helping students see the big picture of the crisis situation and the disequilibrium that accompanies it. Such an understanding allows students to become more like objective, external observers of the crisis and to refocus it in rational ways rather than remaining stuck in their own internal frame of reference and emotional bias. It typically employs the strategy of expansion.

> **RHP:** You sound frozen by what is happening. Let's suppose you were up in the balcony of a movie theater watching the star in a tearjerker movie much like what is going on right now. What would you say to that person?

Helping students refocus or expand their options is a major part of effective listening that mobilizes persons in crisis when they are emotionally, cognitively, and behaviorally stuck. The foregoing examples of these four aspects of listening don't operate in a fragmented or mechanical way, but are fluid and elastic. Listening also operates when attempting to find support, consider safety issues, generate alternatives, and make plans

Taking Action

The acting side of the eight step model is still about listening, but it is indeed about taking action to diffuse the crisis. Students ask us, "Well, when do I stop listening and start acting?" Our answer to that is "You don't!" Like assessment, listening occurs throughout the model. However, when we move over to the acting side of the model, listening moves from an information-gathering activity to a mobilization activity. While our ideal ending point is that students regain their precrisis mobility and equilibrium and the intervener assumes a nondirective operating mode, for the most part the acting side is going to involve the intervener working in a collaborative and sometimes directive mode.

Thus, the acting side of the model still contains restatement and summary clarification, accurate reflective listening, open-ended questions, and owning statements, along with continuing attention to the student's safety. However, in acting, the crisis intervener keeps the focus right on the central core of the student's current concerns and relentlessly works toward paving the way for the student's forward movement from the immediate crisis toward safer and more productive action. The intervener's techniques are geared toward helping the student become aware of and pursue immediate short-term goals. The intervener digresses into external events, past events, the mother and sister, the ex-boyfriend, and background information only when they have a bearing on what is going to be done in the next 24 hours to get the crisis in Chandra's life stabilized. The major focus on acting will be to utilize all the resources the intervener can bring to bear—the student's internal coping mechanisms, external support systems, and the intervener's own arsenal of stabilization techniques—to stop the student's out-of-control behavior and then start her moving in a positive direction. The long-term issues Chandra has with her mother and sister, whether her love life will get better, and what kind of reconstructive surgery needs to be done to her self-concept have no bearing here. The intervener's job, pure and simple, is to get this person up on her feet and moving! And if she is not able to do that, the intervener will need to take over.

So after having said all of this stuff on how to do crisis intervention with emotionally unstable individuals, the question becomes "What cha gonna do when they come for you?" Here are a five tips to send you out the door.

1. *Being role free.* The crisis intervener is genuine and is congruent in both experiencing and communicating thoughts and feelings (Egan, 1975, p. 91). We said it before, and we say it again. You aren't us! Learn this stuff and be yourself!

2. *Opening a bit of oneself up.* When it is appropriate to the situation, you may engage in self-disclosure, allowing others to know you through anecdotes and

expression of your own feelings and thoughts (Egan, 1975, p. 94). But be careful! This is not about you and your crises. You life story is not needed, but at times, sharing yourself puts a very human touch on the situation and creates a bond.

3. *Being nondefensive.* Crisis interveners who behave nondefensively have an excellent understanding of their strengths and weaknesses. Thus, they can be open to negative, even hostile student expressions without feeling attacked or defensive. The crisis intervener who is genuine understands such negative expressions as saying more about the student than about the intervener and tries to facilitate exploration of such comments rather than defend against them (Egan, 1975, pp. 92–93).

4. *Being consistent.* Crisis interveners who are genuine have few discrepancies between what they think, feel, and say and their actual behavior. Crisis interveners who are consistent do not think one thing and tell a student another or engage in behavior that is contrary to their values (Egan, 1975, pp. 93–94). Being inconsistent generally happens when the interventionist is caught in a bind or seems to be at a roadblock with no options. It is easy, then, to lie in regard to expediency. There is a famous line about inmates in an insane asylum that goes something like this: "They may be crazy, but they aren't stupid, and they have long memories." You may get away with lying once, but you won't get away with it a second time.

5. *Being spontaneous.* There is no formula for this business. The crisis intervener communicates freely, using the techniques in here as they fit the particular person in the particular situation at the particular time (Egan, 1975, p. 92). Some of the very best crisis interveners we know are police officers, not PhDs. They take the skills in this chapter and put them together with their street smarts and use them far better than we can. You have street smarts, too, in regard to your student population, so trust yourself, be spontaneous, and you will do the right thing.

The dialogue aptly depicts the crisis intervener owning feelings, using "I" statements, and focusing on the student's emergent concerns rather than allowing the focus to shift to tangential matters or defensive responses. Such statements allow the crisis intervener to retain integrity, squarely face student hostility without becoming hostile in turn, and model a safe and trusting atmosphere in which students see that it is all right for them to demonstrate angry feelings and still be accepted by the crisis intervener. At the same time, the crisis intervener stands by and is consistent with a therapeutic approach without being intimidated by or defensive with the student. The crisis intervener above all has the self-confidence and congruence to make such statements in a way that is facilitative for the student.

Communicating Acceptance

The crisis intervener who interacts with complete acceptance of students exudes an unconditional positive regard for students that transcends their qualities, beliefs, problems, situations, or crises. The intervener is able to prize, care for, and fully accept students, even if they are doing things, saying things, and experiencing situations that are contrary to the intervener's beliefs and values. The intervener is able to put aside student needs, values, and desires and does not require students to make specific responses as a condition of full acceptance.

Even when students persist in projecting negative evaluations onto the crisis intervener, the intervener doesn't have to buy into such notions. If the intervener can truly feel an unconditional positive regard for the student, there will be no need for denial, defensiveness, or diversion from the reality of the intervener's true feelings. If the intervener demonstrates caring and prizing the student, regardless of the student's situation or status, the student will be more likely to accept and prize himself or herself. That is the essence of acceptance in crisis intervention.

ACTING IN CRISIS INTERVENTION: STAYING SAFE

People in the human services business never think they will be assaulted. The facts are, though, that these caring and concerned human service workers who exude the milk of human kindness are not always appreciated by their clientele. Approximately 20% to 50% are assaulted, depending on the type of worker and where it is happening around the world (Guterman, Jayaratme, & Bargal, 1996; Leadbetter, 1993; MacDonald & Sirotich, 2001; Newhill, 2003, pp. 35–54). But you aren't a counselor, social worker, or psychologist and don't deal with food stamp fraud, welfare cheaters, dope addicts, or juvenile delinquents, so what's this mean to you? You don't work with this type of person, but if you deal with college students face-to-face, you most definitely are in the human services business.

Why are you now more at risk? Answers are not easily found, but increased substance abuse (Occupational Safety and Health Administration, 2003), increased psychopathology on campus (Benton, Robertson, Tseng, Newton, & Benton, 2003; Bishop, 2006; Erdur-Baker, Aberson, Barrow, & Draper, 2006), modeling of violent behavior through video games and television (Grossman, 1995), and gangs (Yes! If they are not on your campus you probably go to the University of Antarctica) (Occupational Safety and Health Administration, 2003) are all contributing factors.

The Rehabilitation Act of 1973 and the Americans with Disabilities Act of 1990 made college campuses more receptive and accommodating to people with existing mental illnesses. People who are diagnosed with a mental illness are not especially prone to violence. However, for some disorders, such as paranoid schizophrenia, the potential for their symptoms to turn lethal is high, particularly when they are not taking their medications. College campuses are also prone to attract their fair share of people with problems, including returning veterans with PTSD, students experiencing transient mental health issues, and students who were sexually abused in their youth and now manifest borderline personality disorders. Given the right circumstances and additionally fueled with alcohol, many of these individuals can become homicidal, suicidal, or both (Miller, 2006, pp. 51–59). The problems of dealing with this population have become so persistent and endemic that the *Journal of College Counseling* devoted its Fall 2005 issue to the topic of severe and persistent mental illness on college campuses (Beamish, 2005).

While campuses are still pretty safe places to be, they are not reflective, bucolic, pastoral, ivy-covered halls. Indeed, the recalcitrance of colleges and universities to report campus crime for fear of bad publicity was in large part responsible for the Crime Awareness and Campus Security Act of 1990, otherwise known as the Clery Act, and the crime statistics that colleges are required to now report tell a sobering tale of crime on college campuses. Underlining these statistics is the change from security staff on many college campuses to sworn police officers and sophisticated police departments that have all the trappings of major urban police operations. But if you are on a college campus, you are probably pretty much aware of the foregoing. So what are you, the individual, to do when you are confronted with an irate, angry, out-of-control student? You are probably getting sick to death of us telling you there is no cut-and-dried formula for most of the stuff in this book. Well, there isn't here either. But there are some basic precautions, rules of the road, and don'ts that should give you a fair chance of not ending up in the local ER.

Precautions

Following is a long grocery list of the precautions you need to take when dealing with a potentially violent person (Blair, 1991; Forster, 1994; Greenstone & Leviton, 1993; Kerr, 2009, pp. 108–109; Miller, 2003; Moran, 1984, p. 244; Newell, 2003; Piercy, 1984, p. 143; Thompson & Jenkins, 2004; Turnbull, Aitken, Black, & Patterson, 1990; Weinger, 2001, pp. 33–48; Wood & Khuri, 1984, p. 69). It would be nice if you memorized this list, but you probably won't. However, you might just want to keep it handy for your quick review when you know you are potentially going in harm's way.

1. Past violence is one of the best predictors of future violence. Don't dismiss warnings from records, family and peers, authorities, or fellow students and staff that the student is violent.
2. Bulging neck veins and agitated arm movements mean something, and it generally isn't good. Don't deny the possibility of violence when you first notice early signs of agitation in the student.
3. People who are agitated tend to have expanded personal comfort zones. What may be a normal conversational distance may be way too close. Don't engage in certain behaviors that may be interpreted as aggressive, such as staring directly into the student's eyes for extended periods of time, folding your arms or putting your hands on your hips, pointing fingers, or displaying other facial expressions and body movements that could appear threatening.
4. Don't make promises that cannot be kept. Lying to an agitated individual may get you out of a jam this time, but you and every other staff member who has to interact with the student forever after will have a serious credibility problem.

5. Don't use *why* and *what* questions that put the student on the defensive.
6. Don't allow feelings of fear, anger, or hostility to interfere with your self-control and professional understanding of a student's circumstances.
7. You are not there to win arguments. You are there to gain compliance and diffuse the situation. Don't argue, give orders, or disagree when not absolutely necessary.
8. You aren't a doormat either! Don't be placating by giving in and agreeing to all the real and imagined ills the student is suffering at the hands of the institution.
9. Condescension, satire, put-downs, or any other kinds of discounts do not belong here. Treating persons with respect and dignity allows them to save face.
10. Don't let self-talk about your own importance be acted out in an officious, know-it-all manner. A statement such as "I'm not going to say this again," which shows your supposed authority, is almost guaranteed to make the student cynical about you and test the limits by making you turn that threat into action.
11. Keep your voice tone level and even. If someone is yelling at you, the knee-jerk response is to talk even louder. Don't raise your voice, put a sharp edge on responses, or use threats to gain compliance. Keeping your voice at a low level makes the person have to listen intently to what you have to say.
12. Conversely, don't mumble, speak hesitantly, or use a tone of voice so low that the student has trouble understanding what you are saying.
13. Don't attempt to reason with any student who is under the influence of a mind-altering substance. Get law enforcement there. Blue uniforms tend to sober people up.
14. Don't assume that the student is as reasonable about things as you are. Frustration tends to underlay anger. Frustrated people are not doing very well at getting their problems solved, and by the time you make the scene they may not be reasonable at all. Telling them to be reasonable essentially conveys the message that they are anything but that.
15. Don't dismiss escalating student demands as merely attention-seeking, petulant, or narcissistic behavior. If that is happening, what is the TASSLE rating telling you?

Situational Precautions

In addition to the general precautions listed above, each situation will present issues that must be kept in mind. Some of these situational precautions seem to be common sense while others may be things you would never think of. Each are important and will help to keep you safe when responding to a crisis situation.

1. If you believe there may be violence, get backup. Have someone go with you. Don't become isolated with potentially violent students unless you have taken enough security precautions to prevent or limit a violent outburst.

2. Don't keep the student waiting or leave a potentially violent student alone with freedom to move about. If you believe that is going to be the case, get police there to monitor the student while you take care of business.

3. You are running the show. Don't allow several staff to interact simultaneously with the student in confusing multiple dialogues. Decide beforehand who's going to do the talking.

4. People love to watch fights. People also have allegiances both for and against individuals and groups. They will often accelerate the fight or get involved themselves. Don't allow a crowd to congregate as spectators to an altercation.

5. Don't allow the student to get between you and a safe exit.

6. Don't enter a room ahead of unknown persons or indeed walk into a room where there are unknown visitors. Stay behind and visually frisk them as you go into the room, and do the same before you ever go into the room. On second thought, if people are there who aren't supposed to be there, you don't feel comfortable with them, or they refuse to leave after you request them to, do not go in the room.

7. Don't remain after hours with a potentially violent student when everybody has gone home or is in bed unless proper security is available. Postpone the meeting or, if you can't do that, get a police officer.

8. Don't fail to make contingency plans for violent incidents. Take your personal safety seriously by playing "what if this happens?" scenarios in your mind and with others.

9. Remember that even if you are a floor advisor or run a residence hall, you are not on your own turf when you walk into the student's room. Stay alert from the moment you enter the room until the moment you leave the room.

10. If at all possible, go with a partner or at least have a cell phone or other means of communication to get help in a hurry.

11. Let someone in the office know where you are going and when you will be back.

12. Check out your surroundings. Move into the situation slowly and carefully, and be fully aware of what is going on in the environment around you.

13. Before knocking on a door or entering an office or dorm room, listen carefully for a few seconds for clues as to what may be going on inside. When the door is opened, position yourself on the hinged side of the door, which should give you the best view of the room, and look around carefully before entering.

14. Never stand directly in front of a door. Knock and, as the police do, stand aside, so you are not assaulted or shot through the door. If the student hesitates in opening the door, be very wary of going inside. If you are suspicious about what is going on, politely terminate the appointment and leave.

15. Consider what you are wearing from a safety viewpoint. A tie can get you strangled, and high heels are not what you need in a track meet.

16. Monitor the verbal and nonverbal behavior of all the people in the room. What are they doing, and what must you do to stabilize the situation? If there are intoxicated people present, politely postpone the appointment and leave.

17. If a verbal dispute is going on, first and foremost consider your own safety. If necessary, leave and call the campus police. If you believe you can control the situation or don't seem to have any other choice, attempt to take control as quickly as possible. Separate disputants and have them sit down. Stay calm, and make clear, concise assertive statements about what you want them to do. If that doesn't work, get their attention by making a tangential request: "Stop that! I need to use the telephone to call in." If all else fails, a police whistle gets everybody's attention.

18. Sit in a chair where you can observe what's going on. Seat yourself so you're leaning forward and can easily get out of the chair quickly! If you sense that the situation is deteriorating, leave. If the student stands up, so do you. You are at a serious disadvantage if you are assaulted while sitting.

These injunctions are not a recipe for avoiding violent confrontations, but they are general working procedures that will help the crisis intervener move adroitly with the student through the intervention stages.

STAGES OF INTERVENTION

If at all possible, manage potentially violent situations in a sequential manner. Piercy (1984, pp. 147–148) has developed a nine-stage model for intervention with potentially violent clients in a mental institution. The first six stages, with some adaptations, seem well suited to the college campus: (a) education, (b) avoidance of conflict, (c) appeasement, (d) deflection, (e) time-out, and (f) show of force.

The first five stages all rely heavily on talking instead of acting, and even the sixth uses talking as preferential to force. The agitated student clearly has a limited ability to talk and think through problems, as opposed to acting on them and giving little thought to the consequences (Tardiff, 1984, p. 52).

As we move through the six stages, we will follow Leon, an 18-year-old male resident who is being removed from the residence hall for fighting; Vincent Logan, a residence hall area coordinator; and Sergeant Michele Wright, a crisis intervention team campus police officer, as they make their way, with some starts and stops, through the model.

Stage One: Education

Students need to be educated about what is happening to them and why and how it is happening through reasoning and reassurance. That cannot be done if you are angry. Anger is your worst enemy, and you need to control it. Sticks and stones will break your bones, but words people say are like rubber and glue. They bounce off me and stick on you. One way of keeping your cool is to assume the role of the client's advocate

(Pisarick, 1981). Educating students is the first step in giving them options to chill out, simmer down, and otherwise go about their business. Leon has just appeared at the front desk of Rawls Hall with a television set and is screaming at the top of his lungs.

Leon: TV set for sale! Works great! I want a quarter for it, who'll give me a quarter. All I want is a stinkin' quarter! (The front desk attendant has called Vincent Logan, the residence hall area coordinator, who now enters the scene.)

RHP: My name's Vincent Logan, I'm on the residence hall staff for Rawls. You're Leon Strobensky, right? I believe we have met before. Hi! I understand you're trying to sell a TV for a quarter. Would you like to tell me what's going on?

Leon: Yep. We did meet. You were on the disciplinary committee that kicked me out of here. Can't use the set where I am going in that pig sty dorm. No cable. TV for a quarter!

RHP: Yes, you got into it with your roomie three different times. The last time, he had to go over to the infirmary and get patched up with some stitches. It looks like you're pretty upset right now. I'd like to know what got you to this point today.

Leon: I have to move clear across campus away from all my friends, my classes, everything. It's not fair.

RHP: You certainly have the right to think so, but you couldn't contain yourself with your roomie, you even indicated you picked most of the fights, so you got moved. The option was to move you over to the other side of campus. That wasn't the only option. You could have been moved completely off campus. Just like you have an option now. I understand you're upset and feel this is really unfair, but that was the decision of the disciplinary committee, so you are pretty much bound by it until you can prove you can get along with other folks.

Leon: Screw you, that's no option at all.

RHP: Maybe you don't think so, but you need to think about another option you have, and that is going peaceably and making the move without creating a disturbance and scaring people. People get scared, and even though you don't mean to scare them, that means the police come and you not only don't go back to your room, you don't get your stuff moved into your new room, and it just stays in the hallway, which I know you don't want. Do you need some help in getting moved? If you do, we can get you moved, and you can settle in over at Dunning and start to check out some of the folks and things going on over there, as opposed to have your stuff sitting here in the hallway and spending until midnight getting it moved.

Owning statements that indicate concern over the client's welfare are a good opening. Open-ended questions and some reflection of the client's feelings are crucial to conveying that the client's feelings count for something and are being taken into consideration (Turnbull et al., 1990), but the intervener doesn't allow the emotional catharsis to continue and instead moves to a behavioral, problem-solving mode about moving furniture. The intervener uses the technique of providing options (Newhill, 2003, p. 158; Turnbull et al., 1990) and attempts to deflect Leon away from his escalating emotions to constructive behavior. The student has to make a judgment between getting some help for the troublesome move or doing it himself and running the risk of having further problems if he chooses to continue to escalate.

The intervener next puts the present situation in what Thompson calls "context" (Thompson & Jenkins, 2004, pp. 96–97). Context has to do with reasons, policies, and procedures tied together with the request for compliance. While the last thing Leon may care about are university policies, most people do lots better when they are given reasons for what you are saying; they tend to be more compliant. This opening statement acknowledges the student's feelings but also conveys expectations that he can control himself. By doing so, Vincent sets the tone for behavioral expectations in a clear, caring, firm way (Steveson, 1991). He is using some of Glasser's reality-choice techniques (1998) by letting the student have some choice in the situation, but he is also clearly outlining what the consequences of those choices are. To that end, the student has to make a value judgment about what is best for his health and well-being. Option therapy, in simple terms, says, "You always have a choice" (Slatkin, 2005, p. 64). You need to start deciding as soon as possible who's going to have control over those choices, you or somebody who may make life unpleasant for you (Thompson & Jenkins, 2004, p. 98).

> **RHP:** I hear real clearly that you don't like this and feel it is unfair. Is that right?
> **Leon:** Yes.
> **RHP:** You'd like to get back to Rawls Hall, then, to finish out your college?
> **Leon**: Well, yeah, sure!
> **RHP:** So you'd want something good to come out of this, even if it isn't so great right now?
> **Leon:** Of course.
> **RHP:** Well, if we can get you moved peaceably then, that looks good and says you took your medicine and would be positive regarding the possibility of moving back here next year.

The intervener asks a series of simple questions that will almost surely be answered in the affirmative. By chaining these affirmatives, he sets the student up to respond to the big question (Slatkin, 2005, p. 63). The big question is couched in what Slatkin (2005, p. 58) calls a future conditional strategy by getting a concession now with the possibility of a large reward in the future

> **RHP:** So given all those positive responses I just heard, it sounds like if you go ahead and make the move now, that is the first big step in showing you belong

back in Rawls, so do you want me to get three or four RAs and get your stuff moved now?

The intervener makes a quick judgment to be directive or nondirective. He is directive only to the extent of setting boundaries equivalent to how out of control the student is. His other mission is to establish rapport and credibility with the client and problem solve. He does this by accepting and acknowledging the student where he is and in turn stating the same from the university's perspective. The human service worker's responses are from Glasser's reality therapy (1965) and focus on the issues of becoming involved, looking at alternatives, making value judgments, accepting no excuses, and assuming responsibility and consequences for one's actions.

Stage Two: Avoidance of Conflict

Conflict and confrontation are avoided whenever possible. That does not mean you are a wimp to be run over by being unsure of yourself and stumbling over your words because that will give a bully a green light to run rampant over you (Misino, 2004, p. 112). Matching threat for threat means you will probably go right past the other stages here to a show of force (Dubin, 1981). If the student is fast approaching a point of no return, let him or her ventilate feelings (Slatkin, 2005, p. 64). Although shouting, cursing, and yelling are not pleasant, they are better than hand-to-hand combat. The judgment you have to make is whether they are ventilating and getting the anger out of their system or are they escalating?

> **Leon:** (Starts to escalate again.) Okay, I got a 94 Mustang out there. I'll take 25 bucks for it because I'll have to park it a mile away on the south lot, where'll it probably get stolen, thanks to the frickin' disciplinary committee. Anyone wanna put their money where their mouth is? (Starts to roll his sleeves up and clench his fists.)
>
> **RHP:** I am not going to get into that debate with you, Leon. It's a no-winner for everybody. I would really like to help you get your mind wrapped around this and make the best of it. If you can't do that, I am going to stop talking, and you can sort this out the best you can. If you want to come in my office and sit down, have a cold drink, and chill out. I can do that. If not, then it becomes a police matter. That's not a threat; that's just how it is. Then we are out of it, and it is between you and the police.

If the student retains some semblance of control, a time-out may be the best way of defusing the anger. If not, a show of force will be necessary.

For those students who will not calm down, the next step for the intervener is to make it very clear that violent behavior, by anybody, is unacceptable, and then to indicate what the person's choices and consequences will become if the behavior persists

(Kinney, 1995, p. 49; Wood & Khuri, 1984, pp. 67–68). Those words should be in the form of a plain and simple assertion statement, as the RHP just did in the dialogue, and not in a threatening manner.

Stage Three: Appeasement

Appeasement is probably most appropriate in emergency situations in which the worker has little basis to judge the client's aggressiveness and violence and is unable to obtain immediate assistance. Appeasement is not applicable in a number of settings under ordinary circumstances, but if you do not know with whom you are dealing, appeasement is far better than a trip to the emergency room. In this instance, a review of the scenario can be done later by a threat assessment team to determine what, if any, further action should be taken.

Appeasement can be attempted if the client's demands are simple and reasonable, even if those demands are made in a belligerent manner. Early on, it is better to grant demands and to defer until later the worry about what lessons need to be taught (Piercy, 1984, p. 148). This approach may be difficult for some interventionists to accept, because it is based on the idea that there is no winner or loser in a potentially violent confrontation between an agitated student and the institution (Moran, 1984, p. 234).

The crisis intervener meets this demand because it is easily done and does not seriously conflict with institutional rules. There may be a debriefing afterward with other workers or with a threat assessment team if the student has gotten a high triage rating. But the message should clearly be an understanding among all workers that in emergencies, judgment calls may bend the rules a bit to stay safe and give the intervener time to get help.

Stage Four: Deflection

Deflection of angry feelings is attempted by shifting to less threatening topics. The intervener can deflect the student's anger by redirecting or offering a second best that partially meets the student's needs and partially satisfies him or her. This may be done in a variety of ways. Asking the student to take a physically less threatening position shifts the focus away from agitated motor activity to problem solving (Wood & Khuri, 1984, p. 68).

> **RHP:** I wonder if we could go over to my office to have a soda and talk about how you might get back here?

The intervener literally and figuratively gets the student off his feet and in a less-threatening operating mode by offering him something to drink while sitting and talking. Put together, that sets the stage for a far calmer atmosphere than verbally duking it out in the main entrance of the residence hall (Epstein & Carter, 1988). The intervener may also use some imagery to reframe how the student wishes to look and get out of the situation with some honor and dignity (Slatkin, 2005, p. 65)

RHP: I can see you have a lot of pride in what you do, and how you stand up for yourself, so I want you to imagine walking out of here with a good deal of pride on your own terms, rather than being hauled out of here by the cops.

Stage Five: Time-Out

When students cannot contend with the emotion of the moment, they are asked to go to a reduced-stimulus environment to be alone and think things out. Remember, time-out is not punishment, but a chance to take a breather, think clearly, and possibly make an alternative choice of action.

Stage Six: Show of Force

If the student is unable to proceed to time-out or is otherwise noncompliant or acting out, then a show of force is needed (Piercy, 1984, p. 148). If the student is already agitated enough to warn the crisis interveners that help may be warranted, the interview should be carried out in an open hallway or large meeting room, where the participants are in plain view of other staff members and the student can be restrained easily (Viner, 1982). The show of force indicates that any display of violence or threat of violence will not be tolerated, and it often helps disorganized students regain control of themselves (Wood & Khuri, 1984, p. 68). If this stage is reached, the potential for violence is high, and the worker should not attempt to deal with the student alone. Either by paging for help through an emergency code or by having assistance readily available, the worker needs to be able to summon enough help to demonstrate that compliance is now required.

However, there are times when, through no fault of the intervener, potentially violent situations occur when the worker is alone and not immediately able to call for assistance. The following 13 procedures may keep the intervener out of harm's way (Chavez, 2003; Epstein & Carter, 1988; Moran, 1984, pp. 238–248; Morrison, 1993, pp. 79–100; Thackrey, 1987; Turnbull et al., 1990).

1. *Stay calm and relaxed.* Tensing muscles and agitated movement only fuel the situation and cause the student to expect that something bad is about to happen. Relaxation techniques such as simple deep breathing are extremely helpful, allowing you to stay loose, anticipate student responses, and move quickly.
2. *Practice positive self-talk.* Even in the worst situations, running positive billboards through the mind's eye will help you keep control of the situation.
3. *Do not stare at the client.* Keep casual eye contact because the eyes of the individual will typically move to where a blow might be struck. Focus on an imaginary spot on the client's upper chest, about where the first button on a shirt would be, occasionally glancing at the eyes and other parts of the individual's body. Focusing on the centerline of the client's body will also let you avoid being faked out by extremity movements.

4. *Stay an arm's length or more away.* Make a judgment about how long the client's arms are, and stay an arm's length and a bit more away. Remember that agitated students generally have an expanded sense of personal space and feel threatened when that space is entered.

5. *Stay to the client's weak side.* Know which of the client's hands is dominant and stay to the client's weak side. Especially on males, the watch hand typically indicates the client's weak side. If you cannot determine this for sure, stay to the client's right side since most people are right-handed. In an aggressive stance, a person invariably places the foot of the weak side forward. If the worker keeps to the dominant side of the assailant, any blow the student aims is likely to have less power and be a glancing one because the assailant will have to pivot to the right to get you back on his or her *left* where they have more power and can hit you more easily. Staying on the *right* means the assailant will have to take time to get in a more favorable position and will not be able to use his or her strength as an advantage.

6. *Keep your arms at your sides and your hands open.* Folded arms or hands on hips are bad for two reasons. They imply hostility or authority, and they put the worker at a distinct disadvantage because of the time it takes to unfold them and defend yourself.

7. *Assume a defensive posture.* Stand with your feet slightly spread, face-to-face with the student, but tending a bit to the student's weak side. Move your dominant leg slightly to the rear with your knee locked, ready to pivot and run. Move your other leg slightly forward of your body and bent slightly at your knee. This position will allow you the best chance to stay upright, and staying upright is the best safeguard against being hurt.

8. *Avoid cornering.* When the student is placed in an angle formed by two walls or other objects, with you directly in front of him or her, the only way out is through you.

9. *Avoid ordering.* When a student is threatening violence, attempting to order or command her or him to do something is likely to aggravate the situation further. Staying with the basic empathic listening and responding skills used throughout this book is far more likely to lead to satisfactory results.

10. *Do perceptual checks.* Ask for the student's help. If your current verbal responses are merely agitating the situation, ask the student what solutions or techniques might calm things down.

11. *Admit mistakes.* If you've made an error in judgment, admit it and make an apology. If things have gone this far, do not be afraid to lose face.

12. *Do nothing.* If doing something will make matters worse, do nothing. If the student is determined to leave and help is not immediately available, let the student go. *Never* attempt to touch a student under these circumstances without first indicating what you are about to do and getting the client's agreement for you to do so.

13. *Give validation.* In a sincere and empathic manner, acknowledge that the person has a good reason for feeling that way and let him or her leave.

The cardinal rule for all of these stages is to never, ever deprive the person of personal dignity, respect, or the ability to save face—particularly in front of one's peers (Chavez, 1999; Miller, 2006; Thompson & Jenkins, 2004).

Never Say "Never"; Never Say "Always"

Stay away from all-or-nothing, black-and-white, absolutistic statements. They box you in and don't give you a way out. When you are dealing with a highly irate individual, you want to always have options.

RULES OF THE ROAD

Okay, so you are fired up and ready to rock and roll. Much like your parents giving you final reminders before you went out the door on a date, here are a few rules of the road you need to remember, and after all this, don't forget to have fun!

Everybody's the Same, Everybody's Different

If we have heard one student bemoan his or her outcast state in regard to love's labor lost (somebody put them in the romantic Dumpster, and now they are nothing better than cafeteria waste), we have heard a cast of thousands. Thus, it is easy to say, "Been there, done that," diagnose, and prescribe a solution without ever really listening to what's going on. Because on the bottom line, it is *boring!* While depressives, schizophrenics, personality disorders, and just plain lazy students all have the same common symptoms, they do not have the same problems because of their individuality. To treat them in a cookie-cutter fashion is to say they are a thing that fits in this category, not a person. The students in front of you may be in crisis, but they will also be sensitive to how you treat them. It is that predispositioning business again. If you don't show your respect by your verbal and nonverbal responses that right now they are the most important thing in your world and their story is completely new, thrilling, and captivating, you are not doing your job, and you will be sorry.

It is politically incorrect nowadays to call a person with a mental illness a schizophrenic. Rather, we speak in terms of people-first language and say "a person with schizophrenia." Beyond the stereotyping, the real problem with labeling is that you start treating people the same humdrum way. You convey that you don't care about them as people; they are categories of things. You wouldn't like being treated that way, and they don't either. One of the major signs of burnout in the human service professions is depersonalizing students (Maslach, 1982; Maslach, Jackson, & Leiter, 1996), and that's exactly what you are doing when you see them as problems rather than people. If you do that in crisis intervention, you are likely to get yourself in more trouble than you can possibly imagine.

Redefine the Problem

Many students have complicated and multiple problems in addition to the presenting one. It is not uncommon to get deeply into examining alternatives, and during the course of discussing options and making plans, other problems emerge. Tackle one problem at a time. It may not be the most pressing problem overall, but it should be one that will allow the student to see that control can be restored and the task can be accomplished. Make sure that each problem is clearly and accurately defined from a practical, problem-solving viewpoint.

As in the case of Leon and Jeremy, the problem is someone else's. Many students define the crisis as some external person, event, or thing that has happened. They are unwilling or unable to take ownership for their part in the crisis. They adamantly believe that if the other person, event, or thing were to get fixed, everything would be wonderful. Attempting to solve the crisis of some third party (who isn't present) is useless. The focus must constantly pivot back to the students and to what the students need to do.

Monitoring Yourself

You, the intervener, must be tenacious about not letting students distance themselves from the problem by externalizing it. That is easy to say, but it is difficult to not get caught up in side issues and personalities. As the story unfolds, it is also difficult not to let your own values, beliefs, attitudes, biases, stereotypes, and self-competencies get sucked into your decision making. At all times, interveners must be fully and realistically aware of their physical and psychological limitations and personal readiness to deal objectively with the student and the crisis. Nasty, unhappy, distraught, hysterical, angry, foul-mouthed, and combative students who say bad things about your sainted mother and question your parentage make it all too easy for you to become subjective and reactive when your competencies are questioned. You must not allow that to happen. You must be ready to use the deflection techniques mentioned in the safety section of this chapter to get the monkey off your back and put it where it belongs—on the student. Literally, while you are triaging the student, you need to be triaging yourself, and if you are starting to move into the 20s on the TASSLE, you need to get backup immediately.

In both instances, the intervener stays focused on the student and does not get caught up in side issues such as intervener competency, beliefs, and attitudes. Now the intervener is ready to work on step four, examining alternatives.

Consider Alternatives

In most problem situations, the alternatives are infinite. But students in crisis (and sometimes interveners) have a limited view of the many options available. By using open-ended questions, elicit the maximum number of choices from the student. Then add your own list of possible alternatives to the student's list. For example, "I get the feeling that it might help if you could get in contact with a counselor at the Credit Counseling Bureau. How would you feel about adding that to our list?" Examining, analyzing, and listing alternatives to consider should be as collaborative as possible. The best alternatives are ones that the student truly *owns*. Take care to avoid imposing your alternatives on the student.

The alternatives on the list should be workable and realistic. They should represent the right amount of action for the student to undertake now—not too much, not too little. The student will generally express ownership of an option by words such as "I would really like to call him today." Intervener-imposed options are usually signaled by the intervener's words, such as "*You need to* go to his office and do that right away." Beware of the latter! An important part of the quest for appropriate alternatives is to explore with the student what options worked before in situations like the present one. Often the student can come up with the best choices, derived from coping mechanisms that have worked well in the past. But the stresses created by the immediate crisis may keep students from identifying the most obvious and appropriate alternatives for them. Here the crisis intervener facilitates the student's examination of alternatives.

Plan Action Steps

After developing a short, doable list of alternatives, the intervener needs to move on to step five, making plans. In crisis intervention, the intervener endeavors to assist the student in developing a short-term plan that will help the student get through the immediate crisis, as well as make the transition to long-term coping. The plan should include the student's internal coping mechanisms and sources of help in the environment. The coping mechanisms are usually brought to bear on some concrete, positive, constructive action that students can take to regain better control of their lives. Actions that initially involve some physical movement are preferred. The plan should be realistic in terms of the student's current emotional readiness and environmental supports. It may involve collaboration with the intervener until the student can function independently. The effective crisis intervener is sensitive to the need of the student to function autonomously as soon as feasible.

Use the Student's Coping Strengths

In crisis intervention, it is important not to overlook the student's own strengths and coping mechanisms. Often crisis events temporarily immobilize the individual's usual strengths and coping strategies. If they can be identified, explored, and reinstated, they may make an enormous contribution toward restoring the student's equilibrium and reassuring the student. For example, one woman had previously relieved stress by playing her piano. She told the intervener that she was no longer able to play the piano because her piano had been repossessed. The crisis intervener was able to explore with her several possible places where she could avail herself of a piano in times of stress.

Attend to Student's Immediate Needs

It is important for students in crisis to know that their immediate needs are understood and attended to by the crisis intervener. If a student is extremely lonely, attempt to arrange for the student to be with someone. The student may need to make contact with relatives, friends, former associates, or former friends. The student may need follow-up appointments with the crisis intervener or referral to another intervener, counselor, or agency. The student may simply need to be heard—to ventilate about a loss, a disappointment, or a specific hurtful event.

Get a Commitment

A vital part of crisis intervention is getting a commitment from the student to follow through on the action or actions planned. The crisis intervener should ask the student to verbally summarize the steps to be taken. This verbal summary helps the intervener understand the student's perception of both the plan and the commitment and gives the intervener an opportunity to clear up any distortions. It also provides an opportunity to establish a follow-up checkpoint with the student. The commitment step can serve as a motivational reminder to the student and also encourage and predispose the student to believe that the action steps will succeed. Without a definite and positive commitment from the student, the best of plans may fall short of the objectives worked out by the intervener and the student.

Step seven of the crisis intervention model, the commitment step, does not stand alone. It would be worth little without the foundation of the preceding steps. The actions that a student in crisis owns and commits to are derived from solid planning, which is, in turn, based on systematic examination of alternatives. The three acting steps are based on prior effective listening. All steps are carried out under the umbrella of assessing. Commitment is individually tailored to the specific student crisis situation.

Experienced crisis interveners are generally able to sense how far and how fast the student is able to act. Usually the student is encouraged to commit to as much action as feasible. If we cannot get her or him to make a giant leap forward, we'll accept one small step in a positive direction. The main idea is to facilitate some commitment that will result in the student's movement in a constructive direction.

SUMMARY

Crisis intervention from a practitioner's standpoint incorporates fundamental counseling skills into an eight-step model of systematic helping. The model focuses on facilitative listening and acting within an overarching framework of assessing. The eight-step model is an organized and fluid process of applying crisis intervention skills to the emerging feelings, concerns, and situations that students having most types of trauma might present.

The eight steps in crisis intervention serve to organize and simplify the work of the crisis intervener. The first of these steps, predispositioning, typically seeks to build a relationship that will help students regain stability and show them someone cares what happens to them. Predispositioning also has utility as far as getting the predispositional system of the university into gear by proactively providing education, information, consultation, and communication interlinks with various parties who may play a part in crisis intervention on a systemwide basis. The next three steps include the components of what is typically called *psychological first aid* but in reality is much more than that. Step two explores and defines the problem from the student's point of view. Step three ensures the student's physical and psychological safety. Step four provides support for the student in crisis. Step five examines alternatives available to the student. Step six assists the student in developing a plan of action. Step seven helps the student make a commitment to carry out a definite and positive action plan and also provides for intervener follow-up. Step eight provides follow-up. In a closed system such as a university, follow-up has ramifications not just for the student's welfare but also for the university as a whole.

Assessment of the student and the crisis situation is the keystone for initiating intervention and overarches the model. Assessment techniques include evaluating the severity of the crisis; appraising students' feeling or emoting, behaving, and thinking patterns; assessing the chronic nature and lethality of the crisis; looking into the student's background for contributing factors; and evaluating the student's resources, coping mechanisms, and support systems.

Active listening is a fundamental skill for all successful crisis intervention. Listening includes such techniques as restatement, reflection, a variety of owning or "I" statements, and open- and closed-ended questions. The genetic building blocks of all counseling may be adapted to crisis intervention. Essential components of effective listening and communication include effective attending, empathy, genuineness, and acceptance. Action skills range across nondirective, collaborative, and directive intervener strategies. These strategies may include helping the student focus or expand awareness, obtain guidance, and undergo emotional catharsis; providing support and protection; and mobilizing the student to action.

College-age young adults are high on national incidence of lethal behavior for both suicide and homicide. Because of the expressive nature and emotional dynamics of many of these suicide types, there is a thin line between whether the individual is lethal toward self, others, or both. Thus, interveners need to be aware of the constant potential for lethal behavior and engage in safety practices that keep themselves as well as others out of danger.

REFERENCES

Adler, A. 1958. *What life should mean to you.* New York: Capricorn Books.

Aguilera, D. C. (1998). *Crisis intervention: Theory and methodology* (8th ed.). St. Louis, MO: Mosby.

Alberti, R., & Emmons, M. (2008). *Your perfect right: Assertiveness and equality in life and relationships* (9th ed.). Atascadero, CA: Impact.

Beamish, P. M. (2005). Introduction to the special section—severe and persistent mental illness on college campuses: Consideration for service provision. *Journal of College Counseling, 8,* 138–139.

Benton, S. A., Robertson, J. M., Tseng, W., Newton, F., & Benton, S. L. (2003). Changes in counseling client centered problems across 13 years. *Professional Psychology: Research and Practice, 34,* 66–72.

Bishop, J. B. (2006). College and university counseling centers: Questions is search of answers. *Journal of College Counseling, 9,* 6–19.

Blair, D. T. (1991), Assaultive behavior: Does provocation begin in the front office. *Journal of Psychosocial Nursing and Mental Health Service, 29,* 25–29.

Chavez, L. (2003). 10 things healthyorganizations do to prevent workplace violence. Occupational Hazards, *65,* 22.

Cohen, S. (2004). Social relationships and health. *American Psychologist, 59,* 676–684.

Cormier, W. H., & Cormier, L. S. (1991). *Interviewing strategies for helpers: Fundamental skills and cognitive behavioral interventions* (3rd ed.). Pacific Grove, CA: Brooks/Cole.

de Shazer, S. (1985). *Keys to solution in brief therapy.* New York: W. W. Norton.

Dinkmeyer, D., Jr., & Sperry, L. (2000). *Counseling and psychotherapy: An integrated, individual psychology approach.* Upper Saddle River, NJ: Merrill/Prentice Hall.

Dryden, W. (1984). *Rational emotive therapy: Fundamentals and innovations.* London: Croom Helm.

Dubin, W. R. (1981). Evaluating and managing the violent patient. *Annals of Emergency Medicine, 10,* 481–484.

Egan, G. (1975). *The skilled helper: A model for systematic helping and interpersonal relating.* Pacific Grove, CA: Brooks/Cole.

Egan, G. (1990). *The skilled helper: Model, skills, and methods for effective helping* (4th ed.). Pacific Grove, CA: Brooks/Cole.

Ellis, A. (1962). *Reason and emotion in psychotherapy.* Secaucus, NY: Citadel.

Epstein, M., & Carter, L. (1988). *Training manual for Headquarters staff.* Lawrence, KS: Headquarters.

Erdur-Baker, O., Aberson, C., Barrow, J., & Draper, M. (2006). Nature and severity of college psychological concerns: A comparison of clinical and nonclinical national samples. *Professional Psychology: Research and Practice, 37,* 317–323.

Forster, J. (1994). The psychiatric emergency: Heading off trouble. *Patient Care, 28,* 130.

Gilliland, B. E. (1982). *Steps in crisis counseling.* Memphis: Memphis State University, Department of Counseling and Personnel Services. [Mimeographed handout for crisis intervention courses and workshops on crisis intervention].

Gilliland, B. E., & James, R. K. (1998). *Theories and strategies in counseling and psychotherapy* (4th ed.). Boston: Allyn & Bacon.

Glasser, W. (1965). *Reality therapy: A new approach to psychiatry.* New York: Harper & Row.

Glasser, W. (1998). *Choice theory: A new psychology of personal freedom.* New York: HarperCollins.

Greenstone, J. l., & Leviton S. C. (1993). *Elements of crisis intervention: Crisis and how to respond to them.* Pacific Grove, CA: Brooks/Cole

Grossman, D. (1995). *On killing: The psychological cost of learning to kill in war and society.* Boston: Little & Brown.

Guterman, N. B., Jayaratme, S., & Bargal, R. L. (1996). Workplace violence and victimization experienced by social workers: A cross national study of Americans and Israelis. In G. R. VandenBos & E. Q. Bulatao (Eds.), *Violence on the job: Identifying the risks and developing solutions* (pp. 175–188). Washington, DC: American Psychological Association.

Hoff, L. A., Hallisey, B. J., & Hoff, M. (2009). *People in crisis: Clinical and diversity perspectives* (6th ed.). New York: Routledge.

James, R. K. (2008). *Crisis intervention strategies* (6th ed.). Belmont, CA: Brooks/Cole–Cengage.

Kerr, M. M. (2009). *School crisis prevention and intervention.* Upper Saddle River, NJ: Merrill.

Kinney, J. A. (1995). *Violence at work.* Upper Saddle River, NJ: Prentice Hall.

Leadbetter, D. (1993). Trends in assault on social work staff: The experience of one Scottish department. *British Journal of Social Work, 23,* 613–628.

MacDonald, G., & Sirotich, F. (2001). Reporting client violence, *Social Work, 46,* 107–114.

Maslach, C. (1982). Understanding burnout: Definitional issues in analyzing a complex phenomenon. In W. S. Paine (Ed.), *Job stress and burnout* (pp. 29–40). Newbury Park, CA: Sage.

Maslach, C., Jackson, S. E., & Leiter, M. P. (1996). *Maslach burnout survey–GS manual.* Palo Alto, CA: Consulting Psychologist's Press.

Memphis Police Department. (2008). *Crisis intervention team training manual.* Memphis, TN: Author.

Miller, L. (2006). *Practical police psychology: Stress management and crisis intervention for law enforcement.* Springfield, IL: Charles C Thomas.

Miller, W. R., & Rollnick, S. (2002). *Motivational interviewing: Preparing people for change.* New York: Guilford Press.

Miller, L. (2003). Law enforcement responses to violence against youth. In R. S. Moser & C. E. Franz (Eds). *Shocking violence II: Violent disaster, war, and terrorism affecting our youth* (pp. 165–195). New York: Chalrse C. Thomas.

Misino, D. J. (2004). *Negotiate and win.* New York: McGraw-Hill.

Moran, J. F. (1984). Teaching the management of violent behavior to nursing staff: A health care model. In J. T. Turner (Ed.), *Violence in the medical care setting: A survival guide* (pp. 231–250). Rockville, MD: Aspen Systems.

Morrison, J. M. (1993). Physical techniques. In P. E. Blumenreich & S. Lewis (Eds.), *Managing the violent patient: A clinician's guide* (pp. 79–100). New York: Brunner-Mazel.

Myer, R. A., & James, R. K. (2005). *Crisis intervention workbook and CD-ROM.* Belmont, CA: Thomson Brooks/Cole.

Newhill, C. E. (2003). *Client violence in social work practice: Prevention, intervention, and research.* New York: Guilford Press.

Occupational Safety and Health Administration. (2003). *Guidelines for preventing workplace violence for healthcare and social service workers.* OSHA 3148. Washington, DC: U.S. Department of Labor.

Piercy, D. (1984). Violence: The drug and alcohol patient. In J. T. Turner (Ed.), *Violence in the medical care setting: A survival guide* (pp. 123–152). Rockville, MD: Aspen Systems.

Pisarick, G. (1981, September). The violent patient. *Nursing,* pp. 63–65.

Prochaska, J. O., & DiClemente, C. C. (1982). Transtheoretical therapy: Toward a more integrative model of change. *Psychotherapy: Theory, Research, and Practice, 19,* 276–288.

Prochaska, J. O., & DiClemente, C. C. (1984). *The transtheoretical approach: Crossing the traditional boundaries of therapy.* Malabar, FL: Krieger.

Roberts, A. R. (2005). *Crisis intervention handbook: Assessment, treatment and research* (3rd ed). New York: Oxford University Press.

Rogers, C. R. (1951). *Person centered therapy: Its current practice, implications, and theory.* Boston: Houghton Mifflin.

Slaikeu, K. A. (Ed.). (1990). *Crisis intervention: A handbook for practice and research.* Boston: Allyn & Bacon.

Slatkin, A. A. (2005). *Communication in crisis and hostage negotiations.* Springfield, IL: Charles C Thomas.

Skinner, B. F. (1953). *Science and human behavior.* New York: Free Press.

Steveson, S. (1991). Heading off violence with verbal de-escalation. *Journal of Psychosocial Nursing, 29,* 7–10.

Strentz, T. (2006). *Psychological aspects of crisis negotiation.* Boca Raton, FL: CRC Press.

Tardiff, K. (1984). Violence: The psychiatric patient. In J. T. Turner (Ed.), *Violence in the medical care setting: A survival guide* (pp. 33–55). Rockville, MD: Aspen Systems.

Thackrey, M. (1987). *Therapeutics for aggression.* New York: Human Sciences Press.

Thompson, G. J., & Jenkins, J. B. (2004). *Verbal judo: The art of gentle persuasion.* New York, NY: Harper-Collins.

Thompson, G. J., & Walker, G. A. (2007). *The verbal judo way of leadership*. Flushing, NY: Looseleaf Law Publications.

Turnbull, J., Aitken, I., Black, L., & Patterson, B. (1990). Turn it around: Short-term management for aggression and anger. *Journal of Psychosocial Nursing and Mental Health Services, 28*, 7–13.

Viner, J. (1982). Toward more skillful handling of acutely psychotic patients. Part I: Evaluation. *Emergency Room Report, 3*, 125–130.

Weinger, S. (2001). *Security risks: Preventing client violence against social workers*. Washington, DC: NASW Press.

Wolpe, J. (1990). *The practice of behavior therapy* (4th ed.). New York: Pergamon.

Wood, K. A., & Khuri, R. (1984). Violence: The emergency room patient. In J. T. Turner (Ed.), *Violence in the medical care setting: A survival guide* (pp. 57–84). Rockville, MD: Aspen Systems.

Zdziarski, E. L., Dunkel, W. D., & Rollo, J. M. (2007). *Campus crisis management: A comprehensive guide to planning, prevention, response, and recovery.* San Francisco: John Wiley & Sons.

11

One Day at a Time: Survivorship in the Aftermath

Survivorship is a concept that encompasses reactions of a recognizable group experiencing a loss (Williams, Zinner, & Ellis, 1999). These authors believe survivorship is an opportunity to build a new sense of community that administrators and crisis management teams (CMTs) can use to create a new sense of resourcefulness. The focus of this chapter is to outline ways of taking care of survivors after the crisis. The chapter begins with a brief discussion of characteristics of survivorship. This discussion provides a framework for the remainder of the chapter. Following this section, we discuss the value and role of rituals and memorials as survivors attempt to make meaning of the crisis. Throughout the discussion, we provide some practical questions regarding procedural matters for your campus. We close the chapter with a discussion of approaches that can be used to facilitate survivor recovery.

No one is born knowing how to grieve or mourn a loss. You learn what to feel, how to behave, and what to think about a loss from someone else. These lessons come from a person's culture. Culture, in its broadest meaning (heritage, gender, sexual orientation, race, religious affiliations, and so on), plays a large part in the way someone experiences a loss (James, 2008). University campuses are an amalgamation of different cultures, so expressions of grief and mourning following a loss due to a crisis will take many shapes and forms. Therefore, summarizing the experience into a set of stages or group of tasks is not applicable. We simply cannot account for all the variations of the ways people experience loss. The result is that coordination of the various manifestations of grief and mourning will be a challenge to even the most senior and experienced administrators.

It is important to remember that loss is not limited to a death. Loss can include such things as the damaging beyond repair of a favorite picture or other object. The destruction of a building or other facility on your campus may also cause grief and mourning for some. The destruction of research data can also result in some people having a grief reaction. In summary, the meaning of a loss depends on the survivors' valuing of the object (person, place, thing, idea, and so on) (Williams et al., 1999). Physical proximity, experience, the availability of support, and any changes in day-to-day functioning caused by a loss also play a part in survivorship (Myer & Moore, 2006). The intermixture of these variables directly influences both individuals and groups of people as they try to recover from a loss or other crisis.

SURVIVORSHIP

The experience of survivorship for individuals and groups ranges from negative char-acteristics (Diaz, 2008) and diagnosable mental health issues (Crane & Clements, 2005) to some people emerging with a more positive view of life (e.g., Davis & Nolen-Hoeksema, 2001; Tedeschi & Calhoun, 1995; Watts & Wilson, 1999) or a stron-ger sense of community (Williams et al., 1999). Some individuals and groups may even have little to no reaction to the crisis or loss. These people may simply want to move on as if nothing had happened. Prediction of where individuals or groups will fall on this continuum after a tragic event is truly a guessing game (McGowan, 2006). However, the vast majority will not end up at the extremes of the continuum, but rather some-place in the middle. These survivors can be overlooked as they don't seem to require services immediately, although what may happen in the form of complications from not grieving down the road may be another story indeed. Administrators and CMTs must be prepared to support everyone on this continuum, not just the who that de-velop diagnosable mental illnesses.

Recognition that survivorship is a process rather than an event is critical for re-covery. Each day in this process brings new challenges that will test the patience and steadfastness of administrators and CMTs. You will be tempted at some point, and ev-eryone is, to wonder, "Why don't these people just get on with their lives?" You might also ask, "The crisis is over, so what keeps them from moving on?" or "Why do they keep bringing up these little insignificant problems?" All the time you may be think-ing, "After all, I got over it with no problem." The answer to these questions is that the pace of recovery cannot be predicted, much less scheduled, for individuals (Halpern & Tramontin, 2007) or groups (Williams et al., 1999). Pressuring for closure prior to people's readiness leads to an incomplete emotional picture of the loss or crisis and results in a mixture of ineffective and effective coping (Shalev, 2000). The following section briefly outlines characteristics of survivors that are important to consider during the recovery process.

Shock

Shock is the most common characteristic of survivorship (Diaz, 2008) and a Pandora's box of psychological hornets. The shock is both emotional and social, according to Diaz. The emotional shock reverberates for up to 6 months, as people try to make meaning from the events (Carver, Scheier, & Weintraub, 1989). Groups can even take longer, as they struggle to regain a place and identity on the campus (Williams et al., 1999). Individuals may feel the need to do something out of anger or fear. They might also have difficulty expressing pain and suffer from health problems (Miller, 2002). Many people feel they have lost control of their lives as they struggle to make sense of the events (Halpern & Tramontin, 2007). Survivors may overidentify with the victims (Miller, 2002) and develop survivor's guilt (O'Connor, Berry, Weiss,

Schweitzer, & Sevier, 2000; Spiegel, 1981). For most, none of these issues rises to the level of diagnosable mental disorder (e.g., Stuhlmiller & Dunning, 2000; Ursano, Fullerton, Vance, & Wang, 2000). The shock from a crisis may cause a group to feel humiliated (Diaz, 2008), become overprotective (van der Veer, 1998), or possibly feel shame for not being able to help (Urlic & Simunkovic, 2009). Groups may become dysfunctional, as dynamics within the group become exaggerated (van der Veer, 1998) and communication is disrupted. Overcompensation might occur as the group tries to reestablish a sense of homeostasis. Recognition of these factors associated with survivorship helps administrators and CMTs better understand individuals' and groups' current state and needs.

Displacement

The social aspect of shock is seen through the loss of community by the displacement of groups from familiar surroundings or identity (Diaz, 2008). The experience of a loss of belonging is not unusual (van der Veer, 1998). Myer, Moore, and Hughes (2003) used the idea of refugees to understand the social basis of shock. Take, for example, the faculty members at Central University who were displaced from their offices and labs. Faculty members were moved to a different building for not only offices but also labs and classroom space. Their identity as a department was swallowed by these moves. They no longer had an office to call home. The new offices were not only in a different building but now shared. The classroom space and in some cases lab areas were at a high school. The department these faculty members were moved to also experienced a loss of community by having to double up in offices. The teachers at the high school felt their space was invaded and they could no longer call it their own. An important aspect of recovery is the redevelopment of community (Diaz, 2008). Creating opportunities to reestablish connectiveness is important for survivors. Group activities that facilitate social interaction can go a long way toward restoration of community (Diaz, 2008). Social activities, such as concerts and parties, can be invaluable in helping restore a sense of belonging to the community.

Hierarchy of Suffering

Another aspect of a negative experience following a crisis is the development of a hierarchy of suffering (Bolton, 1999; van der Veer, 1998). This characteristic is seen in both individuals and groups. A hierarchy of suffering means that some people have more of a "right" to be traumatized than others. For example, students who were not outside walking around campus or close to the science building that exploded at Central University might feel they do not have a right to be traumatized. Faculty members who were working off campus that day might also question their right to feel stressed. At the same time, those who were directly involved might feel they have more of a right to be traumatized than anyone else. They may even react with disdain for anyone who seems as upset as they are. This belief cannot be further from the truth. Everyone has a right to grieve and mourn following a loss (Bolton, 1999). Leadership needs to acknowledge this right and support the expression of survivorship. Acknowledgment of being a survivor helps to create a connection with others (Miller, 2002). By making this announcement, administrators and CMTs can cut through the negative valence of being a survivor. This support signals "we're with you" and can be a powerful component of the healing process (Zinner, 1999). Survivors should also be willing to acknowledge their status as survivors. Statements of this nature can also be a catalyst in restoring the sense of community and identity that was lost because of the crisis. Reestablishment of the feeling of community is considered an important step in recovery (Diaz, 2008). Figure 11.1 is the opening statement made by President Tolliver at Central University to an assembly 4 hours following the explosion. In the statement, President Tolliver recognizes the rights of survivors to have their feelings, as well as pointing them to the places where they can receive support.

Participation

The desire to participate in the overall recovery varies from person to person and group to group. Some survivors and survivor groups want to be involved; others may not. However, all survivors should be given the opportunity to participate in whatever way they feel comfortable. At Central University, this process might include staffing the Compassion Center in the field house, escorting volunteers around campus, or baking cookies. Being creative is important when allowing survivors to be involved. To participate, survivors have to be informed of the facts about how a crisis is being handled (Zinner, 1999). For example, in President Tolliver's opening statement (see Figure 11.1), survivors from Central University were pointed toward the Compassion Center as a place to obtain information about the status of people who were injured. As the recovery process develops, other means of communication will also be needed to get information to survivors. These methods might include letters, e-mail, and phone calls to communicate information. Zinner (1999) also believes it is important for groups to be involved in helping other groups as well as individuals within the group. Support can come in many forms, including sending cards, attending memorial services, and visiting the injured in hospitals to allow families to rest or get something to eat. Avoid the temptation to be overprotective and spare survivors the details. Obviously, timing is important in sharing information. You do not want to provide the gory details to someone who is not ready to hear them. The advantage of being informed is that it allows survivors to help in the identification of problems and solutions (Diaz, 2008). Diaz believes that engaging all segments of the affected population in solution-focused activities strengthens community networks and creates an ownership for maintaining a higher quality of life.

A few hours ago a tragedy struck our campus larger than anything we have ever experienced. At this time we know 7 people died and many more were injured. The information is incomplete, and no one knows the exact numbers at this time. We fear the numbers will increase as we search through the rubble of what used to be the science building. Many students, staff, and faculty members joined in the efforts to provide help to anyone who was hurt by the explosion. Calls are coming in from over the entire region with people wanting to know to what they can do. I have had calls from the presidents of other universities pledging support to help in these sad times. Two words—**thank you**—thank you for the support, I am sure we will need this in the coming hours, days, and weeks. The Crisis Management Team is working to start guide the assistance and support to the places where it is needed and to begin the process of recovering.

Right now I want to talk to the survivors. First I want to express my sympathy and the university's sympathy to the family and friends who have lost loved ones. Words cannot express the sadness I feel. Let's take a moment of silence to honor and respect the lives that were lost in the explosion—

I want to also say that you, the survivors, will experience many feelings in the next few days and even weeks to come. Anger, fear, guilt, sadness may be felt by some. Some of you might feel the need to renew your spiritual life or to get closer to family and friends. And some of you may not have strong feelings one way or the other. Regardless of whether you were physically close to the science building or someone; the feelings you have are yours. Not everyone will share nor understand what you are feeling. I ask that you respect those people around you. Accept their feelings, their grief as I do yours.

We have created a compassion center at the field house. Signs are being posted to guide you to the compassion center. We have telephones available, and you can also get current information about the status of the injured. Food and water are available. We request the reporter and other media personnel do not attempt to enter the compassion center. The compassion center is exclusively for survivors. Please honor this request.

Today is a sad day. Our sympathy and support goes out to all survivors.

Figure 11.1   President Tolliver's Opening Statement

REMEMBRANCE SERVICES

Remembrance services are quite common after a crisis. These services provide an opportunity for survivors to participate in rituals that can be helpful in the recovery process. Rituals can be steeped in cultural practices or may be an expression of current pop culture. Although rituals are shrouded in religious connotation, the practice of a ritual is not necessarily a religious act (Wyrostok, 1995). Common rituals that are not necessarily religious include placing flowers at the location of the crisis or loss, sending cards, flying a flag at half-mast, singing songs of remembrance that might be religious or secular, participating in a silent walk around campus, lighting candles, wearing armbands to honor someone who has died, and releasing balloons. Sometimes rituals are created (Witzum & Malkinson, 1999), such as reading the names of the people killed at the World Trade Center every year on 9/11. Rituals are a vital practice that can be used to facilitate health and harmony (Wyrostok, 1995) and promote community connectivity (Zinner & Williams, 1999). Finding ways to create a renewed sense of being connected following a crisis, especially one involving significant losses, is critical (Diaz, 2008).

Rando (1985, p. 336) defines a *ritual* as "a specific behavior or activity which gives symbolic expression to certain feelings and thoughts of the actor(s) individually or as a group. It may be a habitually repetitive behavior or a one-time occurrence." This expression is a tangible experience to relieve discomfort and give survivors a break from routine daily activities (Wyrostok, 1995). According to Wyrostok, this break can jar a system, causing a shift into a new mode of interacting. An example of a repetitive behavior that can be ritualistic is an athletic team wearing black armbands on their uniforms throughout the season. Another ongoing ritual is the playing of "God Bless America" on Sundays at professional baseball games in respect of the lives lost as a result of the terrorist attacks of 9/11.

Allowing survivors to participate in traditional or creative leave-taking ceremonies helps to restore and mobilize a community (Williams et al., 1999). A remembrance service demonstrates a concrete expression of concern and support to families of victims and those most directly affected by a crisis. Services are used to pay respect to the deaths as well as other losses, celebrate the survivors, and highlight resiliency, all of which influence the recovery process (Zinner & Williams, 1999). A remembrance service may be less overwhelming or threatening than ongoing rituals. Survivors may feel more willing to risk the expression of intense emotion for a specified, limited time rather than reexperiencing intense emotion over a long period of time with no end in sight (Wyrostok, 1995).

Remembrance services can be planned and unplanned. While it may seem obvious at first blush that a remembrance service is needed whenever a tragic death or crisis event takes place, making that decision is not always so cut-and-dried. Situations do occur when you may not want to conduct a formal remembrance service (Kerr, 2009). Suicide is a leading example. Extreme caution must be used if a service is conducted in these situations. Anything that glamorizes a suicide could lead to others wanting to and actually committing suicide (Kirk, 1993). Another example is a student tragically dying because of a drug overdose or due to criminal activity. Although these students may be well liked, holding a remembrance service may venerate the act and unwittingly encourage others to follow suit. Policies that provide a course of action in these circumstances can avoid the need to make quick on-the-spot decisions.

Planned Services

Planned services are those that the university sanctions and plans. These services are well thought out and resemble traditional services. Being prepared for a great outpouring of emotions is recommended. The preparation should include having in attendance mental health professionals who are trained in crisis intervention and grief work; enough seating, which may involve several venues; a quiet place to take anyone experiencing acute and uncontrolled emotions; and medical personnel available to assist anyone who may have a physical response (e.g., stroke, heart attack). Guidelines for structuring these services are very important and differ from school to school, depending on policies set by the school. A primary consideration for planning these services is religion. Public universities may want to avoid religious expression; private universities may not have the same restrictions with respect to religion in a remembrance service. However, since many cultures (and religious belief systems) are represented on a campus, policies for these services are needed. An example is the death of a Muslim student from a Middle Eastern background attending a university affiliated with a Christian denomination. A remembrance service that is based on Western culture and Christian in nature might offend other students and the family of the student. To avoid missteps, policies should outline procedures for developing and carrying out services that respect the diversity on your campus.

Unplanned Remembrances

Unplanned remembrances are very common (Kerr, 2009). These are often spontaneous and initiated by students. Preparing for them is very difficult if not impossible. A real concern is the safety of everyone who participates. For example, if the service involves a march down a street, traffic can be a problem. Developing policies and procedures for handling these situations is very important. Preventing a gathering of this type can be seen as cold, uncaring, and heartless, but if a student gets run over while placing flowers on the roadside of a busy interstate, the university will be seen as not vigilant or concerned about student safety. If someone is injured as a result of permitting such a demonstration, attention will center on how the university did not provide a safe place and does not care. Clearly communicating the guidelines for these demonstrations is very important to avoid misunderstandings.

Diversity Issues

Survivors need to feel empowered through remembrance services (Halpern & Tramontin, 2007). The rituals used in the service should reflect the diversity on the university campus and comfort survivors (Griffin, 2007). In addition, the service should be structured to communicate a belief of involvement of the survivors in the recovery process (Halpern & Tramontin, 2007). Yet no matter how much planning takes place, some individual or group may be offended by some aspect of the service or by something that was not included. Using established policies and procedures to guide the development of programs for remembrance services can minimize the chances that someone may be offended. These policies should outline the process for organizing remembrance services with respect to creating the content of a program. Issues such as music, readings, and speakers must all be considered. We recommend that families of victims be consulted in developing a program. Yet caution must be used to avoid statements that are not respectful of a diverse population. Again, policy can help militate against such pronouncements. The following excerpt from a CMT meeting at Central University portrays this situation. In this example, the CMT members debate the appropriateness of allowing a special interest group to participate in the official service or remembrance that is to be held 2 weeks following the explosion.

D day + 9 days, 3:30 p.m., 30 minutes into the meeting to finalize the program for the remembrance service. Basement of field house.

EMP Director Mathews: Okay, whether we want to or not, we have to figure out what we are going to do about the request from—what is the name of the group?
Interim Media Relations Director Lee: (shrugs) The Second Life Gospel Church.
EMP Director Mathews: Okay. Who wants to say anything?
Acting Provost Richardson: My understanding is that two of the people who died in the explosion and several others who were injured attend this church.
Interim Media Relations Director Lee: I almost forgot, this morning we got a request from a community group wanting to have a part in the service. I was told the group represents gay, lesbian, and transgender individuals. It seems one of the people killed was on the board of directors of this group.
Director of Residence Life Shelby: I have heard of this group; it is pretty big.
EMP Director Mathews: Focus, people, we have to sort through this. We have to be careful regardless of what we decide.
Director of Residence Life Shelby: If we let one group participate, we have to let them all.
Director of Facilities Kelly: What is the worst that can happen?
Police Chief Smith: Let's see, fights, protests . . .
Acting Provost Richardson: (interrupts) Mostly, we don't want them saying things to offend someone. But we have to be careful about responding to them. Chon, what do you think?
Interim Media Relations Director Lee: Yes, being careful is important. We have to make sure we respect their views and desire to participate. We cannot just tell them no. What kind of guidelines do we have for this situation?
EMP Director Mathews: Good point, Chon. I almost forgot. The crisis management plan does have something in it about this. It pretty much says that we have the authority to plan the service and that outside groups will be allowed to participate at our discretion.
Director of the Counseling Center Holland: In other words, not much help, right?

EMP Director Mathews: Yes. We will have to address that later, but right now, what do we do?

Director of Residence Life Shelby: How about having a designated location for the members of these groups to gather but not be directly involved in the service? Is that possible?

Director of Facilities Kelly: We might be able to do that, set specific places for them to meet.

The meeting continues as the CMT uses the eight-step model (see Chapter 8) to resolve the problem of granting the requests from these groups. The final solution was that these groups, as well as others requesting to participate, would not be directly involved in the service but would be given space for members of the groups to gather and support one another.

Timing

Care should be used to ensure that the timing and location of planned events encourage participation (Griffin, 2007) and avoid conflicts with other events. Announcements should be clear and communicated as widely as possible. A factor in the timing of a remembrance service is the participation of people representing popular media, print and broadcast. The privacy and dignity of survivors must be safeguarded as much as possible. Allowing representatives from the popular media to have unfettered access to survivors can result in revictimization (Sitterle & Gurwitch, 1999). While the popular press has a right and obligation to report on the services, survivors also have rights. Policies that outline the media role during remembrance services can help avoid conflicts. These policies can be the basis for developing procedures that describe access to survivors with respect to time and location. A press kit and release can be used to communicate guidelines to the media personnel. The information in this release should be specific with respect to access to survivors, list expected behaviors, and describe consequences if the guidelines are not honored.

MEMORIALS

Building memorials is part of human nature. These symbols are a powerful part of the recovery process (Sitterle & Gurwich, 1999) because they have the capacity to evoke unconscious meanings that are not otherwise available to the conscious mind (Wyrostok, 1995).

Sanctioned Memorials

Memorials following crises on university campuses are part of the healing process (Kerr, 2009; Ursano, Fullerton, & Norwood, 1995). These sites become a tangible expression and play a part in giving meaning to the traumatic experience (Wyrostok, 1995). These expressions take many shapes and forms. A plaque on the side of a building commemorating a traumatic event might be used. A classroom or conference room might be dedicated to the memory of the individuals who suffered or died in a crisis. In some situations, an entire building may be dedicated to or named in the memory of individuals who died as the result of disaster. Other types of memorials include endowed chairs, scholarships, funded programs, and flower gardens. The type and magnitude of memorials are limited only by the imagination of those developing them.

Policies about sanctioned memorials should focus on suitability. For example, policies should deal with the appropriateness of memorials for students, staff, or faculty members dying accidentally, because of violent acts, and by suicide. Suicide deaths always cause controversy with respect to creating memorials (Kerr, 2009). In the case of a suicide, care must be taken to allow the expression of grief without glamorizing the death. Policies should also address the nature of the memorial. For example, a memorial that promotes a specific belief system (e.g., Christian, Jewish, Muslim) might not be proper for some university campuses. Policies might also address the types of memorials that are proper. Memorials that require ongoing maintenance might not be suitable unless funds are provided for preservation. These issues should be considered well before the need to make decisions. Ignoring the creation of a policy prior to a traumatic event can lead to emotionally based decisions that may not be the best choice in the long term.

Spontaneous Memorials

After a traumatic event in which lives were lost, spontaneous memorials appear from seemingly nowhere. Clark and Franzmann (2006) explain this occurrence as being the authority of grief. According to these authors, this expression seems to overshadow established authority. Usually these types of memorials are created by individuals or groups as a way to remember the accident and to show respect for those people who died (Kerr, 2009). After the Valentine Day shooting at Northern Illinois University, several memorial sites were created. At the University of Memphis, a memorial was created at the location a student athlete died after being shot. Mementos left at these sites include such things as banners, letters, flowers, balloons, and teddy bears. Many times the items that are left have a religious connotation, such as a cross or Star of David. At times, memorials involve decorating familiar objects because these express loyalty (Fast, 2003). For example, students' desks, doors at residence halls, lockers, and so on might be decorated and become a memorial. We believe that trying to ban this expression will lead to frustration and likely bad public relations. However, policies governing the creation and maintenance of these memorials are strongly recommended (Kerr, 2009).

Halpern and Tramontin (2007) identify a practical issue inherent for spontaneous memorials. They recommend that emotional support be available for those coming to contribute and view the memorial. They recommend having mental health professionals available at these sites to offer assistance on an as-needed basis. This practice appears very prudent, especially in the first few days following a crisis. We recommend that such mental health professionals are clearly identified in some way, for example, with armbands or other clothing that distinguishes them as official representatives of the university. These individuals should not be intrusive or interfere with the expression of grief. Their purpose is to provide temporary support, answer questions, and suggest possible places where additional, ongoing assistance can be found.

Several issues should be considered regarding policies on the creation of spontaneous memorials. The first issue concerns the location and size of the memorial. Location and size are important for safety reasons. The memorial should be situated so that the location does not place anyone visiting it in danger. Having someone injured or even killed because the memorial was located too close to a busy street is a situation to be prevented at all costs. Consideration should be given to the size of the memorial. Memorials should not obstruct the flow of foot or vehicular traffic. Normal traffic patterns may experience disruption but should not be totally interrupted. Just as with sanctioned memorials, the nature of spontaneous memorials is a policy issue. Policies should outline guidelines that emphasize respect for diversity on a university campus. However, monitoring the nature of spontaneous memorials is difficult. Care should be exercised with respect to restricting the nature of these memorials. Finally, the period of time spontaneous memorials will be tolerated is a policy issue. While these memorials do serve an important purpose, they do not need to be sustained with no end in sight. There are two reasons for addressing this issue in policy. The first is grounds-keeping issues. Maintenance staff must be able to perform their jobs without working around these memorials forever. The second issue concerns respect for survivors. After a while, survivors may not want to be constantly reminded of the trauma. They may feel a need get on with life, and having to walk past the memorial every day impedes their personal recovery (Fast, 2003).

SURVIVOR RECOVERY

Administrators and CMTs must recognize that in addition to returning to normal operations, addressing the emotional and social needs of survivors is critical for the recovery process (Diaz, 2008). Ignoring these needs results in an incomplete recovery for individuals (James, 2008) and groups (Shalev, 2000). Community grief may take months to years to resolve, even though public expression through ceremony and ritual may be limited to a few days or weeks and/or a special anniversary (Williams et al., 1999). During this time, the crisis takes on meaning to the community (Park, 2008) and becomes part of communal history (Williams et al., 1999).

During recovery, survivors cycle through high and low points as they attempt to find a renewed sense of meaning in the aftermath of the crisis. According to Diaz (2008), this process involves survivors trusting and feeling safe, feeling supported, finding common ground to work together, and believing that recovery is possible. This process is accomplished through providing appropriate services (Sitterle & Gurwitch, 1999). It is not a one-size-fits-all proposition. Services must meet the need of survivors for where they are in the recovery process and the issues individuals or groups of survivors are experiencing (Nurmi, 1999).

Several methods to support survivors follow. Generally speaking, using more than one method is recommended to make sure the entire campus is involved in the screening of survivors (Foy, Eriksson, & Trice, 2001). The primary foci of these approaches are networking, outreach, and self-care activities. The goal of these efforts is to reestablish a sense of individual and group connectedness to the campus (Zinner & Williams, 1999), as well as emotional well-being (Diaz, 2008).

Screening

Throughout the recovery process, screening survivors for post-traumatic stress disorder (PTSD) is important. Remember that PTSD symptoms may not surface for several months or even longer after a traumatic experience. Therefore, screening is not a one-time isolated event. Screening should take place regularly if not continuously throughout the first year after a traumatic event. Screening can be instrumental in identifying survivors who are experiencing severe trauma, sorting through those experiencing less severe symptoms, and discovering survivors who might be in denial about their feelings. Patience is needed with people in denial, and opportunities given to these survivors to express their feelings and thoughts. Opportunities might include psychoeducational groups or other creative ways to allow the expression of feelings and thoughts in a nonthreatening manner. A plan that outlines procedures and methods for screening will enable you to prevent this part of recovery from slipping through the cracks, which could occur if administrators and CMTs shifted attention to other more pressing issues.

Several methods can be used to screen survivors. Publicizing typical symptoms across campus is one way to start the process. Distributing brochures and putting information on campus web pages are two ways to publicize symptoms. Publishing the symptoms in the campus newspaper for several weeks is another way to communicate with students, staff, and faculty members. Sending e-mail blasts is also an effective method to publicize symptoms. This information can help people self-identify if they need support. Informing residence life staff and others in leadership roles about typical symptoms and asking these people to make referrals as needed is another way to screen for problems that interfere with a person's being able to function.

We recommend that screening should be more than just listing symptoms associated with PTSD. Simply listing these symptoms is not adequate. Brochures, e-mail blasts, articles in the student newspaper, or coverage on the university radio or TV station can also describe problems that many people may experience during recovery. The problems experienced by survivors change over time. Several brochures may be needed to describe the problems survivors may expect at any given time during recovery. These should be made available as appropriate throughout the recovery process. A comprehensive crisis management plan that outlines the distribution of brochures or use of other methods of publicizing problems will ensure that the screening process is not lost among the other recovery activities. A key issue is who takes responsibility for this process. This responsibility will be different for each university. Some campuses may give the responsibility to the student affairs office; others may have the counseling center or health services in charge of distributing brochures. Regardless of which unit has direct responsibility, CMTs should be accountable for making sure the brochures are distributed.

Psychological Debriefing

A *psychological debriefing* is "a single-session semistructured crisis intervention designed to reduce and prevent unwanted psychological sequelae following traumatic events by promoting emotional processing through the ventilation and normalization of reactions and preparation for future experiences" (Bisson, McFarlane, & Rose, 2000, p. 555). Although several models of psychological debriefing are used, the most commonly employed is Critical Incident Stress Debriefing (CISD), developed by Mitchell and Everly (1995). Initially developed for use with intact groups, such as first responders to emergency situations, CISD has been expanded for use with other groups that have been exposed to some type of traumatic event (Robinson, 2000). Debriefing occurs early (1–3 days) following a traumatic experience. Usually, CISD includes some or all of the following: (a) an introduction to the rationale and methods of CISD to group members; (b) explanation of confidentiality; (c) time to describe traumatic events and discuss initial reactions; (d) time for describing emotional responses to the experience; (e) discussion of the recognition, normalization, and management of symptoms; (f) discussion of implementing knowledge and coping strategies; and (g) identification of internal and external sources of support (Foy et al., 2001).

Although evidence of the effectiveness of CISD is debated (Mitchell & Everly, 2000; Robinson, 2000), most people believe CISD can be effective with specific groups (James, 2008). Psychological debriefing is generally considered most effective with groups existing prior to a traumatic event. Possibly because these groups have a level of familiarity, debriefing is not as threatening. One of the primary benefits of CISD is reestablishing a sense of connectedness within the group (Robinson, 2000). For survivors, regaining a sense of belonging is important for recovery (Zinner & Williams, 1999). CISD is also useful for identifying individuals needing further assistance (Mitchell & Everly, 1995). The person leading the session should always be alert for anyone who seems to need additional support. Following the session, the leader is encouraged to identify individuals who are in need of additional support and refer them to sources that can provide the specific type of psychological assistance needed.

In summary, CISD does not appear to be a stand-alone method for supporting survivors. Not everyone responds to its structure and process. While some people may feel their stress and anxieties are reduced by participating in CISD, others may not. In fact, research has found that symptoms for some people increase because of CISD

(James, 2007). Additional services will be needed for these individuals. In addition, recovery will take several months. Reliance on a one-shot session is not practical, given this knowledge.

Natural Debriefing

The idea of using family and friends for support has been growing over the past several years (Ursano et al., 2000). Having someone to talk to with whom you already have a relationship is a pearl beyond price following a traumatic experience. The process of talking with family, friends, and coworkers has become known as *natural debriefing* (Ursano et al., 2000). Natural debriefing is quite common for up to 7 months following a crisis event, according to these authors. Reassurance from the people closest to survivors can have a profound effect on survivors (Myer & Moore, 2006). Survivors receiving support from the people closest to them have fewer long-term stress problems than others (Gray & Litz, 2005). This approach works particularly well with those who are not seriously impaired by the loss (Foa & Meadows, 1997). As we have stated earlier, these are the survivors who are often neglected.

Natural debriefing can easily be included in a plan for recovery, with minimal to no intrusion on other methods. The CMTs might work with the university counseling center and residence halls to develop self-help groups that would permit natural debriefing. Staff members in these two units could identify and contact potential leaders for these groups. Ideally, leaders of the self-help groups should be other students, staff, and faculty members who are emotionally stable and not experiencing debilitating symptoms from the crisis. If professional staff are used, we recommend a coleader who is a peer. The CMTs could support the groups by scheduling meeting rooms and by providing refreshments, which tends to increase participation in these meetings.

The most important element in this model is creating opportunities for talking with family and friends. Administrators at Northern Illinois University and the University of Alabama–Huntsville did this by dismissing classes for a week following the tragedies on their campuses. This action allowed students to return to their homes and receive support from families and others closest to them. Technology can also be used to allow students, staff, and faculty to talk with others about their experience. We recognize that many of these people will have the ability to talk with family members who are not close by through cell phones and the Internet. Enhancing this capacity by video conference with others is one way to improve natural debriefing. The saying that a picture is worth a thousand words applies. Seeing as well as talking to a family member, even if it is through technology, can increase the support that is felt.

Supportive Group Intervention

The appeal of group interventions for survivors rests on the clear relevance of joining with others in therapeutic work for coping with victimization consequences, such as isolation, alienation, and diminished feelings (Foy et al., 2001). Supportive groups may be conducted in different settings. On a college campus, the setting might be the counseling center, a residence life setting, a campus ministry location, health services, or fraternity or sorority residences. These groups work well with an open format that allows new members to be added during the life of the group. Different meeting schedules can be used, but once a week seems to work well. Supportive groups often provide the opportunity for renewing a sense of community that is so needed following a crisis (Diaz, 2008). A real advantage of supportive groups is the identification and preparation of survivors who may benefit from additional therapy or as an adjunctive treatment to individual therapy or trauma-focused group therapy.

Supportive group therapy typically places little emphasis on the details of traumatic events; instead, the focus is group validation of the impact of trauma experience (Foy et al., 2001). The exploration of affects such as hurt, disappointment, frustration, or happiness should be the focus of sessions. This approach is effective in the reduction of psychological distress (Turner, 2000). Supportive group therapy is not limited to the first few weeks after a traumatic event. This approach can be used throughout the recovery process, as survivors continue to work to find meaning in the wake of the trauma.

Compassion Center

Development of a compassion center can provide necessary respite for individuals and groups of survivors (Sitterle & Gurwitch, 1999). These centers provide an island of seclusion for survivors to detach from the campus. Sitterle and Gurwitch (1999) report that compassion centers can develop a sense of community. The purpose of compassion centers evolves over time. Initially, these centers can be used for survivors to gather to wait for information regarding family members or friends. At first, the compassion center might be open 24 hours a day. After the immediacy of the emergency passes, the center might remain open for specific hours. For example, at Central University, a compassion center was located at the stadium for survivors to await word on the status of the victims who were transported to the hospital. During the first few days, the center might be open continuously. Afterwards, the center might be open often but not 24 hours a day. A sign-in and sign-out sheet can enable the staff to know who is at the center. The compassion center could be useful for several weeks for survivors to get information regarding the medical condition of victims who are still in the hospital. Whoever runs such a center needs to recognize that the victims or family members may not want some information shared. As time passes, the compassion center could provide survivors with information such as completing paperwork for insurance claims and referrals to other agencies that can give support.

Staffing compassion centers is important. Whenever the compassion center is open, a person knowledgeable about the current situation, either a volunteer or an employee of the university, should be present. Greeters should be available to welcome every person or family to the center. The names of visitors and their relationship to the victims can be gathered by greeters, who can also direct people to the resources that would be most helpful. Peer counseling can be an important part of a compassion center as well. Peer counseling involves using students to talk with students, staff to talk with staff, and faculty to talk with other faculty.

Compassion centers should always be well supplied. The CMT at Central University worked to outfit the compassion center at the stadium room as quickly as possible. Calls were made to campus computing services, telecommunications, food services, and other units on campus, as well as to the Red Cross to see if they had cots available that could be lent to the university for survivors who have to wait for an extended period of time. Typical supplies for compassion centers include food and water. For example, snacks and sandwiches will always be helpful, and water, coffee, and cold drinks are recommended. In addition, comfortable chairs and tables will help survivors as they wait for information about victims. If possible, centers could also have some crayons, paper, and/ or books available in case younger children come with their parents. Playing soft music may be another way to support survivors. Telephones and computers with Internet access might also be beneficial during the waiting process. After a few days, these computers can be used to access information on referral resources. Finally, electrical outlets will help people recharge the batteries on cell phones or laptop computers.

Psychoeducation

A final way to support survivors is a psychoeducational approach (Griffin, 2007; Halpern & Tramontin, 2007). The goal of this approach is to remove the confusion, mystique, and craziness of being a survivor by anchoring current feelings, behaviors, and thoughts as purposive and reasonable, given the traumatic experience (James, 2008). This approach provides information to survivors in a timely fashion regarding the range of symptoms or problems they might experience. This information includes physical symptoms, psychological problems, social issues, common reactions, and treatment options (Halpern & Tramontin, 2007). In addition, psychoeducation should include information on coping skills, resiliency, and stages of recovery. The following is the introduction used by a group leader at Central University a few weeks after the explosion.

> **Group Leader:** When I talk with someone after they have gone through a terrible experience like you, they ask this question, "Am I crazy?" And my answer is I am 99% sure you are not crazy. This afternoon, we are going to discuss information about some of the problems you may be experiencing. These might include nightmares, guilt feelings, anger, and a lot of others. The point I want to make today is that just because you are having these does not mean you are nuts. You are having an expected reaction to a really awful experience. Sometimes these problems will simply go away after a month or two. If not, I want you to know these problems can be treated. It might take several meetings with some. We will work with you and do this together.

The group leader continues explaining symptoms and the treatment process more specifically. Throughout the discussion, the emphasis is on assuring everyone attending that recovery is possible.

Psychoeducation might also be accomplished through the distribution of flyers, web sites, information meetings, media interviews, and other outreach activities (Halpern & Tramontin, 2007). Outreach can be extended to on-campus groups such as Greek organizations, athletic teams, and other student organizations (Griffin, 2007). A captured audience for doing outreach is classrooms. Northern Illinois University made good use of this strategy following the shooting on its campus. The first day classes resumed after the students returned, mental health professionals, at the discretion of the course instructor, were permitted to speak in the class for about 10 minutes to inform students about problems they might encounter and also the support that had been set up for them. The specific methods to conduct psychoeducation depend on the culture of the university, as well as the severity and nature of the crisis. Griffin (2007) encourages outreach to extend beyond the campus to off-campus groups such as student apartment complexes, campus ministries, campus annexes, and distance education programs.

SUMMARY

Survivorship is a journey that gives meaning to a traumatic experience. Each person and group must walk an individual path to reconnect with their community. This process can take days, weeks, or years as people search for a way to make sense of what happened. Care must be taken to respect the time needed for survivors to recover, not pushing too quickly or slowly in this process. Multiple methods should be used to support survivors as they make their way in the journey to recovery. Engaging in rituals and the creation of memorials are an important part of process. These traditional methods help to bring closure to this part of the effort to understand the impact. Any effort used by administrators and CMTs to facilitate recovery of survivors must recognize and respect the diversity on their campus.

REFERENCES

Bisson, J. I., McFarlane, A. C., & Rose, S. (2000). Psychological debriefing. In E. Foa, T. Keane, & M. Friedman (Eds.), *Effective treatments for PTSD: Practice guidelines from the International Society for Traumatic Stress Studies* (pp. 39–59). New York: Guilford Press.

Bolton, D. (1999). The threat to belonging in Enniskillen: Reflections on the Remembrance Day bombing. In E. S. Zinner & M. B. Williams (Eds.), *When a community weeps: Case studies in group survivorship* (pp. 191–212). Philadelphia: Brunner/Mazel.

Carver, C. S., Scheier, M. F., & Weintraub, J. K. (1989). Assessing coping strategies: A theoretically based approach. *Journal of Personality and Social Psychology, 56,* 267–283.

Clark, J., & Franzmann, M. (2006). Authority from grief, presence, and place in the making of roadside memorials. *Death Studies, 30,* 579–599.

Crane, P. A., & Clements, P. T. (2005). Psychological response to disaster: Focus on adolescents. *Journal of Psychosocial Nursing and Mental Health Services, 43,* 31–39.

Davis, C. G., & Nolen-Hoeksema, S. (2001). Loss and meaning: How do people make sense of loss? *American Behavioral Scientist, 44,* 726–741.

Diaz, J. O. (2008). Integrating psychosocial programs in multisector responses to international disasters. *American Psychologist, 63,* 820–827.

Fast, J. D. (2003). After Columbine: How people mourn sudden death. *Social Work, 48,* 484–492.

Foa, E. B., & Meadows, E. A. (1997). Psychological treatment for posttraumatic stress disorder: A critical review. *Annual Review of Psychology, 48,* 449–480.

Foy, D. W., Eriksson, C. B., & Trice, Gary, A. (2001). Introduction to group interventions for trauma survivors. *Group Dynamics: Theory, Research, and Practice, 5,* 246–251.

Gray, M. J., & Litz, B. T. (2005). Behavioral intervention for recent trauma: Empirically informed practice guidelines. *Behavior Modification, 29,* 189–215.

Griffin, W. (2007). Psychological first aid in the aftermath of crisis. In E. L. Zdziarski II, W. D. Dunkel, & M. Rollo (Eds.), *Campus crisis management: A comprehensive guide to planning, prevention, response, and recovery* (pp. 145–182). San Francisco: John Wiley & Sons.

Halpern, J., & Tramontin, M. (2007). *Disaster mental health: Theory and Practice.* Belmont, CA: Thompson Brooks/Cole.

James, R. (2007). *Crisis intervention strategies* (6th ed.). Belmont, CA: Brooks/Cole-Cengage.

Kerr, M. M. (2009). *School crisis prevention and intervention.* Upper Saddle River, NJ: Merrill.

Kirk, W. (1993). *Adolescent suicide: A school based approach to assessment and intervention.* Champaign, IL: Research Press.

McGowan, K. (2006, March). The hidden side of happiness. *Psychology Today.* Retrieved February 22, 2010 from, www.psychologytoday.com/articles/200602/the-hidden-side-happiness.

Miller, L. (2002). Psychological interventions for terroristic trauma: Symptoms, syndromes, and treatment strategies. *Psychotherapy: Theory, Research, Practice, Training, 39,* 283–296.

Mitchell, J. T., & Everly, G. S., Jr. (1995). *Advanced critical incident stress debriefing.* Ellicott City, MD: International Critical Stress Foundation.

Mitchell, J. T., & Everly, G. S., Jr. (2000). Critical Incident Stress Management and Critical Incident Stress Debriefing:Evolution, effects, and outcomes. In B. Raphael & J. P. Wilson (Eds.), *Psychological debriefing: Theory, evidence and practice* (pp. 71–90). Cambridge: Cambridge University Press.

Myer, R. A., & Moore, H. (2006). Crisis in context: An ecological model. *Journal of Counseling and Development, 84,* 139–147.

Myer, R. A., Moore, H., & Hughes, T. (2003). September 11th survivors and the refugee model. *Journal of Mental Health Counseling, 25,* 245–258.

Nurmi, L. (1999). The sinking of the Estonia: The effect of Critical Incident Stress Debriefing on rescuers. *International Journal of Emergency Mental Health, 1,* 23–32.

O'Connor, L. E., Berry, J. W., Weiss, J., Schweitzer, D., & Sevier, M. (2000). Survivor guilt, submissive behavior, and evolutionary theory: The down-side of winning social comparison. *British Journal of Medical Psychology, 73,* 519–530.

Park, C. L. (2008). Testing the meaning making model of coping with loss. *Journal of Social and Clinical Psychology, 27,* 970–995.

Rando, T. (1985). Creating therapeutic rituals in the psychotherapy of the bereaved. *Psychotherapy, 22,* 336–340.

Robinson, R. (2000). Debriefing with emergency services: Critical incident stress management. In B. Raphael & J. P. Wilson (Eds.), *Psychological debriefing: Theory, practice, and evidence* (pp. 91–107). New York: Cambridge Press.

Shalev, A. Y. (2000). Stress management and debriefing: Historical concepts and present patterns. In B. Raphael & J. P. Wilson (Eds.), *Psychological debriefing: Theory, evidence and practice* (pp. 337–350). Cambridge: Cambridge University Press.

Sitterle, K. A., & Gurwitch, R. H. (1999). The terrorist bombing in Oklahoma City. In E. S. Zinner & M. B. Williams (Eds.), *When a comuunity weeps: Case studies in group suvivorship* (pp. 161–190). Philadelphia: Brunner/Mazel.

Spiegel, D. (1981). Vietnam grief work under hypnosis. *American Journal of Hypnosis, 24*, 33–40.

Stuhlmiller, C., & Dunning, C. (2000). Challenging the mainstream: From pathogenic to salutogenic models of posttrauma intervention. In J. M. Violanti, D. Paton, & C. Dunning (Eds.), *Posttraumatic stress intervention: Challenges, issues, and perspectives* (pp. 10–42). Springfield, IL: Charles C Thomas.

Tedeschi, R. G., & Calhoun, L. G. (1995). *Trauma and transformation: Growing in the aftermath of suffering.* Thousand Oaks, CA: Sage.

Turner, Andrew L. (2000). Group treatment of trauma survivors following a fatal bus accident: Integrating theory and practice. *Group Dynamics: Theory, Research, and Practice, 4*, 139–149.

Urlic, I., & Simunkovic, C. T. (2009). Working through shame in groups for victims of trauma and war. *International Journal of Group Psychotherapy, 59*, 165–179.

Ursano, R. J., Fullerton, C. S., Vance, K., & Wang, L. (2000). Debriefing: Its role in the spectrum of prevention and acute management of psychological trauma. In B. Raphael & J. P. Wilson (Eds.), *Psychological debriefing: Theory, practice and evidence* (pp. 32–42). Cambridge, England: Cambridge University Press.

van der Veer, G. (1998). *Counselling and therapy with refugees and victims of trauma* (2nd ed.). New York: John Wiley & Sons.

Watts, R., & Wilson, M. (1999). The Kempsey bus disaster: The effects of Australia community rescuers. In E. S. Zinner & M. B. Williams (Eds.), *When a community weeps: Case studies in group survivorship* (pp. 73–86). Philadelphia: Brunner/Mazel.

Williams, M. B., Zinner, E. S., & Ellis, R. R. (1999). The connection between grief and trauma: An overview. In E. S. Zinner & M. B. Williams (Eds.), *When a community weeps: Case studies in group survivorship* (pp. 3–22). Philadelphia: Brunner/Mazel.

Witzum, E., & Malkinson, R. (1999). Death of a leader: The social construction of bereavement. In E. S. Zinner & M. B. Williams (Eds.), *When a community weeps: Case studies in group survivorship* (pp. 119–138). Philadelphia: Brunner/Mazel.

Wyrostok, N. (1995). The ritual as a psychotherapeutic intervention. *Psychotherapy: Theory, Research, Practice, Training, 32*, 397–404.

Zinner, E. S. (1999). The *Challenger* disaster: Group survivorship on a national landscape. In E. S. Zinner & M. B. Williams (Eds.), *When a community weeps: Case studies in group survivorship* (pp. 23–48). Philadelphia: Brunner/Mazel.

Zinner, E. S., & Williams, M. B. (1999). Summary and incorporation: A reference frame for community recovery and restoration. In E. S. Zinner & M. B. Williams (Eds.), *When a community weeps: Case studies in group survivorship* (pp. 237–254). Philadelphia: Brunner/Mazel.

12

Leadership Checklist:
Preparing Your Campus for Crisis

This book has been full of what we hope has been useful, applicable information that will help your university survive and thrive following critical incidents that are bound to happen on your campus at some point. We didn't want to finish without taking some time to speak directly to you, the leaders of the university, those in charge of making certain you are prepared, and those who are ultimately held accountable for the outcomes of all things, good and bad, that occur on your watch. Your jobs are not easy; the old saying "with much power comes much responsibility" comes to mind. This ending chapter is our summary to you specifically. We begin by providing a checklist of what we have identified as the primary tasks of leaders regarding crisis management and discuss the details of each briefly.

- Make crisis management a leadership imperative.
- Ensure understanding throughout the university of FERPA, HIPAA, and OSHA and their implications during crises and recovery.
- Develop your crisis management plan as if lives, your campus, and your reputation as a leader depend on it; they may.
- Make the budget available to ensure basic emergency response.
- Insist on multiple copies of disaster plans and infrastructure drawings made accessible in various locations.
- Ensure comprehensive assessment of each critical incident on campus to identify lessons learned.
- Ensure proper communication and dissemination of information.
- Ensure accuracy of student contact information in case of emergency.
- Communicate and partner with outside agencies to prepare for and withstand critical incidents.
- Require regular crisis training and situational exercises.
- Be prepared to take the lead and use methods different from those in daily operations for decision making.
- Seek counsel; stay updated on risk-management recommendations.
- Develop a comprehensive recovery plan
- Be prepared to utilize recovery to achieve long-term goals.

(continued)

> • Determine alternatives to minimize enrollment loss.
> • Identify resources on your campus.
> • Remember: People First!

MAKE CRISIS PLANNING A LEADERSHIP IMPERATIVE

All universities have a list of tasks that require top leadership to set and support. This support is needed for these tasks to be successfully accomplished. We would even go so far as to say that very few systemic programs on a campus can survive, let alone thrive or be successfully implemented, without top administration setting and supporting the initiative as a priority. Crisis planning is one of the initiatives that must be added to the list. This statement is easy to make but very complex to accomplish. Accomplishment means truly understanding the endeavor and the resources, both human and financial, that will be required to succeed and then to make adjustments to make this possible. You are not likely to receive additional funding to support your crisis plan and in this economy may or may not have the ability to add staff to pick up primary responsibilities or to disperse the load of a current staff member who is being reassigned. Effective crisis planning takes a toll, but the toll is much higher when your school experiences the worst-case scenario without crisis planning. The president and cabinet must work out the adjustments and each send a very clear verbal and behavioral message that supports this effort on your campus.

ENSURE UNDERSTANDING OF FERPA, HIPAA, AND OSHA

Everyone on your campus who works in a professional capacity needs to have a basic understanding of what types of information may or may not be shared. During a crisis, everyone tends to do the best they can with the knowledge they have at hand, and out of desperation, some very poor decisions can be made especially without proper preparation. For example, during a critical incident it can be very easy, with the best of intentions, to inappropriately share protected student information. The information may be shared in trying to get resources or assistance, and the best of motivation may be behind the sharing, but you still have rules and regulations determining what information can be shared from a student's official records. A teacher or staff member may know a parent and simply out of caring share that the student seems to be self-isolating and has not been attending classes or turning in assignments since the critical incident on campus. This information regarding attendance, grades, and/or disposition is not appropriate to share, even though it is given with nothing but concern.

DEVELOP A CRISIS MANAGEMENT PLAN

Make campus safety a priority from the highest levels of administration down to include student, staff, and faculty members. Even the person who cleans the building at night when no one else is around needs to be invested in maintaining a safe campus. Pay attention to the efforts of the crisis teams that have been established. Let it be known that you value their effort and depend on those involved to set up policies and plans that will ensure the campus is prepared for whatever comes its way. Remember that these policies and plans are what will ultimately protect you with media, the public, and parents when a critical incident happens on your campus.

MAKE THE BUDGET AVAILABLE

When the need is not immediate, setting a high priority for critical incident resources takes foresight and leadership. This foresight may be especially hard during these difficult economic times for higher education. However, basic safety equipment purchases are purchases you cannot afford to pass on when allocating budgets at the administrative level. In addition, while a specific cost for the human impact of a crisis is not possible to determine, a reasonable expectation of those who choose your institution for education is for those in leadership to make appropriate provisions in case of emergencies to care for immediate physical and emotional implications.

INSIST ON MULTIPLE COPIES OF DISASTER PLANS AND INFRASTRUCTURE DRAWINGS

Require those in leadership positions and frontline personnel to have immediately available a copy of your policies and plans. This means both at the office and at home. Be certain that all necessary contact numbers for your crisis management team and crisis intervention team (home, cell, and office) along with external emergency partners (community services) that you may need are not only in writing in your plan but also programmed into your cell phone. Distance is not an excuse during a critical incident; everyone is still going to you for leadership. Everything goes more smoothly if you have clear procedures in place, and those who need to take action are clear about whom to call on and the appropriate first steps.

ENSURE COMPREHENSIVE ASSESSMENT OF EACH CRITICAL INCIDENT

You can learn lessons from each incident that occurs on your campus. Require your crisis management team to use each incident to improve communication and procedures. Building this process into the plan means that when large events occur, teamwork and confidence based on lessons learned can be utilized. Assess prevention, intervention, and recovery issues, and make changes where needed. Guidance for this assessment was shared in Chapter 6. Do not let this process become a game of second-guessing those making decisions and taking actions; rather, it should be an empowering process of analyses designed to strengthen awareness and confidence. Carefully select the person to facilitate the assessment.

ENSURE PROPER COMMUNICATION AND DISSEMINATION OF INFORMATION

During or directly following a crisis on campus, media will descend even before you have facts about what actually happened. Often text, tweets, video, and photos will be shared before administration is even completely in the loop or the crisis team has had time to come together. An early example of the impact of media during a critical incident occurred in the early morning of November 18, 1999, as the nearly completed Texas A&M bonfire stack collapsed, taking the lives of 12 young people and injuring 27 others. Then Vice President of Student Affairs Malon Southerland remembers the moment, as he has often shared with others in leadership, when his phone rang at his on-campus residence around 5 a.m. with the news that the bonfire had fallen and there were deaths. He has described many times the swiftness with which information, both accurate and rumor, passed across campus and across the state and the country. In more recent incidents, campus leaders experienced a frenzy of activity. Not only do they need to be prepared to address and work with campus and local media but also they must be ready for the implications of unauthorized shared information through media, including student cell phone video and photos of critical incident scenes on Facebook and YouTube. While the administration is still trying to get the right people in place to determine the facts about what has happened and attempting to begin the process of confirming the extent of the incident, identification of victims may already be occurring as families and friends search the Internet for information. This reality needs to be addressed in your media plan for you to be prepared for the implications. Given the technology changes, a completely different level of communication is needed to give a clear report of facts as you know them to your campus community and others as appropriate. If approached properly, your faculty and staff can serve as excellent resources. Training is needed about what and how to communicate after a crisis, and a means of sharing facts must be in place. This system will lessen rumors and fear and also provide excellent resources for sharing recovery resources with your campus community. For example, faculty, student affairs, and housing staff can assist in looking for signs and symptoms of distress in students close to the crisis and make referrals for counseling and other needs. Campuses often overlook the power of the resources at their fingertips—you have amazing professional individuals who usually stand ready and willing to help.

ENSURE THE ACCURACY OF YOUR STUDENT CONTACT INFORMATION

Many universities have improved student communication systems since the incidents at Virginia Tech. Now it is the norm for campuses to be able to contact students through simultaneous e-mail and texting. As a matter of fact, some groups have expressed concern about this growing dependency. The feeling seems to be that so much emphasis is placed on campus communication that many universities that have great warning systems will miss the boat on comprehensive crisis management planning efforts. Between the disasters of Katrina and Rita and the crisis of Virginia Tech, it seems that the focus of most universities has been to respond to state mandates regarding disaster recovery plans (facility and business emphasis) and communication systems. While these are certainly important, they are mere pieces of a much larger issue. With that being said, contact information is an issue for many schools because students tend to move from semester to semester. Updated contact information for students and also for parents is a very serious need during a crisis.

COMMUNICATE AND PARTNER WITH OUTSIDE AGENCIES

Identify agencies and specific professionals in the community that could be of service to your institution in a crisis. This list will obviously include city officials, specific media contacts, and fire and police departments. You may also want to determine specific mental health agencies and staff members, hospitals, physician groups, and other local community safety agents.

REQUIRE REGULAR CRISIS TRAINING AND SITUATIONAL EXERCISES

Regular is the key to success. Many institutions hold informal or formal conversations about how they might handle a specific incident during heightened awareness following a crisis at another campus. All administrators are probably thankful that they didn't have to make the decisions that day and then spend a bit of time thinking of how they may have personally gone about handling a similar situation if they had to. If you want your campus truly prepared when crisis hits, regular training sessions and discussions about how to proceed with various types of critical incidents are essential. It is not about getting the right answer so everyone knows exactly what to do—if it were that easy, there would be no crises. It is about having your personnel know what and how to assess, possible actions, and possible resources at a time when little makes sense.

BE PREPARED TO TAKE THE LEAD AND USE DIFFERENT METHODS

Realize that you may be looking for advice from different sources than your usual right- and left-hand people during times of crisis. Prepare your top advisors for this eventuality, have them assist you in finding the best people for a crisis, and have these individuals play a critical role in policy writing and planning on your campus. You might have experts on campus who have never been asked to participate, and this is a very costly waste. Look in departments of counseling, psychology, social work, criminal justice, and elsewhere for faculty who are specialists in crisis work and can assist. Also be prepared for the difference in leadership and decision-making style that may be required during a crisis. Crisis management is making sense out of chaos, and if your traditional style is inclusion and thoughtfulness, you may need to be prepared for quick, decisive action.

SEEK COUNSEL ON RISK-MANAGEMENT RECOMMENDATIONS

Ask your university legal counsel to review your policies and plans with your crisis management team. You may want to talk about reporting, records, documentation, and official files as part of this conversation. Ask them to read critically and then raise questions for your crisis team. Doing so can solidify your campus plan.

DEVELOP A COMPREHENSIVE RECOVERY PLAN

Putting this step on the checklist may seem ridiculously obvious to many, yet it is amazing how many campuses have a document with a few key individuals involved and are nowhere near ready to handle a crisis on campus. At this juncture in time, given recent national interest, incidents, and media coverage, there is a general expectation of preparedness on the part of universities. It is negligent to be unprepared. A good test of preparedness is to simply walk around campus asking about crisis readiness and campus preparedness—does your staff even know there is a plan? Do those in areas held responsible have basic knowledge about policies and plans? Can your crisis leadership team put their hands on a plan and discuss procedures and possibilities of actions articulately without needing time to prep? There is no time to prep in the middle of a crisis.

BE PREPARED TO UTILIZE RECOVERY TO ACHIEVE LONG-TERM GOALS

This issue is not in any way a suggestion to cash in on a crisis but rather a reminder to consider what the overarching goals are for your institution following a critical incident. Try to take something that may have been anything from negative to horrific and find a way to make some positive impact for your institution. Both Union University and Gustavus Adolphus College are excellent examples of how universities can not only survive but continue to exceed expectations, prosper, and help others following a crisis. These institutions showed incredible resilience after devastation by tornadoes. Their positive approach, spirit, and dedication to moving forward while in the process of crisis and recovery serve as exemplary models. Part of the recovery phase is learning to live normatively again after a crisis, so if there is a change you have been working toward, this may be a time to set new norms that take your university in that changed direction. People tend to want to help and make a difference following a crisis. It is a supreme leadership opportunity to harness the energy and good will offered by those who want to do something and accomplish the goals of your institution. A simple example may be a dream of the institution to develop a new area—a memorial park or educational building, for example.

DETERMINE ALTERNATIVES TO MINIMIZE ENROLLMENT LOSS

It goes without saying that the first thought during a crisis is not enrollment loss, but not long after the initial incident has sunk in, any good administrator thinks of the impact of the possible negative publicity on the institution. Be prepared to step forward with a plan of action with your administration and enrollment management team.

IDENTIFY RESOURCES ON YOUR CAMPUS

A college campus is a gold mine of resources when it comes to campus safety and crisis management. You probably have experts, possibly nationally recognized, on your campus that you may not even be aware of. Depending on the degree programs you offer, you might have faculty who are training and consulting in the area of crisis management who have not been tapped to serve on your crisis team. You may have a counselor in your counseling center who specializes in crisis counseling. Numerous faculty on your campus in the human services areas have received Red Cross certification as part of the training offered at local, state, regional, and national conferences due to the heightened awareness of the need for crisis specialists. A police officer or student affairs staff member may have special education, training, and experience to offer. Do not miss out on your most valuable assets by not identifying, recognizing, or asking.

REMEMBER: PEOPLE FIRST!

In all emergency decisions, set aside the politics of your job, and ask yourself: At the end of the day, if this were happening at an institution where my child attended, if this were my child involved, given the resources I have to work with, what would I want to have happen? What would I need to *know* happened in a bad situation? After all the training, prevention, planning, and rehearsals, there is still much to be said for following your heart in difficult times and doing the right thing by people.

We hope the information provided in this book will assist you in preparation for and endurance through difficult times. Good luck in your endeavors as you lead your campus.

Rick A. Myer, Richard K. "Dick" James, & Patrice Moulton

Author Index

Subject Index